Artificial Intelligence: Concepts, Tools and Techniques

Artificial Intelligence: Concepts, Tools and Techniques

Edited by Mitch Hoppe

MURPHY & MOORE
www.murphy-moorepublishing.com

Murphy & Moore Publishing,
1 Rockefeller Plaza,
New York City, NY 10020, USA

ISBN: 978-1-63987-059-2

Cataloging-in-Publication Data

Artificial intelligence : concepts, tools and techniques / edited by Mitch Hoppe.
    p. cm.
Includes bibliographical references and index.
ISBN 978-1-63987-059-2
1. Artificial intelligence. 2. Fifth generation computers. 3. Neural computers. I. Hoppe, Mitch.
Q335 .A78 2022
006.3--dc23

For information on all Murphy & Moore Publications
visit our website at www.murphy-moorepublishing.com

 MURPHY & MOORE

Contents

Preface

The intelligence exhibited by machines is known as artificial intelligence (AI). The long-term objective of research in AI is to mimic human intelligence. Artificial Intelligence can be classified into artificial general intelligence and artificial biological intelligence. Artificial general intelligence refers to the ability of any intelligent agent to mimic an intellectual task which humans can perform. Artificial biological intelligence aims to understand the natural intelligence of humans. Some of the recent advances in artificial intelligence have been driven by progress in data processing power of modern machines, the use of computational intelligence, statistical methods, and traditional symbolic AI. Some of the tools used include artificial neural networks and mathematical optimization. This book is a valuable compilation of topics, ranging from the basic to the most complex advancements in the field of artificial intelligence. The topics covered herein deal with advanced algorithms as well as the concepts, tools, and techniques that are furthering this discipline. Researchers and students in this field will be assisted by this book.

This book is a comprehensive compilation of works of different researchers from varied parts of the world. It includes valuable experiences of the researchers with the sole objective of providing the readers (learners) with a proper knowledge of the concerned field. This book will be beneficial in evoking inspiration and enhancing the knowledge of the interested readers.

In the end, I would like to extend my heartiest thanks to the authors who worked with great determination on their chapters. I also appreciate the publisher's support in the course of the book. I would also like to deeply acknowledge my family who stood by me as a source of inspiration during the project.

Editor

Applying mean shift and motion detection approaches to hand tracking in sign language

M.M. Hosseini[*], J. Hassanian

Islamic Azad University, Shahrood branch, Shahroodt, Iran.

*Corresponding author: hosseini_mm@yahoo.com (M.M. Hosseini).

Abstract

Hand gesture recognition is very important to communicate in a sign language. In this paper, an effective object tracking and the hand gesture recognition method is proposed. This method is a combination of two well-known approaches, the mean shift and the motion detection algorithm. The mean shift algorithm can track objects based on a color, then when hand passes the face occlusion happens. Several solutions such as the particle filter, kalman filter and dynamic programming tracking have been used, but they are complicated, time consuming and so expensive. The proposed method is so easy, fast, efficient and low costly. The motion detection algorithm in the first step subtracts the previous frame from the current frame to obtain the changes between two images and white pixels (motion level) are detected by using the threshold level. Then the mean shift algorithm is applied for tracking the hand motion. Simulation results show that this method is faster than two times compared with the old common algorithms.

Keywords: *Hand tracking, Motion detection, Mean shift, Hand gesture recognition, sign language.*

1. Introduction

Recently, many research fields of object tracking have involved hand tracking known as a crucial and basic ingredient computer vision. Human beings can simply recognize and track an object immediately even in the presence of high clutter, occlusion, and non-linear variations in the background as well as in the shape, direction or even the size of the target object. However, hand tracking can be a difficult and challenging task for a machine. Tracking for a machine can be used to find the object states. Position, scale, velocity, feature selecting and many other important parameters obtained from a sequential series of images are included, so object tracking uses each image or incoming frame to obtain the weighting coefficients of the entire image. Therefore, it is necessary to specify the special target to track a desired object such as a specific hand. Many solutions are proposed to deal with a hand motion that they use some features to obtain targets such

as colors, area motion and texture, in which [1-2] suggested a solution for an object tracking. Their suggested method converted color frames into gray level images, and then a kernel function is employed. Furthermore, the weights of pixels were obtained each frame. Their proposed method offered several advantages. For instance, it can be very resistant against difficulties such as partial occlusion, blurring caused by camera shaking, deformation of object position and any other sorts of translation. This is due to employing color information as feature vectors in the proposed technique. Wang at el [3] proposed a method based on Hidden Markov Model that they used a Cyber sensory glove and a Flock of Birds motion tracker to extract the features of American Sign Language gestures. The data received from the strain gages in the glove describe the hand shape while the data from the motion tracker describes the trajectory of hand movement. Cheng [4] notes that mean shift is fundamentally a gradient ascent algorithm with an adaptive step size. Since Comaniciu [5], the first introduced mean shift-based on the object tracking, has proven to be a promising alternative for popular particle filtering based on the trackers. In this paper, our method is described in section 2 and the experiment result is shown in section 3, and finally, section 4 draws the conclusions.

2. The Proposed method
Using the hand gesture tracking through the proposed method uses the mean shift algorithm. Occlusion especially happens, when hand reaches the face. Some features are used in the mean shift algorithm such as colors. Since hand (target) and face have the same color, the program cannot recognize the target and the hand tracking faces the problem. Other researchers offered several solutions, such as [5] using the particle filter and [6] using the kalman filter. These methods are complicated and take long time to run and need a large memory, so advanced processor can just satisfy these needs and then they are so expensive. However, this paper suggests an easy and efficient method for solving these problems. This method

limits the tracking range by a) using the mean shift algorithm for motion detection b) eliminating the constant point and then motion range specification, so tracking is done with high accuracy. In this combination method, the color feature is used as a hand distinguished feature. Here, a user in the first frame obtains the hand model as a main purpose of tracking and the color feature and the number of pixels can be extracted by using this model. Then some pixels whose color value is less than hand color value are eliminated with a specific threshold and remained pixels are weighted appropriate to the distance to the hand center (closer, much weighted).

Finally, a range motion is specified through using the motion detection and constant point illustration. Mean shift algorithm calculates the mean of pixels considering the weighting coefficient to obtain hand center. In frames that occlusion happens, motion detection makes track move, because constant points have already been eliminated and when new frames come, the target is obtained by using the proposed combination method again. The block diagram is shown in Figure1.

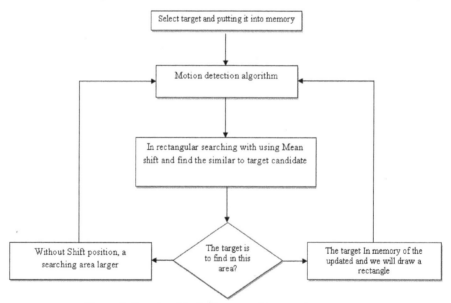

Figure 1.Complete block diagram of integration tracker.

2.1. Motion detection
Motion detection is a famous approach in object tracking that is in fact faster than mean-shift tracker [6]. Motion detection is the easiest of the three motion related detection: tasks, estimation, and segmentation. It results in identifying which image points, or even which regions of the image have moved between two time instants. Using motion

detection algorithm can compare the first frame with the pervious one. It is used in video

compression when it is necessary to estimate changes and to write only the changes, not the whole frame. This algorithm shows an image with white pixels (motion level) on the place where the current frame is different from the previous one. It is already possible to count these pixels, and if the amount of these pixels becomes greater than a predefined threshold level, threshold is produced a motion event. Detecting the motion is calculated the distance in the luminance space between the current image I_k and the last aligned image I_{k-1}^*, obtaining the difference image DI_k, defined as [6]:

$$DI_k(x) = \begin{cases} m & if \ \left| I_k(x) - I_{k-1}^*(x) \right| > T_m \\ 0 & otherwise \end{cases} \quad (1)$$

Where m refers to a factor of increment in the motion, and T_m refers to a motion threshold. DI_k Contains the initial set of points that are candidate to relate to the Moving Visual Object. In order to consolidate the blobs to be detected, a 3×3 morphological closing is used to DI_k. Isolated detected moving pixels are discarded through applying a 3×3 morphological opening. The representation of the motion history image MH_k is then updated by multiplying the previous motion history representation MH_{k-1} with a decay factor, and by adding the difference image DI_k [6]:

$$MH_k = MH_{k-1} * DecayFactor + DI_k \quad (2)$$

Finally, all pixels of MH_k whose luminance is over a motion detection threshold (T_h) are considered as pixels in motion, these pixels can generate the detection image D_{H_k} defined as [6]:

$$D_{H_k}(x) = \begin{cases} 1 & if \quad MH_k(x) > T_h \\ 0 & otherwise \end{cases} \quad (3)$$

a 3×3 morphological closing is applied to the detection image D_{H_k} followed by a 3×3 morphological opening. It is used 3×3 morphology because it can be obtained more smooth and a proper edge from the pictures that cannot be taken by applying 4×4 or 8×8 morphology. Therefore, this solution results in high accuracy in tracking and then the best result.

2.2. Mean shift
In this section mean shift algorithm is adequately presented.

2.2.1. Target representation

At first, a feature space is chosen to characterize the target [7]. The reference *target model* is represented by its pdf q in the feature space. For example, the reference model can be chosen to be the color pdf of the target. The target model can be considered as centered at the spatial location 0, without any general loss. In the subsequent frame a *target candidate* is defined at location y, and is characterized by the pdf $p(y)$. Both pdf-s are estimated from the data. Discrete densities, i.e., m-bin histograms should be used to satisfy the low computational cost imposed by real-time processing. Therefore we have [7]

Target
model:
$$q = \{q_u\}_{u=1,2,...,m}$$
$$\sum_{u=1}^{m} q_u = 1 \quad (I)$$

Target
candidate:
$$p(y) = \{p_u(y)\}_{u=1,2,...,m}$$
$$\sum_{u=1}^{m} p_u = 1 \quad (II)$$

The histogram is enough for our purposes but it is not adequate [8]. Other discrete density estimates can be also applied. We will denote by the formula below.

$$\rho \equiv \rho \left[p(y), q \right] \quad (4)$$

A similarity function exists between p and q. The function $\rho(y)$ plays the role of likelihood and the local maxima in the image shows the presence of objects in the second frame having representations similar to q defined in the first frame. If only spectral information is used to characterize the target, the similarity function can have large variations for adjacent locations on the image lattice and the spatial information is lost. To realize the maxima of such functions, gradient-based optimization procedures are hard to apply and only an expensive exhaustive search can be used. We regularize the similarity function by masking the objects with an isotropic kernel in the spatial domain. When the kernel weights, carrying continuous spatial information are used in defining the feature space representations, and $\rho(y)$ becomes a smooth function in y.

2.2.2. Target model

A target is represented by an ellipsoidal or rectangular region in the image (Figure 2). To eliminate the effect of different target dimensions, all targets are first normalized to a unit circle. This is achieved by independently rescaling the row and column dimensions with h_x and h_y.

Figure 2. Determine target in the first frame (reference image).

Let $\left\{x_i^*\right\}_{i=1,2,...,n}$ be the *normalized* pixel locations in the region defined as the target model. The region is centered at 0. An isotropic kernel, with a convex and monotonic decreasing kernel profile $k(x)$, assigns smaller weights to pixels farther from the center. The robustness of the density estimation increased by using these weights since the peripheral pixels are the least reliable, being often affected by occlusions (clutter) or interference from the background.The function $b:R^2 \rightarrow \left\{1,2,...,m\right\}$ associates to the pixel at location x_i^* the index $b(x_i^*)$ of its bin in the quantized feature space. The probability of the feature $u=1,2,...,m$ in the target model is then calculated as following [7]

$$q_u = C\sum_{i=1}^{n} k\left(\left\|x_i^*\right\|^2\right)\delta\left[b(x_i^*)-u\right] \quad (5)$$

Where 1 is the Kronecker delta function. The normalization constant C is obtained by imposing the condition $\sum_{u=1}^{m} q_u = 1$, from where [7]

$$C = \frac{1}{\sum_{i=1}^{n} k\left(\left\|x_i^*\right\|^2\right)} \quad (6)$$

Since the summation of delta functions for $u=1,2,...,m$ is equal to one.

2.2.3. Target candidates

Suppose that this name $\left\{x_i\right\}_{i=1,2,...,n_h}$ is the *normalized* pixel locations of the target candidate, centered at y in the current frame (Figure 3). The normalization is inherited from the frame containing the target model. Using the same kernel profile $k(x)$, but with bandwidth h, the probability of the feature $u=1,2,...,m$ in the target candidate is given by [7]

$$p_u(y) = C_h\sum_{i=1}^{n_h} k\left(\left\|\frac{y-x_i}{h}\right\|^2\right)\delta\left[b(x_i)-u\right] \quad (7)$$

Where

$$C = \frac{1}{\sum_{i=1}^{n_h} k\left(\left\|\frac{y-x_i}{h}\right\|^2\right)} \quad (8)$$

Figure 3. Target candidate in the second frame of the figure 2.

Is the normalization constant Point out that C_h does not depend on y, since the pixel locations x_i are organized in a regular lattice and y is one of the lattice nodes.

C_h is calculated for specific kernel and different values of h. The number of pixels considered in the localization process is obtained according to h.

2.2.4. Similarity function smoothness

The kernel profile $k(x)$ gives its properties to the similarity function (4).When the target model and candidate are expressed according to (5) and (7). A variable kernel profile leads to a variable similarity function and efficient gradient based optimization procedure can be utilized to find its maxima. The continuous kernel represents an interpolation process between the location and image structure. The used target representations do not limit the similarity and then various functions can obtain ρ. In [9], an experimental evaluation of different histogram similarity has been shown where.

2.2.5. Metric based on Bhattacharyya Coefficient

The similarity function defines a distance between a target model and candidates [7]. This distance should have a metric structure to accommodate comparisons among various targets. We define the distance between two discrete distributions as a formula 9,

$$d(y) = \sqrt{1 - \rho\left[p(y), q\right]} \qquad (9)$$

Where we chose formula 10.

$$\rho(y) \equiv \rho\left[p(y), q\right] = \sum_{u=1}^{m} \sqrt{p_u(y)q_u} \qquad (10)$$

The sample estimate of the Bhattacharyya coefficient between p and q [10, 7]. The Bhattacharyya coefficient is a divergence-type measure [11] that has a straightforward geometric interpretation. It is the cosine of the angle between the m-dimensional unit vectors $(\sqrt{p_1}, \sqrt{p_2}, ..., \sqrt{p_m})^T$ and $(\sqrt{q_1}, \sqrt{q_2}, ..., \sqrt{q_m})^T$. The fact that H and C are distributions is thus explicitly taken into account by representing them on the unit hyper sphere. At the same time, we can interpret (10) as the (normalized) correlation between the vectors $(\sqrt{p_1}, \sqrt{p_2}, ..., \sqrt{p_m})^T$ and $(\sqrt{q_1}, \sqrt{q_2}, ..., \sqrt{q_m})^T$. Properties of the Bhattacharyya coefficient such as its relation to the Fisher measure of information, quality of the sample estimate, and explicit forms for various distributions are shown in [12, 10].

The statistical measure (9) has several desirable properties:

1. It imposes a metric structure (see Appendix). The Bhattacharyya distance [13, p.99] or Kullback divergence [14, p.18] are not metrics when they violate at least one of the distance axioms.

2. It has an obvious geometric interpretation. Note that the L_p histogram metrics including histogram intersection [15]) do not enforce the conditions $\sum_{u=1}^{m} q_u = 1$ and $\sum_{u=1}^{m} p_u = 1$.

3. It utilizes discrete densities, and therefore, it is invariant to the scale of the target (up to quantization effects).

4. It is valid for arbitrary distributions, thus being superior to the Fisher linear discriminate, which yields useful results only for distributions that are separated by the mean-difference [13, p.132].

5. It approximates the chi-squared statistic, while avoiding the singularity problem of the chi square test when comparing empty histogram bins [16]. Divergence based measures were already used in computer vision. The Chern off and Bhattacharyya bounds have been applied in [17] to determine the effectiveness of edge detectors. The Kullback divergence between joint distribution and product of marginal (e.g., the mutual information) has been used in [18] for registration. Information theoretic measures for target distinctness were discussed in [19].

2.2.6. Target Localization

The distance (9) should be minimized as a function of y to find the location corresponding to the target in the current frame [7]. The localization procedure starts from the target position in the previous frame (the model) and searches in the neighborhood. Since our distance function is smooth, the procedure uses gradient information provided by the mean shift vector [20]. More involved optimizations based on the Hessian of (9) can be used [21].

Color information was chosen as the target feature. However, the same framework can be utilized for texture and edges, or any combination of them. In the sequel, it is assumed that the following information is available: (a) detection and localization in the initial objects frame to track (target models) [22, 23]; (b) periodic analysis of each object to account for possible updates of the target models due to significant changes in color [24].

2.2.7. Distance Minimization

Minimizing the distance (9) is equal to maximizing the Bhattacharyya coefficient $\rho(y)$ [7]. The search for the new target location in the current frame starts at the location y_0 of the target in the previous frame. Therefore, the probabilities $\{p(y_0)\}_{u=1,2,...,m}$ of the target candidate at location y_0 in the current frame first have to be computed. Using Taylor expansion around the values $p_u(y_0)$, the linear approximation of the Bhattacharyya coefficient (10) is derived after some manipulations as [7]

$$\rho[p(y),q] \approx \frac{1}{2}\sum_{u=1}^{m}\sqrt{p_u(y_0)q_u} + \frac{1}{2}\sum_{u=1}^{m}p_u(y)\sqrt{\frac{q_u}{p_u(y_0)}} \quad (11)$$

The approximation is satisfactory. When the target candidate $\{p_u(y)\}_{u=1,2,...,m}$ does not change drastically from the initial $\{p_u(y_0)\}_{u=1,2,...,m}$, that is, most often a valid assumption between consecutive frames. The condition $p_u(y_0) > 0$ (or some small threshold) for all $u = 1,2,...,m$, can be enforced by not using the feature values in violation. Recalling (7) results in [7] – you should illustrate the formulas below not just simply dropping them down the text!!!!

$$\rho[p(y),q] \approx \frac{1}{2}\sum_{u=1}^{m}\sqrt{p_u(y_0)q_u} + \frac{C_h}{2}\sum_{u=1}^{n_h}w_i k\left(\left\|\frac{y-x_i}{h}\right\|^2\right) \quad (12)$$

Where

$$w_i = \sum_{u=1}^{m}\sqrt{\frac{q_u}{p_u(y_0)}}\delta\left[b(x_i)-u\right] \quad (13)$$

Therefore, to minimize the distance in the formula (9), the second term in (12) has to be maximized, the first term being independent of y. See that the second term represents the density estimate computed with kernel profile $k(x)$ at y in the current frame, with the data being weighted by w_i (13). The mode of this density in the local neighborhood is the sought maximum that can be found applying the mean shift procedure [20]. In this procedure the kernel is recursively moved from the current location y_0 to the new location y_1 according to the relation

$$y_1 = \frac{\sum_{i=1}^{n_h}x_i w_i g\left(\left\|\frac{y_0-x_i}{h}\right\|^2\right)}{\sum_{i=1}^{n_h}w_i g\left(\left\|\frac{y_0-x_i}{h}\right\|^2\right)} \quad (14)$$

Where $g(x) = -k'(x)$, assume that the derivative of $k(x)$ exists for all $x \in [0,\infty)$, except for a finite set of points. The complete target localization algorithm is presented in the following.

The target model $\{q_u\}_{u=1,2,...,m}$ and its location y_0 in the previous frame.

1. Initialize the location of the target in the current frame with y_0, compute $\{p_u(y_0)\}_{u=1,2,...,m}$, and evaluate $\rho\left[p(y_0),q\right] = \sum_{u=1}^{m}\sqrt{p_u(y_0)q_u}$

2. Obtain the weights $\{w_i\}_{i=1,2,...,n_h}$ according to (13).

3. Find the next location of the target candidate according to (14).

4. Compute $\{p_u(y_1)\}_{u=1,2,...,m}$, and evaluate $\rho\left[p(y_1),q\right] = \sum_{u=1}^{m}\sqrt{p_u(y_1)q_u}$

5. While $\rho\left[p(y_1),q\right] < \rho\left[p(y_0),q\right]$

   Do $y_1 \leftarrow \frac{1}{2}(y_0 + y_1)$

   Evaluate $\rho\left[p(y_1),q\right]$

6. If $\left\|y_1 - y_0\right\| < \varepsilon$ Stop.

Otherwise set $y_0 \leftarrow y_1$ and go to Step 2.

2.2.8. Implementation of the Algorithm

The stopping criterion threshold ε used in Step 6 is obtained by constraining the vectors y_0 and y_1 to be within the same pixel in *original* image coordinates [7]. A lower threshold leads to the sub pixel accuracy. From real-time constraints (i.e., uniform CPU load in time), we also limit the number of mean shift iterations to N_{max}, typically taken equal to 20. In practice, the average number of iterations is much smaller than about 4. Implementation of the tracking algorithm can be much simpler than what is presented above. The Step role 5 is only to avoid potential numerical problems in the mean shift based maximization. These problems can appear because of the linear approximation of the Bhattacharyya coefficient. However, a large set of experiments tracking different objects for long periods of time has shown that the Bhattacharyya coefficient computed at the new location y_1 failed to increase in only 0.1% of the cases. Thus, the Step 5 is not used in practice, and as a result, there is no need to evaluate the Bhattacharyya coefficient in Steps 1 and 4.

We only iterate by computing the weights in Step 2 in the practical algorithm deriving the new location in Step 3, and testing the size of the kernel shift in Step 6. The Bhattacharyya coefficient is computed only after the algorithm completion to evaluate the similarity between the target model and the chosen candidate.

Kernels with Epanechnikov profile [20, 7] are recommended to be used.

$$k(x) = \begin{cases} \dfrac{1}{2}C_d^{-1}(d+2)(1-x) \\ \\ 0 \end{cases}$$

$$\qquad\qquad\qquad (15)$$

if $x \leq 1$

otherwise

In this case, the derivative of the profile, $g(x)$, is constant and (14) reduces to

$$y_1 = \frac{\sum_{i=1}^{n_h} x_i w_i}{\sum_{i=1}^{n_h} w_i} \qquad\qquad (16)$$

i.e., a simple weighted average.

The maximization of the Bhattacharyya coefficient can be also interpreted as a matched filtering procedure. In fact, (10) is the correlation coefficient between the unit vectors $\sqrt{q}$ and $\sqrt{p(y)}$, representing the target model and the candidate. Thus the mean shift procedure finds the local maximum of the scalar field of correlation coefficients. Will call the *operational basin of attraction* the region in the current frame in which the new location of the target can be found by the proposed algorithm. This basin is at least equal to the size of the target model due to the use of kernels. In other words, if in the current frame, the center of the target remains in the image area covered by the target model in the previous frame, and the local maximum of the Bhattacharyya coefficient is a reliable indicator for the new target location. We assume that the target representation provides sufficient discrimination, such that the Bhattacharyya coefficient presents a unique maximum in the local neighborhood. The mean shift procedure finds a root of the gradient as location function that can also correspond to a saddle point of the similarity surface. The saddle points are unstable solutions, and since the image noise acts as an independent perturbation factor across consecutive frames, they cannot affect the

tacking performance in an image sequence. The best algorithm for mean shift is shown in (Figure 4)

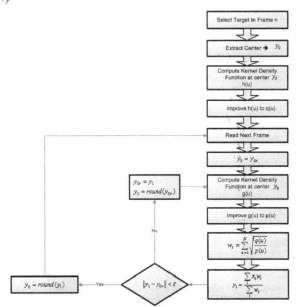

Figure 4.Complete block diagram of the mean shift tracker.

3. Databases

All presented databases in this section are easily available for much research in linguistics and recognition. The data were collected and recorded by Boston University, the database subsets build up benchmark databases that can be used for the automatic recognition of isolated and a continuous sign language, respectively, and so were they defined at the RWTH Aachen University. We briefly describe some commonly used statistical measures w.r.t. automatic recognition in the following: running words are the total number of words in the corpus unique words, which determine the vocabulary size singletons. These are words (or word tuples) that occur only once zerogram-, unigram-, bigram-, trigram- language models describe different linguistic contexts.

3.1. RWTH-BOSTON-104

The RWTH-BOSTON-104 database is based on the sign language published by the national gesture reorganization and the sign language of Boston University. This database has basically registered for studying the language structure and grammar of America sign language (ASL). The RWTH-BOSTON-104 database consists of 201 annotation videos from ASL sentences. These sentences were produced by 3 people (1 man and 2 women) and videos have been taken by the 4 cameras at the same time, 2 of them are located on the forward and show the person forward view, 1 of them is lied beside the person and the last one records the face picture. Videos are taken by speed of 30 frames per second with high resolution. All videos are Gray – Scale except camera related to face picture.

4. Experiments and Results

In this section, the results of applied algorithms on different images have been showed In Figure 5. This shows hand tracking for the usual image by applying just mean shift algorithm. Here 5 frames (Frame 21, 38, 40, 41 and 45) from 76 frames are determined. In this case, hand movements are slow and also resolution and quality of image are acceptable. As illustrated, this algorithm could not track the hand as an object tracking properly.

Figure 6 shows hand tracking for the usual image by applying just motion detection algorithm. This algorithm could not track just hand as an object

tracking. As seen in some frames face, the other hand has been chosen as a target.

Figure 7 shows hand tracking for the usual image by applying the combination of motion detection and mean shift algorithms. This algorithm could track just hand as an object tracking better than above algorithms.

Figure 8 shows hand tracking for the complicated image by applying the combination of motion detection and mean shift algorithms. In Figure 8, the resolution and quality of images are not so proper, images are noisy and blurring, and hand movements are faster than the old ones but as seen, this algorithm could track the hand as an object tracking so efficiently. These pictures have been taken from the deaf forum Iran's site but the old pictures are related to the main database, RWTH-BOSTON-104.

Figure 5. Hand tracking for the usual image by applying just mean shift algorithm.

Figure 6. Hand tracking for the usual image by applying just motion detection algorithm.

Figure 7. Hand tracking for the usual image by applying the combination of mean shift and motion detection algorithms.

Figure 8. Hand tracking for complicated image by applying mean shift and motion detection algorithms.

This algorithm in spite of some other famous algorithm used for target tracking, such as dynamic programming tracking [25], which is proper in real time works. Due to using the mean shift algorithm, the less computation is needed to track the target and it is faster than other common algorithms, such as it is 2 times faster than dynamic programming tracking when we use the same processor. Also, it needs less memory to track the target; therefore, it is useful for implementation practically.

5. Conclusions

Mean shift algorithm is just based on the color feature and sometimes loses the hand completely, so it always cannot track the hand correctly such as complicated images that the hand is lost because face and hand skin have the same color and then occlusion happens. Mean shift algorithm cannot consider the multimode levels, so it converges on the local maximum and cannot track the hand efficiently if there is the same color object with the hand. Motion detection algorithm is based on the object motion and cannot track just the hand as a target. The old solutions are complicated, time consuming and so expensive. However, the proposed method is so easy, fast, and efficient and low costly. The used combination method can track the hand properly when there are noise and parasite in the background. Because, it is able to consider the multimode levels and detect the hand as an object tracking. Simulation results showed our method could track more appropriately than the both of mean shift and motion detection algorithms. It is so efficient even in complicated images.

References

[1] Birchfield, S., 1998. "Elliptical Head Tracking Using Int ensity Gradients and Color Histograms," Proc.IEEE Conf. ComputerVision and Pattern Recognition, pp: 232-237.

[2] Black, M. and D. Fleet, 2000. "Probabilistic Detection and Tracking of Motion Boundaries," Int'l J.Computer Vision, 38(3): 231-245.

[3] Honggang Wang, Ming C. Leu and Cemil OZ. "American Sign Language Recognition Using Multi-dimensional Hidden Markov Models," journal of

information science and engineering 22, 1109-1123 (2006).

[4] Y. Cheng. "Mean shift, mode seeking, and clustering". IEEE Transactions on Pattern Analysis and Machine Intelligence, 1995, Vol.17, No. 8, pp. 790-799.

[5] D. Comaniciu, V. Ramesh, P. Meer. "Kernel-based object tracking". IEEE Transactions on Pattern Analysis and Machine Intelligence, 2003, Vol. 25, No. 5, pp. 564-577.

[6] Ruiz-del-Solar, J. and Vallejos, P.: Motion Detection and Tracking for an AIBO Robot Using Motion Compensation and Kalman Filtering. RoboCup 2004 Symposium, Lecture Notes in Computer Science (accepted).

[7] D. Comaniciu, V. Ramesh, P. Meer, Kernel-based object tracking, IEEE Transactions on Pattern Analysis and Machine Intelligence 25 (5) (2003) 564–577.

[8] D. W. Scott, Multivariate Density Estimation. Wiley, 1992.

[9] J. Puzicha, Y. Rubner, C. Tomasi, and J. Buhmann, "Empirical evaluation of dissimilarity measures for color and texture," in Proc. 7th Intl. Conf. on Computer Vision, Kerkyra, Greece, 1999, pp. 1165–1173.

[10] T. Kailath, "The divergence and Bhattacharyya distance measures in signal selection," IEEE Trans. Commun. Tech., vol. 15, pp. 52–60, 1967.

[11] J. Lin, "Divergence measures based on the Shannon entropy," IEEE Trans. Information Theory, vol. 37, pp. 145–151, 1991.

[12] Djouadi, O. Snorrason, and F. Garber, "The quality of training-sample estimates of the Bhattacharyya coefficient," IEEE Trans. Pattern Anal. Machine Intell., vol. 12, pp. 92–97, 1990.

[13] K. Fukunaga, Introduction to Statistical Pattern Recognition. Academic Press, second edition, 1990.

[14] T. Cover and J. Thomas, Elements of Information Theory. John Wiley & Sons, New York, 1991.

[15] M. Swain and D. Ballard, "Color indexing," Intl. J. of Computer Vision, vol. 7, no. 1, pp. 11–32, 1991.

[16] F. Aherne, N. Thacker, and P. Rockett, "The Bhattacharyya metric as an absolute similarity measure for frequency coded data," Kybernetika, vol. 34, no. 4, pp. 363–368, 1998.

[17] S. Konishi, A. Yuille, J. Coughlan, and S. Zhu, "Fundamental bounds on edge detection: An information theoretic evaluation of different edge cues," in Proc. IEEE Conf. on Computer Vision and Pattern Recognition, Fort Collins, 1999, pp. 573–579.

[18] P. Viola and W. Wells, "Alignment by maximization of mutual information," Intl. J. of Computer Vision, vol. 24, no. 2, pp. 137–154, 1997.

[19] J. Garcia, J. Valdivia, and X. Vidal, "Information theoretic measure for visual target distinctness," IEEE Trans. Pattern Anal. Machine Intell., vol. 23, no. 4, pp. 362–383, 2001.

[20] D. Comaniciu and P. Meer, "Mean shift: A robust approach toward feature space analysis," IEEE Trans. Pattern Anal. Machine Intell., vol. 24, no. 5, pp. 603–619, 2002.

[21] W. Press, S. Teukolsky, W. Vetterling, and B. Flannery, Numerical Recipes in C. Cambridge University Press, second edition, 1992.

[22] Lipton, H. Fujiyoshi, and R. Patil, "Moving target classification and tracking from real-time video," in

IEEE Workshop on Applications of Computer Vision, Princeton, NJ, 1998, pp. 8–14.

[23] M. Black and D. Fleet, "Probabilistic detection and tracking of motion boundaries," Intl. J. of Computer Vision, vol. 38, no. 3, pp. 231–245, 2000.

[24] S. McKenna, Y. Raja, and S. Gong, "Tracking colour objects using adaptive mixture models," Image and Vision Computing Journal, vol. 17, pp. 223–229, 1999.

[25] P. Dreuw, T. Deselaers, D. Rybach, D. Keysers, H. Ney: Tracking Using Dynamic Programming for Appearance-Based Sign Language Recognition. In Proceedings of the 7th International Conference of Automatic Face and Gesture Recognition, Southampton, UK, 2006.

2

Application of statistical techniques and artificial neural network to estimate force from sEMG signals

V. Khoshdel and A. Akbarzadeh*

Center of Excellence on Soft Computing & Intelligent Information Processing, Mechanical Engineering Department, Ferdowsi University of Mashhad, Mashhad.

*Corresponding author: Alireza.Akbarzadeh@um.ac.ir (A. Akbarzadeh).

Abstract

This paper presents an application of the design of experiment(DoE) techniques to determine the optimized parameters of the artificial neural network (ANN)model, which are used to estimate the force from the electromyogram (sEMG) signals. The accuracy of the ANN model is highly dependent on the network parameter settings. There are plenty of algorithms that are used to obtain the optimal ANN settings. However, to the best of our knowledge, no regression analysis has yet been used to model the effect of each parameter as well as presenting the percent contribution and significance level of the ANN parameters for force estimation. In this paper, the sEMG experimental data is collected, and the ANN parameters are regulated based on an orthogonal array design table to train the ANN model. The Taguchi method helps us to find the optimal parameters settings. The analysis of variance (ANOVA) technique is then used to obtain the significance level as well as the contribution percentage of each parameter I order to optimize ANN' modeling in the human force estimation. The results obtained indicate that DoE is a promising solution to estimate the human force from the sEMG signals.

Keywords: *Artificial Neural Network, Taguchi Method, Analysis of variance, EMG signals.*

1. Introduction

The rehabilitation robot has recently received much attention by the physiotherapists and robot researchers. There are some reasons for this increasing attention. The rehabilitation robot can consistently apply therapy over long time periods without tiring. In addition, the use of sensors can highly improve the quality of therapy. Moreover, it can provide some types of therapy exercises that a therapist cannot do. Furthermore, the robot can decrease the cost of a physiotherapy process. There is also a great need from many patients with movement disabilities to have session physiotherapy. Finally, the rehabilitation robot can be easily programmed by a physiotherapist to perform the suggested exercises [1]. Muscle activity can be recorded from selected muscles using surface EMG electrodes (sEMG), while the user moves his arm. The muscular activity can be transformed to the force and kinematic variables that are used as the inputs in the robot control by a decoding procedure.

The sEMG signals are one of the most common biological signals thaht help us in the robot control according to the user's intention. The sEMG signals can directly reflect the muscle activation level in real time [2-8]. In voluntary movements, force is associated with the motor unit recruitment and variations in the motor unit firing frequency [9]. At the same muscle length and under the isometric conditions, a greater number of recruited motor units with greater discharge frequencies (i.e. muscle activation) lead to a greater force generation. Therefore, a linear relationship between EMG and muscle force is assumed. Although, Precise estimation of muscle force based on the sEMG signals in real time provides valuable information for a robot control system in order to perform effective therapeutic exercises, while the sEMG signals are random, continuous, and non-linear in nature [10, 11]. Therefore, the sEMG signals should be processed in order to get a simple model for its amplitude and then map this amplitude for joint force. Various methods have been proposed for the sEMG-based force estimation such as mathematical models, artificial neural network (ANN), and neurofuzzy. It has been shown that ANN will yield efficient to estimate the voluntary limb force [12]. It has been shown that the setting of network parameters, such as the number of neurons, number of hidden layers, and learning rate have great influences on the accuracy of ANN model. However, selection of the ANN design parameters is still an open question in the force estimation for the rehabilitation robots. Design of experiment (DoE), as a statistical technique, is widely used to study the relationship between the factors involved, and affecting the outputs of the process. Additionally, it can be used to systematically identify the optimum setting of factors to reach the desired output. In this paper, we used DoE to find the best setting of the ANN parameters in order to achieve a minimum error in force estimation. The applications of DoE techniques to optimize the ANN parameters have been reported in the literature [13-18]. It has been found that some factors such as the number of neurons in the hidden layers, transfer function, and training function have significant effects on the ANN performance. Therefore, in this paper, the sEMG experimental data was collected, and the ANN parameters were regulated based on an orthogonal array design table to train the ANN model. The Taguchi method helps us to find the optimal parameter settings. The analysis of the variance (ANOVA) technique is then used to obtain the significance level as well as the contribution percentage of each parameter to optimize the ANN modeling in the human force estimation. The results of human force estimation have indicated that DoE is a promising solution to optimize the ANN modeling. This paper is organized as followss: Section 2 explain how ANN is used for the sEMG-based force estimation. The Taguchi method is introduced in section 3. In section 4, the experimentation procedure is presented. The results obtained and the concluding discussion are presented in sections 5 and 6.

2. Force estimation

In the control system of the rehabilitation robots, the estimated force is used as an input signal. Nevertheless, the raw sEMG signals are not suitable as input signals for controllers, and must be processed prior to use. In this paper, each EMG channel is independently processed in three steps, as follows. Step 1: The raw EMG signals must be filtered. In this step, a a 5th ordered notch filter is used to remove the 60 Hz noise resulting from the power supply. Step 2: The EMG signal should be rectified. The absolute value for the EMG signals is calculated in this step. Step 3: The online

moving average (OMA) of the rectified EMG signals is calculated as follows:

$$E(t) = \sqrt{\frac{1}{N}\sum_{i=0}^{N} E(t-i)^2}$$ (1)

where, N is the number of segments ($N=100$) and $E(t)$ is the value of the rectified EMG at its sampling point. The signal processing procedure is shown in figure 1. Finally, the processed EMG (PEMG) signals are ready to be used as an input for the ANN estimator.

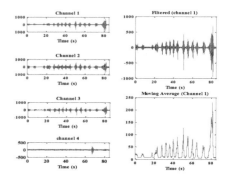

Figure 1. EMG process for neural network estimation.

MLP and cascade are the two most common ANN structure that are used for force estimation. The detailed structural design for te feed-forward condition for MLP and Cascade is depicted in figure 2.

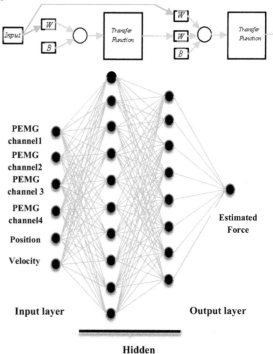

Figure 2. Cascade (up) and MLP (down) neural network structure.

We proposed the PEMG signals and the of human dynamics information as the inputs for estimation. Hence, the relationship between the sEMG signals and the human force can been proposed as:

$$\mathbf{F}_{h_{est}} = \begin{bmatrix} PE_{ch1}(t) \\ PE_{ch2}(t) \\ PE_{ch3}(t) \\ PE_{ch4}(t) \\ \theta \\ \dot{\theta} \end{bmatrix} W^{hl1}_{6 \times n} W^{hl2}_{n \times m} W^{ol}_{m \times 1} \qquad (2)$$

where, $F_{h_{est}}$ is the estimation of human force, $PE_{ch\,i}(t)$ is the processed EMG signal for the ith channel, and θ and $\dot{\theta}$ are the angular position and velocity, respectively. $W^{hl1}_{6 \times n}$ and $W^{hl2}_{6 \times n}$ are the neural network weight matrices of the hidden layers, and $W^{ol}_{6 \times n}$ is the weight matrix of the output layer.

Selection of the ANN design parameters is still an open challenge. For example, the network performance may deteriorate by a large number of hidden neurons. In addition, to store the huge numbers of network variables, a huge memory is required, and hence, training becomes complicated. However, the network cannot adjust the weight and bias properly during training, if a very low number of neurons are selected in the hidden layer, which result in over-fitting. Over-fitting makes the network excessively complex, and thus, the non-generalized network generates random error, and provides a very poor classification. Figure3 depicts the design parameters of ANN that largely affect the ANN performance.

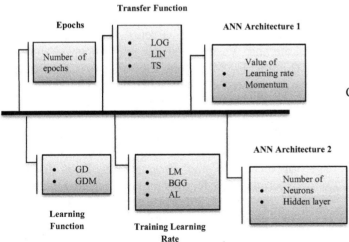

Figure 3. Design parameters of ANN.

Due to the lack of a specific rule for finding the optimal ANN parameters for an optimized network performance, a statistical technique is performed to investigate the appropriate network topology for force estimation.

3. Taguchi Method

In the Taguchi method, constructed on the fractional factorial experiment, the independent parameters are divided into design parameters and noise parameters [19]. The design parameters are those for which the designer chooses values as a part of the design process and the noise parameters are defined for modelling uncertainty in the design.

In the design process, we choose the design parameter values such that the design goals are maximized despite the noise parameter actions. This means that a robust tuning technique using the Taguchi method would enable the regulators not only to reduce the control errors but also to decrease variations in those values while remaining insensitive to changes in system dynamics and variations in operating points.

By implementing this approach, the researchers can significantly decrease the time required for experimental investigations. DoE using the Taguchi method is briefly outlined below [20]:

A. **_Identification of objectives_**: the first step of the Taguchi method is to identify a specific objective. In this paper, the objective is the ANN parameters, which are used to minimize the estimation error.

B. **_Determining the quality characteristic_**: in Taguchi method, the quality characteristics are classified into one of the following three types: nominal-the-best, smaller-the-better, and larger-the-better. In this study, the smaller-the-better type is used to decrease the estimation error.

C. **_Selecting the controllable factors and noise factors_**: one of the most important steps involved is the selection of the factors to be tested for their influence on the quality characteristic. Actually, if we select the controllable factors and noise factors carelessly, this can lead to false conclusions and may require the experiments to be repeated. The desired number of levels must be determined after selecting the factors. In this paper, the ANN parameters are used as the controllable factors, and we do not have any noise factor. The numbers of levels for the ANN parameters are defined in table 2. In the next step, we should assign a physical value to each level of controllable factors.

D. **Selecting an orthogonal array:** it is clear that testing all combinations of the factor levels is required in the full factorial experiment. For example, a study involving 6 factors with three levels for each factor would require $3^4 \times 2^2 = 324$ experiments. Orthogonal arrays produce smaller and less-costly experiments. Using an L_27 (3^5) orthogonal array, for example, a study involving 5 factors with three levels for each factor can be conducted with only 27 experiments. In addition to being efficient, the procedures used for using orthogonal arrays are straightforward and easy to use. In this paper, in order to reduce the number of experiments, an L_36 (3^6) orthogonal array is selected. This array implies only 36 experiments.

E. **Conducting the experiment and analysis:** conducting the experiments includes execution of the experiment as developed in the planning and design phases. The analysis phase of experimentation is related to calculations for converting raw data into the representative signal-to-noise ratio (SNR). SNR, as a measurement tool for determining robustness, is a critical component to an optimal parameter design. SNR can be adopted as the index of the system ability to perform well regardless of the noise by including the impact of noise factors on the process. By successfully applying this concept to experimentation, it is possible to determine the design parameters of ANN that can produce the minimum estimation errors while maximizing SNR.

In the case of the smaller-the-better quality characteristic, SNR can be written as Eq. 3:

$$ITAE = \int F_m - F_{est} dt \qquad (3)$$

where, F_m is the measured force, F_{est} is the estimated force, and ITEA is the integral force error. Consequently, SNR can be defined as:

SNR= $-10\log ITAE$ \qquad (4)

The Taguchi method reduces the number of experiments over the full-factorial approach. Therefore, to provide the levels of confidence in the results, it is valuable to use the statistical analysis of experiments, which are called the analysis of variance (ANOVA). Furthermore, ANOVA identifies and ranks the variables that affect the variance of the output signal. ANOVA

is one of the main steps in using the Taguchi method.

4. Experimental
4.1 Setup and sEMG data collection
Four channels of sEMG signals are used as the main input signals in order to estimate the participants real force. Locations of the sEMG electrodes are shown in figure 4. Each channel mainly corresponds to one muscle, as shown in table 1. To determine the magnitude of the sEMG signals of the knee extensors, our participants were seated on a dynamometer (Biodex - System3, Biodex Medical Systems Inc., USA) with a hip angle of 85°.

Figure 4. The locations of sEMG electrodes.

Table 1 . Muscles for each sEMG channel.

EMG Channel	Ch-1	Ch-2	Ch-3	Ch-4
Muscle	Vastus Lateralis	Rectus Femoris	Vastus Medialist	Bicep Femoris

Electrodes (Ag/AgCl) with an electrolytic gel interface were positioned above the midpoint of the muscle belly (with 2 cm distance on inter-electrodes) of the Rectus Femoris, Vastus Lateralis, Vastus medialis, and Biceps Femoris (Figure 3). Moreover, the reference electrodes were located on the patella bone. The skin was carefully shaved and cleaned with alcohol in order to reduce the skin impedance. To reduce the motion artefacts of the electrodes, they were further secured to the skin with an elastic tape, together with the preamplifier. Prior to the experiment, the leg was passively shaken to check the mechanical artefacts of the sEMG signals from each muscle. Several tests (e.g. contractions against manual resistance in knee flexion and extension) were performed to visualize whether a good signal was produced from each muscle. When artefacts or poor signals were observed, the preparation procedure was repeated. ME6000 was used to record the sEMG signal from muscle in

Sport Sciences Research Institute of IRAN (SSRI). The data collected from the EMG sensor was sampled using a 2000 Hz sampling frequency.

4.2 Design of experiments(DoEs)

The experimental region was decided as per Taguchi design approach. The number of levels for each controllable process parameter was provided in table 2. A wide experimental region was covered so that the sensitivity to noise factors did not change with small variations in these factor settings, and to obtain optimum regions for the process parameters. Therefore, each parameter was analysed at different levels of the ANN parameters. The cascade-forward back-propagation and MLP back-propagation ANN with three training functions(LM, Boydon – Fletcher – Goldfarb – Shanno, GDA) were considered in this study. The number of neurons was varied from 1 to 10 and the number of hidden layer was varied from 2 to 4. Three transfer functions (PURELIN, LOGSIG, and TANSIG) were used in this work. The two different learning functions gradient descent (GD) and gradient descent with momentum (GDM), frequently used for ANN were also considered. These factors and their levels used for DoE are shown in table 2. After deciding the parameters and their levels, the Taguchi design approach was applied to decide the experimental region. An orthogonal array L_36, which was designed for these factors is shown in table 3.

Table 2. ANN parameters levels.

Parameters	Range	Levels		
		1	2	3
Learning Function(LF)	-	GD	GDM	-
Training Function(TrF)	-	LM	BFGS	GDA
Number of hidden Layers(NL)	2-4	2	3	4
Number of neurons(Nn)	1-10	1	5	10
Topology of ANN(TP)	-	MLP	Cascade	
Transfer Function(TF)	-	TAN	PUR	LOG

The experiments were conducted as per L_36 orthogonal array for the set of parameters shown in table 3. MSE was calculated for all trials as per the L_36 orthogonal array to understand the process parameter characteristics and optimum setting of user-defined parameters.

By plotting the average response value for each factor level (Figure 5), relative comparisons of the slope between the points plotted can be made.

Table 3. Orthogonal for different factors of ANN.

NO	TP	LF	TrF	NL	Nn	TF	ITAE
1	1	1	1	1	1	1	215.4
2	1	1	2	2	2	2	220.0
3	1	1	3	3	3	3	251.5
4	1	1	1	1	1	1	215.4
5	1	1	2	2	2	2	220.0
6	1	1	3	3	3	3	251.5
7	1	1	1	1	2	3	236.6
8	1	1	2	2	3	1	183.4
9	1	1	3	3	1	2	223.7
10	1	2	1	1	3	2	252.3
11	1	2	2	2	1	3	216.4
12	1	2	3	3	2	1	246.7
13	1	2	1	2	3	1	551.0
14	1	2	2	3	1	2	205.9
15	1	2	3	1	2	3	215.1
16	1	2	1	2	3	2	216.3
17	1	2	2	3	1	3	215.0
18	1	2	3	1	2	1	213.8
19	2	1	1	2	1	3	176.2
20	2	1	2	3	2	1	170.6
21	2	1	3	1	3	2	249.5
22	2	1	1	2	2	3	183.8
23	2	1	2	3	3	1	694.5
24	2	1	3	1	1	2	254.0
25	2	1	1	3	2	1	321.2
26	2	1	2	1	3	2	250.2
27	2	1	3	2	1	3	211.3
28	2	2	1	3	2	2	317.9
29	2	2	2	1	3	3	245.3
30	2	2	3	2	1	1	187.7
31	2	2	1	3	3	3	213.1
32	2	2	2	1	1	1	188.9
33	2	2	3	2	2	2	199.2
34	2	2	1	3	1	2	555.2
35	2	2	2	1	2	3	247.6
36	2	2	3	2	3	1	294.6

With this best combination of design parameters, SNR increased to about 100%. The results obtained were confirmed by the ANOVA analysis.

The percentage contributions are shown in table 4. The main purpose of this analysis was to estimate the effect of each factor on the results.

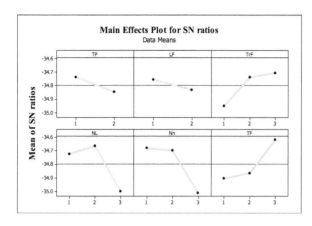

Figure 5. Main effects plot for SNRs.

Table 4. Percentage contribution.

Controller Parameter	Percentage contribution	P-value
TP	12.01 %	0.236
LF	9.02 %	0.617
Trf	10.12 %	0.817
NL	19.42 %	0.138
Nn	19.01 %	0.147
TF	14.22 %	0.390
ANOVA Error	16.20 %	

The ANOVA analysis shows that *NL* and *Nn* have the biggest percentage contributions. This confirms the results show in figure 5, which illustrates that SNR values for the levels of *NL* and *Nn* differ significantly. It is important to note that the error contribution computed with ANOVA gives an idea of the confidence in the results.

P-values, which report the significance level of the parameters are shown in the second column of table 4. The trend confirms that at stage 4, while NL and Nn have minimum P-value, which means that these parameters significantly contribute toward ANN estimation, LF and TrF do not have important effects on the improvement of SNR.

To compare the proposed optimized ANN with manual tuning ANN parameters, the result of Simulink in MATLAB were compared. The Total error of estimation across 84 seconds was 3.45 for MATLAB manual tuning ANN and 6.32 for the *proposed optimized ANN.*

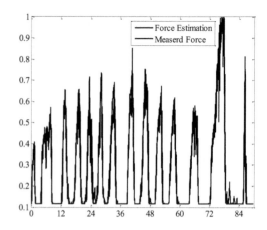

Figure 6. Force estimation by the optimized ANN.

We can vividly assert that the proposed method is more efficient than manual tuning.

The force estimated by the optimized ANN based on the Taguchi method is shown in figure 6, where the black line represents the measured force by load cells and red line represents the force estimated by ANN. As we can vividly realize, the performance of optimized ANN is well, and it can estimate the human force appropriately.

5. Results and Discussion
The highlights of this paper can be summarized as follows:

- Use of the DoE technique, presented in this paper, allow the researchers to obtain the optimum combinations of the ANN parameter settings with a minimal number of experiments among a large possible number of experiments. Using the Taguchi L_36 design, only 36 experiments were gathered and used to train the ANN model. The minimum number of experiments results in time and cost savings.
- By a close observation of the experimental table, it can be observed that the optimal combination settings suggested by the Taguchi method, is not any of the existing runs of the table.
- Verification runs, using the optimum ANN parameters, showed that the ANN model produced acceptable results.
- The authors believe that the optimum settings of the ANN parameters are largely problem-dependent. Optimization process should be performed for each application, as the significant factors might be different for ANN trained for different purposes.

6. Conclusion

The objective of this paper was to use the Taguchi method to determine the optimal ANN parameters for the human force estimation. To the best of the author's knowledge, application of the statistical technique and ANN to estimate human force from the sEMG signals as not yet been reported in the literature. Using an L_36 orthogonal array, only 36 experiments were designed, and an effective ANN model was trained. Using the Taguchi technique, additional combinations of experiments, not originally tested, were able to be predicted. The results obtained indicate that the best settings for the ANN parameters are learning function: GDM, training function: BFGS, umber of hidden layer: 5, number of neurons: 5, type of ANN: MLP and transfer function: GDA. Additionally, contribution of the parameters in the regression model indicates that Nn and NL have the most percent contribution while LF has the least one. The results obtained demonstrate that the Taguchi method is an effective tool in identifying the optimal ANN parameters.

References

[1] Fateh, M. M. & Khoshdel, V. (2015). Voltage-based adaptive impedance force control for a lower-limb rehabilitation robot. Advanced Robotics, vol. 29, no. 15, pp. 961-971.

[2] Khoshdel, V. & Akbarzadeh Tootoonchi, (2015). A. Robust Impedance Control for Rehabilitation Robot. Modares Mechanical Engineering, vol. 15, no. 8, pp. 429-437.

[3] Jain, R. K., Datta, S. & Majumder, S. (2013). Design and control of an IPMC artificial muscle finger for micro gripper using EMG signal. Mechatronics, vol. 23, no. 3, pp. 381.

[4] Dellon, B. & Matsuoka, Y. (2007). Prosthetics, exoskeletons, and rehabilitation (grand challenges of Robotics). IEEE Robot. Autom. Mag., vol. 14, no. 1, pp. 30–34.

[5] Wu, S., Waycaster, G. & Shen, Xi. (2011). Electromyography-based control of active above-knee prostheses. Control Engineering Practice, vol 19, no. 8, pp. 875–882.

[6] Kiguchi, K., Kariya, S., Watanabe, K., Izumi, K. & Fukuda, T. (2001). An exoskeletal robot for human elbow motion support—Sensor fusion, adapta tion, and control. IEEE Trans. Syst., Man, Cybern. B, Cybern., vol. 31, no. 3, pp. 353–361.

[7] Rosen, J., Brand, M., Fuchs, M. & Arcan, M. (2001). A myosignal-based powered exoskeleton system. IEEE Trans. Syst., Man, Cybern. A, Syst., Humans, vol. 31, no. 3, pp. 210–222.

[8] Kiguchi, K., Rahman, M. H., Sasaki, M. & Teramoto, K. (2008). Development of a 3DOF mobile exoskeleton robot for human upper limb motion assist," Robot. Autonom. Syst. vol. 56, no. 8, pp. 678–691.

[9] Fleischer C. & Hommel, G. (2008). A human - exoskeleton interface utilizing electromyography. IEEE Trans. Robot. vol. 24, no. 4, pp. 872–882.

[10] Moritani, T. & Muro, M. (1987). Motor unit activity and surface electromyogram power spectrum during increasing force of contraction. Eur J Appl Physiol Occup Physiol. vol. 56, no. 3, pp. 260-265.

[11] Hogan, N. & Mann, R. W. (1980). Myoelectric signal processing, Optimal estimation applied to electromyography—Part1: Derivation of the optimal myoprocessors. IEEE Transactions on Biomedical Engineering, vol. 27, no. 7, pp. 396-410.

[12] Siegler S., Hillstrom H. J, Freedman, W., & Moskowitz, G. (1985). Effect of myoelectric signal processing on the relationship between muscle force and processed EMG. Am. J. Phys Med, vol. 64, no. 3, pp. 130-149.

[13] Lin, T. Y, Ping, H. C., Hsu, T. H. & Wang, L. C. (2011). A systematic approach to the optimization of artificial neural networks. In: IEEE 3rd International conference on communication software and networks (ICCSN), vol. 6, pp. 76-79.

[14] Inhira, E. & Yokoi, H. (2007). An optimal design method for artificial neural networks by using the design of experiments. J Adv Comput Intell Inform, vol. 11, pp. 593-599.

[15] Kim, Y. S. & Yum, B. J. (2004). Robust Design of Multilayer Feed Forward Neural Networks: An Experimental Approach. Appl. Artif. Intell., vol. 17, pp. 249-263.

[16] Packianather, M. S., Drake, P.R. & Rowland, H. (2000). Optimizing the Parameters of Multilayered Feed Forward Neural Networks through Taguchi Design of Experiments. Qual. Reliab. Eng. Int., vol. 16, pp. 461-473.

[17] Yang, S. M. & Lee, G. S. (1999). Neural Network Design by using Taguchi Method. J. Dyn. Syst. Meas. Contr, vol. 121, pp. 560-563.

[18] Khaw, J. F. C., Lim, B. S. & Lim, L. E. N. (1995). Optimal Design of Neural Networks using the Taguchi Method. Neuralcomputing, vol. 7, pp. 225-245.

[19] Roy, R. K. (2001). Design of Experiments Using the Taguchi Approach: 16 Steps to Product and Process Improvement. Wiley, (2001).

[20] Lee, K. & Kim, J. (2000). Controller gain tuning of a simultaneous multi-axis PID control system using the Taguchi method. Control Engineering Practice, vol. 8, no. 8, pp. 949-958.

3

Discrete time robust control of robot manipulators in the task space using adaptive fuzzy estimator

M. M. Fateh* and S. Azargoshasb

Electrical Engineering Department, University of Shahrood, Shahrood, Iran.

Corresponding author: mmfateh@shahroodut.ac.ir (M. M. fateh).

Abstract

This paper presents a discrete-time robust control for electrically driven robot manipulators in the task space. A novel discrete-time model-free control law is proposed by employing an adaptive fuzzy estimator for the compensation of the uncertainty including model uncertainty, external disturbances and discretization error. Parameters of the fuzzy estimator are adapted to minimize the estimation error using a gradient descent algorithm. The proposed discrete control is robust against all uncertainties as verified by stability analysis. The proposed robust control law is simulated on a SCARA robot driven by permanent magnet dc motors. Simulation results show the effectiveness of the control approach.

Keywords: *Discrete Control, Uncertainty Estimator, Free-model Control, Adaptive Fuzzy Estimator, Task-space, SCARA Robot.*

1. Introduction

The Advantages of digital systems to analogue systems lead us to pay more attention on developing the discrete control theory and using digital controllers. Digital control systems are superior to continuous time control systems from different points of view. For instance, digital systems are more flexible to changes, more immune to environmental noises and less computational [1]. The stability analysis of discrete control system has been rigorously studied. Stability analysis of discrete-time fuzzy-model-based control systems with time delays has been introduced in [2].was presented [2]. Stability analysis and stabilization of discrete-time T-S fuzzy time-varying delay systems has been studied in [3]. A model reference adaptive control approach for the synchronization of a discrete-time chaotic system is using output tracking control has been performed [4]. The important purposes in these researches are the improvement of the control performance and to ensure the system stability at the presence of problems such as uncertainties, nonlinearities, sampling period and discretizing errors. Discrete control of robot manipulators has achieved a great deal of research in various forms of control algorithms. The

discrete repetitive linear controls namely Q-filter, convolution, learning and basis function were offered and compared in [5]. Among them, the Q-filter algorithm as an internal control shows the fastest execution speed, the lowest computational complexity, and ease of design and implementation. However, tracking errors cannot converge to zero due to nonlinearity of the robotic system. Many research efforts have paid attention to the model-based control. However, a precise model is not available in practice. In addition, complex models may not be used in the control laws for avoiding computational burden and practical difficulties. Therefore, a simpler model such as nominal model is preferred to design a controller. As a result, the control system faces uncertainty raised from differences between the nominal model and actual system. Generally, the uncertainty may include the parametric uncertainty, unmodeled dynamics, external disturbances and discretization error. The control performance is thus dependent on how well the uncertainty can be estimated and compensated. In order to overcome model uncertainties, a discrete sliding-mode control was developed for robot manipulators [6]. Another approaches model-free discrete control for uncertain robot manipulators was presented using a fuzzy estimator [7]. Alternatively, this paper presents a model-free control by estimation of the uncertainty. In the last few decades, adaptive and robust control of robot manipulators in the task-space [8-9] and joint-space [10] have been extensively studied. The task-space control is much complicated than the joint-space control in the presence of uncertainties. Among the control strategies used for the robot manipulators, the torque control strategy is more complicated than the voltage control strategy [11]. Position control of flexible joint robots using torque control strategy is a challenging task, while voltage control strategy has considerably simplified this problem [12-13]. Nowadays, various fuzzy systems are widely used in adaptive and robust control of robot manipulators [14-15] due to their universal approximation property [16]. These researches can be considered as different efforts made towards a common objective which is estimation and compensation of uncertainty. For example, using the T–S model of discrete-time chaotic systems, an adaptive control algorithm was presented based on some conventional adaptive control methods [17]. Another approach based on adaptive fuzzy sliding mode control has been presented for the position control of robotic manipulators [18]. Most learning algorithms such as the gradient descent algorithm require some training data for estimation a function as a fuzzy system or a neural network for example. In estimation of uncertainty, the problem with this procedure is that the training data is not available unknown. To solve this problem, this paper finds a relationship between the tracking error and the estimation error to perform the gradient descent algorithm. Thus, the need for providing training data will be eliminated. One of the most challenging problems in designing a robust controller is to employ an uncertainty bound parameter which should be known in advance or estimated [19-20]. The value of uncertainty bound parameter is very crucial. Overestimation of this parameter will result in saturation of input and higher frequency of chattering in the switching control laws, while underestimation will increase the tracking error [21]. By estimation the uncertainty, a new robust control approach is proposed which is free from the uncertainty bound parameter. In this paper, a discrete-time robust adaptive fuzzy control has been proposed for position control of a robot manipulator using voltage control strategy in task space. In the proposed method, the consequence parts of fuzzy

rules are tuned via adaptive laws using a gradient descent algorithm. Most of robust control approaches are based on linear parameterization property of the manipulator dynamic equation. Consequently, the regressor matrix should be identified which requires a tedious procedure. However, the model free control approach presented in this paper does not need the regressor analysis. As result, it is much simpler and less computational. This paper is organized as follows: Section 2 introduces modeling of the electrical robot manipulator driven by geared permanent magnet dc motors. Section 3 presents the proposed discrete control law. Section 4 describes the discrete adaptive fuzzy method to estimate and compensate the uncertainties. Section 5 deals with stability analysis and performance evaluation. Section 6 presents the simulation results and finally, section 7 concludes the paper.

2. Modeling

Consider an electrical robot driven by geared permanent magnet dc motors. The dynamics of robot manipulator [22] is expressed as

$$\mathbf{D(q)\ddot{q} + C(q,\dot{q})\dot{q} + G(q) = \tau} \tag{1}$$

where, $\mathbf{q} \in R^n$ is the vector of joint positions, $\mathbf{D(q)} \in R^{n \times n}$ the inertia matrix of manipulator, $\mathbf{C(q,\dot{q})\dot{q}} \in R^n$ the vector of centrifugal and Coriolis torques, $\mathbf{G(q)} \in R^n$ the vector of gravitational torques, and $\boldsymbol{\tau} \in R^n$ the vector of joint torques. The vectors and matrices are shown bold for clarity. We assume that the mechanical system is perfectly rigid. The electric motors provide the joint torques $\boldsymbol{\tau}$ by

$$\mathbf{J\ddot{\theta}_m + B\dot{\theta}_m + r\tau = \tau_m} \tag{2}$$

where, $\boldsymbol{\tau}_m \in R^n$ is the torque vector of motors, $\boldsymbol{\theta}_m \in R^n$ the position vector of motors, and $\mathbf{J,B,r} \in R^{n \times n}$ the diagonal matrices for inertia, damping, and reduction gear of motors, respectively. The vector of joint velocities $\dot{\mathbf{q}}$ is obtained by the vector of motor velocities $\dot{\boldsymbol{\theta}}_m$ through the gears as

$$\mathbf{r\dot{\theta}_m = \dot{q}} \tag{3}$$

Note that vectors and matrices are represented in the bold form for clarity. In order to obtain the motor voltages as the inputs of system, consider the electrical equation of geared permanent magnet dc motors in the matrix form as

$$\mathbf{RI_a} + \mathbf{L\dot{I}_a} + \mathbf{K_b r^{-1} \dot{q}} = v \tag{4}$$

where, $v \in R^n$ is the vector of motor voltages, and $\mathbf{I_a} \in R^n$ the vector of motor currents. $\mathbf{R, L, K_b} \in R^{n \times n}$ represent the diagonal matrices for the armature resistance, inductance, and back-emf constant of the motors, respectively. The motor torque vector $\boldsymbol{\tau}_m$ as the input for the dynamic (2) is produced by the motor current vector

$$\mathbf{K_m I_a} = \boldsymbol{\tau}_m \tag{5}$$

where, $\mathbf{K_m}$ is the diagonal matrix of the torque constants. A model for the electrically driven robot in the state space is introduced by the use of (1)–(5) as

$$\dot{\mathbf{x}} = \mathbf{f(x)} + \mathbf{bv} \tag{6}$$

Where

$$\mathbf{f(x)} = \begin{bmatrix} \mathbf{x_2} \\ (\mathbf{Jr^{-1}} + \mathbf{rD(x_1)})^{-1}(-(\mathbf{Br^{-1}} + \mathbf{rC(x_1, x_2)})\mathbf{x_2} - \mathbf{rG(x_1)} + \mathbf{K_m x_3}) \\ -\mathbf{L^{-1}(K_b r^{-1} x_2 + Rx_3)} \end{bmatrix},$$

$$\mathbf{b} = \begin{bmatrix} \mathbf{0} \\ \mathbf{0} \\ \mathbf{L^{-1}} \end{bmatrix}, \mathbf{x} = \begin{bmatrix} \mathbf{q} \\ \dot{\mathbf{q}} \\ \mathbf{I_a} \end{bmatrix} \tag{7}$$

The state space (6) is a nonlinear multivariable multi-input/multi-output system. The complexity of the model (6) faces serious challenges in the field of robot control. In order to consider the actuator dynamics, the voltages of motors denoted by V were considered as the inputs of the robotic system (6). To simplify the control problem, the majority of the control approaches have not considered the actuator dynamics by using the joint torques τ as the inputs of the system. However, the control performance will be degraded in the high-speed application. Another issue is that the previous control approaches presented for robot manipulators have been based on the second order dynamics of the robot manipulator in a companion form whereas the model (6) is neither the second order nor the companion form.

3. Proposed discrete robust adaptive fuzzy control

From the matrix (4), the voltage equation for the ith motor can be written in the scalar form as

$$RI_a + L\dot{I}_a + K_b r^{-1} \dot{q} + \varphi = v \tag{8}$$

The variable φ denotes the external disturbance. Equation (8) includes both the input v and the joint velocity $\dot{q}$, thus can be considered for position control of the robot manipulator. With the advantage of simplicity, it is preferred for control purposes compared to the complex system (6). The task space velocity $\dot{X}(t)$ is related to joint space velocity $\dot{q}(t)$ as [9]

$$\dot{X} = J(q)\dot{q} \tag{9}$$

where, $J(q) \in R^{n \times n}$ is the Jacobian matrix from joint space to task space. The derivative of (9) respect to time can be written as

$$\ddot{X} = J(q)\ddot{q} + \dot{J}(q)\dot{q} \tag{10}$$

$\dot{J}(q)$ exists if the desired path is smooth. Assuming there are no singular points in the desired path in task space such that the Jacobian matrix is of full rank. One can easily obtain from (9) that $\dot{q} = J^{-1}(q)\dot{X}$.

In this paper, it us assumed that the manipulator operates in a region where $J^{-1}(q)$ is nonsingular. Thus, the voltage (8) can be rewritten as

$$RI_a + L\dot{I}_a + K_b r^{-1} J^{-1}(q)\dot{X} + \varphi = v \tag{11}$$

Equation (11) can be rewritten as

$$\hat{J}^{-1}\ddot{X} + g = v \tag{12}$$

where, $\hat{J}^{-1}$ is an estimate and inverse of J, and g is expressed as

$$g = RI_a + L\dot{I}_a + K_b r^{-1} J^{-1}\dot{X} + \varphi - \hat{J}^{-1}\ddot{X} \tag{13}$$

In order to propose a model-free controller, one can consider the system (12) in which g is referred to as the uncertainty. One can obtain from (12) a linear discrete system using a sampling period T that is a small positive constant. Substituting kT into t for $kT \le t < (k+1)T$ and $k = 1, 2, \ldots$ the discrete time model of the system can be given by

$$\hat{J}_k^{-1}\ddot{X}_k + g_k + \varepsilon_1 = v \tag{14}$$

where, $\ddot{X}_k = \ddot{X}(kT)$, $\hat{J}_k^{-1} = \hat{J}^{-1}(kT)$ and $g_k = g(kT)$ and the discretizing error ε_1 is expressed as

$$\varepsilon_1 = \hat{J}^{-1}\ddot{X} - \hat{J}_k^{-1}\ddot{X}_k + g - g_k \tag{15}$$

A discrete adaptive fuzzy control law is proposed as

$$\hat{J}_k^{-1}(\ddot{X}_{d,k} + k_d \dot{e}_k + k_p e_k) + f_k = v \qquad (16)$$

where, v is the output of the controller which is given to the voltage input of the motor. $e_k = X_{d,k} - X_k$ is defined as the tracking error, $\dot{e}_k = \dot{X}_{d,k} - \dot{X}_k$ is derivative the tracking error of e_k, and k_p and k_d are the control design parameters. The term f_k is an adaptive fuzzy system for compensating uncertainty. $\ddot{X}_{d,k}$ denotes the discrete-time value of the desired joint acceleration $\ddot{X}_d(t)$ using a zero order hold converter defined as

$$\ddot{X}_{d,k} = \ddot{X}_d(kT) \quad \text{for } kT \le t < (k+1)T$$
$$\text{and } k = 0,1,2... \qquad (17)$$

4. Discrete adaptive fuzzy estimation of the uncertainty

Applying control law (16) to the discrete-time model of the system (14) obtains the closed loop system,

$$\hat{J}_k^{-1}(\ddot{e}_k + k_d \dot{e}_k + k_p e_k) = g_k + \varepsilon_1 - f_k \qquad (18)$$

where, $\ddot{X}_{d,k} - \ddot{X}_k = \ddot{e}_k$, (18) can be written as

$$\hat{J}_k^{-1}(\ddot{e}_k + k_d \dot{e}_k + k_p e_k) = G_k - f_k \qquad (19)$$

where,

$$G_k = g_k + \varepsilon_1 \qquad (20)$$

Suppose that f_k is the output of an adaptive fuzzy system with inputs of e_k, $\dot{e}_k$ and $\ddot{e}_k$. If two fuzzy sets are given to each fuzzy input, the whole control space will be covered by eight fuzzy rules. The linguistic fuzzy rules are proposed in the Mamdani type of the form

$$FR_l : \text{if } e_k \text{ is } A_1^l \text{ and } \dot{e}_k \text{ is } A_2^l \text{ and } \ddot{e}_k \text{ is } A_3^l$$
$$\text{then } f_k = C_l \qquad (21)$$

where, FR_l denotes the lth fuzzy rule for $l = 1,...,8$. In the lth rule A_1^l, A_2^l, A_3^l and C_l are the fuzzy membership functions belonging to the fuzzy variables e_k, $\dot{e}_k$, $\ddot{e}_k$ and f_k respectively. Two Gaussian membership functions named as Positive (P) and Negative (N) are defined for the input e_k in the operating range of manipulator as shown in figure 1. The same membership functions as for e_k are assigned to $\dot{e}_k$ and $\ddot{e}_k$. Eight symmetric Gaussian

membership functions are defined for f_k in the form of

$$\mu_l(f_k) = \exp\left(-\left(\frac{f_k - \bar{y}_k^l}{\sigma}\right)^2\right) \quad \text{for } l = 1,...,9 \quad (22)$$

where, σ and $\bar{y}_k^l$ are the design parameters. σ is constant whereas $\bar{y}_k^l$ is adjusted by an adaptive law.

The fuzzy rules should be defined such that the tracking control system goes to the equilibrium point. We may use an expert's knowledge, the trial and error method, or an optimization algorithm to design the fuzzy controller. The obtained fuzzy rules are given in table 1 in [7]. In this paper, f_k is adapted using a gradient descent algorithm to minimize the tracking error.

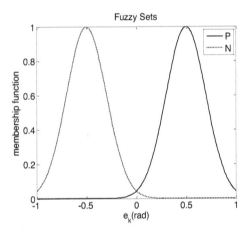

Figure 1. Membership functions of the input e_k .

If we use the product inference engine, singleton fuzzifier, center average defuzzifier, and Gaussian membership functions, the fuzzy system [23] is of the form

$$f_k(e_k, \dot{e}_k, \ddot{e}_k) = \frac{\sum_{L=1}^{8} \bar{y}_k^l z_k^l}{\sum_{L=1}^{8} z_k^l} \qquad (23)$$

where,

$$z_k^l = \mu_{A_1^l}(e_k) \mu_{A_2^l}(\dot{e}_k) \mu_{A_3^l}(\ddot{e}_k) \qquad (24)$$

where, $\mu_{A_1^l}(e_k) \in [0,1]$, $\mu_{A_2^l}(\dot{e}_k) \in [0,1]$ and $\mu_{A_3^l}(\ddot{e}_k) \in [0,1]$ are the membership functions for the fuzzy sets $\mu_{A_1^l}$, $\mu_{A_2^l}$ and $\mu_{A_3^l}$ respectively, and $\bar{y}_k^l$ is the center of fuzzy set C_l. The objective is to design a fuzzy system f_k so that the estimation error is minimized.

$$E_k = \frac{1}{2}(G_k - f_k)^2 \qquad (25)$$

The parameter which should be adjusted online is $\bar{y}_k^l$. The adaptation law in the gradient descent algorithm is given by [26]

$$\bar{y}_{k+1}^l = \bar{y}_k^l - \alpha \frac{\partial E_k}{\partial \bar{y}_k^l} \qquad (26)$$

where, α is a positive constant which determines the speed of convergence and $\frac{\partial E_k}{\partial \bar{y}_k^l}$ is calculated as

$$\frac{\partial E_k}{\partial \bar{y}_k^l} = -\frac{z_k^l(G_k - f_k)}{\sum_{L=1}^9 z_k^l} \qquad (27)$$

Note that G_k is an unknown function. So it is unavailable and cannot be used in the adaptation law. To solve the problem, this paper proposes a novel technique. Substituting (19) into (27) yields to

$$\frac{\partial E_k}{\partial \bar{y}_k^l} = -\frac{z_k^l(\hat{J}_k^{-1}(\ddot{e}_k + k_d \dot{e}_k + k_p e_k))}{\sum_{L=1}^9 z_k^l} \qquad (28)$$

The proposed model (14) is purposeful. The used technique for calculating $\frac{\partial E_k}{\partial \bar{y}_k^l}$ in (28) for the gradient descent algorithm implies that the algorithm does not require data as input-output pairs for the unknown function. Substituting (28) into (26) yields to adaptive rule

$$\bar{y}_{k+1}^l = \bar{y}_k^l + \alpha \frac{z_k^l(\hat{J}_k^{-1}(\ddot{e}_k + k_d \dot{e}_k + k_p e_k))}{\sum_{L=1}^9 z_k^l} \qquad (29)$$

5. Stability

A proof for the boundedness of the state variables $\mathbf{q}$, $\dot{\mathbf{q}}$ and $\mathbf{I_a}$ is given by stability analysis. In order to analyze the stability, the following assumptions are made:

Assumption 1 The desired trajectory $X_{d,k}$ must be smooth in the sense that $X_{d,k}$ and its derivatives up to a necessary order are available and all uniformly bounded [22].

As a necessary condition to design a robust control, the external disturbance must be bounded. Thus, the following assumption is made:

Assumption 2 The external disturbance φ is bounded as $|\varphi(t)| \le \varphi_{\max}$.

Assumption 3 we assume that the robot is operating in a finite task space such that the Jacobian matrix is full rank. Assuming there are no singular points in the desired path in task space such that the inverse of Jacobian matrix, $\hat{J}_k^{-1}$ is bounded.

The closed loop system (19) can be represented as

$$\hat{J}_k^{-1}(\ddot{e}_k + k_d \dot{e}_k + k_p e_k) = w \qquad (30)$$

where, $w = G_k - f_k$. The linear second order differential (30) with $k_p > 0$, $k_d > 0$ and the boundedness of $\hat{J}_k^{-1}$ is stable based on the Routh-Horwitz criteria. The output e_k is bounded if the input w be bounded. The gradient descent algorithm obtains the reduction of error expressed by $E_k = \frac{1}{2}(G_k - f_k)^2$ in (25). Therefore, $w = G_k - f_k$ is bounded. In the system (30), the boundedness of input w implies that

Result 1. e_k, $\dot{e}_k$ and $\ddot{e}_k$ are bounded.

We have $X_k = X_{d,k} - e_k$. According to the Assumption 1, $X_{d,k}$ is bounded. Thus,

Result 2. The task space position X_k is bounded.

Since $\mu_{A_1^l}, \mu_{A_2^l}, \mu_{A_3^l} \in [0\ 1]$, thus according to (24) one can imply that $|z_k^l| \le 1$. Thus,

Result 3. The function z_k^l is bounded.

Parameter $\bar{y}_{k+1}^l$ was expressed as (29), in which, parameters k_p and k_d are constant, and $\hat{J}_k^{-1}$ is bounded. As expressed in Result 1, e_k, $\dot{e}_k$ and $\ddot{e}_k$ are bounded. The boundedness of z_k^l was given in Result 3. Therefore,

Result 4. The parameter $\bar{y}_{k+1}^l$ is bounded.

From (23), Result 3 and Result 4, it can be concluded that

Result 5. Function f_k is bounded.

Considering control law (16) and using Assumption 1 and 3 for boundedness of $\ddot{X}_{d,k}$ and $\hat{J}_k^{-1}$, Result 5 for boundedness of f_k, and Result 1 for boundedness of e_k and $\dot{e}_k$ verifies that

Result 6. Motor voltage v is bounded.

According to [13], in an electrically driven robot when the motor voltage is bounded, it is proven that

Result 7. The motor velocity $\dot{q}$, and the motor current I_a are bounded.

Since

$$q = \int_0^t \dot{q}\, dt \qquad (31)$$

As expressed in Result 7, $\dot{q}$ is bounded, and according to boundedness t, Therefore

Result 8. , The joint position q is bounded.

As a result, the joint position q in Result 8, the joint velocity $\dot{q}$, and the motor current I_a in Result 7 are bounded. Applying this reasoning for all joints imply that

Result 9. The state vectors $\mathbf{q}$, $\dot{\mathbf{q}}$, and $\mathbf{I_a}$ are bounded.

Therefore, the stability is proven.

6. Simulation results

The control law (16) is simulated using a three link SCARA robot driven by permanent magnet dc motors presented by [24]. The parameters of motors are given in table 2 in [7]. In the simulations, the arm which consists of the first three joints is used to perform the proposed task-space control law. The fourth joint is locked. The maximum voltage of each motor is set to $v_{max} = 40$.

Simulation 1 In this simulation, the desired trajectory in the task-space is defined as

$$X_d = \left[0.75 - 0.1\cos(\frac{\pi kT}{3}); 0.65 - 0.1\sin(\frac{\pi kT}{3}); 0\right]^T \qquad (33)$$

To consider the kinematical uncertainties, $\hat{J}(q)$ is selected as $\hat{J}(q) = 0.8J(q)$. The adaptation rule (29) is set to $\bar{y}_k^l(0) = 0$, $\alpha = 0.285$, $k_d = 108$ and $k_p = 388$. The external disturbance is given zero.

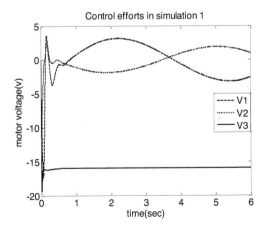

Figure 2. The control efforts in simulation 1.

Figure 2 illustrates the control efforts which are satisfactory. The motor voltages are smooth and under the maximum permitted voltage. The

tracking performance in the xy plane and along the z axis are shown in figure 3 and figure 4, respectively. The tracking performance confirm that the parameters are well adapted as shown in figure 5.

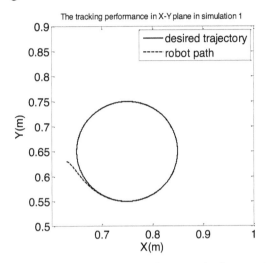

Figure 3. The tracking performance in the xy plane.

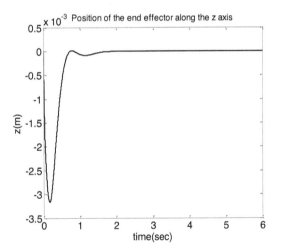

Figure 4. The tracking performance along the z axis.

Simulation 2: In this simulation, the desired trajectory in the task-space is defined as (33). To consider the kinematical uncertainties, $\hat{J}(q)$ is selected as $\hat{J}(q) = 0.8J(q)$. The adaptation rule (29) is set to $\bar{y}_k^l(0) = 0$, $\alpha = 0.29$, $k_d = 100$ and $k_p = 380$. The external disturbance is inserted to the input of each motor as a periodic pulse function with a period of 2 S, amplitude of 2 V, time delay of 0.7 S, and pulse width 30% of period.

The motor voltages behave well under the maximum permitted value of 40V as shown in figure 6. The effects of disturbances in tracking performance are represented in figure 7.

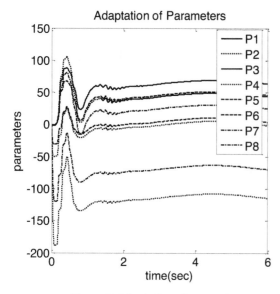

Figure 5. Adaptation of parameters.

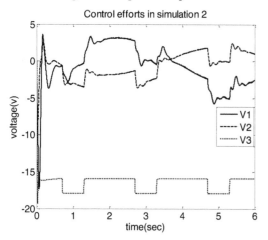

Figure 6. Control efforts in simulation 2 for disturbance rejection.

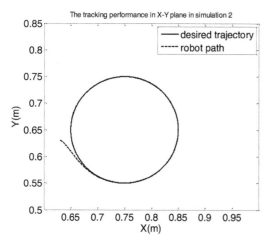

Figure 7. The tracking performance in the xy **plane in simulation2 for disturbance rejection.**

7. Conclusion

This paper has developed a discrete-time model-free robust control for electrically driven robot manipulators in task space. The adaptive fuzzy system has estimated the lumped uncertainty very well. The proposed gradient descent algorithm has been able to minimize the estimation error without using any data for the lumped uncertainty. The gradient descent algorithm has performed adaptively to reduce the tracking error in the presence of uncertainties. The proposed method has shown a very good performance such that the value of tracking error are ultimately bounded to small values. The proposed control algorithm has guaranteed the stability analysis and simulation results have shown the effectiveness of the method. The control approach is robust with a very good tracking performance.

References

[1] Ogata, K. (1987). Discrete-Time Control Systems. Prentice-Hall, NJ.

[2] Lam, H. K. & Leung, F. H. F. (2008). Stability analysis of discrete-time fuzzy-model-based control systems with time delay: Time delay-independent approach. Fuzzy Sets and Systems, vol. 159, no. 8, pp. 990-1000.

[3] Wu, L., Su, X., Shi, P. & Qiu, J. (2011). A new approach to stability analysis and stabilization of discrete-time T-S fuzzy time-varying delay systems. IEEE Transactions on Systems, vol. 41, no. 1, pp. 273-286.

[4] Lee, W. K., Hyun, C. H., Lee, H., Kim, E. & Park, M. (2007). Model reference adaptive synchronization of T–S fuzzy discrete chaotic systems using output tracking control. Chaos, Solitons and Fractals, vol. 34, no. 5, pp. 1590-1598.

[5] Kempf, C., Messner, W., Tornizuka, M. & Horowitz, R. (1993). Comparison of four discrete-time repetitive control algorithms. IEEE Cont Syst Mag, vol. 13, no. 6, pp. 48-54.

[6] Shoja Majidabad, S. & Shandiz, H. T. (2012). Discrete-time based sliding-mode control of robot manipulators. International Journal of Intelligent Computing and Cybernetics. vol. 5, no. 3, pp. 340-358.

[7] Fateh, M. M., Azargoshasb, S. & Khorashadizadeh, S. (2013). A model-free discrete control for robot manipulators using a fuzzy estimator. The International Journal for Computation and Mathematics in Electrical and Electronic Engineering, Accepted 1-Nov-2013.

[8] Liu, C., Cheah, C. C. & Slotine, J. J. E. (2006). Adaptive Jacobian tracking control of rigid-link electrically driven robots based on visual task-space information. Automatica, vol. 42, no. 9, pp. 1491-1501.

[9] Cheah, C. C., Liu, C. & Slotine, J. J. E. (2006). Adaptive Jacobian tracking control of robots with uncertainties in kinematic, dynamic and actuator models. IEEE Trans. Automatic control. vol. 51, no. 6, pp. 1024-1029.

[10] Sage, H. G., De Mathelin, M. F. & Ostertag, E. (1999). Robust control of robot manipulators. a survey. Int. J. Control, vol. 72, no. 16, pp. 1498-1522.

[11] Fateh, M. M. (2010). Robust voltage control of electrical manipulators in task-space. Int. J. Innov. Comput. Info. Control, vol. 6, no. 6, pp. 2691-2700.

[12] Fateh, M. M. (2012). Nonlinear control of electrical flexible-joint robots. Nonlinear Dyn. vol. 67, no. 4, pp. 2549-2559.

[13] Fateh, M. M. (2012). Robust control of flexible-joint robots using voltage control strategy. Nonlinear Dyn. vol. 67, no. 2, pp. 1525-1537.

[14] Wai, R. J. & Muthusamy, R. (2013). Fuzzy-neural-network inherited sliding-mode control for robot manipulator including actuator dynamics. IEEE Transactions on Neural Networks and Learning Systems, vol. 24, no. 2, pp. 274-287.

[15] Yoo, B. K. & Ham, W. C. (2000). Adaptive control of robot manipulator using fuzzy compensator. IEEE Transactions on Fuzzy Systems, vol. 8, no. 2, pp. 186-199.

[16] Wang, L. X. (1994). Adaptive fuzzy systems and control. Prentice Hall.

[17] Feng, G. & Chen, G. (2005). Adaptive control of discrete-time chaotic systems: a fuzzy control approach. Chaos, Solitons and Fractals, vol. 23, no. 2, pp. 459-467.

[18] Erbatur, K., Kaynak, O., Sabanovic, A. & Rudas, I. (1996). Fuzzy adaptive sliding mode control of a direct drive robot. Robotics and Autonomous Systems, vol. 19, no. 2, pp. 215-227.

[19] Qu, Z. & Dawson, D.M. (1996). Robust tracking control of robot manipulators. IEEE Press, Inc., New York.

[20] Talole, S. E. & Phadke, S. B. (2008). Model following sliding mode control based on uncertainty and disturbance estimator. Journal of Dynamic Systems, Measurement, and Control, vol. 130, no. 3, pp. 1-5.

[21] Fateh, M. M. (2010). Proper uncertainty bound parameter to robust control of electrical manipulators using nominal model. Nonlinear Dynamics, vol. 61, no. 4, pp. 655-666.

[22] Spong, M. W., Hutchinson, S. & Vidyasagar, M. (2006). Robot Modelling and Control. Wiley, Hoboken.

[23] Wang, L. X. (1997). A Course in Fuzzy Systems and Control. Prentice-Hall, New York.

[24] Fateh, M. M. & Babaghasabha, R. (2010). Impedance control of robots using voltage control strategy. Nonlinear Dynamics, Accepted 19 May 2013.

4

Holistic Farsi handwritten word recognition using gradient features

Z. Imani[1*], A.R. Ahmadyfard[1] and A. Zohrevand[2]

1. Electrical Engineering Department, University of Shahrood, Shahrood, Iran.
2. Computer Engineering & Information Technology Department, University of Shahrood, Shahrood, Iran.

*Corresponding author:z.imani13@gmail.com (Z Imani).

Abstract
In this paper we address the issue of recognizing Farsi handwritten words. Two types of gradient features are extracted from a sliding vertical stripe which sweeps across a word image. These are directional and intensity gradient features. The feature vector extracted from each stripe is then coded using the Self Organizing Map (SOM). In this method each word is modeled using the discrete Hidden Markov Model (HMM). To evaluate the performance of the proposed method, FARSA dataset has been used. The experimental results show that the proposed system, applying directional gradient features, has achieved the recognition rate of 69.07% and outperformed all other existing methods.

Keywords: *Handwritten Word Recognition, Directional Gradient Feature, Intensity Gradient Feature, Hidden Markov Model, Self-organizing Feature Map, FARSA Database.*

1. Introduction

Due to being fraught with such difficulties as high variability of handwritten words' style and shape, uncertainty of human-writing, skew or slant writing, segmentation of words into characters ,and the size of lexicon, cursive handwritten word recognition has become a challenging area in pattern recognition[1]. Farsi handwritten recognition, which this paper addresses, is very similar to Arabic in terms of strokes and structure. The only difference is that Farsi has four more characters. Therefore, Farsi word recognition system can also be used for Arabic words [2]. Handwritten word recognition systems may work online or offline. In the online system, words are written using special tools like pen and tablet. In this way available information such as writing direction and writing speed facilitates the process of recognition. In the online method, handwritten recognition is occurs concurrently with writing [3,4,5], while in off-line method handwritten words exist prior to the recognition. The data were first collected using a pen and a paper and then scanned. Since in the offline method, additional tools for collecting data are not used, the recognition is more complex. In this paper we address the problem of recognizing Farsi

handwritten words in an offline manner. In recent years, several studies have been conducted in this area, as reported below.
In [6] a holistic system for recognition of Farsi/Arabic handwritten words using the right-left discrete Hidden Markov Models (HMM) was proposed. The histogram of chain-code directions for vertical stripes on word image was used as feature vector [6]. The extracted feature vectors were used as the input data to the Kohonen self-organization vector quantization. A database including 17000 images of 198 words was used for evaluating this system. Finally by smoothing the probabilities of observation symbols, recognition rate of 65% was achieved [6].
In [7] Dehghan et al generated a fuzzy codebook using the same feature vectors. The recognition rate of 67% was reported for this system, using an HMM classifier [7].
In [2], a method for recognizing handwritten Iranian cities' name was proposed. In this method K-means clustering was used for vector quantization and words were modeled using the discrete HMM. For this method a recognition rate of 80.75% was reported [2]. In [8] the authors proposed an off-line Arabic/Farsi handwritten

recognition algorithm using RBF network. The features utilized in this method were wavelet coefficients being extracted from the profiles of smoothed word image in four standard directions. A database including 3300 images of 30 common Farsi names was used to evaluate this system. This method achieved 96% recognition rate.

AlKhateeb et al [9] dealt with the problem of offline Arabic word recognition. They used a set of intensity features to train an HMM classifier for each word. The results were re-ranked using structure-like features (including a number of sub-words and diacritical marks) to improve recognition. This method achieved 89% recognition rate using re-ranking.

Imani et al [10] used chain-code and distribution of stoke pixels across a sliding frame as a hybrid method for feature extraction stage, then they used an HMM for classification. This method was applied on FARSA database [11] and a recognition rate of 68.88% was achieved.

In this paper we addressed the off-line Farsi handwritten words recognition problem. To do so, we extracted gradient features from a sliding window, which sweeps across the word image. In this paper, we proposed two recognition systems. In one of the systems, the magnitude of image gradient was used and in the other one, the direction of image gradient was utilized in order for representing the word image. In either of the two systems, the feature vector, being extracted from a sliding window, was quantized through using a vector quantization algorithm. Then, for each word class some sequences of code indexes, (that were taken from its sample image), from the sample images of that class were used to train its discrete Hidden Markov Model. As it was shown in the experimental results, directional gradient features outperform intensity gradient features in terms of recognition rate. In fact, the intensity gradient features are performed in typewritten recognition in [12]. However using features based on the direction of script gradient improves the recognition rate. FARSA is an appropriate dataset of handwritten Farsi words which was introduced by Imani et al [11]. We evaluate the proposed methods in this paper using FARSA database.

The rest of the paper is organized as follows. In the next section, the proposed word recognition system will be introduced. In section 3, the employed classification features are explained. The vector quantization for feature coding vector is presented in section 4. In section 5, the system's classification method will be described. The experimental results are reported in section 6.

Finally, the paper will be drawn to a conclusion in section 7.

2. Proposed method

The word recognition system contains three stages: preprocessing, feature extraction and classification. The block diagram of the proposed Farsi handwritten word recognition is demonstrated in figure 1.

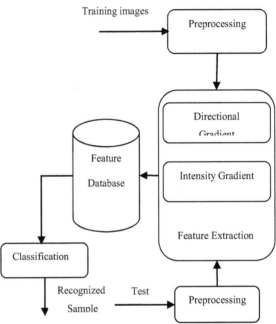

Figure1. Block diagram of the proposed system.

2.1. Preprocessing

The pre-processing stage plays a very crucial role in word recognition in order to represent various samples of a word in an invariant manner [3]. The stage consists of the following steps:

- Binarization and noise removal: The gray level image of a word is binarized by thresholding. Then those connected components with an area less than the predefined threshold are deleted.

- Cropping: In order to increase the processing speed and to decrease memory usage, the binary image is cropped by its bonding box. Then, the image is resized by 45 pixels in height.

- Skeletonization and dilation: First, the word image skeleton is extracted (Figure 2.b).Then, it is dilated (Figure 2.c) by a 4×4 square structure element. This step aims at making the system independent of stroke width [3].

3. Extracting feature from word image

In order to represent the word image as a pattern

to the recognition system we need to represent it using discriminative features. We use a number of white pixels, horizontal and vertical edges, together with the histogram of gradient directions, within a sliding window, to describe the word image.

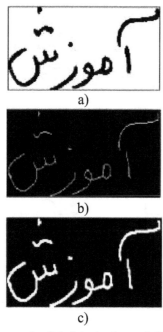

Figure2. An example of skeletonization and dilation. a) Original image. b) Word skeleton. c) Dilation on word skeleton.

3.1 Sweep word image using sliding stripe

A sliding stripe is used to scan word image from right to left. Accordingly each word image is divided into several narrow windows with an overlap of 50%.Using this strategy, word image can be represented as a sequence of script primitives [10]. Each window is twice as wide as each stroke in the word image as suggested in [6]. Thus, in this study we widen the window to 8 pixels and heighten it to the word image height.

A set of simple features are extracted from pixels falling within that window. In order to extract proper features from each window of the word image, the window is divided horizontally into a number of zones. In this paper two types of gradient features are extracted from each window zone.

3.2. Gradient feature extraction

By applying a low pass Gaussian filter, we convert the binary image of Farsi script into a gray scale image. Here we made use of horizontal and vertical Sobel operators to determine the gradient of word image in x and y directions namely G_x and G_y. These two Sobel operators are shown in figure 3. We also calculated the gradient's direction:

$$\theta(x,y) = tan^{-1}(G_y/G_x) \tag{1}$$

−1	−2	−1		−1	0	1
0	0	0		−1	0	2
1	2	1		−1	0	1
	(a)				(b)	

Figure3. Sobel masks, (a) horizontal mask and (b) vertical mask.

3.3. Using intensity and magnitude of gradient components as a feature set

In order to describe image inside a sliding window, the window is divided into 9 horizontal cells and 3 features are extracted from each individual cell. The features are: image intensity, horizontal component, and vertical components extracted from the Sobel operators (Figure 4).

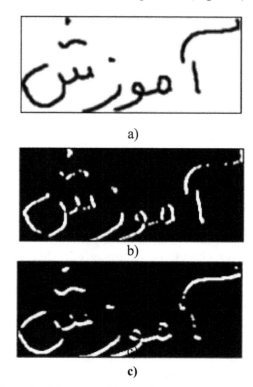

Figure4. a) Input word image. b) Vertical derivative of (a). c) Horizontal derivative of (a).

The intensity feature represents the number of white pixels within each sliding window cell. The number of horizontal and vertical edges is counted in each sliding window cell [12]. Accordingly, there are 3 features for each cell and each sliding window has 9 horizontal cells, so 27feature values for each sliding window are extracted.

3.4. Gradient direction as feature

In (1), $\theta(x,y)$ returns the direction of gradient vector (G_x, G_y) in the range of [-π, π]. The gradient direction at each pixel is quantized to 8 intervals of $\pi/4$ each (Figure 5).Each sliding window, as introduced in the previous section, is divided into 5 horizontal cells whose histograms are shown in four normalized directions. Thus we represent a sliding window on image word using a feature vector including 20 components.

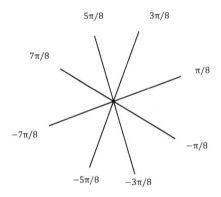

Figure 5. Quantizing the gradient direction with four symbols.

4. Vector quantization

In this research for 198 classes of database, 533000 extracted frame from the training set is used as input to the Kohonen Self Organization vector quantization (SOM in Neural Network MATLAB Toolbox) to obtain a codebook with 49 symbols. After generating the codebook a given feature vector is mapped to a symbol from 1 to 49, which is the closest code word by the Euclidean distance measure. The histogram distribution of feature vectors in codebook has been shown in figure 6. Thus, each word image is now identified by an observation sequence. The sequences are given as input to the Hidden Markov Models.

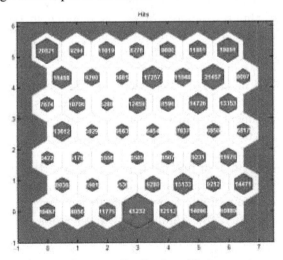

Figure6. Histogram distribution of feature vectors.

5. Hidden Markov Model classification

The Hidden Markov Models (HMMs) are widely used for text recognition. The HMMs are statistical models being originally used for speech recognition efficiency. Since the HMM has put in a good performance in speech recognition, and because of the similarities between speech recognition and cursive handwriting, it has been extended to Farsi handwriting word recognition [3,13,14].

HMM can be represented using three parameters as follows:

$$\lambda = (\pi, A, B) \tag{2}$$

λ stands for an HMM model, π is the vector of the initial state probabilities, A is the state transition matrix and B is the matrix of observation symbol probabilities:

$$\pi = \{\pi_i | \pi_i = P(S_1 = i)\} \tag{3}$$

$$A = \{a_{ij} | a_{ij} = P(S_t = j | S_{t-1} = i)\} \tag{4}$$

$$B = \{b_j(o_k) | b_j(o_k) = P(O_t = o_k | S_t = j)\} \tag{5}$$

where, a_{ij} is the probability that system at time t is in j^{th} state assuming that system at time t-1 was in i^{th} state. In (5), $b_j(o_k)$ is the probability that we observe o_k at time $t, o_t = o_k$, assuming that system at this time is in j th state. Here, N equals to the number of states, T to the length of the sequence of observations to the number of possible observations (form the training set), and $S = \{s | 1 \leq s \leq N\}$ [15].

To design an HMM classifier, several procedures are needed to be performed including (i) deciding the number of states and observations,(ii) choosing HMM topology, (iii) model training using selected samples and (iv) testing and evaluation [9].

The number of chosen states is proportioned to the word length. Indeed for each word, the number of states is considered proportional to the minimum number of frames in the word picture. In this paper, a right-to-left HMM is employed. Each state could have a self-transition, or a transition to the next or two next states. In the training stage, the model is optimized using the training data through an iterative process. The Baum-Welch algorithm, a variant of the Expectation Maximization (EM) algorithm, is utilized to maximize the observation sequence probability $p(O | \lambda)$ of the chosen model, $\lambda = (\pi, A, B)$, for optimization[9].

It is well known that if adequate training data is not provided, the HMM parameters especially the observation symbol probabilities, are usually poorly estimated. As a result, the recognition rate is degraded even if a very slight variation in the testing data occurs. A proper smoothing of the estimated observation probability can overcome this problem without a need for more training data. The parameter smoothing method as proposed in [16] is used. After training all of the HMMs by the Baum-Welch algorithm, the value of each observation probability in each state is raised by adding a weighted-sum of the probabilities of its neighboring nodes in the SOM as follows:

$$b_j^{new}(k,l) = b_j^{old}(k,l) + \sum_{\substack{(k,l) \neq \\ (p,q)}} W_{(k,l),(p,q)} b_j^{old}(p,q) \qquad (6)$$

where, the weighting coefficient $W_{(k,l),(p,q)}$ defined as the function of distance between two nodes (p,q) and (k,l) in the map:

$$W_{(k,l),(p,q)} = SF. c^{(d_{(k,l),(p,q)}-1)} \qquad (7)$$

(c) Is a constant chosen to be equal to 0.5. The smoothing factor (Sf) controls the degree of smoothing, and $d_{(k,l),(p,q)}$ is the hexagonal distance between two nodes with the coordinates (k,l) and (p,q) in the codebook map.

In testing stage, an observed sequence of test images is given to all of the HMM models to find the best model that can generate the data. Viterbi's algorithm is used to match a single model to the observed sequence of symbols. The reader is referred to [17] for more details about HMM.

6. Experimental results
In this section, firstly, the collected database, namely FARSA, is introduced. Then, the results of applying the proposed method to the database are reported.

6.1. FARSA database
Farsi scripts have four more characters than the Arabic ones in their character set. Therefore, the most accurate recognition result can be obtained only by using the proper dataset for the language [18]. So the standard Arabic database cannot be used for Farsi and there is no proper handwritten database available in Farsi.

A proper database must include a significant number of samples for each class of words in the dictionary. We prepare a database including 30000 images of 300 formal words which are common in Farsi Language. The handwritten words are scanned with 300-dpi resolution and 256 gray levels. The database is called FARSA [11].

6.2. Experiments and results
In this paper, 198 word classes of the FARSA

were used to evaluate the proposed system. The number of word classes was chosen to compare the proposed method with the methods in [6, 10] which had used the same number of word classes. A subset including 19800 samples of the images in the FARSA database was chosen. Out of which about 70% of samples were chosen randomly as the training database and the rest were utilized for the test.

All of the HMM models are initialized using the same parameters. The performance of the word recognition system is illustrated in table1 by a top-n recognition rate (the percentage of test words recognized as true class lies among the first n positions in the candidate list). The criterion for ranking of a HMM model is the log-likelihood of a given test image being produced by the HMM model.

Table 1 reports the results achieved through comparing two types of gradient feature extraction. As can be seen, directional gradient features are more appropriate than intensity gradient features for handwritten word recognition. The amplitude of gradient performed very well as feature for typewritten recognition in [12]. But in handwritten, due to a variety of text and change the font stretch as seen in table 1, the directional gradient features work better. As shown in table 1 the recognition rate using the angle of gradient improves the recognition rate about 16%.

As mentioned previously, due to the variation of handwritten words in a class and because of the limited number of training data, the recognition rate is not considerable. The proposed method was repeated after smoothing the observation probabilities of the HMMs. As reported in [10] the appropriate smoothing factor is 0.001. In this experiment, we report the results of smoothing the HMM parameters with proper smoothing factor in table1.In another experiment, we consider three codebook sizes. Figure 7 shows the results of an experiment in which directional gradient feature extraction method is adopted. As can be seen, the recognition rate of a codebook being 49 in size outdoes that of the one being 36 in size. But the results for 49 and 64 are almost identical. On the other hand, figure 8 shows that the computational complexity and training system time for 64 is much higher than 49. So we choose 49 as the codebook size.

On the other hand, figure 8 shows that the computational complexity and training system time for 64 is much higher than 49. So we choose 49 as the codebook size.

Table1. Comparison of recognition results with two types feature extraction.

Lexicon size = 198	Directional Gradient feature	Intensity Gradient features	Feature vector size	Top1	Top5	Top10
Without smoothing	✓		20	58.83	76.81	81.80
With smoothing SF=0.001	✓		20	69.07	88.35	92.73
Without smoothing		✓	27	47.17	68.50	75.35
With smoothing SF=0.001		✓	27	53.48	77.89	85.39

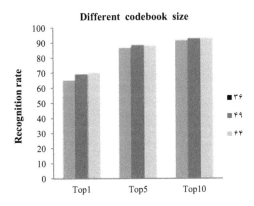

Figure7. Comparison of recognition results with different codebook size.

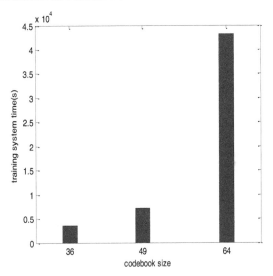

Figure8. Training system time for different codebook size.

Table 2 shows that the performance of the proposed word recognition systems compared with three existing methods [6,7,10].

In an earlier work [10], a combination of chain code histogram features and intensity features were used during the extraction stage and the feature vectors were 25 in length.

It can be seen that, despite in this work we use less features in compare with an earlier work [10], the performance has been improved.

7. Conclusion

We proposed an offline system for recognizing of Farsi handwritten words. Directional and intensity gradient features were employed.

The extracted feature vector was coded using a vector quantization algorithm. The codes were utilized as an observation in order to train the HMM model for each word class.

Table2. Recognition rate of proposed method compared to other method.

Method	lexicon size	Number of training images	Number of testing images	Top-1	Top-5	Top-10
DHMM+smoothing [6]	198	10200	6800	65.05	86.08	90.83
FVQ/HMM[7]	198	10200	6800	67.18	87.55	92.06
The previous method [10]	198	13800	5900	68.88	87.54	91.75
The proposed system	198	13800	5900	**69.07**	**88.35**	**92.73**

The proposed system was evaluated using a newly prepared database, namely FARSA database.

The experimental results for directional gradient features outperformed intensity gradient features

and the results achieved through adopting the proposed method were far better than those achieved through employing the existing methods.

References

[1] Sagheer, M.W., He, C. L., Nobile, N. & Suen, C. Y. (2010). Holistic Urdu Handwritten Word Recognition Using Support Vector Machine. Proceedings of the 20th International Conference on Pattern Recognition, Istanbul, Turkey, 2010.

[2] Vaseghi, B., Shahpour, A., Ahmadi, M. &Amirfattahi, R. (2008). Off-line Farsi /Arabic Handwritten Word Recognition Using Vector Quantization and Hidden Markov Model, Proceedings of the 12th IEEE International Multi topic Conference. Karachi, Pakistan, 2008.

[3] Märgner, V. & ElAbed, H. (2012). Guide to OCR for Arabic Scripts. London: Springer-Verlag.

[4] Ghods, V., Kabir, E. & Razzazi, F. (2013). Effect of delayed strokes on the recognition of online Farsi handwriting. Pattern Recognition Letters, vol. 34, no. 5, pp. 486–491.

[5] Ghods, V., Kabir, E. & Razzazi, F. (2013). Decision fusion of horizontal and vertical trajectories for recognition of online Farsi subwords. Journal of Engineering Applications of Artificial Intelligence, vol. 26, no. 1, pp. 544–550.

[6] Dehghan, M., Faez, K., Ahmadi, M. & Shridhar, M. (2001). Handwritten Farsi (Arabic) word recognition: a holistic approach using discrete HMM. Pattern Recognition, vol. 34, no. 5, pp. 1057–1065.

[7] Dehghan, M., Faez, K., Ahmadi, M. & Sridhar, M. (2001). Unconstrained Farsi handwritten word recognition using fuzzy vector quantization and hidden Markov models. Pattern Recognition Letter, vol. 22, no. 2, pp. 209–214.

[8] Bahmani, Z., Alamdar, F., Azmi, R. & Haratizadeh, S. (2010). Off-line Arabic/Farsi handwritten word recognition using RBF neural network and genetic algorithm. IEEE International Conference on Intelligent Computing and Intelligent Systems, Xiamen, China, 2010.

[9] AlKhateeb, J. H., Ren, J., Jiang, J. & Al-Muhtaseb, H. (2011). Offline handwritten Arabic cursive text recognition using Hidden Markov Models and re-ranking. Pattern Recognition Letters, vol. 32, no. 5, pp. 1081–1088.

[10] Imani, Z., Ahmadyfard, A.R., Zohrevand, A. & Alipour, M. (2013) .offline Handwritten Farsi cursive text recognition using Hidden Markov Models. 8th iranian conference on machine vision and image processing, Zanjan, Iran, 2013.

[11] Imani, Z., Ahmadyfard A. R. & Zohrevand A. (2013). Introduction to Database FARSA: digital image of handwritten Farsi words. 11th Iranian Conference on Intelligent Systems in Persian, Tehran, Iran, 2013.

[12] Khorsheed, M. S. (2006). Mono-font cursive Arabic text recognition using speech recognition system. In Structural, Syntactic, and Statistical Pattern Recognition, Springer Berlin Heidelberg, pp.755-763.

[13] Khorsheed M.S. (2002). Off-line Arabic character recognition – a review. Pattern Analysis and Application, vol. 5, no. 1, pp. 31-45.

[14] Günter, S. & Bunke, H. (2004). HMM-based handwritten word recognition: on the optimazation of the number of states, training iterations and Gaussian components. Pattern Recognition, vol. 37, no. 10, pp. 2069–2079.

[15] Al-Muhtaseb, H. A., Mahmoud, S. A. & Qahwaji. R.S. (2008). Recognition of off-line printed Arabic text using Hidden Markov Models, Signal Processing journal, vol. 88, no. 12, pp. 2902–2912.

[16] Zhao, Z., & Rowden, C. G. (1992). Use of Kohonen self-organising feature maps for HMM parameter smoothing in speech recognition. In IEE Proceedings F (Radar and Signal Processing), IET Digital Library, vol. 139, no. 6, pp. 385–390.

[17] Rabiner, L. R. (1989). A tutorial on hidden Markov models and selected applications in speech recognition. Proceedings of the IEEE, vol. 77, no. 2, pp. 257–286.

[18] Haghighi, P. J., Nobile N., He, C. L. & Suen, C. Y. (2009). A New Large-Scale Multi-purpose Handwritten Farsi Database, Proc. International Conference on Image Analysis and Recognition, Halifax, NS, Canada, 2009.

5

Trajectory tracking of under-actuated nonlinear dynamic robots: Adaptive fuzzy hierarchical terminal sliding-mode control

Y. Vaghei and A. Farshidianfar[*]

Mechanical Engineering Department, Ferdowsi University of Mashhad, Mashhad, Iran.

*Corresponding author: farshid@um.ac.ir (A. Farshidianfar).

Abstract Under-actuated nonlinear dynamic systems trajectory tracking, such as space robots and manipulators with structural flexibility, has recently been investigated for hierarchical sliding mode control since these systems require complex computations. However, the instability phenomena possibly occur especially for long-term operations. In this paper, a new design approach of an adaptive fuzzy hierarchical terminal sliding-mode controller (AFHTSMC) is proposed. The sliding surfaces of the subsystems construct the hierarchical structure of the proposed method in which the top layer includes all of the subsystems' sliding surfaces. Moreover, a terminal-sliding mode has been implemented in each layer to ensure the error convergence to zero in finite time besides chattering reduction. In addition, online fuzzy models are employed to approximate the two nonlinear dynamic system's functions. Finally, a simulation example of an inverted pendulum is proposed to confirm the effectiveness and robustness of the proposed controller.

Keywords: *Adaptive Fuzzy System, Hierarchical Structure, Terminal Sliding Mode Control, Under-actuated System.*

1. Introduction

In the recent years, interests toward developing under-actuated systems have been increased. Many of mechanical systems often have the under-actuation problem in which the system is not able to follow arbitrary trajectories in configuration space. This occurs if the system has a lower number of actuators than its degrees of freedom. In this condition, the system is said to be trivially under-actuated. These systems cover a wide range of applications in our everyday lives such as overhead cranes, space robots, automobiles with non-holonomic constraints, and legged robots [1-3].

Many researchers investigated the control of under-actuated systems. In this paper, the focus is on variable structure systems (VSS) due to their effective control scheme in dealing with uncertainties, noise, and time varying properties [4,5]. One of the robust design methodologies of VSS is the sliding mode control chooses switching manifolds, which are usually linear hyper-planes that guarantee the asymptotic stability shown by the Lyapunov's stability theorem [6,7]. In high precision applications, fast

convergence may not be delivered without strict control. Hence, in order to overcome this problem, a terminal sliding mode (TSM) control has recently been developed. It enables the fast finite time convergence and ensures less steady state errors. However, the existence of the singularity problem in the conventional TSM controller design methods is a common drawback [8,9]. Several methods have been proposed to solve this problem.

The TSM control methods can be divided into two approaches: the indirect approach and the direct approach, in which the controllers require discontinuous control leading to undesirable chattering. In an indirect approach [10], scientists implemented switching from terminal sliding manifold to linear sliding manifold in order to avoid the singularity problem. In addition, some efforts have been made to transfer the trajectory to a specified open non-singular region [11]. Also, a direct approach has been investigated for a class of nonlinear dynamical systems with parameter uncertainties and external disturbances in [12]. Later, fuzzy TSM controllers [13] were introduced to solve the problems caused by these two approaches and under-actuated systems with unknown nonlinear system functions [14,18]. In addition, there has been growing attention paid to the adaptive fuzzy TSM in various control problems [19].

In further studies, efforts have been made to overcome the problems of the fuzzy sliding mode control and fuzzy TSM control. Hierarchical structures shown their effectiveness according to their ability to achieve the ideal decoupling performance with guaranteed stability [20]. The implementation of these structures enables us to decouple a class of nonlinear coupled systems into several subsystems. Also, the sliding surfaces, which govern the states' responses, are defined for each subsystem. In these systems, first, a sliding surface is defined for each subsystem. Then, the first-layer sliding surface constructs the second-layer sliding surface. This process continues to achieve the last sliding mode surface (hierarchical surface). In literature, the Lyapunov theorem has been employed to prove the stability of the closed-loop system for the single-input system. There are a few studies on the effectiveness of the adaptive fuzzy law derivation for the coupling factor tuning [21-23]; however, the chattering and fast convergence problems are still remained unsolved.

As can be clearly seen in the aforementioned studies, the implementation of the adaptive fuzzy system besides the sliding mode and hierarchical structure could not solve the chattering and fast time convergence problems; therefore, in this study, our main objective is to propose a novel control method, named as the adaptive fuzzy hierarchical terminal sliding mode control (AFHTSMC), which enables us to use the advantages of terminal sliding mode control besides the adaptive fuzzy hierarchical structure for uncertain under-actuated nonlinear dynamic systems control. The main features of the proposed AFHTSMC are as follows: 1) The implementation of the TSM control, which guarantees the fast finite time convergence and reduces the chattering and steady state errors. This superior property becomes admirable in the applications requiring high precision; 2) The unknown nonlinear system functions are approximated by the adaptive fuzzy systems with adaptive learning laws; 3) The hierarchical structure of the proposed method is also a very effective tool to guarantee the stability, especially for complex and high nonlinear dynamic systems. In Section II, the system's description and the control objectives are presented. Then

AFHTSMC development for dealing with the trajectory tracking control problem of uncertain under-actuated nonlinear dynamic systems is introduced in Section III. Section IV is dedicated to the Lyapunov stability analysis of the proposed closed-loop system. The simulations, results and discussions are presented in Section V for an inverted pendulum on a cart. Finally, concluding remarks are made in Section VI.

2. System description and problem formulation

An under-actuated single-input-multi-output system with uncertainty and nonlinear coefficients is defined in (1).

$$\begin{cases} \dot{x}_1(t) = x_2(t) \\ \dot{x}_2(t) = f_1(x) + b_1(x)\,u(t) + d_1(x,t) \\ \dot{x}_3(t) = x_4(t) \\ \dot{x}_4(t) = f_2(x) + b_2(x)\,u(t) + d_2(x,t) \\ \qquad \vdots \\ \dot{x}_{2n-1}(t) = x_{2n}(t) \\ \dot{x}_{2n}(t) = f_n(x) + b_n(x)\,u(t) + d_n(x,t) \end{cases} \tag{1a}$$

$$y(t) = [x_1(t)\; x_3(t)\;...\; x_{2n-1}(t)]^T \tag{1b}$$

where, $x(t) = [x_1(t)\; x_2(t)\;...\; x_{2n}(t)]^T \in \mathfrak{R}^{2n}$ is the system state variable, $f_i(x)$ and $b_i(x)$, i=1,2, …, n are unknown nominal nonlinear functions, $(0 \le d_i(x,t) \le \rho_i,\ i=1,2,\ ...,\ n)$ are bounded time-varying disturbances, and $u(t)$ and $y(t)$ are the control input and the system output, respectively. The contribution of this paper is to design the hierarchical terminal sliding mode controller with adaptive fuzzy learning laws for a class of uncertain under-actuated nonlinear dynamic systems (UUND). Figure 1 shows that the adaptive learning laws are applied to adjust the parameter vectors of fuzzy systems for approximation of uncertain nonlinear system functions.

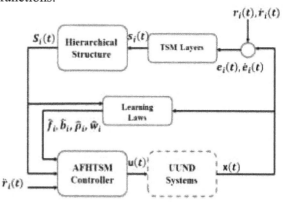

Figure 1. The schematic overall control block-diagram.

Also, the performance of the bounded trajectory tracking and asymptotical trajectory tracking are addressed. Finally, the simulation results of an inverted pendulum on a movable cart with bounded external disturbance are investigated.

3. AFHTSMC development
3.1. The terminal sliding surfaces
In this section, initially, the conventional terminal sliding surfaces are defined in (2-4).

$$s_i(t) = \dot{e}_i(t)^{\gamma_i} + c_i e_i(t) \tag{2}$$

where, for i=1,2,...,n, the reference inputs are $r_i(t)$, c_i and $\gamma_i = \frac{p}{q}$ are positive constants, and p and q are odd positive integers.

$$e_i(t) = x_{2i-1}(t) - r_i(t) \tag{3}$$

$$\dot{e}_i(t) = x_{2i}(t) - \dot{r}_i(t) \tag{4}$$

However, the singularity problem may occur in this structure because of the term $c_i \frac{q}{p} e_i^{\frac{q-p}{p}}(t)\dot{e}_i(t)$ in the control input. If the $2q > p > q$ is chosen, the term $e_i^{\frac{q-p}{p}}(t)$ will be equal to $e_i^{\frac{2q-p}{p}}(t)$ which will be nonsingular. On the other hand, if little control to enforce $e_i(t) \neq 0$ is made while $\dot{e}_i(t) \neq 0$, the singularity problem occurs. Hence, an indirect approach has been implemented to avoid this problem and define the terminal sliding surfaces in (5).

$$s_i(t) = \dot{e}_i(t)^{\gamma_i} + c_i e_i(t) \tag{5}$$

It has to be noticed that the derivative of $s_i(t)$ along the system's dynamics does not result in terms with negative (fractional) powers by using (5) and the singularity is avoided by switching between (2) and (5), where the error and its derivative are bounded as in [20]. In this problem, designing a switched control that drives the plant state to the switching surface and maintain it on the surface upon interception is the most important achievement. As can be seen, the system motion is governed by c_i, which is an integer number. This number's value indicates the effect of error on the sliding surface and it is selected based on the $\dot{e}_i(t)^{\gamma_i}$ value, while $s_i(t)$ in each layer has a crucial effect on the system's control. It is important to mention that high values of c_i increase the effect of e_i in each layer and may result in misleading the controller; hence, appropriate values of c_i are required to maintain a high precision control system. Further studies can be found in section 3.2.

3.2. The hierarchical structure
In the next step, after the definition of the sliding

surfaces, higher hierarchical levels ($S_i(t)$) are created by lower TSM surfaces ($s_i(t)$) as shown in figure 2. The ith hierarchical layer sliding surface is defined in (6).

$$S_i(t) = \lambda_{i-1} S_{i-1}(t) + s_i(t) \tag{6}$$

where, λ_{i-1} is constant when $\lambda_0 = S_0 = 0$. The value of the λ_{i-1} parameter indicates the effectiveness of the last hierarchical layers in comparison with the current sliding surface. Larger values of λ_{i-1} increase the value amount that is given to the prior layers instead of the highest hierarchical sliding surface. This parameter has to be adjusted so as to satisfy the Lyapunov theorem and the required accuracy.

Furthermore, the control input for the ith layer $u_i(t)$ consists of the equivalent and the switching control terms besides the last control input $u_{i-1}(t)$, which is shown in (7).

$$u_i(t) = u_{i-1}(t) + \hat{u}_{eq,i}(t) + \hat{u}_{sw,i}(t) \tag{7}$$

where, $u_0 = 0$ and

$$\hat{u}_{eq,i}(t) \tag{8}$$
$$= -\frac{\left[\hat{f}_i(x|\hat{\theta}_{f_i}) - \ddot{r}_i(t) + c_i\gamma_i^{-1}\dot{e}_i^{2-\gamma_i} + \right.}{\left. ksgn(s_i) \right]}{\hat{b}_i(x|\hat{\theta}_{b_i})}$$

$$\hat{u}_{sw,i}(t) \tag{9}$$
$$= -\sum_{l=1}^{i-1} \hat{u}_{sw,l}(t)$$
$$- \frac{\left\{ \sum_{l=1}^{i}[\sum_{\substack{m=1 \\ m \neq l}}^{i}(\prod_{j=m}^{i} a_j)\hat{b}_m(x|\hat{\theta}_{b_m})] \right\}}{\sum_{m=1}^{i}(\prod_{j=m}^{i} a_j)\hat{b}_m(x|\hat{\theta}_{b_m})}$$

where, $\hat{f}_i$, $\hat{b}_i$ are the approximations of the unknown nonlinear functions. $f_i(x)$ and $b_i(x)$ are defined in (13,14). $\ddot{r}_i(t)$ is the second derivative of reference input , $a_j = \lambda_j$ as $j \neq i$ and $a_j = 1$ as $j = i$, i=1,2,...,n.

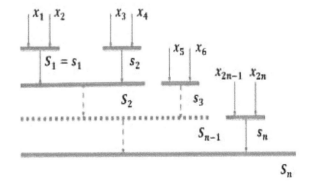

Figure 2. The hierarchical TSM layers construction.

3.3. Adaptive fuzzy inference system

In order to improve the system effectiveness, the unknown uncertain continuous nonlinear functions, $f_i(x)$, $b_i(x)$ and $\rho_i(x)$ are to be learned by the learning functions. The fuzzy rule base is defined in (10).

$$R^{(l)}: \text{IF } x_1 \text{ is } F_1^l \text{ and } \dots \text{ and } x_{2n} \text{ is } F_{2n}^l, \quad (10)$$
$$\text{THEN } y \text{ is } G^l$$

where, F_i^l and G_i^l are the input and the output of the fuzzy systems, respectively. The crisp point x is mapped from fuzzy sets U to a crisp point V, based on the fuzzy IF-THEN rules and by means of the fuzzifier and defuzzifier. The output of the fuzzy system is shown in (11), based on singleton fuzzifier, center-average deffuzification, and product inference engine.

$$y = \theta^T \xi(x) \quad (11)$$

in which, $\theta^T = [\theta^T\ \theta^T\ \dots\ \theta^T] \in \Re^M$ are the points that have the maximum value of membership functions that G^l is able to achieve and $\xi(x) = [\xi^1(x)\ \xi^2(x)\ \dots\ \xi^M(x)]^T$ are basis functions defined as in (12).

$$\xi^l(x) = \frac{\prod_{i=1}^{2n} \mu_{F_i^l}(x_i)}{\sum_{l=1}^{M} \prod_{i=1}^{2n} \mu_{F_i^l}(x_i)} \quad (12)$$

where, $\mu_{F_i^l}(x_i)$ is the membership function of the fuzzy set. The approximation of the unknown nonlinear functions $f_i(x)$, $b_i(x)$ and $\rho_i(x)$ are defined as in (13-15).

$$\hat{f}_i(x|\hat{\theta}_{f_i}) = \hat{\theta}_{f_i}^T \xi(x) \quad (13)$$

$$\hat{b}_i(x|\hat{\theta}_{b_i}) = \hat{\theta}_{b_i}^T \xi(x) \quad (14)$$

$$\hat{\rho}_i(x|\hat{\theta}_{\rho_i}) = \hat{\theta}_{\rho_i}^T \xi(x) \quad (15)$$

Also, the optimal parameters will be defined in (16-18).

$$\theta_{f_i}^* = \arg_{\hat{\theta}_{f_i}(t) \in \Omega_{\hat{\theta}_{f_i}}} \min \sup_{x(t) \in \Omega_x} \{|\hat{f}_i(x|\hat{\theta}_{f_i}) \quad (16)$$
$$- f_i(x)|\}$$

$$\theta_{b_i}^* = \arg_{\hat{\theta}_{f_i}(t) \in \Omega_{\hat{\theta}_{b_i}}} \min \sup_{x(t) \in \Omega_x} \{|\hat{b}_i(x|\hat{\theta}_{b_i}) \quad (17)$$
$$- b_i(x)|\}$$

$$\theta_{\rho_i}^* = \arg_{\hat{\theta}_{\rho_i}(t) \in \Omega_{\hat{\theta}_{\rho_i}}} \min \sup_{x(t) \in \Omega_x} \{|\hat{\rho}_i(x|\hat{\theta}_{\rho_i}) \quad (18)$$
$$- \rho_i(x)|\}$$

And the learning laws of parameter vectors are designed as in [19, 20].
In addition, the upper bound of uncertainties is defined in (19).

$$\dot{\tilde{\omega}} \quad (19)$$
$$= \begin{cases} \gamma_w |S_i(t)| & \text{if } |\tilde{\omega}| < N_w \\ \gamma_w |S_i(t)| - \delta_w |S_i(t)| \tilde{\omega}(t) & \text{if } |\tilde{\omega}| \geq N_w \end{cases}$$

where, $\gamma_w > 0$ is the learning gain and $\delta_w > 0$ is the projection gain.
Hence, (20, 21) are obtained for AFHTSMC.

$$S_n(t) = \sum_{m=1}^{n} \left(\prod_{j=m}^{i} a_j\right) s_m(t) \quad (20)$$

$$u_n(t) = \sum_{l=1}^{n} \hat{u}_{sw,l}(t) + \hat{u}_{eq,l}(t) \quad (21)$$

4. Stability analysis

The following Lyapunov functions are considered in order to prove the stability of the proposed control method. Here, it has been assumed that the learning parameters are bounded and no projection term is required for the learning laws.

$$V_i = \left\{ S_i^2 + \sum_{m=1}^{i} \left[\frac{\tilde{\theta}_{f_m}^T \tilde{\theta}_{f_m}}{\gamma_{f_m}} + \frac{\tilde{\theta}_{b_m}^T \tilde{\theta}_{b_m}}{\gamma_{b_m}} + \frac{\tilde{\theta}_{\rho_m}^T \tilde{\theta}_{\rho_m}}{\gamma_{\rho_m}} \right] \right. \quad (22)$$
$$\left. + \tilde{\omega}^2/\gamma_\omega \right\}/2$$

$$\dot{V}_i = S_i \dot{S}_i + \frac{\tilde{\omega}\dot{\tilde{\omega}}}{\gamma_\omega} + \sum_{m=1}^{i} \left[\frac{\tilde{\theta}_{f_m}^T \dot{\tilde{\theta}}_{f_m}}{\gamma_{f_m}} + \frac{\tilde{\theta}_{b_m}^T \dot{\tilde{\theta}}_{b_m}}{\gamma_{b_m}} \right. \quad (23)$$
$$\left. + \frac{\tilde{\theta}_{\rho_m}^T \dot{\tilde{\theta}}_{\rho_m}}{\gamma_{\rho_m}} \right]$$

$$\dot{V}_i = S_i \sum_{m=1}^{n} \left(\prod_{j=m}^{i} a_j\right) \dot{s}_m(t) + \frac{\tilde{\omega}\dot{\tilde{\omega}}}{\gamma_\omega} \quad (24)$$
$$+ \sum_{m=1}^{i} \left[\frac{\tilde{\theta}_{f_m}^T \dot{\tilde{\theta}}_{f_m}}{\gamma_{f_m}} + \frac{\tilde{\theta}_{b_m}^T \dot{\tilde{\theta}}_{b_m}}{\gamma_{b_m}} + \frac{\tilde{\theta}_{\rho_m}^T \dot{\tilde{\theta}}_{\rho_m}}{\gamma_{\rho_m}} \right]$$

$$= S_i \sum_{m=1}^{n} \left(\prod_{j=m}^{i} a_j\right) [c_m \dot{e}_m \quad (25)$$
$$+ \gamma_m \dot{e}_m^{\gamma_m - 1} (f_m + b_m u + d_m - \ddot{r}_m) + \frac{\tilde{\omega}\dot{\tilde{\omega}}}{\gamma_\omega}$$
$$+ \sum_{m=1}^{i} \left[\frac{\tilde{\theta}_{f_m}^T \dot{\tilde{\theta}}_{f_m}}{\gamma_{f_m}} + \frac{\tilde{\theta}_{b_m}^T \dot{\tilde{\theta}}_{b_m}}{\gamma_{b_m}} + \frac{\tilde{\theta}_{\rho_m}^T \dot{\tilde{\theta}}_{\rho_m}}{\gamma_{\rho_m}} \right]$$

$$\leq S_i \sum_{m=1}^{n} \left(\prod_{j=m}^{i} a_j\right) [c_m \dot{e}_m \quad (26)$$
$$+ \gamma_m \dot{e}_m^{\gamma_m - 1} (f_m + b_m u - \ddot{r}_m)$$
$$+ |S_i| \sum_{m=1}^{i} \left|\left(\prod_{j=m}^{i} a_j\right) \gamma_m \dot{e}_m^{\gamma_m - 1} \rho_m\right| + \frac{\tilde{\omega}\dot{\tilde{\omega}}}{\gamma_\omega}$$
$$+ \sum_{m=1}^{i} \left[\frac{\tilde{\theta}_{f_m}^T \dot{\tilde{\theta}}_{f_m}}{\gamma_{f_m}} + \frac{\tilde{\theta}_{b_m}^T \dot{\tilde{\theta}}_{b_m}}{\gamma_{b_m}} + \frac{\tilde{\theta}_{\rho_m}^T \dot{\tilde{\theta}}_{\rho_m}}{\gamma_{\rho_m}} \right]$$

$$= S_i \sum_{m=1}^{n} \left(\prod_{j=m}^{i} a_j \right) [c_m \dot{e}_m \tag{27}$$
$$+ \gamma_m \dot{e}_m{}^{\gamma_m-1} ([f_m - \hat{f}_m^*] + [\hat{f}_m^* - \hat{f}_m] + \hat{f}_m + [b_m u$$
$$- \hat{b}_m^* u] + [b_m^* u - \hat{b}_m u] + b_m u - \ddot{r}_m)$$
$$+ |S_i| \sum_{m=1}^{i} \left| \left(\prod_{j=m}^{i} a_j \right) \right| \gamma_m \dot{e}_m{}^{\gamma_m-1} \{ [\rho_m - \hat{\rho}_m^*]$$
$$+ [\hat{\rho}_m^* - \hat{\rho}_m] + \hat{\rho}_m \} + \frac{\widetilde{\omega}\dot{\widetilde{\omega}}}{\gamma_\omega}$$
$$+ \sum_{m=1}^{i} \left[\frac{\tilde{\theta}_{f_m}^T \dot{\tilde{\theta}}_{f_m}}{\gamma_{f_m}} + \frac{\tilde{\theta}_{b_m}^T \dot{\tilde{\theta}}_{b_m}}{\gamma_{b_m}} + \frac{\tilde{\theta}_{\rho_m}^T \dot{\tilde{\theta}}_{\rho_m}}{\gamma_{\rho_m}} \right]$$

$$\leq S_i \omega + S_i \sum_{m=1}^{n} \left(\prod_{j=m}^{i} a_j \right) [c_m \dot{e}_m \tag{28}$$
$$+ \gamma_m \dot{e}_m{}^{\gamma_m-1} ([\hat{f}_m^* - \hat{f}_m] + \hat{f}_m + [b_m^* u - \hat{b}_m u] + b_m u$$
$$- \ddot{r}_m)$$
$$+ |S_i| \sum_{m=1}^{i} \left| \left(\prod_{j=m}^{i} a_j \right) \right| \gamma_m \dot{e}_m{}^{\gamma_m-1} \{ [\hat{\rho}_m^* - \hat{\rho}_m] + \hat{\rho}_m \}$$
$$+ \frac{\widetilde{\omega}\dot{\widetilde{\omega}}}{\gamma_\omega} + \sum_{m=1}^{i} \left[\frac{\tilde{\theta}_{f_m}^T \dot{\tilde{\theta}}_{f_m}}{\gamma_{f_m}} + \frac{\tilde{\theta}_{b_m}^T \dot{\tilde{\theta}}_{b_m}}{\gamma_{b_m}} + \frac{\tilde{\theta}_{\rho_m}^T \dot{\tilde{\theta}}_{\rho_m}}{\gamma_{\rho_m}} \right]$$

$$= S_i \omega + S_i \sum_{m=1}^{n} \left(\prod_{j=m}^{i} a_j \right) [c_m \dot{e}_m \tag{29}$$
$$+ \gamma_m \dot{e}_m{}^{\gamma_m-1} ([\theta_{f_m}^*{}^T \xi - \hat{\theta}_{f_m}{}^T \xi] + \hat{f}_m + [\theta_{b_m}^*{}^T \xi$$
$$- \hat{\theta}_{b_m}{}^T \xi] + b_m u - \ddot{r}_m)$$
$$+ |S_i| \sum_{m=1}^{i} \left| \left(\prod_{j=m}^{i} a_j \right) \right| \gamma_m \dot{e}_m{}^{\gamma_m-1} \{ [\theta_{\rho_m}^*{}^T \xi - \hat{\theta}_{\rho_m}{}^T \xi]$$
$$+ \hat{\rho}_m \} + \frac{\widetilde{\omega}\dot{\widetilde{\omega}}}{\gamma_\omega} + \sum_{m=1}^{i} \left[\frac{\tilde{\theta}_{f_m}^T \dot{\tilde{\theta}}_{f_m}}{\gamma_{f_m}} + \frac{\tilde{\theta}_{b_m}^T \dot{\tilde{\theta}}_{b_m}}{\gamma_{b_m}} + \frac{\tilde{\theta}_{\rho_m}^T \dot{\tilde{\theta}}_{\rho_m}}{\gamma_{\rho_m}} \right]$$

$$= S_i \omega + S_i \sum_{m=1}^{n} \left(\prod_{j=m}^{i} a_j \right) [c_m \dot{e}_m \tag{30}$$
$$+ \gamma_m \dot{e}_m{}^{\gamma_m-1} (\hat{f}_m + b_m u - \ddot{r}_m)$$
$$+ |S_i| \sum_{m=1}^{i} \left| \left(\prod_{j=m}^{i} a_j \right) \right| \gamma_m \dot{e}_m{}^{\gamma_m-1} \{ \hat{\rho}_m \} + \frac{\widetilde{\omega}\dot{\widetilde{\omega}}}{\gamma_\omega}$$
$$- S_i \sum_{m=1}^{i} \left(\prod_{j=m}^{i} a_j \right) \tilde{\theta}_{f_m}^T \xi + \sum_{m=1}^{i} \tilde{\theta}_{f_m}^T \hat{\theta}_{f_m}^T / \gamma_{f_m}$$
$$- S_i \sum_{m=1}^{i} \left(\prod_{j=m}^{i} a_j \right) \tilde{\theta}_{b_m}^T \xi u + \sum_{m=1}^{i} \tilde{\theta}_{b_m}^T \hat{\theta}_{b_m}^T / \gamma_{b_m}$$
$$- |S_i| \sum_{m=1}^{i} \left(\prod_{j=m}^{i} a_j \right) |\tilde{\theta}_{\rho_m}^T \xi + \sum_{m=1}^{i} \tilde{\theta}_{\rho_m}^T \hat{\theta}_{\rho_m}^T / \gamma_{f_m}$$

Hence, we replace the terms $\hat{f}_m^*, \hat{f}_m, b_m^*$ and $\hat{b}_m$ by $\theta_{f_m}^*{}^T \xi$, $\hat{\theta}_{f_m}{}^T \xi$, $\theta_{b_m}^*{}^T \xi$ and $\hat{\theta}_{b_m}{}^T \xi$, respectively. This leads to (29) and discretization gives (30). Substituting the learning laws and the control law of the ith layer and the learning upper

bound of uncertainties into the above equation yields (31-35).

$$= |S_i|\omega + \frac{\widetilde{\omega}\dot{\widetilde{\omega}}}{\gamma_\omega} + S_i \sum_{m=1}^{n} \left(\prod_{j=m}^{i} a_j \right) [c_m \dot{e}_m \tag{31}$$
$$+ \gamma_m \dot{e}_m{}^{\gamma_m-1} \left(f_m + b_m \hat{u}_{eq,m} \right.$$
$$+ b_m \left(\sum_{\substack{l=1 \\ l \neq m}}^{i} \hat{u}_{eq,l} + \sum_{l=1}^{i} \hat{u}_{sw,l} \right) - \ddot{r}_m \right)]$$
$$+ |S_i| \sum_{m=1}^{i} \left| \left(\prod_{j=m}^{i} a_j \right) \right| \gamma_m \dot{e}_m{}^{\gamma_m-1} \rho_m$$

$$= |S_i|\omega + \frac{\widetilde{\omega}\dot{\widetilde{\omega}}}{\gamma_\omega} + S_i \sum_{m=1}^{n} \left(\prod_{j=m}^{i} a_j \right) [c_m \dot{e}_m \tag{32}$$
$$+ \gamma_m \dot{e}_m{}^{\gamma_m-1} \left(f_m + b_m \sum_{l=1}^{i} \hat{u}_{sw,l} + \hat{u}_{eq,l} - \ddot{r}_m \right)]$$
$$+ |S_i| \sum_{m=1}^{i} \left| \left(\prod_{j=m}^{i} a_j \right) \right| \gamma_m \dot{e}_m{}^{\gamma_m-1} \rho_m$$

$$= |S_i|\omega + \frac{\widetilde{\omega}\dot{\widetilde{\omega}}}{\gamma_\omega} + S_i \sum_{m=1}^{n} \left(\prod_{j=m}^{i} a_j \right) [\tag{33}$$
$$\gamma_m \dot{e}_m{}^{\gamma_m-1} \left(b_m \left(\sum_{\substack{l=1 \\ l \neq m}}^{i} \hat{u}_{eq,l} + \sum_{l=1}^{i} \hat{u}_{sw,l} \right) \right)]$$
$$+ |S_i| \sum_{m=1}^{i} \left| \left(\prod_{j=m}^{i} a_j \right) \right| \gamma_m \dot{e}_m{}^{\gamma_m-1} \rho_m$$

$$\leq |S_i|\omega + \frac{\widetilde{\omega}\dot{\widetilde{\omega}}}{\gamma_\omega} - K|S_i|\dot{e}_m{}^{\gamma_m-1}\omega \tag{34}$$
$$\leq -K_1 S_i^2 - K|S_i|\dot{e}_m{}^{\gamma_m-1}\omega < 0 \tag{35}$$

5. Simulations and discussions

The inverted pendulum on a movable cart is considered to verify the effectiveness of the proposed controller (Figure 3). Here, the system functions are described in (36-39).

$$f_1(x) = \frac{\{m_t g \sin x_1 - m_p L \sin x_1 \cos x_1 x_2^2\}}{L/2 \left(\frac{4m_t}{3} - m_p \cos^2 x_1 \right)} \tag{36}$$

$$f_2(x) = \frac{\left\{ -\frac{4m_p L}{2} x_2^2 \sin \frac{x_1}{3} + m_p g \sin x_1 \cos x_1 \right\}}{\left(\frac{4m_t}{3} - m_p \cos^2 x_1 \right)} \tag{37}$$

$$b_1(x) = \cos \frac{x_1}{\frac{L}{2}\left(\frac{4m_t}{3} - m_p\cos^2 x_1\right)} \qquad (38)$$

$$b_2(x) = \frac{4}{3\left(\frac{4m_t}{3} - m_p\cos^2 x_1\right)} \qquad (39)$$

where, $m_t = m_p + m_c$ and x_1 , x_2 , x_3 , x_4 are respectively the pendulum's angle with respect to the vertical axis, the angular velocity of the pendulum with respect to the vertical axis, the position of the cart, and the velocity of the cart. The magnitudes of the constant parameters of the system are shown in table 1.

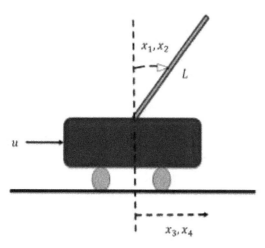

Figure 3. The inverted pendulum on a movable cart.

The simulations have been done by MATLAB 2012 software. Since the term x_i is used in the Lyapunov function and adaptation laws, it has to be fuzzified in order to achieve the results for the output of the system. Hence, x_i is input variable of the fuzzy system and u is its output variable, respectively. The membership functions are assumed to be triangular because they result in entropy equalization in probability density function.

Table 1. The constant parameter's magnitudes of the system.

Parameter	Magnitude	Description
m_c	1 Kg	Mass of the cart
m_p	0.05 Kg	Mass of the pendulum
L	1 m	Length of the pendulum
g	$9.806\ \frac{m}{s^2}$	Acceleration due to gravity

Also, the reconstruction will be error-free if a ½ overlap between neighbouring fuzzy sets is considered. When interfacing fuzzy sets are being constructed by numerical datum, these two characteristics are implemented. Based on the aforementioned reasons, the membership functions are designed as shown in figures 4 and 5.

As can be clearly seen, each of the inputs and the outputs are partitioned by seven membership functions called as negative big (NB), negative medium (NM), negative small (NS), zero (Z), positive small (PS), positive medium (PM), and positive big (PB). Of course, one can alter the membership functions type and number in order to improve the results.

In this research, the reference inputs are set as $r_1(t) = 5.5\sin(t)$ (degree) and $r_2(t) = \sin(t)$ (m). The hierarchical terminal sliding surfaces are selected as $s_1(t) = \dot{e}_1(t)^{\gamma_1} + c_1 e_1(t)$ and $s_2(t) = \dot{e}_2(t)^{\gamma_1} + c_2 e_2(t)$ where $c_1 = 2$, $c_2 = 1$ and $\gamma_1 = \gamma_2 = \frac{9}{7}$. The initial values are chosen as $x(0) = [\frac{\pi}{6}, 0, 0, 0]$. In addition, we assume the external disturbance to be a low frequency signal, $d_1(x, t) = 0.75 x_1^2(t)\sin(\sin(t)\ x_1 x_3)$, and a high frequency signal, $d_2(x, t) = 0.75 x_3 x_4 \sin(100(t))$.

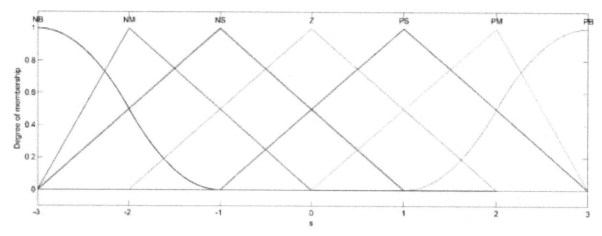

Figure 4. The membership functions of the input variables.

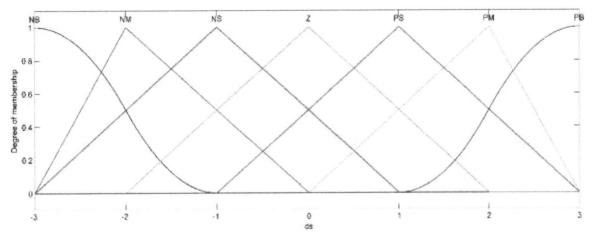

Figure 5. The membership functions of the output variable.

In order to verify the reliability of the proposed AFHTSMC, long-term operation simulations are presented and compared with Adaptive Fuzzy Hierarchical Sliding Mode Control (AFHSMC) [19] as shown in figures 6-9. The position tracking plots for the pendulum and the cart (Figure 6 and 7) demonstrate the perfect match of the two control methods for a hundred seconds. As can be clearly seen for AFHTSMC, the small undesirable fluctuations disappear in the very first steps of the control algorithm and the desired oscillatory motion continues over a long period of time. Figure 8 represents a significant effect of the TSM implication on the control method by comparing the top hierarchical surfaces of the aforementioned methods. As it is shown the TSM results have a higher rate of convergence. Also, asymptotical trajectory tracking is obtained immediately and the transition time (0.42 seconds) is much less than that of [19] (3.65 seconds). In addition, the variations of the top

hierarchical surface decreases significantly in AFHTSMC, compared to AFHSMC. Therefore, the combination of the TSM control and hierarchical structure enables the fast finite time convergence of the uncertain nonlinear dynamic system. Therefore, the proposed method is much more convenient when fast convergence properties and high precision are required. The control input variations after learning are also presented in figure 9, in which the AFHTSMC shows smoother force results. This happens because of the TSM requirement to avoid the singularity problem. Although there may exist a large amplitude of force before learning, it does not affect the system because of the AFHTSMC's fast convergence. However, there still exists small fluctuations. In addition, in most of the high precision applications, we do not need very large forces. Hence, the force variations are between small ranges that do not affect the system performance.

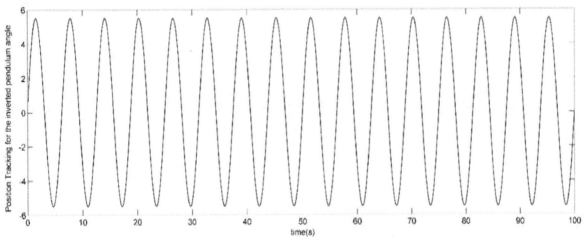

Figure 6. The position tracking vs. time for the pendulum angle (blue dashed line is the reference signal, the solid blue line is the output signal and the red dashed line is for the AFHSMC).

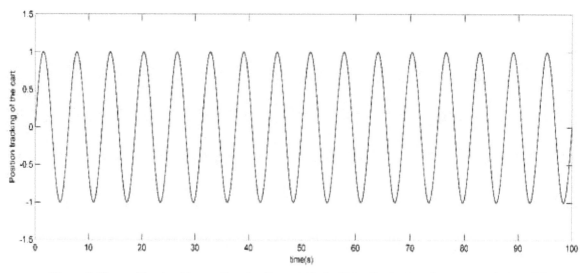

Figure 7. The position tracking vs. time for the cart (dashed blue line is the reference signal, the solid blue line is the output signal and the dashed red line is for the AFHSMC).

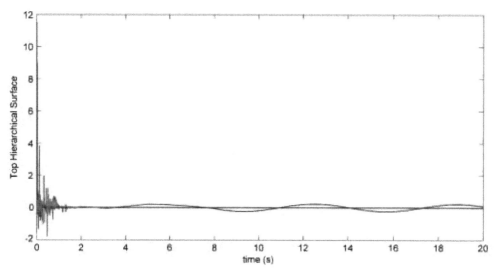

Figure 8. Second level hierarchical terminal sliding surface vs. time (blue and red solid lines represents the AFHTSMC and the AFHSMC top hierarchical surface, respectively).

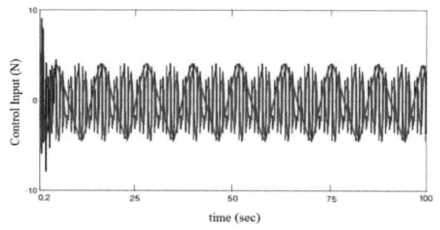

Figure 9. The control input (u) vs. time (The blue solid line and the red solid line show the force values for AFHTSMC and AFHSMC, respectively).

It is clear that larger learning rates can accelerate the convergence properties though the instability phenomena possibly occur in AFHSMC, especially in long-term applications. However, the implementation of the AFHTSMC reduces the requirement to implement very large learning rates, and is a major drawback of the previous studies. In addition, as demonstrated in the simulation results, applying Lyapunov stability theorem with the AFHTSMC guarantees the robustness to the bounded external disturbance, stability, and finite time convergence in trajectory tracking of the system.

6. Conclusions

In this study, the AFHTSMC has been proposed for a class of uncertain nonlinear dynamic systems. The control algorithm was designed based on the Lyapunov stability criterion. The combination of the TSM and the adaptive fuzzy hierarchical system, which is the main novelty of this paper, enables the system to converge much faster to the desired trajectory compared with the other methods in literature. Also, applying the TSM in the adaptive fuzzy hierarchical system is much more effective in chattering reduction. Furthermore, the hierarchical structure decouples the class of nonlinear coupled systems to subsystems with guaranteed stability, and the direct adaptive fuzzy scheme works online but does not require prior knowledge of dynamic parameters. Computer simulations for an inverted pendulum on a cart have demonstrated the long-term stability, robustness, and validity. The AFHTSMC can be extended to other applications with multi-input-multi-output (MIMO) structures. We will focus on the fuzzy Type-2, neuro-fuzzy, and evolutionary fuzzy systems in the hierarchical TSM in our future study.

References

[1] Santiesteban, R., Floquet, T., Orlov, Y., Riachy, S. & Richard, J. P. (2008). Second Order Sliding Mode Control of Under-actuated Mechanical Systems II: Orbital Stabilization of an Inverted Pendulum with Application to Swing Up/Balancing Control, International Journal of Robust Nonlinear Control, vol. 56, no. 3, pp.529-543.

[2] Udawatta, L., Watanabe, K., & Izumi K. (2004). Control of three degrees of freedom under-actuated manipulator using fuzzy based switching, Artificial Life Robotics, vol. 8, no. 2, pp. 153- 158.

[3] Chiang, C. C., & Hu, C. C. (2012). Output tracking control for uncertain under-actuated systems based fuzzy sliding-mode control approach, IEEE International Conference on Fuzzy Systems Proceedings, Brisbane, Australia, 2012.

[4] Utkin, V. I. (1992). Sliding Modes in Control Optimization, Berlin, Heidelberg. New York: Springer-Verlag.

[5] Zinober, A. S. I. (1993). Variable Structure and Lyapunov Control, London, Heidelberg. New York: Springer-Verlag.

[6] Slotine, J. J. E. & Li, W. (1991). Applied Nonlinear Control, New Jersey: Prentice Hall.

[7] Utkin, V., Guldner, J. & Shi, J. (1999). Sliding Mode Control in Electromechanical Systems, Taylor and Francis Ltd.

[8] Yu, X.H. & Zhihong, M. (1996). Model reference adaptive control systems with terminal sliding modes, International Journal of Control, vol. 64, pp. 1165–1176.

[9] Yu, X., Zhihong, M., Feng, Y. & Guan, Z. (2002). Nonsingular terminal sliding mode control of a class of nonlinear dynamical systems, 15th Terminal world congress (IFAC), Barcelona, Spain, 2002.

[10] Zhihong, M. & Yu, X.H. (1997). Terminal sliding mode control of MIMO linear systems, IEEE Transactions on Circuits Systems: I, Fundamental Theory Applications, vol. 44, pp. 1065–1070.

[11] Wu, Y., Yu, X. & Man, Z. (1998) Terminal sliding mode control design for uncertain dynamic systems, Systems Control Letters, vol. 34, pp. 281–287.

[12] Feng, Y., Yu, X. & Man, Z. (2002). Non-singular terminal sliding mode control of rigid manipulators, Automatica, vol. 38, pp. 2159–2167.

[13] Tao, C. W., Taur, J. S. & Chan, M. L. (2004). Adaptive fuzzy terminal sliding mode controller for linear systems with mismatched time-varying uncertainties, IEEE Transactions on Systems Man and Cybernetics B. Cybernetics, vol. 34, pp. 255–262.

[14] Chiang, C. C. & Hu, C. C. (2012). Output tracking control for uncertain under-actuated systems based fuzzy sliding-mode control approach, IEEE International Conference on Fuzzy Systems Proceedings, Brisbane, Australia, 2012.

[15] Aghababa, M. P. (2014). Design of hierarchical terminal sliding mode control scheme for fractional-order systems, IET Science, Measurement & Technology, vol. 9, no. 1, pp. 122-133.

[16] Mobayen, S. (2015). Fast terminal sliding mode tracking of non-holonomic systems with exponential decay rate, IET Control Theory and Applications, vol. 9, no. 8, pp. 1294-1301.

[17] Mobayen, S. (2014), An adaptive fast terminal sliding mode control combined with global sliding mode scheme for tracking control of uncertain nonlinear third-order systems, Nonlinear Dynamics, DOI:10.1007/s11071-015-2180-4.

[18] Hwang, C. L., Wu, H. M. & Shih, C. L. (2009). Fuzzy sliding-Mode under-actuated control for autonomous dynamic balance of an electrical bicycle, IEEE Transactions on Control Systems and Technology, vol. 17, no. 3, pp. 783–795.

[19] Nekoukar, V. & Erfanian, A. (2011). Adaptive fuzzy terminal sliding mode control for a class of MIMO uncertain nonlinear systems, Fuzzy sets and systems, vol. 179, pp. 34-49.

[20] Lin, C. M. & Mon, Y. J. (2005). Decoupling control by hierarchical fuzzy sliding-mode controller, IEEE Transactions on Control Systems and Technology, vol. 13, no.4, pp. 593–598.

[21] Qian, D., Yi, J. & Zhao, D. (2008). Control of a class of under-actuated systems with saturation sing hierarchical sliding mode, IEEE International Conference on Robotics and Automation Proceedings, Pasadena, CA, USA, 2008.

[22] Hwang, C. L., Chiang, C. C. & Yeh, Y. (2014). Adaptive Fuzzy Hierarchical Sliding-Mode Control for the Trajectory Tracking of Uncertain Under-actuated Nonlinear Dynamic Systems, IEEE Transactions on Fuzzy Systems, vol. 22, no. 2, pp. 286-299.

[23] Li, T. & Huang, Y., (2010). MIMO adaptive fuzzy terminal sliding-mode controller for robotic manipulators, Information Siences, vol. 180, pp. 4641-4660.

6

High impedance fault detection: Discrete wavelet transform and fuzzy function approximation

M. Banejad* and H. Ijadi

Electrical Engineering Department, Shahrood University of Technology, Shahrood, Iran.

Corresponding author: m.banejad@shahroodut.ac.ir (M. Banejad).

Abstract

This paper presents a method including a combination of the wavelet transform and fuzzy function approximation (FFA) for high impedance fault (HIF) detection in distribution electricity network. Discrete wavelet transform (DWT) is used in this paper as a tool for a signal analysis and after studying different types of mother signals, detailed types and feeder signal, the best case is selected. In the next step, the DWT is used to extract the features. The extracted features are used as the FFA Systems inputs. The FFA system uses the input-output pairs to create a function approximation of the features. The FFA system is able to classify the new features. The combined model is used to model the HIF. This combined model has the high ability to model different types of HIF. In the proposed method, different kind of loads including nonlinear and asymmetric loads and HIF types are studied. The results show that the proposed method has high capability to distinguish between no fault and HIF states accurately.

Keywords: *High Impedance Fault, Fuzzy Function Approximation, Wavelet Transform, Distribution Network, Arc Fault.*

1. Introduction

Safety is one of the important issues in distribution electricity networks. Lack of security in the power network may lead to damage to humans and equipment. The prevention is the best solution to avoid the harmful events. The HIF is one of the issues that results in death and financial damages. The HIF occurs when a conductor contacts with the ground or high impedance object. As the impedance of the current path is high, the current value in this type of fault is low and usually ranges from 0A to 100A [1]. Hence, by the conventional over current relay, it is not possible to detect this kind of fault; it is treated as a normal load current raise.

The HIF can occur in two forms. In the first form, a conductor breaks and falls to the ground. In the second form, an electrical conductor is not disconnected but only is to be connected to a high impedance object (such as tree branches and leaves). The HIFs are usually associated with an electric arc, which may cause a fire. Due to the nonlinearity nature of the fault, the HIF current

contains various frequency harmonic components including low and high frequency components. It should be noted that other network components have also broad frequency harmonics. Therefore, the HIF should be studied precisely. The researchers have performed several HIF experiments and have studied the associated voltage and current to obtain models that are to be used in the simulations. As the HIF has a random nature and the fault current is influenced by many parameters, developing a model that covers all conditions is difficult. However, since the developed model is based on practical experiments, the researchers considered some aspects of the HIF characteristics.

The first model of HIF was introduced in 1985. In this model, the HIF was modeled by a single resistor in the fault location [2]. After five years, with respect to the presence of ARC in the HIF, an arc based model is presented [3]. In this model, the HIF is presented in anti-parallel two diodes, each one is in series with a DC voltage source and series impedance. The two diodes as well as the voltage sources show the diode voltage threshold. The series impedance also controls the current. Three years later, branch impedances were replaced with two nonlinear resistors [4]. Also in 2005, the arrangement of fixed and variable resistors in two half cycles were presented [5]. In addition to the electrical aspects for HIF modeling, the dynamical aspects of the HIF arc are used. This is possible by using the dynamical relationships of electrical arc [6,7]. Also, a combinational method which uses the both aspects were employed in [8]. In this reference, a dynamical relationship is considered for a variable resistor placed in a path out of the diodes routs. The advantage of this method is that the arc model results are close to the practical experiments. Also, in this model, the routes of the two diodes can represent the non-similarity between positive and negative half cycle of high impedance fault in [9], two voltage sources with random value were used to create random characteristics for the HIF current.

Researchers have proposed various methods for the detection of the HIF. These methods usually start by measuring available signal at the feeder and preparing them for analysis. Then, the signal processing tools are for feature extraction and obtaining discriminative. The latter has been used to discriminate between normal and HIF situations. Finally, the fault classification is performed using simple or intelligent algorithms. References [10] and [11] used discrete Fourier transform to find the voltage signal harmonics and feeder current. In order to extract frequency feature of the HIF, some signal processing tools such as Fourier transform and Kalman filter have been utilized. Also, the magnitude of the harmonics was founded through using Kaman filter [12]. In the power system, time-frequency based methods are used. This leads to more use of the wavelet transform. This fact is due to the time varying behavior of the power system phenomena especially HIF. The wavelet transform based methods were for analysis the measured signal in [13,14].

After extracting features, the HIF should be distinguished from normal operating conditions. Sequential algorithms such as described in [15] to check the appropriate features, if the feature exceeds the threshold value, it means that the HIF has been occurred. Intelligent methods such as artificial neural network (ANN), perform classification the training data. In [12,16,17] different methods of training, the ANN was used in HIF detection. A combination of the ANN and

sequential algorithm was used in [18] and the method employed in [14] is based on the a neuron-fuzzy method.

In this paper, firstly the signal is decomposed using DWT. In the next stage, the wavelet output is used to find appropriate features for classification. In order to consider the more realistic case, a combined model of the HIF is used. In the classification stage, an FFA intelligent method for is presented.

In this paper, firstly the wavelet transform and FFA are briefly explained. Then, the proposed method is provided. After that, the component modeling is described. Finally, the simulation results and discussion are described.

2. Wavelets for signal analysis

The wavelet analysis is a signal-processing tool that has successful applications in various fields especially in power engineering. Some applications of the wavelet are in the field of power quality [19], power system protection [20], power system transient [21].

Unlike Fourier transform, the wavelet analysis is able to provide simultaneous time and frequency information. Hence, it is a useful tool for analysis of transient signal that contains high frequency and low frequency components. There are two discrete and continuous wavelet transforms. The DWT is used to process digital data. The DWT for the function x is given by:

$$DWT(m,k) = \frac{1}{\sqrt{a_0^m}} \sum_n x[n].g[\frac{k - na_0^m}{a_0^m}] \qquad (1)$$

Where x[n] is a digital signal, g is the mother wavelet, a0 and k are scale factors, respectively. Also n and m are real numbers.

The DWT can be implemented by using a multistage filter with the mother wavelet as the low pass filter and high pass filter [22]. The center frequency is varied by changing the scale and time shift in the mother wavelet. This shows that the wavelet transform can suitably extract unwanted transient signals and frequency components of a waveform. There are different types of mother wavelets, which can extract specific features of the signal. It should be noted that the selection of the mother wavelet is important in feature extraction. This selection depends on the type of application. Suitable mother wavelet should have a greater difference between the normal and faulted output signal. As a result, the suitable mother wavelet creates a better output. With regards to the specifications of the mother wavelet, several mother wavelets are considered as the suitable ones. In order to find the most suitable mother wavelet, several mother wavelets can be examined.

The DWT is considered as a multistage filter with mother wavelet, which acts as the high pass and low pass filter. The output of the low pass filter gives the details of the low-frequency component of the signal. In addition, the output of the high pass filter gives the details of the high-frequency component of the signal. To obtain more details from the input signal, we can change the mother wavelet or levels of detail. This analysis called multi-resolution analysis shown in figure 1.

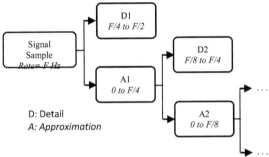

Figure 1. Diagram of multi-resolution analysis of wavelet.

3. Fuzzy system for approximation of function

The FFA is a method for nonlinear system modeling. Some types of fuzzy system are written as a closed nonlinear formula. These closed formulas simplify the fuzzy system computation. In addition, the fuzzy system can be treated an approximation of a function using the closed formula. It is very important to choose suitable number of fuzzy rules in design of fuzzy systems. Because choosing many fuzzy rules will complicate the fuzzy system, which may not be needed for the problem. On the other hand, choosing limited number of fuzzy rules, may lead to incorrect result. The important notion of employing fuzzy system for approximation function is to use mapped if-then fuzzy based on the output Mamdani fuzzy system according to (2). The specification of this fuzzy system is given in [23].

In (2), the input-output pairs create if-then rules. This equation presents an the FFA, where F is the function approximation,(x_i, y_i) are input-output pairs as training data, n is number of training data, m is input data dimension, x is input variable, x_i is input training data, y_i is output training data and parameter σ is the standard deviation of the Gaussian membership function.

$$F(x) = \frac{\sum_{i=1}^{n} y_i * exp(-(\frac{(x-x_i)^2}{\sigma^2}))}{\sum_{i=1}^{n} exp(-(\frac{(x-x_i)^2}{\sigma^2}))} \qquad (2)$$

In this equation by choosing a suitable value for the parameter σ in the fuzzy system, it is possible to adapt any n-pairs input with any precision. If the number of pairs of input - output is large, then the function will have a better approximation. Smaller σ results in smaller adaptive error and the less F(x) smoothness. If F(x) is not being smooth, it is possible not to generalize it for the paired that do not lie in the set, not in a learning set. So σ should be chosen carefully to balance adaption popularities [23].

4. Proposed HIF detection methodology

The proposed method for identifying the HIF is based on DWT and FFA. In the first step of the proposed method, the feeder signal (voltage or current) is measured and then stored with 100 kHz sampling frequency for the duration of one second. In the next step, the signal processing is performed with DWT through choosing the best mother wavelet and details. Then, the features are built using the output of DWT. These features can discriminate between the no fault and HIF states. In the last step, the HIF classification is performed by FFA and training data. Figure 2 shows this process briefly.

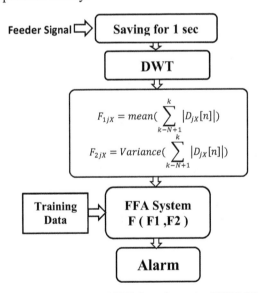

Figure 2. Process of HIF detection using DWT &FFA.

It is worthwhile to note that both voltage and current signals are examined separately, then after investigating the result, it will be decided which of these signals should be used in the simulation.

In the above algorithm, the following questions should be answered:

1- Which one of the measured signals provides the best accuracy?

2- Which one of the mother wavelet and what level of detail provides the best accuracy?

3- How to create the discriminating features using the wavelet output?

4- How does FFA the classify the HIF?

In response to the first question, it should be noted that, in this paper, phase voltage, phase current and summation of all phases voltage have separately been examined and simulated. From the results, the signal that creates the highest detection accuracy, is selected as an appropriate signal.

In response to the second question, it should be noted that in this paper, 17 types of mother wavelet ('db2','db4', 'db5', 'db8','db14','db20', 'sym5', 'sym8', 'coif4', 'bior2.6', 'bior5.5', 'bior6.8', 'rbio2.2', 'rbio3.1', 'rbio3.3', 'rbio4.4') and seven levels of details for all types of measured signal have been separately investigate. Among them, each one that has the highest detection accuracy, is selected as an appropriate mother wavelet and details.

The response to the third question is given in the following. As, the output of the wavelet is not the number and it is a function discrete of variables. Thus, this cannot be considered as the input of an intelligent algorithm or classification algorithm. Therefore, the appropriate input signal should extract features from the output of the wavelet, which expresses the desired behavior of the signal. In this paper, firstly, summation absolute detail (SAD) is taken from the output wavelet. The SAD calculated as follows [24]:

$$SAD_{jX}[k] = \sum_{k-N+1}^{k} |D_{jX}[n]| \qquad (3)$$

In (3), D_{jx} is the detail of the wavelet output at Level j for Signal X, k and N are real numbers. Next, two features of output wavelet are extracted. These two features for signal X at level j are the mean and variance denoted by F_{1jx} and F_{2jx}. The two features used as inputs of the classification system. These two features calculated as:

$$F_{1jX} = mean(SAD_{jX}[k]) \qquad (4)$$

$$F_{2jX} = variance(SAD_{jX}[k]) \qquad (5)$$

In response to the fourth questions is that as FFA needs input-output pairs as the training data for the FFA. These pairs are the mean and variance of SAD output for no fault and HIF cases, respectively. The value of output pairs the HIF case is one, and value of output pairs for no fault and normal load situations is zero. Expanding (2) for the two inputs (n=2) yields.

$$F_{HIF} = F(F_1, F_2)$$
$$\frac{\sum_{i=1}^{n} y_i * exp(\frac{-(F_1-F_{1i})^2}{\sigma_1^2}).exp(\frac{-(F_2-F_{2i})^2}{\sigma_2^2})}{\sum_{i=1}^{n} exp(\frac{-(F_1-F_{1i})^2}{\sigma_1^2}).exp(\frac{-(F_2-F_{2i})^2}{\sigma_2^2})} \qquad (6)$$

$$y_i = \begin{cases} 1 & for\ HIF \\ 0 & for\ NF \end{cases}$$

Where F_{HIF} is the FFA of HIF, n is the number of training data, F_1 & F_2 are input features, F_{1i} & F_{2i} are input training data, y_i is output training data and parameter σ is the standard deviation.

In (6), y_i is also equal to one for HIF training data and equal to zero for no fault. Thus, if the function F (F_1, F_2) is equal to one for the new data of features, this represents the occurrence of HIF in the network. Alternatively, if the function F (F_1, F_2) is equal to zero, for it means that the network is working normally.

5. Component modeling and system under study

The study system in this paper is a radial distribution network as shown in figure 3. The parallel feeders are connected to a 63 kV slack bus via a63/20 kV substation transformer and the system frequency is 50 Hz. The parallel feeders (lines) have different lengths. Lines lengthare10, 20 and 30km.To have a better accuracy, the π model is used for the lines.

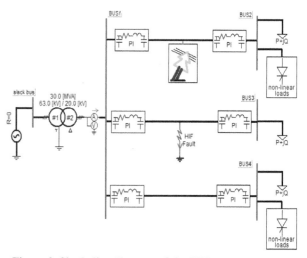

Figure 3. Single line diagram of the MV network under study.

Different loads for consumers in the buses are also used. The different loads are:

- Constant power (with different Power rating and different Power Factor)

- Induction machine (with constant and random torque)

- Electric arc furnace

- Load switching

- Thyristor load (3-Phase, 1-Phase, fixed angle, random angle, R&L load)
- Asymmetric loads (R & L & C)

In addition to different electrical loads, normal operating states are simulated such as capacitor bank switching, saturation transformer and change the situation the tap changer.

In this paper, a combined HIF model is employed in the simulation. This model combines the dynamical relationship arc and electrical model. In this model, the HIF is represented by anti-parallel two diodes, each one is in series with a DC voltage source and series dynamic resistors. The dynamic model of a dynamic resistor depends on the HIF currents. This model is shown in figure 4.

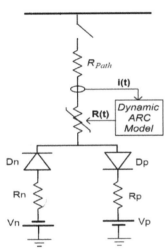

Figure 4.The combined model of HIF.

In figure 4, the dynamic resistance of arc model is calculated from the following equations [25]:

$$g = \int \frac{1}{\tau}(G - g)\, dt \qquad (7)$$

$$G = \frac{|i|}{u_{st}} \qquad (8)$$

$$u_{st} = (u_0 + r|i|)l \qquad (9)$$

$$R = \frac{1}{g} \qquad (10)$$

Where, g is the time-varying arc conductance, G is the stationary arc conductance, τ is time constant, i is the arc current, u_0 is constant voltage parameter per arc length, r is resistive component per arc length and l is the arc length [25].

The used model in this paper can satisfy several features of the behavior of HIF. For example, to create an asymmetry in the positive and negative half-cycle the two routes diodes are modeled differently. In order to create the random behavior for the HIF, the randomness in the resistance

value or in the value of source voltage or even dynamic parameters such as the length of the arc are modeled. With the available parameters of the combined HIF model, many HIF models can be simulated. In this paper, some of the discrepancies in the used model are:

- Path resistance
- Dynamic parameters (l, r, u_0)
- Random variation of the dynamic parameter around their nominal values
- Resistor and voltage source in parallel branches.(R_n,R_p,V_n, V_p)
- Random variation resistor and voltage source around their nominal values
- Location and phase of the HIF fault

The reason of using of different changes in model parameters, is to create various features of HIF that are to be justified by the real situations.

6. Simulation and data analysis

In this section, the simulations and data analysis are given based on the proposed method. The simulation has two distinct parts. In the first part, the simulation of the HIF is performed based on the proposed method and models of the component introduced in Sections 4 and 5, respectively. The schematic diagram of the process of the application of the proposed algorithm is given in figure 5.

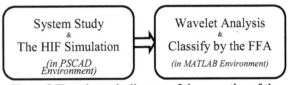

Figure 5.The schematic diagram of the execution of the proposed algorithm.

The number of systems running in PSCAD is 100. Among the total runs of 100, 50% is devoted for the no fault and 50% for the HIF case.

6.1. HIF simulation

In this section, some typical currents of the HIF model simulation in this paper, have been investigated. Figures 6 to 8 show typical current of HIF model for different cases. Also, figure 9 shows the voltage-current characteristic of one type of the HIF models.

In figure 6, constant amplitude of current HIF is seen. This is due to the constant parameters. Also, the parameter values routes of the two diodes are identical, the positive and negative half cycles are symmetric. But, in figure 7, the arc length parameter randomly is randomly changed. Hence, the random behavior in amplitude of current HIF can be observed and even in the current amplitude, it reaches to zero.

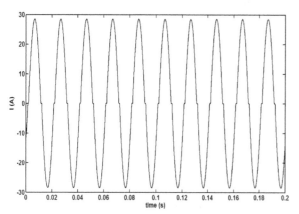

Figure 6. A typical current of HIF with constant amplitude.

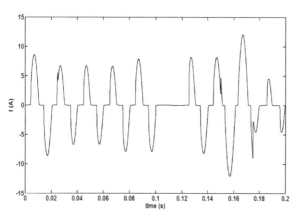

Figure 7. A typical current of HIF with random behavior.

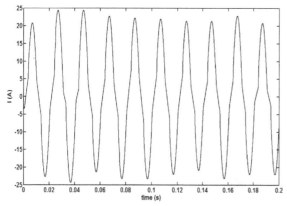

Figure 8. A typical current of HIF with randomness and asymmetry behavior.

In figure 8, the value of DC voltage parameters in the two diodes route change randomly and asymmetrically. Hence, in the current of the HIF model, the random behavior and asymmetry in the two half cycles can be seen easily. These figures demonstrate some are capabilities of the combined model.

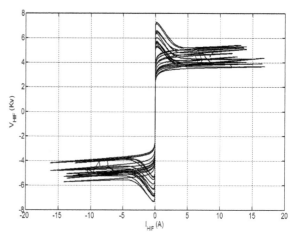

Figure 9. A typical voltage current characteristic of HIF with random behavior.

6.2. Wavelet analysis of the proposed method

At the beginning of this section, the discrimination between normal situation and HIF case is investigated. Then, the features are constructed using DWT output. Finally, the results of the algorithm analyzed.

6.2.1. Output of DWT

For different electrical network events and different measured signals or mother wavelet, the wavelet output can vary dramatically. For example, several wavelet outputs for no fault work and HIF event for phase voltage with mother wavelet db14 are examined.

Figure 9 shows the detail parts of the wavelet output for the case of switching load. As can be seen in this figure, the detailed output wavelet has a non-zero value for a short time period and for the rest of the time, its value is equal to zero. Wavelet detailed outputs in figure 10, belongs to the case of the saturation transformer. Comparing with the previous figure shows that the details in figure 9 output are smaller and have a repetitive jumps and smaller value and for Detail 4. The value is nearly zero (except in the beginning of the time).

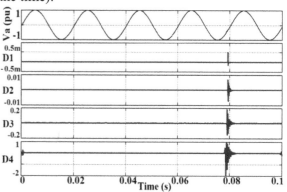

Figure 9. DWT details for switching load.

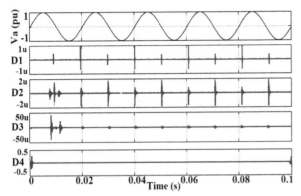

Figure 10. DWT details for saturation Transformer.

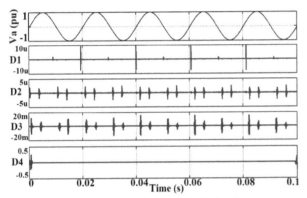

Figure 11. DWT details for electric Arc furnace.

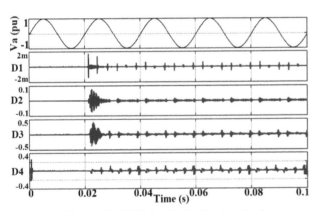

Figure 12. DWT details for thyristorload.

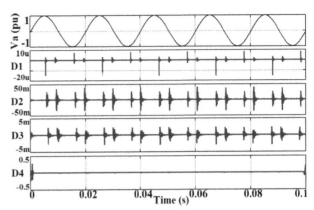

Figure 13. DWT details for Diode load.

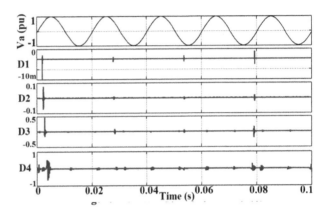

6.2.2. Feature extraction from the output of DWT

As stated previously, the output of DWT is not an integer number. Hence, at first, the value of SAD is computed from the output wavelet. If for example in (3), let X to be V_a (voltage of Phase a), j to be 4 and mother wavelet to be, db14, then SAD_{4Va} is computed and the result is shown in figure 15. The values of SAD_{4Va} in figure show several of no fault work and several HIF cases.

The values of SAD are the difference between no fault and several HIF cases. But, it should be noted that this visual interpretation of the extract feature needs to be converted a mathematical form. According to figure 15, that amount SAD of HIF case is larger than amount SAD for no fault. But, it is not always true. Also, for the HIF case, that abrupt change SAD of HIF is more than the no fault, and again it is not always the case. The two main differences in the outputs of SAD, mean and variance have chosen as the extracted feature for distinguishing between the normal working situations and HIF cases. Generally, these two features are can be different which depends on the type of mother wavelet, detail and measurement signals.

To select the best of two features, they are drawn in two-dimensional coordinates for normal

Also, figure 11 shows the wavelet detailed outputs for the case of electric arc furnace. The details behavior seen in figure is similar to the transformer saturation case. However, the case of the thyristor load (shown in Figure 12) has a different behavior.

The wavelet detailed outputs for the case of the diode load is illustrated figure 13. As this figure indicates there is an asymmetry in the first three details and small value in Detail 4. For the case of HIF, the wavelet Detail outputs are given in figure 14. In this figure, the amplitude of Detail 4 is greater than the corresponding detail in the previous cases. This issue helps us to find a discriminative feature to distinguish between no fault work and HIF case.

working and HIF cases as shown. For example, if two features (F1,F2) extracted from the output wavelet of the sum of three voltage phase by mother wavelet Demy and Detail 6, then figure 16 shows two features relative to each other.

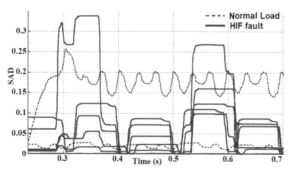

Figure 15. SAD for several cases.

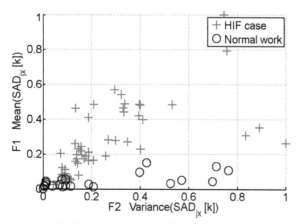

Figure 16. F1 versus F2 using (Vabc) with Mother WT demy and detail 6.

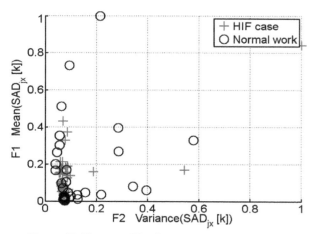

Figure 17. F1 versus F2 using Va with Mother WT db14 and detail 7.

Also, figure 17 shows two features from the output wavelet of Va by db14 mother wavelet and Detail 7. In figure 16 for most of the cases, the features corresponding to the normal working cases are closer to the coordinates. By changing

the mother wavelet and the signal type, this closeness can be varied. In general, as a better discriminative criterion is made, the better is feature will be selected.

6.3.1. Result analysis and discussion

In order to find the best features as the different features, the two factors of $F1_{jx}$ and $F2_{jx}$ are determined and classified from 17 mother wavelets, 7 detailed levels including voltage, current and sum of the voltage feeder for three phases were performed and classified. The accuracy of results is different for each type. In the FFA system, 80 input-output pairs for training and 20 input-output pairs for testing were considered. Some of the results of the simulation for 833 cases are given in table 1.

Table 1.The best detection using WT &FFA.

Row	Feeder Signal	Mother WT	Detail	Accuracy (%)
1	Vabc	Demy	D6	94.19
2	Vabc	Rbio3.3	D4	93.93
3	Vabc	Sym5	D5	93.16
4	Vabc	Bior5.5	D5	92.97
5	Vabc	Coif4	D5	92.85
6	Vabc	Bior6.8	D5	92.83
7	Vabc	Sym8	D5	92.80
8	Vabc	Demy	D5	92.73
9	Vabc	Bior2.6	D4	92.64
10	Vabc	Db14	D5	92.40
⋮	⋮	⋮	⋮	⋮
39	Vx	Rbio2.2	D7	89.83
⋮	⋮	⋮	⋮	⋮
103	Ix	Db5	D5	83.51
⋮	⋮	⋮	⋮	⋮
833	Vx	Db8	D1	52.79

According to these results, it can be seen that the best classification accuracy is 94.19%, which is a correct diagnosis. In the best classification for the case of the sum of three-phase voltage, the used mother wavelet is 'Demy' with Detail 6.

This means that to have better accuracy in the proposed algorithm, firstly the three phase voltages should be measured. Then, some of the measured voltages are used as the inputs for the wavelet transform. In the next step, the wavelet transform with Demy mother wavelet is employed. After that, the value of SAD is computed according to (3) to compute Detail 6. Then, the features of F1 and F2 are computed using (4) and (5). Finally, the two features are applied to the FFA as the inputs.

With choosing a suitable mother wavelet, detailed level in the result shows the proposed method is able to discriminate between no fault and HIF cases with high accuracy.

6.3.2. Implication issues

Implication issues for the proposed algorithm show that the findings based on the phase voltage has less accuracy compared with the findings based on three-phase voltage. Nevertheless, still the phase voltage based results has high accuracy as much as 89.83%, which is acceptable. The use of phase current does not yield an accuracy as high as the previous ones and the use of the phase current is not recommended for detection the HIF.

7. Conclusion

In this paper, a new HIF detection method based on the combination of FFA and DWT, is proposed. This method is an alternative method for diagnosing of HIF from no fault case. In this method, the feature is extracted using wavelet output. By investigating different mother wavelets, feeder signals and detail types, the base case is selected.

In the proposed method, the FFA system is used for classification. The FFA system uses training data to perform classification. The 80 training data used in this paper. The FFA system is able to perform classification accuracy.

In addition, an accurate combined model used to model the HIF. This combined model has the high ability to model different types of HIF. In order to study the performance of the proposed method for different types of HIF case and different normal working conditions such as thyristor load and arc furnace were examined. The obtained results have a very good accuracy as high as 94.19%. This indicates that the proposed algorithm has correct performance under different operating conditions in the electricity distribution networks.

References

[1] Aucoin, B. M., & Jones, R. H. (1996). High impedance fault detection implementation issues. IEEE Transactions on Power Delivery, vol. 11, no. 1, pp. 139-148.

[2] Aucoin, M. (1985). Status of High Impedance Fault Detection. IEEE Transactions on Power Apparatus and Systems, vol. 104, no. 3, pp. 637-644.

[3] Emanuel, A. E., Cyganski, D., Orr, J. A. & Gulachenski, E. M. (1990). High impedance fault arcing on sandy soil in 15 kV distribution feeders: contributions to the evaluation of the low frequency spectrum. IEEE Transactions on Power Delivery, vol. 5, no. 2, pp. 676-686.

[4] Sharat, A. M., Snider, L. A. & Debnath, K. (1993). A neural network based back error propagation relay algorithm for distribution system high impedance fault detection. 2nd International Conference on Operation and Management in Advances in Power System Control, vol. 2, no. 1, pp. 613-620.

[5] Lai, T. M., Snider, L. A., Lo, E. & Sutanto, D. (2005). High-impedance fault detection using discrete wavelet transform and frequency range and RMS conversion. IEEE Transactions on Power Delivery, vol. 20, no. 1, pp. 397-407.

[6] Darwish, H. A. & Elkalashy, N. I. (2005). Universal arc representation using EMTP. IEEE Transactions on Power Delivery, vol. 20, no. 2, pp. 772-779.

[7] Michalik, M., Rebizant, W., Lukowicz, M., Seung-Jae, L., Sang-Hee, K. & Michalik, M. (2006). High-impedance fault detection in distribution networks with use of wavelet-based algorithm.IEEE Transactions on Power Delivery, vol. 21, no. 4, pp. 1793-1802.

[8] Michalik, M., Rebizant, W., Lukowicz, M., Seung-Jae, L. & Sang-Hee, K. (2005). Wavelet transform approach to high impedance fault detection in MV networks, Power Tech IEEE Russia, Russia, 2005.

[9] Vahidi, B., Ghaffarzadeh, N., Hosseinian, S. H. & Ahadi, S. M. (2010). An Approach to Detection of High Impedance Fault Using Discrete Wavelet Transform and Artificial Neural Networks. Simulation, vol. 86, no. 4, pp. 203-215.

[10] Khorashadi-Zadeh, H. (2004). A novel approach to detection high impedance faults using artificial neural network. 39th International in Universities Power Engineering, vol. 1, no. 1, pp. 373-376.

[11] Zadeh, H. K. (2005). An ANN-Based High Impedance Fault Detection SchemeDesign and Implementation. International Journal of Emerging Electric Power Systems Research, vol. 4, no. 2, pp. 1-14.

[12] Samantaray, S. R., Dash, P. K. & Upadhyay, S. K. (2009). Adaptive Kalman filter and neural network based high impedance fault detection in power distribution networks. International Journal of Electrical Power & Energy Systems, vol. 31, no. 4, pp. 167-172.

[13] Ming-Ta, Y., Jhy-Cherng, G., Jin-Lung, G. & Chau-Yuan, C. (2005). Detection of High Impedance Faults in Distribution System,Transmission and Distribution Conference and Exhibition. Asia and Pacific, 2005.

[14] Etemadi, A. H., & Sanaye-Pasand, M. (2008). High-impedance fault detection using multi-resolution signal decomposition and adaptive neural fuzzy inference system. Generation, Transmission & Distribution, vol. 2, no. 1, pp. 110-118.

[15] Chul-Hwan, K., Hyun, K., Young-Hun, K., & Sung-Hyun, B. (2002). A novel fault-detection technique of high-impedance arcing faults in transmission lines using the wavelet transform. IEEE Transactions on Power Delivery, vol. 17, no. 4, pp. 921-929.

[16] Abohagar, A. A. & Mustafa, M. W. (2012). Back propagation neural network aided wavelet transform for high impedance fault detection and faulty phase selection. IEEE International Conference on Power and Energy, Malaysia, 2012.

[17] Vico, J., Adamiak, M., Wester, C. & Kulshrestha, A. (2010). High impedance fault detection on rural electric distribution systems. Rural Electric Power Conference, USA, 2010.

[18] Baqui, I., Zamora, I., Mazón, J. & Buigues, G. (2011). High impedance fault detection methodology using wavelet transform and artificial neural networks. Electric Power Systems Research, vol. 81, no. 7, pp. 1325-1333.

[19] Van Long, P., Kit-Po, W., Watson, N. & Arrillaga, J. (2000). Sub-harmonic state estimation in power systems. In the: Power Engineering Society Winter Meeting, vol. 2, no. 1, pp. 1168-1173.

[20] Silveira, P. M., Seara, R. & Zurn, H. H. a. (1999). An approach using wavelet transform for fault type identification in digital relaying. In the: Power Engineering Society Summer Meeting, vol. 2, no. 1, pp. 937-942.

[21] Meliopoulos, A. P. S., & Chien-Hsing, L. (2000). An alternative method for transient analysis via wavelets. IEEE Transactions on Power Delivery, vol. 15, no. 1, pp. 114-121.

[22] Torres G, V., & Ruiz P, H. F. (2011). High Impedance Fault Detection Using Discrete Wavelet Transform. Robotics and Automotive Mechanics Conference in Electronics, Cuernavaca, Mexico, 2011.

[23] Li-Xin, W. (1997), A Course In Fuzzy Systemsand Control. Prentice Hall, International Edition.

[24] Elkalashy, N. I., Lehtonen, M., Darwish, H. A., Taalab, A. M. I. & Izzularab, M. A. (2008). DWT-Based Detection and Transient Power Direction-Based Location of High-Impedance Faults Due to Leaning Trees in Unearthed MV Networks. Power Delivery, IEEE Transactions on, vol. 23, no. 1, pp. 94-101.

[25] Kizilcay, M., & Pniok, T. (1991). Digital simulation of fault arcs in power systems. European Transactions on Electrical Power, vol. 1, no. 1, pp. 55-60.

7

Video-based face recognition in color space by graph-based discriminant analysis

S. Shafeipour Yourdeshahi [1*], H. Seyedarabi[1] and A. Aghagolzadeh [2]

1. Faculty of Electrical and Computer Engineering, University of Tabriz, Tabriz, Iran.
2. Faculty of Electrical and Computer Engineering, Babol University of Technology, Babol, Iran.

*Corresponding author: shafeipour@tabrizu.ac.ir (S. Shafeipour).

Abstract

Video-based face recognition has attracted significant attention in many applications such as media technology, network security, human-machine interfaces, and automatic access control system in the past decade. The usual way for face recognition is based upon the grayscale image produced by combining the three color component images. In this work, we consider grayscale image as well as color space in the recognition process. For key frame extractions from a video sequence, the input video is converted to a number of clusters, each of which acts as a linear subspace. The center of each cluster is considered as the cluster representative. Also in this work, for comparing the key frames, the three popular color spaces RGB, YCbCr, and HSV are used for mathematical representation, and the graph-based discriminant analysis is applied for the recognition process. It is also shown that by introducing the intra-class and inter-class similarity graphs to the color space, the problem is changed to determining the color component combination vector and mapping matrix. We introduce an iterative algorithm to simultaneously determine the optimum above vector and matrix. Finally, the results of the three color spaces and grayscale image are compared with those obtained from other available methods. Our experimental results demonstrate the effectiveness of the proposed approach.

Keywords: *Face Recognition; Key Frame; Intra-class; Inter-class; Color Component.*

1. Introduction

Face recognition has been one of the most popular research areas in computer vision during the recent decades due to its many applications such as media technology, surveillance systems, access control, and human-machine interfaces. However, by far, no comprehensive technique has been proposed to provide a robust solution to all problems. Most of the algorithms proposed are still image-based, and they have been proven successful in solving some of the problems such as pose, lighting and expression variations, occlusion, and low image resolutions. Recently, due to the much development in media technology and the increased demands on security, video-to-video face recognition has received a significant attention.

One of the most important properties of a video sequence is its temporal continuity. Using this property, we can increase the recognition rate. In this regard, in the past decade, researchers have begun to use the spatiotemporal data [1]. A wide variety of popular approaches in this field try to represent a video sequence as a linear subspace or a nonlinear manifold [2]. Then the similarity between two sequences is obtained by measuring the distance between two subspaces. Most of these methods compute principal angles between two spaces. In these methods, the recognition process relies mainly on the representation of the video sequence as a linear subspace [3]. In [4], manifold has been partitioned into a number of linear subspaces by Maximal Linear Patch, and manifold to manifold distance has been converted to measure the similarity between pairwise linear models. In [5], Wang et al. have introduced a discriminative learning method called Manifold

Discriminant Analysis (MDA) to solve the recognition problem. Therefore, MDA tries to determine the mapping matrix in the grayscale images, where local models from the manifolds with different class labels can be better separated, and meanwhile, the local data compactness within each manifold can be better enhanced.

Some methods are based upon the still image techniques, which try to select key frames from a video sequence and then apply still image-based face recognition algorithms. Therefore, these techniques focus on extracting all key-frames from the video sequence as the representative frames.

On the other hand, color plays an effective role in the biometrics works. The RGB color space is an additive color model, and all the other color spaces that may be more appropriate for many types of visual task can be derived from this color space [6-10]. For example, the HSV color space has been chosen in image retrieval [11], and it has been demonstrated that the YCbCr color space is more useful than the RGB color model for the face detection tasks [12, 13]. A conventional way of face recognition is to convert the RGB color space into a grayscale image by combining the three color component images. In [14], Wang et al. have shown that the human visual system uses color cues for recognition, and using color space can improve the recognition rate.

In this paper, we compare the three color spaces RGB, YCbCr, and HSV in video-based face recognition using the graph-based discriminant analysis. Then we introduce our proposed method, which includes face detection in video sequence, clustering in order to obtain the key frames, and graph-based discriminant analysis in color space. Extensive experimental evaluation of the proposed model and its comparison for the three color spaces and other available methods are discussed in section 3, followed by discussion of the results.

2. Proposed algorithm

The proposed algorithm is based upon converting video sequences into some clusters, each of which acting as a linear subspace. The center of each cluster is considered as the cluster representative. The recognition process is completed by comparing the key frames. In this paper, two intelligent ways are proposed for clustering. For comparing the key frames, we consider the grayscale image as well as the color space. The three popular color spaces RGB, YCbCr, and HSV are used for the mathematical representation

of each frame and the recognition process used for the graph-based discriminant analysis.

By introducing the intra-class and inter-class similarity graphs to the color space, the problem changes to determining the color component combination vector and mapping matrix. In this paper, two equations are achieved using a number of mathematical oprations, and an optimal solution is achieved by designing an iterative algorithm. Figure 1 shows a block diagram of the proposed algorithm. In the following parts, the details of our proposed method are explained.

2.1. Face detection in video sequence

Face detection is an essential early step in the face recognition systems. Real-time face detection is very significant in a video-based face recognition. The Cascade AdaBoost face detector, proposed by Viola and Jones [15], and face detection based on color information [16] are two main methods for a real time face detection. A better face region is normalized via finding the distance between two eyes. There are many methods for eye detection. The most important ones consist of template matching, eigen space, and Hough transform. For face detection in other frames, this point is used that the neighbouring regions within successive video frames tend to be highly correlated. Therefore, a search window is determined around the face region in the first frame, and by calculating the correlation between the current face region and the next frame into the search window, in which the highest correlation to conclude is the face region in the next frame. This procedure is repeated for the entire frames. Determining the size of the search window has a major role in the calculation.

2.2. Clustering and key frames

Several approaches have been presented for clustering and constructing local linear models from nonlinear manifold [17-19]. Most of them use iterative-based clustering methods such as k-means to classify a given data through a certain number of clusters. The most important problem with this method is the number of clusters required to be specified by the user. Also the linearity of the local model has a low accuracy, and therefore, the clustering result is not optimal.

Two different algorithms have been proposed for clustering videos. In the first algorithm, data containing face detection in successive frames in the video sequence is used. In other words, the motion vectors obtained by the successive frames can predict the movements of the head and perform clustering.

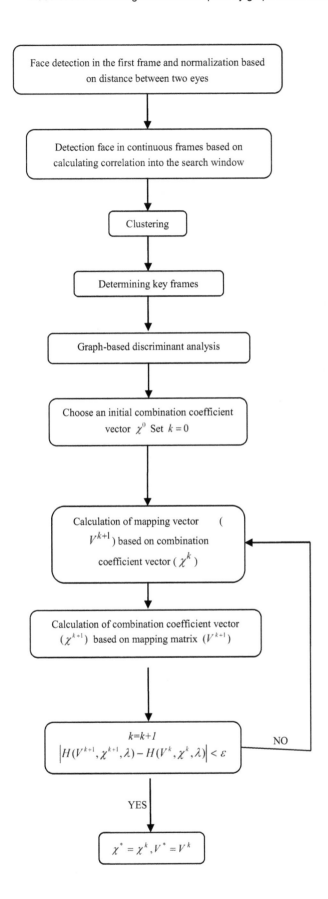

Figure 1. The block diagram of the proposed algorithm.

This method has the following advantages:

• Determining the number of clusters and linear model is quite intelligent, and with the implementation of this method, the number of clusters depends on moving the head in each video sequence.

• Linearity of the model has a high accuracy.

• This method is very simple because of the existence of the motion vector information.

• Due to changes in the direction of motion vector, we can predict the head direction.

In this clustering method, the key frames are selected based on the motion vectors with the most changes in the horizontal and vertical directions.

In the second clustering method, the first frame of each video is chosen as the center of the first cluster. Then by calculating the correlation between the first key frame and the next one and its comparison with the suitable threshold, it can be determined whether the second frame belongs to the first cluster. To obtain the second cluster, the first frame that does not belong to the first cluster is determined as the center of the second cluster. Similarly, this process is continued to successive frames until all frames are assigned to the clusters. It should be noticed that after obtaining all clusters, their key frames are compared with a specified threshold for merging. An appropriate choice of the threshold is important in determining the number of clusters.

2.3. Graph-based discriminant analysis in color space

The usual way for face recognition is to use grayscale images. In the present study, we used color information, and compared the three popular color spaces RGB, YcbCr, and HSV. The RGB color space is an additive color model, and all the other color spaces can be derived from it. In this color space, each pixel is represented by the three components red, green, and blue. If we can represent an image by separating the intensity of the color information, some processing steps would be faster.

MPEG compression, which is used in digital component video standard, is coded in the YCbCr color space. In this color space, the luminance and color information are separated. The Y component describes brightness, and Cb and Cr describe a color difference rather than a color. The HSV (hue, saturation, value) color space was designed with an emphasis on the visual perception. In the following part, face recognition is achieved using the graph-based discriminant analysis.

Let A_i be a color image with three columns, and each color component be a column vector. We suppose that the resolution of each color component is $m \times n$. Therefore, the color image A_i is expressed as an $N \times 3$ matrix: $A_i = [\alpha_{1i}, \alpha_{2i}, \alpha_{3i}]$, where $\alpha_{1i}, \alpha_{2i}, \alpha_{3i}$ are three color components related to a color space (RGB, HSV or YCbCr) and $N = m \times n$.

In this work, we tried to find the optimal coefficients to combine the three color components of the above color spaces. Suppose that Z_i is a combined image, given by (1):

$$Z_i = x_1\alpha_{1i} + x_2\alpha_{2i} + x_3\alpha_{3i} = [\alpha_{1i}, \alpha_{2i}, \alpha_{3i}]\chi = A_i\chi \qquad (1)$$

where, x_1, x_2, x_3 are their coefficients. Therefore, our attempt was to find the coefficients so that Z_i was the optimal description of A_i for face recognition.

A graph in our model refers to a collection of vertices or nodes and a collection of edges that connect pairs of vertices. Given n points $\{Z_1, .., Z_n\}$ from the underlying manifold M, and each Z_i belonging to class c_i, the similarity score between two points with three color components is defined by:

$$K_{i,j} = \min\|\alpha_{li} - \alpha_{lj}\|^2 \quad l = 1,2,3 \qquad (2)$$

where, $\|\bullet\|$ denotes the Euclidean norm. The two-adjacency graphs for inter-class and intra-class are defined by:

$$S_b(i,j) = \begin{cases} 1 & if \quad K_{i,j} \geq \varepsilon \quad c_i \neq c_j \\ 0 & otherwise \end{cases} \qquad (3)$$

$$S_w(i,j) = \begin{cases} 1 & if \quad K_{i,j} \leq \varepsilon \quad c_i = c_j \\ 0 & otherwise \end{cases} \qquad (4)$$

where, c_i is the class label for Z_i, and c_j is the class label for Z_j, and S_w and S_b are the intra-class similarity graph and the inter-class similarity graph, respectively.

Our aim was to minimize the distance between points of the connected points of S_w, and to maximize the distance between points of the connected points of S_b in the feature space. Therefore, the points on M manifold were mapped to a new manifold M', i.e., $\phi : Z_i \to Y_i$. The matching score between two points in the new manifold can be computed using the Euclidean distance measures. Such a mapping can be expressed by minimizing and maximizing the following two objective functions, respectively [20]:

$$\min \frac{1}{2}\sum_{i,j}(Y_i - Y_j)^2 S_w(i,j) \qquad (5)$$

$$\max \frac{1}{2}\sum_{i,j}(Y_i - Y_j)^2 S_b(i,j) \qquad (6)$$

where, $Y_i = V^T Z_i = V^T A_i\chi$. The minimization problem from (5) can be written as follows:

$$\begin{aligned} &\min\frac{1}{2}\sum_{i,j}((V^T A_i\chi)^2 + (V^T A_j\chi)^2 - 2(V^T A_i\chi V^T A_j\chi))S_w(i,j) \\ &= \sum_{i,j}V^T A_i\chi S_w(i,j)\chi^T A_i^T V - \sum_{i,j}V^T A_i\chi S_w(i,j)\chi^T A_j^T V \\ &= V^T A_\chi(D_w - W_w)A_\chi^T V \\ &= V^T A_\chi L_w A_\chi^T V \end{aligned}$$
$$(7)$$

and the maximization problem from (6) can be written as:

$$\begin{aligned} &\max\frac{1}{2}\sum_{i,j}((V^T A_i\chi)^2 + (V^T A_j\chi)^2 - 2(V^T A_i\chi V^T A_j\chi). \\ &.S_b(i,j)) = V^T A_\chi L_b A_\chi^T V \end{aligned} \qquad (8)$$

where, $L_w = D_w - W_w$ and $L_b = D_b - W_b$ are the Laplacian matrix, W_w and W_b are the weight matrices, D_w and D_b are the diagonal matrices, and $A_\chi = [A_1\chi | A_2\chi ... A_N\chi]$. It should be noticed that this calculation shows that L_w is a positive semi-definite. Equation 7 can be written as:

$$\begin{aligned} &\arg\min_{V\chi} V^T A_\chi L_w A_\chi^T V \\ &= \arg\min_{V\chi}(V^T A_\chi D_w A_\chi^T V - V^T A_\chi W_w A_\chi^T V) \\ &= \arg\min_{V\chi}(1 - V^T A_\chi W_w A_\chi^T V) \\ &\text{subject to } V^T A_\chi D_w A_\chi^T V = 1 \end{aligned} \qquad (9)$$

The constraint $V^T A_\chi D_w A_\chi^T V = 1$ eliminates the arbitrary scaling factor. Therefore, Equation 9 can be re-written as follows:

$$\begin{aligned} &= \arg\max_{V\chi}(V^T A_\chi W_w A_\chi^T V) \\ &\text{subject to } V^T A_\chi D_w A_\chi^T V = 1 \end{aligned} \qquad (10)$$

Similarly, Equation 8 can be re-written as a maximization problem, as follows:

$$\arg\max_{V\chi}(V^T A_\chi L_b A_\chi^T V) \qquad (11)$$

Integrating (10) and (11), we have:

$$\arg\max_{V\chi}(V^T A_\chi \beta L_b A_\chi^T V + V^T A_\chi (1-\beta)W_w A_\chi^T V) \quad (12)$$

$$= \arg\max_{V\chi}(V^T A_\chi(\beta L_b + (1-\beta)W_w)A_\chi^T V)$$

subject to $V^T A_\chi D_w A_\chi^T V = 1$ \quad (13)

$$H(V,\chi,\lambda) = V^T A_\chi(\beta L_b + (1-\beta)W_w)A_\chi^T V -$$

$$- \lambda(V^T A_\chi D_w A_\chi^T V - 1) \quad (14)$$

where, β is a suitable constant and $0 \le \beta \le 1$. To find V and χ, we first took the derivative of $H(V,\chi,\lambda)$ in (14) with respect to V:

$$\frac{\partial H(V,\chi,\lambda)}{\partial V} = 2A_\chi(\beta L_b + (1-\beta)W_w)A_\chi^T V - 2\lambda A_\chi.$$

$$.D_w A_\chi^T V \quad (15)$$

Equating the derivative to zero, $\frac{\partial H(V,X,\lambda)}{\partial V} = 0$, and thus we can write:

$$A_\chi(\beta L_b + (1-\beta)W_w)A_\chi^T V = \lambda A_\chi D_w A_\chi^T V \quad (16)$$

Secondly, Equations 5 and 6 can be re-written as follow ($0 \le \delta \le 1$):

$$H(V,\chi,\lambda) = \sum_i V^T A_i \chi\chi^T A_i^T V \beta D_b(i,i) +$$

$$+ \sum_{i,j} V^T A_i \chi\chi^T A_j^T V[(1-\beta)S_w(i,j) - \beta S_b(i,j)] -$$

$$- \lambda(\sum_i V^T A_i \chi\chi^T A_i^T V D_w(i,i) - 1) \quad (17)$$

Therefore, we can write:

$$\frac{\partial H(V,\chi,\lambda)}{\partial \chi} = 2[\sum_i A_i^T V\beta D_b(i,i)V^T A_i + \sum_{i,j} A_j^T V.$$

$$((1-\beta)S_w(i,j) - \beta S_b(i,j))V^T A_i]\chi -$$

$$- 2\lambda \sum_i A_i^T V D_w(i,i)V^T A_i\chi \quad (18)$$

Equating the derivative to zero, $\frac{\partial H(V,\chi,\lambda)}{\partial \chi} = 0$, therefore we have the following equation:

$$[\sum_i A_i^T V\beta D_b(i,i)V^T A_i + \sum_{i,j} A_j^T V((1-\beta)S_w(i,j) -$$

$$- \beta S_b(i,j))V^T A_i]\chi = \lambda \sum_i A_i^T V D_w(i,i)V^T A_i\chi \quad (19)$$

Therefore, we have the following two equations:

Equation I:

$$A_\chi(\beta L_b + (1-\beta)W_w)A_\chi^T V = \lambda A_\chi D_w A_\chi^T V$$

subject to $V^T A_\chi D_w A_\chi^T V = 1$ \quad (20)

Equation II:

$$[\sum_i A_i^T V\beta D_b(i,i)V^T A_i + \sum_{i,j} A_j^T V((1-\beta)S_w(i,j) -$$

$$- \beta S_b(i,j))V^T A_i]\chi = \lambda \sum_i A_i^T V D_w(i,i)V^T A_i\chi$$

subject to $\sum_i V^T A_i \chi\chi^T A_i^T V D_w(i,i) = 1$ \quad (21)

For solving the above two equations, we used the generalized Eigen-equation $P\eta = \kappa Q\eta$ [21]. From the above theorem, the solutions to the above equations can be chosen as the eigenvectors of the generalized equation (for equation II, associating to the largest eigenvalue). Therefore, we can easily calculate the optimum points χ and V by an iterative algorithm. Suppose that $\chi = \chi^k$ is the initial value for χ in the k-th iteration. First we calculated $V = V^{k+1}$ from (20). In the second step, we calculated $\chi = \chi^{k+1}$ based on $V = V^{k+1}$. In the next iteration, $\chi = \chi^{k+1}$ was used as the initial value. This algorithm performs the above two steps successively until it converges. It should be pointed out that convergence may be determined after n+1 times of iterations, if $\left|H(V^{n+1},\chi^{n+1},\lambda) - H(V^n,\chi^n,\lambda)\right| < \varepsilon$. Then we chose χ^{n+1} and V^{n+1}.

Given a test vide sequence, we first partitioned it into some clusters, and then using χ^{n+1} and V^{n+1} the center of each cluster was mapped to the new space. Therefore the similarity between manifolds could be obtained by calculating the distance between the cluster representatives in the new space.

3. Experimental results

The described algorithm was evaluated using the Honda/UCSD database [22] and the CMU MoBo database [23]. The first video database, Honda/UCSD, has been collected by K. C. Lee et al., and is used for video-based face recognition. The spatial and temporal resolution of each video sequence is 640×480 and 15 frames per second, respectively. In this database, every person turns his/her head in different speeds and rotations. Some of these sequences include a partial occlusion. The second database, MoBo (Motion of Body), was originally collected for the purpose of human identification from distance. The considered subset contained 96 sequences of 24 different subjects walking on a treadmill. Each person had 4 videos.

For each video sequence, after the detection of face and eye, the face area was marked by a square with the dimensions $2.8d \times 2.8d$, where d is the distance between the two eyes. Figure 2 shows this face area. Figure 3 the illustrates the face regions detected in some frames of the Honda/UCSD database. As described earlier, in the first method of clustering, the face regions obtained at the position of the frames within the search window are used.

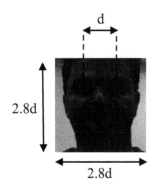

Figure 2. Face area marked by distance between two eyes.

Figure 3. Faces detected in one of the video sequences of Honda/UCSD database.

The search window dimension is 10×10 pixels. Changes in the horizontal and vertical directions, compared to the previous frame, are shown, respectively, with dx and dy. In other words, dx and dy are the motion vectors.

Figure 4 illustrates the variation of dx and dy in consecutive frames of a video sequence in the Honda/UCSD database. As an example shown in the figure, with the shift to the right human head, the motion vectors are moved to the right. Accordance with the motion vectors, clustering can be done. As described in the first clustering method, the key frames are selected based on the highest $|dx| + |dy|$ within the cluster. These frames in addition to the first frame of a video sequence are considered as the key frames.

The second approach to clustering was performed in successive frames by comparing the correlations. The number of clusters was determined according to the threshold value. In this simulation, this value was set as 0.7. Figure 5 illustrates seven clusters obtained by this method.

In the second clustering method, centers of each cluster were selected as the key frames.

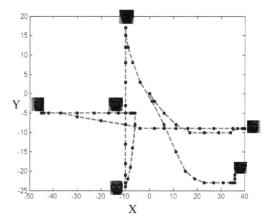

Figure 4. Variation of dx and dy in one video sequence of the Honda/UCSD database.

Figure 6 shows the key frames of two video sequences in the Honda/UCSD database. Experiments were performed for 5 randomly selected training/test combinations to report the identification rates. In order to evaluate the proposed approach, all faces were normalized, followed by histogram equalization to eliminate the lighting effects, and then face recognition experiments were conducted on the three color spaces (RGB, YcbCr, and HSV) and the grayscale image.

The initial value for χ was set as $\chi^0 = [1/3, 1/3, 1/3]$ (averaging the three color component images). After describing the iterative process for training, the algorithm generated one optimal color component combination coefficient vector $\chi^l = [x_{1l}, x_{2l}, x_{3l}]^T$ and the optimal discriminant mapping matrix. The vector χ^l determined one discriminating color component $Z^l = x_{1l}\alpha_1 + x_{2l}\alpha_2 + x_{3l}\alpha_3$.

We designed the algorithm on the grayscale images and the three popular color spaces (RGB, YCbCr and HSV), and then compared the performance of our algorithm with two still image techniques (Eigenface and Fisherface) [24], NN matching in LLE + k-means clustering [18], Mutual Subspace Method (MSM) [25], Manifold to Manifold Distance (MMD) method [26], Regularized Nearest points (RNP) [27], Collaboratively Regularized Nearest points (CRNP) [28] and Collaborative Mean Attraction (CMA) [29].

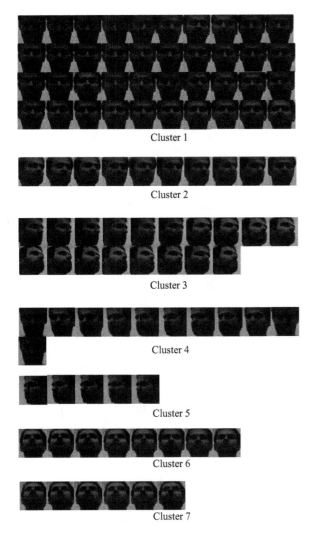

Cluster 1

Cluster 2

Cluster 3

Cluster 4

Cluster 5

Cluster 6

Cluster 7

Figure 5. Clusters obtained by comparing correlation.

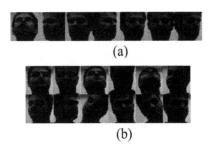

(a)

(b)

Figure 6. Center of clusters for two video sequences of Honda/UCSD database.

Table 1 shows the average recognition rate by different color space databases and the seven methods in the Honda/UCSD and CMU MoBo databases. It also shows that the proposed algorithm, in color space, achieves a better performance than the classical methods using grayscale images. Therefore, color plays an effective role in face recognition. In the best performance, the algorithm achieves an average recognition rate of 97.6% for the YCbCr color space (in Honda/UCSD database), which is a nearly 7% increase compared with the proposed method using the grayscale images.

4. Conclusions and future work

In this work, we proposed a novel method for a video-based face recognition in color space. For extracting the key frames from the video, the input sequences were converted into a number of clusters, each one acting as a linear subspace. Also to compare the center of each cluster, three popular color spaces (RGB, YCbCr and HSV) were used for the mathematical representation of each frame, and graph-based discriminant analysis was applied for the recognition process.

Table 1. Average recognition rate by different color spaces

in Honda /UCSD database and CMU MoBo database.

Different methods	Average rate of recognition Honda/UCSD	Average rate of recognition CMU MoBo	Ref.
Eigenface	74.2	81.0	[24]
FisherFace	79.2	88.3	[24]
LLE+K-means	91.8	89.8	[18]
MSM	88.2	85.1	[25]
MMD	96.9	93.6	[26]
RNP	87.1	94.7	[27]
CRNP	97.4	94.4	[28]
CMA	94.9	94.6	[29]
Proposed Grayscale	90.9	88.7	Proposed
Proposed RGB	93.8	91.1	Proposed
Proposed HSV	96.4	93.8	Proposed
Proposed YCbCr	97.6	95.1	Proposed

We introduced an iterative algorithm to simultaneously determine the optimal color component combination vector and mapping matrix. Our experimental results also indicate that the recognition performance with color images is significantly better than grayscale images.

In the future works, we intend to explore new methods for computing the manifold to manifold distance in color space, which mainly emphasize the similarity of data variation modes between two manifolds, and compare them with the result of the proposed method.

References

[1] Aggarwal, G., Chowdhury, A. R. & Chellappa R. A. (2004). system identification approach for video-based face recognition. In 17th International Conference on Pattern Recognition, vol. 4, pp. 175-178.

[2] Lee, K. C., Ho, J., Yang, M. H. & Kriegman, D. (2003). Video-based Face Recognition Using Probabilistic Appearance Manifolds. IEEE Computer Society Conference on Computer Vision and Pattern Recognition, pp. 313-320.

[3] Wang, R., Shan, S., Chen, X., Dai, Q. & Gao, W. (2012). Manifold-Manifold Distance and its Application to Face Recognition With Image Sets. IEEE Trans. on Image Processing, vol. 21, no. 10, pp. 4466-4479.

[4] Wang, R., Shan, S., Chen, X., Chen, J. & Gao, W. (2011). Maximal Linear Embedding for Dimensionality Reduction. IEEE Trans. on Pattern Analysis and Machine Intelligence, vol. 33, no. 9, pp. 1776-1792.

[5] Wang, R. & Chen, X. (2009). Manifold discriminant analysis. In CVPR, pp. 429-436.

[6] Torres, L., Reutter, J. Y. & Lorente, L. (1999). The importance of the color information in face recognition. In Proc, IEEE Int. Conf. Image Processing, vol. 3, pp. 627–631.

[7] Rajapakse, M., Tan J. & Rajapakse J. (2004). Color channel encoding with NMF for face recognition. In Proc. IEEE Int. Conf. Image Processing, vol. 3, pp. 2007–2010.

[8] Yang, J., Zhang, D., Xu, Y. & Yang, J. Y. (2006). Recognize color face images using complex eigenfaces. In D. Zhang, A. K. Jain, (ed.): Advances in Biometrics, Int. Conf. Lecture Notes in Computer Science, Springer-Verlag Berlin Heidelberg, vol. 3832, pp. 64–68.

[9] Phung, S. L., Bouzerdoum, A. & Chai, D. (2002). A novel skin color model in YCbCr color space and its application to human face detection. In IEEE International Conference on Image Processing (ICIP'2002), vol. 1, pp. 289–292.

[10] Yang, J. & Liu, C. (2008). Color Image Discriminant Models and Algorithms for Face Recognition. IEEE Transactions on Neural Networks, vol. 19, no. 12, pp. 2088-2098.

[11] Vadivel, A., Sural, S. & Majumdar, A. (2005). Human color perception in the HSV space and its application in histogram generation for image retrieval. In SPIE Procedings seetings, San Jose CA, United states of America, pp. 598-609.

[12] Hsu, R. L., Abdel-Mottaleb, M. & Jain, A. K. (2002). Face detection in color images. IEEE Trans. on Pattern Analysis and Machine Intelligence, vol. 24, no. 5, pp. 696-706.

[13] Dios, J. J. de. & Garcia, N. (2003). Face detection based on a new color space YCgCr. In Proc. IEEE Int. Conf. Image Processing, vol. 3, pp. 909–912.

[14] Wang, S. J., Yang, J., Zhang, N. & Zhou, C. G. (2011). Tensor Discriminant Color Space for Face Recognition. IEEE Transactions on Image Processing, vol. 20, no. 9, pp. 2490-2501.

[15] Viola, P. & Jones, M. (2001). Rapid Object Detection Using a Boosted Cascade of Simple Features. Proc. Conf. Computer Vision and Pattern Recognition, vol. 1, pp. 511-518.

[16] Wang, Y. & Yuan, B. (2001). A novel approach for human face detection from color images under complex background. Pattern Recognition, vol. 34, no. 10, pp. 1983–1992.

[17] Fan, W. & Yeung, D. Y. (2006). Locally Linear Models on Face Appearance Manifolds with Application to Dual-Subspace Based Classification. CVPR, vol. 2, pp. 1384–1390.

[18] Hadid, A. & Pietikäinen, M. (2004). From Still Image to Video-Based Face Recognition: An Experimental Analysis. Proceedings of the Sixth IEEE international conference on Automatic face and gesture recognition, pp. 813–818.

[19] Kim, T. K., Arandjelović, O. & Cipolla, R. (2005). Learning over Sets Using Boosted Manifold Principal Angles (BoMPA). Proc. British Machine Vision Conf., pp. 779–788.

[20] Yan, S., Xu, D., Zhang, B., Zhang, H. J., Yang, Q. & Lin, S. (2007). Graph embedding and extensions: A general framework for dimensionality reduction. IEEE Trans. Pattern Anal. Mach. Intell., vol. 29, no. 1, pp. 40–51.

[21] Lancaster, P. & Tismenetsky M. (1985). The Theory of Matrices (Second Edition). Academic Press, INC. Orlando, Florida.

[22] Lee, K., Ho, J., Yang, M. & Kriegman, D. (2005). Visual tracking and recognition using probabilistic appearance manifolds. Computer Vision and Image Understanding, vol. 99, no. 3, pp. 303–331.

[23] Gross, R. & Shi, J. (2001). The cmu motion of body (mobo) database. Technical Report CMU-RI-TR-

01-18, Robotics Institute, Carnegie Mellon University, Pittsburgh, PA.

[24] Belhumeur, P. N., Hespanha, J. P. & Kriegman, D. J. (1997). Eigenfaces vs. Fisherfaces: Recognition Using Class Specific Linear Projection. PAMI, vol. 19, no. 7, pp. 711–720.

[25] Yamaguchi, O., Fukui, K. & Maeda, K. (1998). Face Recognition Using Temporal Image Sequence. FG, pp. 318–323.

[26] Wang, R., Shan, S., Chen, X., Dai, Q. & Gao, W. (2008). Manifold-Manifold Distance with Application to Face Recognition based on Image Sets. IEEE Conference computer vision and pattern recognition. pp. 1-8.

[27] Yang, M., Zhu, P., Gool, L. V. & Zhang, L. (2013). Face recognition based on regularized nearest points between image sets. In The 10th IEEE International Conference on Automatic Face and Gesture Recognition. FG, pp. 1-7.

[28] Wu, Y., Minoh, M. & Mukunoki, M. (2013). Collaboratively Regularized Nearest Points for Set Based Recognition. Proceedings of the British Machine Vision Conference, BMVA Press, pp. 1-10.

[29] Wu, Y., Mukunoki, M. & Minoh, M. (2014). Collaborative Mean Attraction for Set Based Recognition. The 17th Meeting on Image Recognition and Understanding (MIRU).

8

Governor design for hydropower plants by intelligent sliding mode variable structure control

L. Yu* and D. Qian

School of Control & Computer Engineering, North China Electric Power University, Changping District, Beijing, China.

Corresponding author: yulufly2009@163.com(L.Yu).

Abstract

This work proposes a neural-fuzzy sliding mode control scheme for a hydro-turbine speed governor system. Considering the assumption of elastic water hammer, a nonlinear mode of the hydro-turbine governor system is established. By linearizing this mode, a sliding mode controller is designed. The linearized mode is subject to uncertainties. The uncertainties are generated in the process of linearization. A radial basis function (RBF) neural network is introduced to compensate for the uncertainties. The update formulas for the neural networks are derived from the Lyapunov direct method. For the chattering phenomenon of the sliding mode control, a fuzzy logic inference system is adopted. In the sense of Lyapunov, the asymptotical stability of the system can be guaranteed. Compared with the internal mode control and the conventional PID control method, some numerical simulations verify the feasibility and robustness of the proposed scheme.

Keywords: *Hydropower Plant, Speed Governor, Water Hammer, Neural Network, Fuzzy Logic, Sliding Mode Control, Chattering.*

1. Introduction

With the increasing acute global energy crisis, hydropower, an ideal renewable and clean energy, has been given a widely social concern. It is generally known that the hydropower generation has a great development potential and a broad market prospect. A hydro-turbine governor system is an important part of the hydropower plants [1], and the speed governor plays a vital role in controlling the hydro-turbine speed. Therefore, research work on the hydro-turbine governor system has becomes significant.

A hydro-turbine governor system is a complex nonlinear object, which features time- variant and non-minimum phases. For the non- linear governor system, various mathematical models and control methods have been presented.

Many different mathematical models have been proposed in terms of the hydropower plants. For example, Paolo [2] has presented a detailed numerical model for the dynamic behavior of the Francis turbine, and has considered the effects of water hammer on the turbine. Chen [3] has introduced a novel model of a hydro-turbine system with a surge tank, and has studied the non-linear dynamical behaviors of the hydro-turbine system.

According to many different mathematical models, various control methods have been proposed. Tan [4] has designed a PID tuning of load frequency controller based on a two-degree-of-freedom internal model control. Using a high-gain observer to replace the coordinate transformation, Liu [5] has presented a nonlinear robust control strategy, which is only required to measure the rotor speed. Kishor [6] has used the H-infinity method to approximate the non-linear part of the penstock-turbine transfer function, and has studied the hydraulic transient characteristics. Qian [7] has presented a GA- based fuzzy sliding mode control approach for speed governing of a hydro-turbine. Most of the methods mentioned above only focus on the accurate linear model and the non-linear dynamical analysis. However, few papers have paid attention to the uncertainties generated in the process of linearization of the non-linear mode, and the influence of elastic water hammer upon the security and stability of a hydro-turbine governor system.

In order to further investigate the hydro -turbine governor system, a novel non-linear mathematical model with elastic water hammer was developed. By linearizing the nonlinear mode, the sliding mode controller was designed. The advantage of the sliding mode control method is that in the sliding motion, the designed controller shows strong robustness and high control accuracy in the presence of uncertainties and external disturbances. However, the designed sliding mode controller based on the linearized model cannot stabilize the non-linear governor system. Furthermore, a chattering phenomenon [8] exists in the conventional sliding mode control method. Therefore, in this work, we presented a neural-fuzzy sliding mode control scheme, which combines with the merits of the fuzzy set theory [9-10], neural networks [11-12], and sliding mode control [13-14]. A radial basis function (RBF) neural network was introduced to compensate for the uncertainties generated in the process of linearization of the non-linear mode [15]. The update formula of the network was deduced from the Lyapunov direct method so that the weight convergence and system stability could be simultaneously guaranteed. Considering the chattering phenomenon of the sliding mode control, a fuzzy logic inference system was adopted to regulate the gain of the switching control law according to the system performance [16]. In the sense of Lyapunov, the asymptotically stability of the whole system could be guaranteed. The simulation results obtained demonstrated the effectiveness of the proposed scheme to improve the dynamic performance of the system and attenuate the chattering phenomenon.

This paper is organized as follows. Under the assumption of elastic water hammer, the detailed nonlinear mathematical model of a hydro-turbine governor system is given in Section 2. The design of a new neural-fuzzy sliding mode controller is reported in Section 3. The simulation results for the different states in the hydro-turbine governor system are illustrated in Section 4. Finally, conclusions are given in Section 5.

2. Mode of hydro-turbine governor system
2.1 Penstock and hydro-turbine

When penstocks are short or medium in length, the hydraulic turbine model is adequate under the assumption of the inelasticity of penstocks and the incompressibility of fluid. However, considering the hydropower plants with long conduits, it has to take into account the effects of elasticity of penstock and compressibility of fluid. Water hammer is produced by the rapid velocity changes

of the flowing fluid in the pipelines. The emergence of elastic water hammer can cause serious problems for the hydraulic turbine, and then affects the whole power system. Therefore, the stability study of the hydroelectric power plant with elastic water hammer is of paramount importance. In this paper, the mathematic models of the water tunnel and penstock components are presented under the assumption of elastic water hammer. The elastic water hammer is represented by a delay block of $e^{-T_{rs}}$. Three components interconnected with each other constitute the nonlinear governing system, as shown in figure 1.

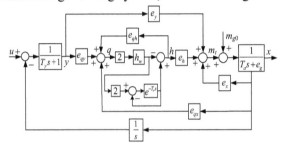

Figure 1. Transfer function block diagram of a hydro-turbine governor system.

Considering a small variation around an operating point, the linearized equation of the Francis hydro-turbine can be given as

$$m_t = e_x x + e_y y + e_h h$$
$$q = e_{qx} x + e_{qy} y + e_{qh} h \tag{1}$$

The six hydro-turbine constants e_x, e_y, e_h, e_{qx}, e_{qy}, and e_{qh} can be defined as:

$$e_x = \frac{\partial m_t}{\partial x}, e_y = \frac{\partial m_t}{\partial y}, e_h = \frac{\partial m_t}{\partial h}, e_{qx} = \frac{\partial q}{\partial x}, e_{qy} = \frac{\partial q}{\partial y}, e_{qh} = \frac{\partial q}{\partial h}$$

The effects of surge tank are ignored, and the transfer function of penstock with the incremental head and flow can be written as

$$\frac{\Delta h(s)}{\Delta q(s)} = -2h_w th(0.5T_r s) \tag{2}$$

Compared with the traditional simplified method of the Taylor series expansion, this paper presents a new simplified nonlinear method, as shown in function (3).

When the hyperbolic tangent function is converted to an exponential function, the transfer function of penstock with the incremental head and flow can be given as

$$G_h(s) = \frac{\Delta h(s)}{\Delta q(s)} = -2h_w th(0.5T_r s)$$
$$= -2h_w(1 - 2\frac{e^{-T_r s}}{1 + e^{-T_r s}}) \tag{3}$$

The new method takes into accounts the higher order terms of the system model. Therefore, the accuracies of the hydraulic tunnel and the penstock are greatly improved. In figure 1, the red section means the hydraulic turbine part taking elastic water hammer; this relation only depends on the length of penstock. Considering the elastic water hammer, the hydro-turbine transfer function relating to the mechanical power and the wicket gate opening can be derived and written as

$$\frac{\Delta m_t(s)}{\Delta y(s)} = e_y \frac{1 - 2h_w e \tanh(0.5T_r s)}{1 + 2h_w e_{qh} \tanh(0.5T_r s)} \quad (4)$$

where, $e = e_{qy}e_h/e_y - e_q$, and h_w is the normalized hydraulic impedance of penstock, the water inertia time is $T_w = T_r h_w$, the penstock reflection time is $T_r = 2L/a$, penstock length is L, and the water wave velocity is a.

2.2 Wicket gate and servomechanism

The servomotor is used to amplify the control signal, and to provide power to operate the guide vane. Neglecting small time constants, the transfer function relating to the control signal u and the wicket gate servomotor stroke y can be written as:

$$\frac{\Delta y(s)}{\Delta u(s)} = \frac{1}{T_y s + 1} \quad (5)$$

where, T_y is the response time of the wicket gate servomotor

2.3 Generator and network

If the generator unit supplies for an isolated load, the dynamic process of the synchronous generator unit only relating to the moment of inertia can be described as

$$\frac{\Delta x(s)}{\Delta[(m_t - m_{g0})(s)]} = \frac{1}{T_a s + e_g} \quad (6)$$

where, m_t is the turbine torque (in per unit), m_{g0} is the load torque (in per unit), T_a is the generator unit mechanical time (in seconds), and e_g is the load self-regulation fact.

3. Control designed and analysis
3.1 Design of RBF network-based sliding mode controller

Taking into account the linearized small-signal model of an ideal Francis turbine, the expression of penstock with inelastic water hammer and non-friction can be obtained by the Taylor series expansion.

$$\frac{\Delta h(s)}{\Delta q(s)} = -2h_w th(0.5T_r s) = -T_w s \quad (7)$$

Thus a 3-order mode of state space is obtained by linearization of the simplified model, where the system state variables are independent and measurable. The wicket gate servomotor stroke relative deviation $x_3 = y$, the turbine torque relative deviation $x_2 = m_t$ and the turbine speed relative

deviation $x_1 = x$. To eliminate the speed deviation, the integral of x_1 is utilized as an additional state x_4, which is defined as

$$x_4 = \int_0^\infty x_1 dt \quad (8)$$

The state space expression for the hydro-turbine governor system with model uncertainties and external disturbances is described as follows.

$$\dot{x} = (A + \Delta A)x + (B + \Delta B)u + F(d(t) + g(t))$$
$$= Ax + Bu + f \quad (9)$$
$$y = C^T x$$

where, $x = [x_1 \ x_2 \ x_3 \ x_4]^T$ is the state vector; ΔA and ΔB are unknown or uncertain; $d(t)$ values are disturbances including the parameter variations and load disturbances; $g(t)$ is the external indefinite disturbance; f is the uncertainties consisting of all unknown parts and disturbances; and $C^T = [1 \ 0 \ 0 \ 0]$ is the output matrix.

$$A = \begin{bmatrix} -\dfrac{e_g - e_x}{T_a} & \dfrac{1}{T_a} & 0 & 0 \\[2mm] 0 & -\dfrac{1}{e_{qh}T_w} & \dfrac{e_{qy}e_h - e_{qh}e_y}{T_y e_{qh}} + \dfrac{e_y}{e_{qh}T_w} & \dfrac{e_{qy}e_h - e_{qh}e_y}{T_y e_{qh}} \\[2mm] 0 & 0 & -\dfrac{1}{T_y} & -\dfrac{1}{T_y} \\[2mm] 1 & 0 & 0 & 0 \end{bmatrix}$$

$$B = [0 \quad -\frac{e_{qy}e_h - e_{qh}e_y}{T_y e_{qh}} \quad \frac{1}{T_y} \quad 0]^T$$

$$F = [\frac{1}{T_a} \quad 0 \quad 0 \quad 0]^T$$

$$f = \Delta Ax + \Delta Bu + F(d(t) + g(t))$$

The sliding mode controller consists of two stages. First the sliding surface is defined as

$$s = c^T x = c_1 x_1 + c_2 x_2 + c_3 x_3 + c_4 x_4 \quad (10)$$

where, c_i ($i = 1,2,3,4$) is the sliding surface coefficient vector, which is positive constant.

Secondly, the sliding mode control law is designed, which is composed of the equivalent control law and the switching control law

$$u = u_{eq} + u_{sw} \quad (11)$$

where, u_{eq} forces the system trajectory to the sliding mode stage, and is defined as the equivalent control law. u_{sw} keeps the system trajectory on the sliding surface and is defined as the switching control law.

Furthermore, u_{eq} can be obtained by

$$\dot{s} = c^T \dot{x} = 0 \quad (12)$$

Substituting (8) into (12) yields

$$u_{eq} = -(c^T B)^{-1} c^T Ax \quad (13)$$

Take into account the following positive definite function as a Lyapunov candidate function:

$$V(t) = \frac{1}{2}s^2 \qquad (14)$$

Differentiating $V(t)$ with respect to time t yields:

$$
\begin{aligned}
\dot{V}(t) &= s\dot{s} \\
&= s[c^T \dot{x}] \\
&= s[c^T(Ax + Bu + f)] \qquad (15) \\
&= s[c^T(Ax + Bu_{eq}) + c^T Bu_{sw} + c^T f] \\
&= s[c^T Bu_{sw} + c^T f]
\end{aligned}
$$

The switching control is obtained as:

$$u_{sw} = -(c^T B)^{-1}[ks + \eta sign(s)] \qquad (16)$$

where, η, k are positive constants.

Substituting (16) into (15) yields:

$$\dot{V}(t) = -ks^2 - \eta|s| + c^T fs \le -ks^2 - (\eta - |c^T f|)|s| \qquad (17)$$

where, $\eta = \eta_0 + c^T \bar{f}$, and η_0 is positive constant. If the upper bound of the uncertain parts $c^T \bar{f} = \sup c^T f$ is certainty, it can judge the stability of the system by using the Lyapunov stability theory.

Considering the influence of uncertainties on the stability and robustness of the system, a RBF neural network is adopted to approximate the uncertainties. The system state vector x is defined as the network input, and $\hat{f}$ is the estimated f value as the network output. The update formula of the network can be deduced using the Lyapunov direct method.

$$\hat{f}(x) = W^T h(x) \qquad (18)$$

$$f(x) = W^{*T} h(x) + \varepsilon \qquad (19)$$

where, W is the weight matrix of the RBF neural network, and W^* is the optimal weight of the RBF neural network; ε is the approximation error of the RBF neural network, and $h(x)$ is the radial basis function, which it is determined by:

$$h(x) = \exp(\frac{\|x - c_f\|^2}{2b_f^2}) \qquad (20)$$

where, c_f and b_f depict the center and width of the hidden neuron of the RBF network. We can make the following assumptions:

1. There exists an optimal weight W^*, so that the output of the optimal network satisfies $c^T|W^{*T}h(x) - \bar{f}| \le \varepsilon_0$, where ε_0 is a positive constant.
2. The norm of the system uncertainties and its upper bound satisfy the following relationship $c^T|\bar{f} - f| \ge \varepsilon_1 \ge \varepsilon_0$, where ε_1 is a positive constant.

To get the update formulas, a new Lyapunov function is needed to redefine, as follows:

$$V(t) = \frac{1}{2}s^2 + \frac{1}{2}\alpha^{-1}\hat{W}^T\hat{W} \qquad (21)$$

where, $\hat{W} = W^* - W$, $\dot{\hat{W}} = -\dot{W}$, and α is a positive constant.

Differentiating $V(t)$ with respect to time t yields:

$$\dot{V}(t) = s\dot{s} + \alpha^{-1}\hat{W}^T\dot{\hat{W}} \qquad (22)$$

The adaptive law of RBF network is defined as:

$$\dot{W} = c^T \alpha |s| h(x) \qquad (23)$$

By substituting (17) and (23) into (22), $\dot{V}(t)$ is obtained as:

$$
\begin{aligned}
\dot{V}(t) &= s\dot{s} - \alpha^{-1}(W^* - W)^T\dot{W} \\
&= s[-ks - (\eta - c^T\hat{f})sgn(s)] - \alpha^{-1}(W^* - W)^T c^T \alpha h(x)|s| \\
&= s[-ks - (\eta - c^T\hat{f})sgn(s)] - \alpha^{-1}[W^{*T}\exp(\frac{\|x-c_f\|^2}{2b_f^2}) \\
&\quad - W^T\exp(\frac{\|x-c_f\|^2}{2b_f^2})]c^T\alpha|s| \\
&\le -ks^2 - \eta_0|s| - c^T(\bar{f} - \hat{f})|s| \\
&\quad - c^T(W^{*T}\exp(\frac{\|x-c_f\|^2}{2b_f^2}) - |f|)|s| \\
&\le -ks^2 - \eta_0|s| - (\varepsilon_1 - \varepsilon_0)|s|
\end{aligned}
$$
$$(24)$$

According to the assumptions 1 and 2, the Lyapunov function (22) satisfies $\dot{V}(t) \le 0$, i.e. the system (9) with the uncertainties is asymptotic stability in the sense of Lyapunov once the control law (11) is adopted.

3.2 Design of fuzzy sliding mode controller

Although the sliding mode control is one of the effective non-linear control approaches, its drawback is the chattering phenomenon, which is determined by the switching function and its gain. To solve this chattering problem, the key is how to minimize reasonably the switching control signal. Therefore, a fuzzy logic inference system is introduced to regulate the gain of the switching control law to alleviate the chattering problem.

The design of a fuzzy logic controller having one input and one output was proposed. The number of fuzzy control rules can be minimized since only one input variable s. As mentioned earlier in Section 2, u_{eq} is the equivalent control law, and u_{sw} is the switching control law. The fuzzy control rules can be expressed as follow:

   I.   If s is ZO, then u is u_{eq}.

   II. If s is NZ, then u is $u_{eq} + u_{sw}$.

where the fuzzy sets ZO and NZ represent zero and non-zero，and the sliding surface variable s is the input of the fuzzy controller. When the s value is zero, then the control law of the fuzzy sliding mode controller is only determined by the equivalent control. Similarly, when the s value is non-zero, then that is composed of the equivalent control and the switching control.

However, in practice application, only two control rules cannot be enough to completely describe the operation of a non-linear hydro-turbine governor system. In order to eliminate this weakness and attenuate the chattering phenomena simultaneously, five items of fuzzy rules based on the theory of sliding mode control were presented by incorporating the fuzzy logic control.

The fuzzy logic system can be briefly described as follows. The sliding surface variable s is regarded as the input of fuzzy controller, and the weighting of the switching control law $w1$ is chosen as the output of fuzzy controller. The fuzzy control rules are designed according to the operation experiences. By fusing the prior knowledge about the sliding mode control, we know that when the system states are far from the sliding surface, a large $w1$ value is needed. Otherwise, a small $w1$ value is required. To determine the final control action, the fuzzy rules can be designed as follow:

I.   If s is PB, then $w1$ is PB.
II. If s is PM, then $w1$ is PM.
III. If s is ZO, then $w1$ is ZO.
IV. If s is NM, then $w1$ is PM.
V.   If s is NB, then $w1$ is PB.

where, NB, NM, ZO, PM, and PB are negative big, negative medium, zero, positive medium, and positive big, respectively. Figure 2 shows the membership functions of the linguistic labels NB, NM, ZO, PM, and PB for the term s, and the membership functions of the linguistic labels NB, NM, ZO, PM, and PB for $w1$.

The output of the designed fuzzy inference system is shown in figure 3. Finally, the output of the fuzzy controller $w1$ can be obtained by the output singleton fuzzy sets and the center-of-gravity defuzzification method.

The final value of the switching law by the fuzzy logic law is defined as:

$$u'_{sw} = w1 \times u_{sw} \qquad (24)$$

The final total control law u is obtained as:

$$u = u_{eq} + w1 \times u_{sw} \qquad (25)$$

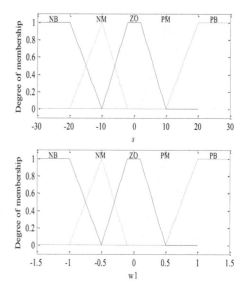

Figure 2. Membership functions of s and $w1$.

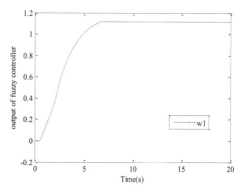

Figure 3. Output surface of the fuzzy interface system.

4. Numerical simulation

The hydro-turbine governor system was supplied for an isolated network with a single-penstock /single-Francis turbine. The parameters of the hydropower plant were defined as $T_r=2$, $h_w=0.55$, $T_y=0.5$, and $T_a=6.65$. Table 1 shows the time-varying transferred coefficients of the hydro-turbine governor system, and the initial states $x_0=[0\ 0\ 0\ 0]^T$. The parameters for the sliding surface s were chosen to be $c_1=50.39$, $c_2=3.32$, $c_3=6.74$, and $c_4=22.4$ from Acker command of MATLAB by placing the pole of Ackermann's formula in the vector $[-1\ -2-2i\ -2+2i\ -8]$.

The center c_f and width b_f of the hidden neuron of the RBF network were designed as random numbers in the interval $(0, 1)$. The parameter α was selected to be 10^8. n^* was selected to be 6, which is the number of hidden neurons. The parameters k and η were determined to be $k=0.2$, $\eta=0.05$.

For comparison with the dynamic and steady-state performances of different control methods, we adopted the internal mode control and the conventional PID control.

Table 1. Some coefficients of hydraulic turbine system.

Point	e_x	e_y	e_h	e_{qx}	e_{qy}	e_{qh}	e_g
Case 1	-1.00	1.00	1.50	0.00	1.00	0.50	0.21
Case 2	-0.26	1.92	0.92	0.00	1.06	0.35	0.21

4.1. Load rejection

To demonstrate the dynamic nonlinear characteristic of the presented scheme, 10% load disturbance was applied as the interference signal. Under the operating condition Case 1, the comparisons among the neural-fuzzy sliding mode control, the internal mode control and the conventional PID control are shown in figure 4. According to this figure, compared with the internal mode control, the overshoot of the state variables with the fuzzy sliding mode control x_1, x_2, x_3 in the hydro-turbine governor system decreased, and the regulation time was greatly shortened. Compared with the conventional PID control, the dynamic performance of the state variables improved significantly, where the regulation time of the controlled system was shortened, the fluctuation times were reduced, and the accuracy of the stable states was improved. According to figure 5, the chattering phenomena of the control input u improved significantly. The numerical simulation results obtained show that the proposed scheme has strong anti-interference and preferable dynamic characteristics.

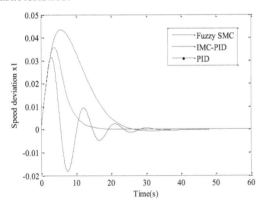

Figure 4(a). Speed deviation x_1.

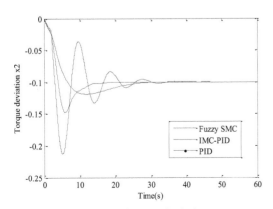

Figure 4(b). Torque deviation x_2.

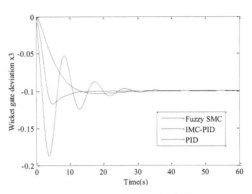

Figure 4(c). Water gate deviation x_3.

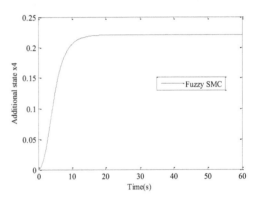

Figure 4(d). Additional state x_4.

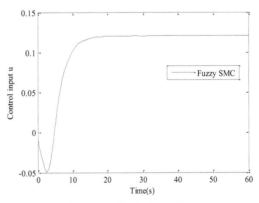

Figure 5. Control input u.

4.2. Robustness testing

In order to verify the robustness of the neural-fuzzy sliding mode governor, 10% of the load rejection under the operating conditions Case 1 and Case 2 was tested. The controller parameters were kept unchanged. According to figure 6, the state variables of the hydro-turbine governor system could still have a good robustness when the system parameters changed. In practical applications, the proposed neural-fuzzy sliding mode governor possesses a great advantage. It can significantly extend the lifetime of equipment and improve the safety and reliability of the hydroelectric power plants.

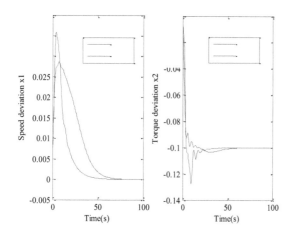

Figure 6(a). Speed deviation x1 and torque deviation x2.

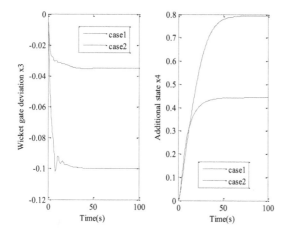

Figure 6(b). Water gate deviation x_3 and additional state x_4.

5. Conclusion

In this work, a novel non-linear mathematical model for a hydro-turbine governor system with elastic water hammer was established. Considering the previous nonlinear systems used to reach an ideal dynamic performance, a neural-fuzzy sliding mode governor was proposed. The non-linear mathematic model for hydropower plants was linearized, and a radial basis function (RBF) neural network was introduced for compensate for the error between the linearized and non-linear models. In order to eliminate the chattering phenomenon, a fuzzy logic inference system was designed to regulate the gain of the switching control law. Compared with the internal mode control and the conventional PID control, the proposed neural-fuzzy sliding mode governor improved the dynamic and steady-state performance of the system. The

numerical simulation results demonstrated the feasibility, robustness, and stability of the proposed method.

References

[1] Fang, H. Q., Chen, L. & Dlakavu, N. et al. (2010). Basic modeling and simulation tool for analysis of hydraulic transients in hydroelectric power plants. IEEE Transactions on Energy Conversion, vol. 23, no. 3, pp. 834-841.

[2] Xu, C. & Qian, D.W. (2016). Governor design for a hydropower plant with an upstream surge tank by GA-based fuzzy reduced-order sliding mode. Energies, vol. 8, no. 12, pp. 13442-13457.

[3] Chen, D. Y., Ding, C. & Ma, X. Y. (2013). Nonlinear dynamical analysis of hydro-turbine governing system with a surge tank. Applied Mathematical Modelling, vol. 37, no. 14, pp. 7611-7623.

[4] Tan, W. (2010). Unified tuning of PID load frequency controller for power systems via IMC. IEEE Transactions on power systems, vol. 25, no. 1, pp. 341-350.

[5] Qian, D. W. & Yi, J. Q. (2012). L_1 adaptive governor design for hydro-turbines. ICIC Express Letters, Part B Applications, vol. 3, no. 5, pp.1171-1177.

[6] Kishor, N (2009). Oscillation damping with optimal pole-shift approach in application to a hydro plant connected as SMIB system. IEEE Systems Journal, vol. 3, no. 3, pp. 317-330.

[7] Qian, D. W., Yi, J. Q. & Liu, X. J. (2010). GA-based fuzzy sliding mode governor for hydro-turbine. International Conference on Intelligent Control and Information Processing, Dalian, China, 2010.

[8] Liu, D. T., Yi, J. Q. & Zhao, B. D. (2003). Fuzzy tuning sliding mode control of transporting for an overhead crane. Second International Conference on Machine Learning and Cybernetics, Xi'an, China, vol. 4, pp. 2541-2546, 2003.

[9] Lin, F. J. & Wai, R. J. (2001). Sliding-mode-controlled slider-crank mechanism with fuzzy neural network. IEEE Transactions on Industrial Electronics, vol. 48, no. 1, pp. 60-70.

[10] Çam, E. (2007). Application of fuzzy logic for load frequency control of hydroelectrical power plants. Energy Conversion and Management, vol. 48, no. 4, pp. 1281-1288.

[11] Qian, D. W., Zhao, B. D. & Yi, J. Q. (2013). Neural sliding-mode load frequency controller design of power systems. Neural Computing and Applications, vol. 22, no. 2, pp.279-286.

[12] Xiao, Z. H., Guo, J. & Zeng, H. T. (2009). Application of fuzzy neural network controller in hydropower generator unit. Kybernetes, vol. 38, no. 10, pp. 1709-1717.

[13] Ding, X. B. & Sinha, A. (2011). Sliding mode/H_∞ control of a hydro-power plant. American Control Conference. San Francisco, American, 2011.

[14] Qian, D. W., Yi, J. Q. & Liu, X. J. (2011). Design of reduced order sliding mode governor for hydro-turbines. American Control Conference (ACC), pp. 5073-5078, July, 2011.

[15] Salhi, I., Doubabi, S. & Essounbouli, N. (2010). Application of multi-model control with fuzzy switching to a micro hydro-electrical power plant. Renewable Energy, vol. 35, no.9, pp. 2071-2079.

9

Prediction of rock strength parameters for an Iranian oil field using neuro-fuzzy method

M. Heidarian[*], H. Jalalifar and A. Rafati

Department of Petroleum Engineering, Shahid Bahonar University, Kerman, Iran.

Corresponding author: Mohamadheidarian64@yahoo.com(M. Heidarian).

Abstract

Uniaxial compressive strength (UCS) and internal friction coefficient (μ) are the most important rock strength parameters. They could be determined by either laboratory tests or empirical correlations. Sometimes, for many reasons, laboratory analysis is not possible. On the other hand, due to changes in the rock composition and properties, none of the correlations could be applied as an exact universal one. In such conditions, the proposed artificial intelligence method could be an appropriate candidate for estimation of the strength parameters. In this work, the adaptive neuro-fuzzy inference system (ANFIS), which is one of the artificial intelligence techniques, was used as a dominant tool to predict the strength parameters for one of the Iranian SW oil fields. A total of 655 datasets (including the depth, compressional wave velocity, and density data) were used. 436 and 219 datasets were randomly selected among the data for construction and verification of the proposed intelligent model, respectively.

To evaluate the performance of the model, the root mean square error (RMSE) and correlation coefficient (R^2) values between the reported values for the drilling site and the estimated ones were computed. A comparison between RMSE for the proposed model and that for the recent intelligence models shows that the proposed model is more accurate than the others. Acceptable accuracy and using conventional well-logging data are the highlight advantages of the proposed intelligence model.

Keywords: *Uniaxial Compressive Strength, Internal Friction Coefficient, Well-Logging, Adaptive Neuro-Fuzzy Inference System.*

1. Introduction

Uniaxial compressive strength (UCS) and internal friction coefficient (μ) are the most important rock strength parameters. These parameters have very high usage in the mechanical and geomechanical studies of rocks. Specially, in the stress-strain analysis problems such as wellbore stability, these parameters are essential. The values for UCS and μ are determined by either core analysis (laboratory method) or empirical correlations. Laboratory methods are very expensive and time-consuming. In addition, in practice, many geomechanical problems in reservoirs must be addressed when core samples are unavailable for laboratory testing. In fact, core samples of overburden formations, where many wellbore instability problems are encountered, are almost never available for testing [1]. To solve this problem, a number of empirical relations have been proposed that relate rock strength to the parameters measurable with geophysical well logs [1,2-8]. It should be noticed that each one of these correlations has been developed from the specific ranges of the well log data. Due to changes in the rock composition and properties, which result in changes in the data, none of the correlations could be applied as an exact universal one because the accuracy of no correlation is guaranteed for the data that is different from the one used for developing it. In such conditions, to overcome these problems, intelligence techniques could be very useful and helpful. In the recent years, there has been an increasing interest in developing intelligence models for prediction of the rock strength properties in the world. A review of the published-related studies is presented here.

Noorani and Kordani (2011) tried to estimate the uniaxial compressive strength of intact rocks using a neuro-fuzzy (NF) model and a multiple regression (MR) one. For this purpose, they used 15 laboratory datasets (including porosity, saturation, dry density, tensile strength, Schmidt Hammer number (SHN), sound velocity, point load index (PLI), and UCS). Among the data used, they used, respectively, 12 and 3 datasets as the training data and test data. To evaluate the performance of the models, the root mean square error (RMSE) index was calculated; it was 6.1 for the NF model and 13.63 for the MR one [9].

Amani and Moeini (2012) used the artificial neural network (ANN) and the adaptive neuro-fuzzy inference system (ANFIS) to predict the shear strength of the reinforced concrete (RC) beams. The ANN model, with multi-layer perceptron (MLP), using a back-propagation (BP) algorithm, was used to predict the shear strength of the RC beams. Six important parameters were selected as the input parameters including concrete compressive strength, longitudinal reinforcement volume, shear span-to-depth ratio, transverse reinforcement, effective depth of beam, and beam width. The ANFIS model was also applied to a database, and the results obtained were compared with the ANN model results and empirical codes. The first-order Sugeno fuzzy was used. Comparison between the models and the empirical formulas showed that the ANN model with the MLP/BP algorithm provided a better prediction for the shear strength [10].

Dadkhah and Esfahani (2013) applied two soft-computing approaches, neuro-fuzzy inference system (ANFIS) and genetic programming (GP), for the prediction of UCS. Block punch index (BPI), porosity, P-wave velocity, and density were used as the inputs for both methods, and were analyzed to obtain the training data and testing data. Of all the 130 datasets, the training and testing sets consisted of randomly-selected 110 and 20 sets, respectively. The results obtained showed that the ANFIS and GP models were capable of accurately predicting the uniaxial compressive strength (UCS) used in the training and testing phase of the study. The GP model results better predicted UCS compared to the ANFIS one [11].

Ceryan (2014) applied support vector machines (SVMs), relevance vector machines (RVMs), and ANN, which are intelligent technique-based, to predict UCS for the volcanic rocks in Turkey. In these models, the porosity and P-durability index representing microstructural variables were used as the input variables. Their results indicated that the SVM and RVM performances were better than the ANN model. Also the RVM run time was considerably faster, and it yielded the highest accuracy [12].

Mishra et al. (2015) applied some soft-computing techniques including ANN, FIS, and ANFIS to estimate UCS of intact rocks by the index tests. BPI, point load strength (PLS), SHN, and ultrasonic P-wave velocity (Vp) were used as the input data. Various statistical parameters (VAF, RMSE, and correlation coefficient) were determined to check the predictive performances of these models. On the basis of these statistical parameters, it can be said that all the three models are equally robust in estimating UCS from the corresponding index test results. However, the fuzzy inference system (Sugeno-type) emerges to be a more competent analysis technique than the other two models in this regard [13].

In this work, by using the adaptive neuro-fuzzy inference system (ANFIS), an intelligence model was proposed for the estimation of UCS and μ using the conventional well-logging data (including depth, compressional wave velocity, and density data) in one of the Iranian SW oil fields. Some advantages of this work are as follow:

- The estimation technique is relatively simple, cheap, and quick.
- The inputs (depth, compressional wave velocity, and density data) are available in most wells.
- Generally, well logs can provide a continuous record over the entire well, so the well-log data, as the input, can be estimated over the whole well.
- In the ranges of the data used, the proposed model is intelligent.

2. Materials and method
2.1. Methodology
Adaptive neuro-fuzzy inference system (ANFIS) was used as the dominant tool. It is a combination of fuzzy logic and ANN. For example, when the number of training pairs is small, the results obtained for the neural network system may be poor. In such conditions, if fuzzy systems are combined with a neural network system, the results can improve [14]. An ANFIS system, which was first introduced by Jang in 1993, constructs a FIS, whose membership function parameters are adjusted using a back-propagation algorithm either alone or in combination with a least-squares type of method [15]. This adjustment allows the fuzzy systems to learn from the data they are modeling [16]. ANFIS is capable

of mapping the unseen inputs to their outputs by learning the rules from the previously-seen data [17]. An ANFIS system has five layers including an input layer, an input MF layer (for input fuzzification), a rule layer, an output MF layer (for defuzzification of outputs), and an output layer. Figure 1 shows the structure of an ANFIS system.

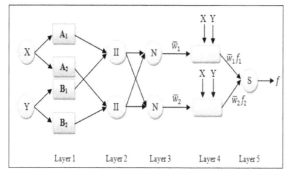

Figure 1. Structure of a simple ANFIS system.

2.2. Data analysis

This work was focused on one of the Iranian southwest oil fields. From the studied field, 655 wire-line log data was obtained and used to develop an intelligence model for prediction of either UCS or μ. The data consisted of the depth, compressional wave velocity (V_p), and density (RHOB log). Ranges of the data used are shown in table 1.

2.3. Constructing the model

Appropriate assignment of the inputs and outputs is the first step in any modeling process with intelligence systems. In this study, since the UCS and μ determinations were the objective, they were assigned as the output variables. The depth, compressional wave velocity (V_p), and density (RHOB log) were assigned as the input variables (Figure 2).

Table 1. Data ranges used.

PVT Property	Number of Points		Range		Mean	
	Training data	Test data	Training data	Test data	Training data	Test data
Depth (m)	436	219	3922-4916	3930-49150	4421	44419
Wave velocity ($\mu s\ ft^{-1}$)	436	219	43.6-93.89	45.16-93.19	51.316	51.406
Density (g cm^{-3})	436	219	2.3-3.04	2.29-3.04	2.782	2.782
Uniaxial compressive strength (MPa)	436	219	1.9-100	2.01-89.91	64.93	64.87
Internal friction coefficient	436	219	0.2-0.72	0.2-0.71	0.6096	0.6128

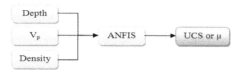

Figure 2. Schematic of output and input parameters of system (ANFIS).

A total of 655 input-output datasets, which were obtained using the wire-line logs in one of the SW Iranian oil fields were used. The data was divided into two groups. One group included 436 datasets, which were selected randomly and used for constructing the model, and the other one included 219 datasets that were used for validation of the model. There are three methods including Genfis1 and Genfis2, and Genfis3 to generate the fuzzy inference system (FIS) structure. They generate the fuzzy inference system structure from the data using the subtractive clustering and fuzzy c-means (FCM) clustering, respectively. After the accuracy tests, it was found that the Genfis2 result was better than Genfis1 and Genfis3 for either the UCS or the μ prediction. Therefore, to generate the FIS structure, Genfis2 was used. The properties of the constructed model are listed in table 2. Figure 3 shows the structure of the constructed model. After constructing the model, it was implemented

twice. First, it was implemented to predict UCS, and, once again, it was implemented to predict μ. The results obtained for a comparison made between the values reported from the drilling site, which were obtained using the wire-line logs, and the values estimated from the test data using the intelligence model are shown in figures 4 and 5.

Table 2. Properties of constructed model (Genfis2).

Inference type	Method
AND	prod
OR	probor
Implication	Prod
Aggregation	max
Difuzzification	wtaver

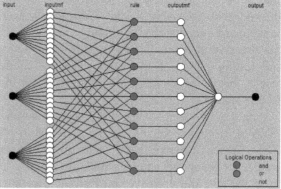

Figure 3. Constructed model to predict either uniaxial compressive strength or internal friction coefficient.

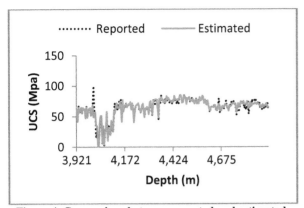

Figure 4. Comparison between reported and estimated values for the model in test data for uniaxial compressive strength (UCS).

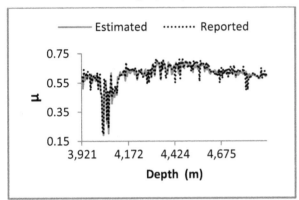

Figurer 5. Comparison between reported and estimated values for the model in the test data for internal friction coefficient (µ).

3. Results and discussion

In this study, the adaptive neuro-fuzzy inference system (ANFIS) was applied for prediction of the uniaxial compressive strength (UCS) and internal friction coefficient (µ) in one of the Iranian southwest oil fields. ANFIS is one of the powerful artificial intelligence techniques that is a combination of the fuzzy logic and neural networks, and combines the advantages of both systems. After constructing and running the model, the correlation coefficient (R^2) between the reported values from the drilling site and the values estimated from the intelligence model was computed in the test data. They were 0.890 and 0.892 for µ and UCS, respectively (Figures 6 and 7). Also for a more accurate performance evaluation of the model, the root mean square error (RMSE) in the test data was computed using (1), which was compared with the accuracy of the recently-proposed intelligence and predictive models (Table 3).

$$RMSE = \sqrt{\sum_{i=1}^{n} \left[(X)_{experimenal} - (X)_{predicted} \right]^2 / N} \quad (1)$$

where, $X_{expimental}$ and $X_{predicted}$ are, respectively, the field reported and the model estimated values for either UCS or µ. N is the number of dataset used. According to table 3, the accuracy of the proposed model is more acceptable than that for the others. Moreover, in the previous models, most of the input data are obtained by laboratory tests, which are very time- and money-consuming. However, in the proposed model, the conventional wire-line logs, which are available in most wells, are applied as the input data.

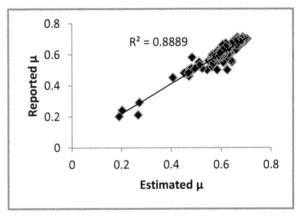

Figure 6. Correlation between experimental and predicted values from ANFIS in test data internal friction coefficient (µ).

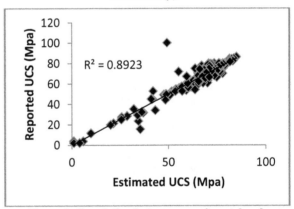

Figure 7. Correlation between experimental and predicted values from ANFIS in test data for uniaxial compressive strength (UCS).

4. Conclusion

For several reasons such as time and money limitations, laboratory determination of the rock strength properties (UCS and µ) is sometimes impossible. In such conditions, the experimental correlations are usually applied. Several correlations have been proposed. However, since the accuracy of no correlation is guaranteed for the data that is different from the one used for developing it, none of the correlations could be applied as a universal one. In this study, using the adaptive neuro-fuzzy inference system (ANFIS), an intelligence model was proposed to predict either UCS or µ for an Iranian SW oil field. For evaluation of the model accuracy, the correlation coefficient (R^2) between the values predicted from the model and the reported ones were calculated. They were 0.890 and 0.892 for μ and UCS, respectively. The results obtained for the proposed model could be acceptable, and this model could be applied as an appropriate one to predict UCS and μ when laboratory analysis is not possible. Acceptable accuracy and using conventional well-logging data are the highlight advantages of the proposed intelligence model.

Table 3. A comparison between proposed model and recent intelligence and predictive models.

Num.	Model	Year	Technique	Used variables		Number of data		RMSE	
				Input	Output	Training	Test	UCS	μ
1	Yurdakul et al. [18]	2011	ANN	SHN	UCS	25	6	7.92	-
2	Yurdakul et al.	2011	MR	SHN	UCS	25	6	46.51	-
3	Noorani & Kordani	2011	NF	φ, S, ρ, S_T, SHN, V_u, PLI	UCS	12	3	6.1	-
4	Noorani & Kordani	2011	MR	φ, S, ρ, S_T, SHN, V_u, PLI	UCS	12	3	13.63	-
5	Martins et al. [19]	2012	MR	φ, ρ, V_u, E_m	UCS	45	10	11.09	-
6	Martins et al.	2012	ANN	φ, ρ, V_u, E_m	UCS	45	10	11.49	-
7	Martins et al.	2012	SVM	φ, ρ, V_u, E_m	UCS	45	10	11.12	-
8	Mishra & Basu [20]	2013	FIS	φ, ρ, BPI, PLS, SHN, Vp	UCS	44	16	8.21	-
9	Mishra & Basu	2013	MR	φ, ρ, BPI, PLS, SHN, Vp	UCS	44	16	6.89	-
10	Ceryan	2104	SVM	φ, PDI	UCS	24	23	11.87	-
11	Ceryan	2104	RVM	φ, PDI	UCS	24	23	10.77	-
12	Ceryan	2104	ANN	φ, PDI	UCS	24	23	14.69	-
13	Mishra et al.	2015	ANN	BPI, PLS, SHN, Vp	UCS	44	15	16.9	-
14	Mishra et al.	2015	FIS	BPI, PLS, SHN, Vp	UCS	44	15	9.54	-
15	Mishra et al.	2015	ANFIS	BPI, PLS, SHN, Vp	UCS	44	15	13.72	-
16	This study	-	ANFIS	depth, Vp, ρ (RHOB log)	UCS, μ	436	219	5.24	0.025

where:
SHN: Schmidt Hammer number
PLS: point load strength
S_T : tensile strength
φ: porosity

BPI: Block punch index
PDI: P-durability index
V_u: ultrasonic velocity
S: saturation

PLI: point load index
E_m : modulus of elasticity
Vp: P-wave velocity
ρ: density

References

[1] Chang, Ch., Zoback. M. D. & Khaksar, A. (2006). Empirical relations between rock strength and physical properties in sedimentary rocks. Journal of Petroleum Science and Engineering, vol. 51, no. 3, pp. 223–237.

[2] Bradford, I. D. R., Fuller, J., Thompson, P. J. & Walsgrove, T. R. (1998). Benefits of assessing the solids production risk in a North Sea reservoir using elastoplastic modeling. SPE/ISRM Eurock, Trondheim, Norway, 1998.

[3] Fjaer, E., Holt, R. M., Horsrud, P., Raaen, A. M. & Risnes, R. (1992). Petroleum Related Rock Mechanics. Amsterdam: Elsevier.

[4] Freyburg, E. (1972). Der Untere und mittlere Buntsandstein SW_Thuringen in seinen gesteinstechnicschen Eigenschaften. Ber. Dtsch. Ges. Geol. Wiss., vol. 17, no. 6, pp. 911–919.

[5] Horsrud, P. (2001). Estimating mechanical properties of shale from empirical correlations. SPE Drilling & Completion, vol. 16, no. 2, pp. 68–73.

[6] McNally, G. H. (1987). Estimation of coal measures rock strength using sonic and neutron logs. Journal of Applied Geophysics, vol. 24, no. 4-5, pp. 381–395.

[7] Moos, D., Zoback, M. D. & Bailey, L. (1999). Feasibility study of the stability of openhole multilaterals, SPE Mid-Continent Operations Symposium, Oklahoma City, Oklahoma, 1999

[8] Vernik, L., Bruno, M. & Bovberg, C. (1993). Empirical relations between compressive strength and porosity of siliciclastic rocks. International Journal of Rock Mechanics and Mining Sciences & Geomechanics Abstracts, vol. 3, no. 7, pp. 677–680.

[9] Noorani, R. & kordi, H. (2011). A Robust Approach to Estimate the Uniaxial Compressive Strength of Intact Rocks. 6th National Congress on Civil Engineering, Semnan University, Semnan, Iran, 2011.

[10] Amani, J. & Moeini, R. (2012). Prediction of shear strength of reinforced concrete beams using adaptive neuro-fuzzy inference system and artificial neural network. Scientia Iranica, Transactions A: Civil Engineering, vol. 19, no. 2, p.p. 242-248.

[11] Dadkhah, R. & Esfahani, N. (2013). Application of genetic programming to modeling of uniaxial compressive strength. Middle-East Journal of Scientific Research, vol. 15, no. 6, pp. 840-845.

[12] Ceryan, N. (2014). Application of support vector machines and relevance vector machines in predicting uniaxial compressive strength of volcanic rocks. Journal of African Earth Sciences, vol. 100, pp. 634–644.

[13] Mishra, D. A., Srigyan, M., Basu, A. & Rokade, P. J. (2015). Soft computing methods for estimating the uniaxial compressive strength of intact rock from index tests. International Journal of Rock Mechanics & Mining Sciences, vol. 80, pp. 418–424.

[14] Jalalnezhad, M. J. (2012). Prediction of gas hydrates formation rate in gas production and transport operations, using fuzzy logic. Master science thesis, petroleum department, Shahid Bahonar university of Kerman, Kerman, Iran. 2012.

[15] Jang, J. S. R., (1993). ANFIS: adaptive-network-based fuzzy inference systems. IEEE Transactions on Systems, vol. 23, no. 3, pp. 585–665.

[16] MATLAB user's guide. (2007). Fuzzy logic Toolbox user's guide (MATLAB CD-ROM). Mathworks, Inc, Natick, MA, USA, pp. 299.

[17] Feili, M. A., Ranjbar, M., Nezamabadi –Poor, H., Schaffie, M. & Ashena. R . (2011). Development of Neural Fuzzy System for Advanced Prediction of Bottomhole Circulating Pressure in Underbalanced Drilling Operations. Journal of Petroleum Science and Technology, vol. 29, no. 21, pp. 2282–2292.

[18] Yurdakul, M., Ceylan, H. & Akdas. H. (2011). A predictive model for Uniaxial compressive strength of carbonate rocks from Schmidt hardness. The 45th US Rock Mechanics/Geomechanics Symposium. San Francisco, CA, June 26–29, 2011.

[19] Martins, F., Begonha, A. & Braga, M. (2012). Prediction of the mechanical behavior of the Oporto granite using Data Mining techniques. Expert Systems with Applications, vol. 39, pp. 8778–8783.

[20] Mishra, D. A. & Basu, A. (2013). Estimation of uniaxial compressive strength of rock materials by index tests using regression analysis and fuzzy inference system. Engineering Geology, vol. 160, pp. 54–68.

10

IRDDS: Instance reduction based on Distance-based decision surface

J. Hamidzadeh

Faculty of Computer Engineering & Information Technology, Sadjad University of Technology, Mashhad, Iran.

Corresponding author: j_hamidzadeh@sadjad.ac.ir (J. Hamidzadeh).

Abstract

In instance-based learning, a training set is given to a classifier for classifying new instances. In practice, not all information in the training set is useful for classifiers. Therefore, it is convenient to discard irrelevant instances from the training set. This process is known as instance reduction, which is an important task for classifiers since through this process the time for classification or training could be reduced. Instance-based learning methods are often confronted with the difficulty of choosing the instances, which must be stored to be used during an actual test. Storing too many instances may result in large memory requirements and slow execution speed. In this paper, first, a Distance-based Decision Surface (DDS) is proposed and is used as a separate surface between the classes, and then an instance reduction method, which is based on the DDS is proposed, namely IRDDS (Instance Reduction based on Distance-based Decision Surface). Using the DDS with Genetic algorithm selects a reference set for classification. IRDDS selects the most representative instances, satisfying both of the following objectives: high accuracy and reduction rates. The performance of IRDDS is evaluated on real world data sets from UCI repository by the 10-fold cross-validation method. The results of the experiments are compared with some state-of-the-art methods, which show the superiority of the proposed method, in terms of both classification accuracy and reduction percentage.

Keywords: *Instance Reduction, Distance-based Decision Surface, Support Vector Machine, Genetic Algorithm.*

1. Introduction

In the pattern recognition, supervised classification is a procedure that assigns a label to an unclassified sample, trained by a set of previously classified samples. Classification is one of the most important goals of pattern recognition [1].

In the literature of data classification, there are some methods that classify data based on distance between new data and training samples. Instance reduction is a crucial task in some instance-based learning methods. Instance-based learning methods are often confronted with the difficulty of choosing the instances, which must be stored to be used during an actual test. Storing too many instances may result in a large memory occupation and decrement in execution speed. Actually, some training sets may contain non- or a little information, which can be either noisy or redundant. Therefore, a process will be needed to discard unwanted information from the training

set. In literature, this discarding process is known as the instance reduction process. As a result, after some of the instances have been removed from the training set, the amount of memory needed for storage and the time required for an actual test are reduced.

One main challenge in designing an instance reduction algorithm is the maintenance of border, central, or other sets of points. In this research, we have decided to maintain the border points because the internal ones do not affect the decision boundaries as much as the non-boundaries do [2-5]. Hence, the internal points can be removed with a low impact on classification accuracy. A large number of border points may be needed to define a border completely, so some methods maintain central points in order to use those instances which are the most typical of a particular class to classify instances close to them. This can affect the decision boundaries, because the decision boundaries depend on not only where the instances of one class lie, but also where those of the other classes lie.

In instance reduction, we often face a trade-off between the sample size and the classification accuracy [6]. A successful algorithm often reduces the size of the training set significantly without a significant reduction on classification accuracy. In some cases, classification accuracy can be even increased with the reduction of instances, when noisy instances are removed or decision boundaries are smoothed. A recently survey of different methods for data reduction can be seen in [7].

This paper focuses on the problem of reducing the size of the stored set of instances while trying to maintain classification accuracy. This is first accomplished by providing a survey of methods which have been employed to reduce the number of instances (that are needed in learning methods) and then by proposing an instance reduction technique based on the Distance-based Decision Surface (DDS) [8], namely IRDDS (Instance Reduction based on Distance-based Decision Surface). In [8], a weighted quadratic decision surface is derived. In this paper, we have derived an unweighted decision surface of order one.

The remainder of the paper is organized as follows: In section 2, a survey of instance reduction methods is presented. In section 3, the proposed Distance-based Decision Surface is introduced in subsection 3.1. The proposed instance reduction method (IRDDS) is introduced in subsection 3.2. Finally, the statistical stability of the proposed method is proved in subsection 3.3. An evaluation of the proposed method is presented in section 4 and its performance is compared to some state-of-the-art methods. Finally, in section 5, conclusions and future research direction are presented.

2. Survey of instance reduction methods and distance-based classifiers

Several methods have been proposed for instance reduction, some of which are surveyed in this section. Most of the methods discussed here use T as original instances in the training set and $S \subseteq T$ (S as a subset of T) as their representatives.

The Condensed Nearest Neighbor (CNN) [9] and the Edited Nearest Neighbor (ENN) [10] rules are the first two methods of instance reduction. The CNN begins by selecting one instance which belongs to any class from T randomly and puts it in S, and then each instance in T is classified by using only the instances in S. If an instance is

misclassified, it will be added to S in order to ensure that it will be classified correctly. This process will be repeated until there are no misclassified instances in T. Instance Based Learning Algorithms (IBn), introduced in [11], can be considered as editing methods. IB2 is an online learning method, similar to CNN, IB2 works by adding to an initially empty set (S) those instances that are not correctly classified by the edited set (S). Within this setting, a newly available instance that is not added to the edited set does not need to be stored. Since noisy instances are very likely to be misclassified, they are almost always maintained in the edited set. In order to overcome this weakness, the IB3 method uses a wait and see evidence gathering method to determine which of the kept instances are expected to perform well during classification.

The Reduced Nearest Neighbor (RNN) rule was introduced by Gates [12]. RNN algorithm starts with $S = T$ and removes each instance from S until further removal does not cause any other instances in T to be misclassified. RNN is computationally more expensive than Hart's Condensed Nearest Neighbor (CNN) rule, but it always produces a subset of CNN. Thus, RNN is less expensive in terms of computation and storage during the classification stage. Since the removed instance is not guaranteed to be classified correctly, this algorithm is able to remove noisy and internal instances while maintaining border points.

Another variant of CNN is the Generalized Condensed Nearest Neighbor (GCNN) [13], which is similar to CNN. However, GCNN assigns instances that satisfy an absorption criterion to S. The absorption is calculated in terms of the nearest neighbors and its rivals (the nearest instances of the other classes). An instance is absorbed or included in S if its distance compared to its nearest neighbor and its nearest rivals are not more than a threshold.

In ENN algorithm, S starts out the same as T, then any instance in S which does not agree with the majority of its k nearest neighbors is removed. This removes noisy instances as well as close border cases. It also maintains all internal points, which keep it from reducing the storage requirements as much as most of the other reduction methods do. A variant of this method is the Repeated ENN (RENN). The RENN applies the ENN algorithm repeatedly until all remaining instances have the majority of their neighbors with the same class. Another extension of ENN is all k-NN method [14]. This algorithm works as follows: for i = 1 to k, flag any instances which are not classified correctly by its i nearest neighbors, as bad. When the loop is repeated for k times, any instances which are flagged as bad are removed.

In order to reduce storage requirements and remove noisy instances, an instance t should be removed if all k of its neighbors are from the same class or even from a class other than t. This process removes noisy instances as well as internal ones, while maintaining border ones. Unlike most previous methods, there are some methods such as DROP1 to DROP5 which pay more attention to the order according to which instances have been removed [2]. In these methods, each instance t has k nearest neighbors (ordered from the nearest to the farthest) and those instances that have t as one of their k nearest neighbors are called the associates of t (sorted from the nearest to the farthest). The Iterative Case Filtering algorithm (ICF) was proposed in [15]. ICF is based on the Coverage and Reachable sets which are the neighboring set and associate set, respectively. The neighborhood set for an instance such as t is all the instances between t and the nearest enemy of t. The nearest enemy of t is the nearest instance from the other classes. Those instances that have t as one of their k nearest neighbors are called the associates set of t, where t is the training set. In this method, an instance t is flagged for removal if |Reachable(t)| > |Coverage(t)|, which means that more cases can solve t than t can solve itself, then all the instances flagged for removal will be deleted. Another method that finds border instances is proposed in [3], namely Prototype Selection by Clustering (PSC), which applies clustering algorithm. Two types of clustered regions are in PSC method, namely homogeneous and heterogeneous clusters. In homogeneous cluster, all instances are from the same class, whereas, in heterogeneous clusters, they are from different classes. Thus, two types of instances are in PSC, one of which is the mean of the instances in each homogeneous cluster and the other is from heterogeneous clusters as a border instance.

Evolutionary algorithms have been used for instance reduction, with promising results. The basic idea is to maintain a population of chromosomes, which represents solutions to the problem and evolves over time through a process of competition. In this evaluation, both data reduction and classification accuracy are considered. The examples of application of genetic algorithm and other evolutionary algorithms for instance reduction can be found in [16-18]. The CHC evolutionary algorithm [16] and Steady-State Memetic Algorithm (SSMA)

[17] are the most known evolutionary algorithms. In terms of instance selection, the SVM (Support Vector Machines) not only is a classifier but also an instance selection method. SVBPS (Support Vector Based Prototype Selection) is a wrapper method which is based on SVM [19]. It works doing a double selection; the first one applies SVM to obtain the support vectors and the second one applies DROP2 over the support vectors. FRPS (Fuzzy Rough Prototype Selection) is a fuzzy-based method which is introduced in [20]. It uses fuzzy rough set theory to express the quality of the instances and uses a wrapper method to determine which instances to be removed.

Nikolaidis and et. al. introduced a multi-stage method for instance reduction and abstraction in [5], namely Class Boundary Preserving (CBP) algorithm. CBP is a hybrid method which selects and abstracts instances from training set that are close to the class boundaries. In the first stage of CBP, using ENN algorithm smooths the class boundaries. In the second stage, it tries to distinguish between border and non-border instances by using the geometric characteristics of the instance distribution. In the third stage, border instances are pruned by using the concept of mutual neighborhood, and in the last stage, the non-border instances are clustered.

Hamidzadeh and et. al. introduced a Large Symmetric Margin Instance Selection method, namely LAMIS [21]. LAMIS removes non-border instances and keeps border ones. This method presents an instance reduction process through formulating it as a constrained binary optimization problem and solves it by employment filled function algorithm. In LAMIS, the core of instance selection process is based on keeping the hyperplane that separates a two-class data, to provide large margin separation. These authors introduced another instance reduction method in [4]. This method is based on hyperrectangle clustering, called Instance Reduction Algorithm using Hyperrectangle Clustering (IRAHC). IRAHC removes interior instances and keeps border and near border ones. This method presents an instance reduction process based on hyperrectangle clustering. A hyperrectangle is an n-dimensional rectangle with axes aligned sides, which is defined by min and max points and a corresponding distance function. The min-max points are determined by using the hyperrectangle clustering algorithm. In IRAHC, the core of instance reduction process is based on the set of hyperrectangles.

A survey of the related classifiers is given below. Classification can be done based on sample properties, one of which is distance. Distance is a numerical description of how much objects are departed. In the Euclidean space $\Re^n$, the distance between two points is usually given by the Euclidean distance (2-norm distance). Based on other norms, different distances are used such as 1-, p- and infinity-norm. In classification, various distances can be employed to measure the closeness, such as the Euclidean, Mahalanobis [22] or bands distance [23].

In literature of data classification, there are some methods that classify data based on the distance between new unseen data and training samples. One of the classifiers is Minimum Distance Classifier (MDC) [1]. It classifies an unknown sample into a category to which the nearest prototype pattern belongs. In this classifier a Euclidean distance is used as the metric. Senda et al. based on karhunen-loeve expansion omit the redundant calculations of MDC [24].

3. The proposed method

In this section, first we propose a distance-based decision surface and then a new method for instance reduction, namely IRDDS (Instance Reduction based on Distance-based Decision Surface) is introduced. IRDDS is based on the proposed DDS. For two given classes, we calculate the average distances of all the training samples. Unclassified samples are classified as a class that has the smaller average distance. Applying such a rule leads to derive a formula to be used as the decision surface. Afterwards, we present an instance reduction method based on DDS by employing genetic algorithm.

The proposed Distance-based Decision Surface is introduced in subsection 3.1. Also, a kernel extension of DDS is introduced in this subsection. The proposed instance reduction method (IRDDS) is introduced in subsection 3.2. Finally, the statistical stability of the proposed method is proved in subsection 3.3.

The steps of IRDDS are described as follow: In the first step of IRDDS, the original training sample is considered. In the second step of IRDDS, a proper distance-based surface, namely DDS, is obtained by using parameter tuning which is described in subsections 3.1 and 3.2. In the next two steps, the instance reduction is done based on DDS using Genetic Algorithm. This step of IRDDS is described in subsection 3.2. Finally, the reduced training sample is obtained through IRDDS.

3.1. Distance-based Decision Surface (DDS)

In this subsection, we derive a formula to

determine the decision surface between two classes of samples. Let $d_1(x, x_i)$ denote distance of the test sample x to the training sample of the first class and denote distance of the test sample x to the training sample of the second class. DDS is based on the distance between unclassified sample x and samples of two classes. The goal is to determine decision surface in a way that the average distances from the two classes are equal. Hence, (1) is employed to determine the decision surface.

$$\frac{1}{n_1}\sum_{i=1}^{n_1}d_1(x,x_i)=\frac{1}{n_2}\sum_{j=1}^{n_2}d_2(x,x_j) \tag{1}$$

The average distance of x from all samples in each class is shown in (1), so a decision surface can be derived. In (1), and are used as the number of training samples for the first and second classes respectively. It should be noted that d(*,*) calculates the distance between two points and the same distance function is used in (1). We can derive a linear equation as a decision surface from (1). Therefore, to classify a new unclassified sample, we have presented a formula as the decision surface.

Here, we use the Euclidean distance (2-norm). Thus, substituting distances with this norm gives (2).

$$\begin{aligned}x^Tx\,(n_2n_1)-2x^T\left(n_2\sum_{i=1}^{n_1}x_i\right)+n_2\sum_{i=1}^{n_1}x_i^Tx_i=\\ x^Tx\,(n_1n_2)-2x^T\left(n_1\sum_{j=1}^{n_2}x_j\right)+n_1\sum_{j=1}^{n_2}x_j^Tx_j\end{aligned} \tag{2}$$

The proposed decision surface is derived where a and b are defined as in (3) and (4), respectively,

$$a=2n_1n_2\,((\sum_{j=1}^{n_2}x_j)/n_2-(\sum_{i=1}^{n_1}x_i)/n_1) \tag{3}$$

$$b=n_2\sum_{i=1}^{n_1}x_i^Tx_i-n_1\sum_{j=1}^{n_2}x_j^Tx_j \tag{4}$$

$$F(x)=ax+b=0 \tag{5}$$

A linear decision surface is shown in (5), which is called Distance-based Decision Surface (DDS). To classify a test sample such as x, it is sufficient to determine the sign of (5). Input test sample cannot properly be classified if the sign of decision surface is neither positive nor negative. In this situation the label of the sample is randomly assigned.

Kernel methods are powerful statistical learning techniques, which are widely applied to various learning algorithms [25]. Kernel methods can be employed to transform samples into a high dimensional space. In the high dimensional space, various methods can be employed to separate samples linearly. A mapping function denoted can be employed to transform samples into a high dimensional space. By using kernel function, the inner products between the images of the data can be substituted in the feature space. As a result, we have (6).

$$K(x,y) = <\varphi(x), \varphi(y)> = \varphi(x)^T \varphi(y) \qquad (6)$$

Thus, using (1) and Euclidean distance in the high dimensional feature space gives (7).

$$n_2 \times \sum_{i=1}^{n_1} \left[(\varphi(x) - \varphi(x_i))^T (\varphi(x) - \varphi(x_i)) \right] =$$
$$n_1 \times \sum_{j=1}^{n_2} \left[(\varphi(x) - \varphi(x_j))^T (\varphi(x) - \varphi(x_j)) \right] \qquad (7)$$

Using (6) in (7) gives:

$$n_2 \times \sum_{i=1}^{n_1} \left[k(x,x) - 2k(x,x_i) + k(x_i,x_i) \right] =$$
$$n_1 \times \sum_{j=1}^{n_2} \left[k(x,x) - 2k(x,x_j) + k(x_j,x_j) \right] \qquad (8)$$

Using Radial Basis Function (RBF) kernel in (8) gives:

$$n_1 \sum_{j=1}^{n_2} \exp(-\frac{\|x-x_j\|^2}{2\sigma^2}) - n_2 \sum_{i=1}^{n_1} \exp(-\frac{\|x-x_i\|^2}{2\sigma^2}) = 0 \qquad (9)$$

As a result of using this kernel function, we have a nonlinear decision surface as shown in (9).

3.2. Reduction based on DDS using genetic algorithm

In the context of data reduction, we are required to reduce instances while maintaining the data classification accuracy. Hence, in the reduction of instances, we often face a trade-off between the sample size and the classification accuracy. Therefore, instance reduction is a multi-objective optimization problem that attempts to maximize the classification accuracy and, at the same time, minimizes the sample size. The issue of measuring the classification accuracy is associated with the sample quality issue, in which we aim to achieve the best representative sample with the minimum size. In DDS algorithm, it is better to use the stored instances during generalization in order to avoid excessive storage, time complexity, and possibly to improve generalization by avoiding noise and overfitting. DDS maintains all the training instances. It learns very quickly, because it needs only to read the training set without any further processing. Hence, it

generalizes better for many applications. However, it has relatively large memory requirements because it stores all the training instances. It must make computation through all available instances in order to classify a new input sample, so it is slow during the classification task. Moreover, since it stores all instances in the training set, noisy instances are stored as well, and can degrade the classification accuracy. On the other hand, when some of the instances are removed from the training set, the storage requirements and time needed for generalization are correspondingly reduced. This subsection focuses on the problem of reducing the size of the stored set of instances while trying to maintain or even improve the classification accuracy. In this subsection, we propose a new method for instance reduction that is based on DDS, namely IRDDS (Instance Reduction based on Distance-based Decision Surface).

Genetic Algorithms (GA) are optimization processes inspired in natural evolution laws. In this paper, a binary genetic algorithm is applied to optimize the bit-stream in order to implement instance reduction based on DDS. Hence, the process is carried out for instance reduction (for two classes) by applying a binary GA as follows:

a) The binary chromosome consists of n1+n2 gens, where n1 and n2 are the number of instances in the first and second classes, respectively. Each gene can have two possible states: 0 or 1. If the gene is 1, then its associated instance will be maintained. If it is 0, then its associated instance will be discarded.

b) The cost function (fitness function) that must be minimized can be defined as follows:

The cost function is the combination of the two following terms: the reverse of sample reduction rate and the classification error rate. The cost function = A + B, where A equals weight multiplied by inverse of RedRate, and B equals (1-weight) multiplied by error_rate. The sample reduction rate (RedRate) is defined as the discarded training sample size divided by the original training sample size.

c) GA is applied in order to obtain a subset of the training samples that minimizes the cost function.

The weight parameter that is used in the cost function is found to obtain a quite good trade-off between storage requirements and achieved error rate for the experiments, which have been conducted in this paper. The weight parameter takes values in interval [0, 1]. Regarding the parameters, we preserved the value of weight=0.5 as the best choice, due to the fact that it was analysed in the previous work related to instance selection [26]. During the training process, the cost function over the validation set is calculated for the best individual of each population. The individual that achieves the lowest cost value over the validation set is selected as the final individual. The other GA parameters that have been used in the experiments are reported in the next section.

3.3. Statistical stability of the proposed method

Statistical stability is the most fundamental, which means the patterns, which are identified by the algorithm, and really genuine patterns of the data source but not just an accidental relation occurring in the finite training set. This property can be considered as the statistical robustness of the output in the sense that if we rerun the algorithm on a new sample from the same source, it should identify a similar pattern. Proving that a given pattern is indeed significant and is the concern of 'learning theory', a body of principles and methods that estimate the reliability of pattern functions under appropriate assumptions about the way in which the data was generated. The Rademacher complexity measures the capacity of a class. It assesses the capacity of the class by its ability to fit random noise. The difference between empirical and true estimation over the pattern class can be bounded in terms of its Rademacher complexity [27].

The following theorem can be used to derive an upper-bound of the generalization error in terms of Rademacher complexity for the proposed method [27].

Theorem: Let P be a probability distribution on Z, where Z be training samples drawn according to P with probability at least $1-\delta$, the proposed function f (or DDS classifier) satisfies:

$$P(y \neq f(x)) \leq \hat{P}_n (y \neq f(x)) +$$

$$2\sqrt{\frac{E(k(X,X))}{n}} + \sqrt{\frac{\ln(\frac{1}{\delta})}{2n}} \qquad (10)$$

where, function f is as:

$$f(x) = \sum_{i=1}^{n} \mu_i k(x, x_i) \qquad (11)$$

For obtaining the upper bound in theorem 1, at first, we prove (12). This inequality shows the empirical complexity measure of the proposed function f.

$$\hat{G}_n(f) \leq \frac{2}{n} \left[\sum_{i=1}^{n} k(x_i, x_i) \right]^{\frac{1}{2}} \qquad (12)$$

$$F = \left\{ \sum_{i=1}^{n} \mu_i k(x, x_i) : n \in N, x_i \in X \right\} \subseteq$$
$$\left\{ <w, \Phi(x) > : \|w\| \leq 1 \right\} \qquad (13)$$

According to the Sup properties, Cauchy Schwarz and Jensen's inequality, we have

$$\hat{G}_n(F) \leq \frac{2}{n} E \left[(\sum_{i=1}^{n} \sum_{j=1}^{n} g_i g_j k(x_i, x_j))^{\frac{1}{2}} | X_i \right]$$
$$\leq \frac{2}{n} \left(\sum_{i=1}^{n} \sum_{j=1}^{n} E \left[g_i g_j k(x_i, x_j) | X_i \right] \right)^{\frac{1}{2}} \qquad (14)$$

Finally, we obtain (15) and the theorem proved.

$$G_n(F) = E(\hat{G}_n(F)) \leq E \left(\frac{2}{n} \left(\sum_{i=1}^{n} k(x_i, x_i) \right)^{\frac{1}{2}} \right) =$$
$$\frac{2}{n} E(\sqrt{\sum_{i=1}^{n} k(x_i, x_i)}) = \frac{2}{n} E(\sqrt{n \times \|\varphi(x)\|^2}) = \qquad (15)$$
$$\frac{2}{n} E(\|\varphi(x)\| \times \sqrt{n}) = \frac{2}{\sqrt{n}} R$$

4. Experimental results

In this section, at first, SVM and DDS classifiers have been compared, and then IRDDS is compared with the some state-of-the-art instance reduction methods. Extensive experiments have been conducted to evaluate the performance of the proposed method against five state-of-the-art instance selection methods using some real world data sets.

In order to validate IRDDS, experiments have been conducted over the real world data sets which have been taken from the UCI data set repository [28]. The selected data sets and their characteristics are shown in table 1. In this table, #samples, #features, and #classes denote the number of instances, the number of attributes, and the number of classes, respectively.

The data sets are grouped into two categories depending on the size they have (a horizontal line divides them in the table). The small data sets have less than 1000 instances and the larger data sets have more than 1000 instances. In each group, the data sets have been sorted increasingly depending on their #classes.

In the first experiment, SVM and DDS classifiers have been compared. To this end, the classifiers have been tested on the first group of the data sets (the small size data sets).

Table 1. Selected data sets of UCI data repository [28].

No.	Data Set	#samples	#features	#classes
1	Ionosphere	351	34	2
2	Sonar	208	60	2
3	Wdbc	569	30	2
4	Liver	345	6	2
5	Haberman	306	3	2
6	Heart	267	44	2
7	Pima	768	8	2
8	Musk	476	167	2
9	Trans	748	4	2
10	Iris	150	4	3
11	Vehicle	846	18	4
12	Glass	214	9	7
13	Ecoli	336	7	8
14	Vowel	990	10	11
15	Census	299,285	41	2
16	Satimage	4435	36	6
17	Segment	2310	19	7
18	Shuttle	43500	9	7
19	Yeast	1484	8	10
20	Pendigits	3498	16	10
21	Poker	350,000	10	10
22	Letter	15000	16	26

The experimental results (without instance reduction for the DDS) are summarized in table 2. Note that the values in table 2 denote the error classification rates in percentage. For multiclass classification, we can use classification by pairwise coupling. In this paper, we have used the voting approach in comparison to the classifier output approaches for the extension of two-class classifier as multiclass classifier.

In order to show the performance of IRDDS, it was compared against the other reduction methods, which include BEPS, LAMIS, DROP3, IRAHC and PSC, using k-NN with k=3 and the Euclidean distance. All the methods have been tested on all the data sets in terms of classification error rate and reduction percentage performance measures. Table 3 shows the results obtained using the competing methods. For each method,

the average classification error rates (Err) and the reduction percentages (Red) are shown. As already mentioned, instance reduction is a multi-objective optimization problem.

Therefore, table 5 presents both classification error rates and instance reduction percentages for all the competing methods and all the data sets. The reduction percentages are the ratio of the number of discarded instances to the number of instances in the original data set multiplied by 100.

Table 2. The classification error rates (percent) and their parameters.

Data Set	SVM			DDS	
	C	δ	Rate	δ	Rate
Ionosphere	2	4	**3.99**	0.1	5.12
Sonar	0.8	8	14.42	0.4	**11.06**
Wdbc	4	2	4.92	1	**2.99**
Liver	2	4	**26.96**	8	32.46
Haberman	2	2	24.84	12	**24.18**
Heart	1	4	**16.85**	0.8	17.60
Pima	4	4	**27.08**	4	29.43
Musk	0.2	16	17.15	0.2	**14.20**
Trans	8	2	**18.45**	8	19.10
Iris	0.2	2	3.33	0.2	**2.67**
Vehicle	2	8	23.95	1	**19.10**
Glass	4	2	28.50	0.1	28.50
Ecoli	4	4	**12.80**	0.1	13.39
Vowel	1	2	24.15	0.4	**19.84**

In table 5, for each data set, the best methods have been highlighted in terms of its instance reduction percentage or error rate. As can be seen, in the cases of problems, which IRDDS could not attain the highest reduction percentage, this method has almost the lowest error rate.

Overall, among the competing methods, IRDDS exhibits the best average of instance reduction percentage.

As already mentioned, instance reduction is a two-objective optimization problem and a gain in one objective becomes unpleasant with the other objective. Therefore, table 3 presents both classification error rates and reduction percentages for all the competing methods and all the data sets. There are some major factors that affect different performances of IRDDS and the other methods used for instance reduction in each problem or data set. First of all, the complexity of classes in each problem is a key factor in instance reduction percentage. Secondly, there are noises and outliers in each problem differently. In table 4, average ranks in terms of error rate and reduction percentage are shown separately.

Table 4 indicates that, it is clear that IRDDS exhibits good average rank in terms of both error rate and reduction percentage. IRDDS obtains the best classification error rate and the second best

instance reduction percentage ranks among the competing methods. Overall, IRDDS exhibits good results in both classification error rates and instance reduction percentages.

In order to compare the execution speed of the competing methods, the average computation times of IRDDS and the other methods measured in seconds per run are reported in table 5. It includes training time. Time required to reduce the training set averaged over the training sub sets in 10-fold cross validation.

Table 3. Average error rates (Err) and reduction percentages (Red) of IRDDS and the other methods.

Data Set	BEPS		LAMIS		DROP3		IRAHC		PSC		IRDDS	
	Err	Red	Err	Red	Err	Red	Err	Red	Err	Red	Err	Red
Ionosphere	15.20	68.24	15.13	79.62	17.32	55.70	**14.86**	89.87	18.94	43.79	**14.86**	**96.90**
Sonar	14.09	80.12	12.23	**90.35**	27.55	72.11	**10.23**	90.01	20.24	64.59	15.23	75.87
Wdbc	14.90	45.87	17.31	66.93	18.93	28.12	16.89	66.72	21.62	43.59	**4.85**	**89.75**
Liver	34.68	54.13	32.79	**77.92**	35.02	66.84	32.45	76.36	44.64	54.13	**25.30**	60.55
Haberman	26.70	80.30	23.54	**83.51**	33.40	80.90	**22.62**	84.85	36.38	64.70	23.74	48.28
Heart	**21.38**	27.85	32.13	88.95	36.22	88.11	31.72	**88.15**	35.59	46.92	22.72	85.07
Pima	26.03	58.43	24.29	89.21	30.30	**94.46**	**23.53**	89.06	29.83	56.94	25.13	67.15
Musk	16.03	81.60	15.01	48.38	28.72	47.49	14.63	48.50	27.84	31.59	**13.80**	**82.50**
Trans	25.80	71.24	24.93	89.47	30.19	82.07	25.78	89.02	28.73	43.76	**25.19**	**91.10**
Iris	4.31	69.32	3.47	73.87	4.27	68.10	3.87	75.68	5.34	**79.55**	**3.0**	71.26
Vehicle	35.19	90.32	32.69	91.40	47.07	90.10	**29.95**	90.13	38.75	67.45	32.92	**92.18**
Glass	23.78	87.35	20.85	**89.63**	27.68	77.46	**19.85**	88.45	40.91	61.55	24.95	60.23
Ecoli	13.87	71.40	**15.12**	**88.71**	19.45	74.16	15.49	87.03	18.62	73.84	18.29	81.38
Vowel	**8.50**	76.94	9.14	84.96	9.31	65.41	8.54	85.14	15.75	54.76	8.91	**87.19**
Census	27.43	54.10	26.18	73.90	22.65	65.98	28.70	54.60	24.65	**77.78**	**19.32**	66.50
Satimage	6.04	82.35	**5.13**	75.87	7.07	74.80	11.25	54.10	7.33	62.85	6.50	**84.02**
Segment	7.01	68.02	**6.12**	56.29	9.60	**80.36**	18.13	60.20	13.45	44.29	10.75	48.12
Shuttle	19.10	58.97	17.84	62.54	26.81	49.31	21.16	46.10	13.67	69.10	**13.08**	**70.23**
Yeast	44.60	78.06	43.01	82.97	43.82	82.86	42.67	83.70	46.96	56.80	**42.11**	**84.36**
Pendigits	6.01	75.23	5.19	90.04	3.46	85.18	4.28	90.63	5.68	**93.77**	**2.15**	31.52
Poker	28.34	62.95	32.14	65.10	29.73	73.56	27.98	48.20	42.93	73.96	**21.36**	**76.10**
Letter	7.01	67.30	6.14	82.59	15.76	48.38	5.62	83.97	20.65	81.67	**4.18**	**85.10**

Table 4. Average ranks in terms of error rate and reduction percentage ranks.

Average rank	BEPS	LAMIS	DROP3	IRAHC	PSC	IRDDS
Error rate (Err)	3.43 (4)	3.24 (3)	4.65 (5)	2.80 (2)	5.26 (6)	2.11 (1)
Reduction percentage (IR)	4.33 (5)	2.48 (1)	3.96 (4)	3.04 (3)	4.45 (6)	2.73 (2)

Table 5: Average computational times of IRDDS and the other methods measured in seconds per run.

Data set	BEPS	LAMIS	DROP3	IRAHC	PSC	IRDDS
Ionosphere	6.1(5)	3.8(2.5)	7.5 (6)	3.2(1)	4.1 (4)	3.8 (2.5)
Sonar	0.98(1)	1.43(5)	1.3 (3)	1.3(3)	1.7 (6)	1.3 (3)
Wdbc	37.1(5)	5.28(2)	87.34 (6)	4.8(1)	5.8 (3)	19.4 (4)
Liver	3.8(1)	15.18(5)	5.0 (2)	14.8(3)	16.8 (6)	15.03 (4)
Haberman	4.0(5)	2.30(2)	4.1 (6)	2.1(1)	2.6 (3)	3.5 (4)
Heart	1.12(1)	2.46(6)	2.2 (2)	2.4(4.5)	2.3 (3)	2.4 (4.5)
Pima	38.6(5)	5.6(3)	83.5 (6)	4.7(1)	6.5 (4)	5.1 (2)
Musk	19.8(5)	4.15(3)	75.10(6)	3.5(2)	4.3(4)	1.2(1)
Trans	37.9(5)	5.8(3)	82.06(6)	5.3(2)	6.4(4)	5.2(1)
Iris	0.7(1)	3.04(5)	0.8 (2)	2.9(3.5)	3.16 (6)	2.9 (3.5)
Vehicle	26.6(5)	6.2(2)	86.38(6)	5.3(1)	7.10(4)	6.34(3)
Glass	1.6(4)	1.16(1)	1.5 (2)	1.6(4)	1.7 (6)	1.6 (4)
Ecoli	7.5(5)	2.91(3)	8.2 (6)	2.8(1.5)	3.2 (4)	2.8 (1.5)
Yeast	71.8(5)	6.8(2)	76.90(6)	5.8(1)	7.13(4)	6.95(3)
Vowel	51.6(5)	6.4(2)	58.12(6)	6.2(1)	8.39(3)	8.40(4)
Census	487,131.12(5)	32,452.06(3)	500,260.8(6)	28,325.87(1)	73,629.1 (2)	85,201.0 (4)
Satimage	119.6(1)	154.42(4)	130.92(2)	149.18(3)	184.36(5)	192.10(6)
Segment	89.6(3)	83.41(2)	7624.9 (6)	79.80(1)	107.67 (5)	96.05 (4)
Shutlle	8943.7(2)	613.34(1)	9938.12(3)	10276.38(4)	11083.64(5)	12541.18(6)
Pendigits	97.4(1)	123.62(4)	11587.3 (6)	98.70(2)	158.5 (3)	146.93 (5)
Poker	13,350.11(3)	6430.24(2)	728,851.6(6)	852.23(1)	93,436.8 (4)	142,106.4(5)
Letter	492.6(1)	517.17(3)	504.02(2)	601.4(4)	716.84(6)	698.76(5)
Average rank	3.39	3.06	4.70	2.07	4.22	3.57

5. Conclusions and future research

In this paper, a new instance reduction procedure is presented. The introduced method employs a Distance-based Decision Surface (DDS) and Genetic algorithm, called IRDDS. In IRDDS, we proposed a decision surface for a binary classification process. An input test sample with respect to the decision surface can be assigned to one of the two classes.

The experiment results show IRDDS is the best among all the other methods. IRDDS obtains the best classification error rate and the second best instance reduction percentage ranks among the competing methods. Overall, IRDDS exhibits good results in both classification error rates and instance reduction percentages. The performance of IRDDS is demonstrated through the experiments, and the results show that IRDDS has good robustness in noisy cases. The results clearly demonstrate that IRDDS often yields the most robust performance over the data sets.

IRDDS is an offline method. As future research, we are interested in extending it to use for online applications, such as data stream.

References

[1] Duda, R. O., et al. (2001). Pattern classification. New York: Wiley Interscience Publication.

[2] Wilson, D. R. & Martinez, T. R. (2000). Reduction techniques for instance-based learning algorithms. Machine Learning, vol. 38, pp. 257–286.

[3] Olvera-Lo´pez, J. A., Carrasco-Ochoa, J. A. & Martı´nez-Trinidad, J. F. (2010). A new fast prototype selection method based on clustering. Pattern Analysis and Applications, vol. 13, no. 2, pp. 131-141.

[4] Hamidzadeh, J., Monsefi, R., & Yazdi, H. S. (2015). IRAHC: Instance Reduction Algorithm using Hyperrectangle Clustering. Pattern Recognition, vol. 48, pp. 1878–1889.

[5] Nikolaidis, K., Goulermasn, J. Y. & Wu, Q. H. (2011). A class boundary preserving algorithm for data condensation. Pattern Recognition, vol. 44, pp. 704–715.

[6] Liu, H. & Motoda, H. (2002). On Issues of Instance Selection. Data Mining Knowledge Discovery, vol. 6, pp. 115-130.

[7] Garcı´a, S., Derrac, J., Cano, J. R. & Herrera, F. (2012). Prototype selection for nearest neighbor classification: taxonomy and empirical study. IEEE Transactions on Pattern and Machine Intelligence, vol. 34, no. 3, pp. 417 – 435.

[8] Hamidzadeh, J., Monsefi, R. & Sadoghi Yazdi, H. (2012). DDC: distance-based decision classifier. Neural Computation & Application, no. 21, pp. 1697–1707.

[9] Hart, P. (1968). The condensed nearest neighbor rule. IEEE Transaction on Information Theory, vol. 14, pp. 515–516.

[10] Wilson, D. (1972). Asymptotic properties of nearest neighbor rules using edited data. IEEE Transactions on Systems, Man and Cybernetics, vol. 2, pp. 408–421.

[11] Aha, D. W. & Kibler D. (1991). Instance-based learning algorithms. Machine Learning, vol. 6, no. 1, pp. 37–66.

[12] Gates, G. W. (1972). The Reduced Nearest Neighbor Rule. IEEE Transactions on Information Theory, vol. 18, no. 3, pp. 431-433.

[13] Chien-Hsing, C., Bo-Han, K. & Fu, C. (2006). The generalized condensed nearest neighbor rule as a data reduction method. Proceedings of the 18th international conference on pattern recognition, IEEE Computer Society, Hong-Kong, pp. 556–559, 2006.

[14] Tomek I. (1976). An experiment with the edited nearest-neighbor rule. IEEE Transactions on Systems, Man and Cybernetics, vol. 6, no. 6, pp. 448–452.

[15] Brighton, H. & Mellish, C. (2002). Advances in instance selection for instance-based learning algorithms. Data Mining and Knowledge Discovery, vol. 6, no. 2, pp. 153–172.

[16] Cano, J. R., Herrera, F. & Lozano, M. (2003). Using evolutionary algorithms as instance selection for data reduction in KDD: an experimental study. IEEE Transactions on Evolutionary Computation, vol. 7, no. 6, pp. 561–575.

[17] Garcia, S., Cano, J. R. & Herera, F. (2008). A memetic algorithm for evolutionary prototype selection: a scaling up Approach. Pattern Recognition, vol. 41, pp. 2693–2709.

[18] Olvera-Lopez, A. J., Carrasco-Ochoa, J. F., Martinez-Trinidad, J. A. & Kittler, J. (2010). A review of instance selection methods. Artificial Intelligence Review, vol. 34, pp. 133–143.

[19] Li, Y., Hu, Z., Cai, Y. & Zhang, W. (2005). Support vector based prototype selection method for nearest neighbor rules. Lecture Notes in Computer Science, vol. 3610, pp. 528-535.

[20] Verbiest, N., Cornelis, C. & Herrera, F. (2013). FRPS: A Fuzzy Rough Prototype Selection method, Pattern Recognition, vol. 46, no. 10, pp. 2770-2782.

[21] Hamidzadeh, J., Monsefi, R., & Yazdi, H. S. (2014). Large symmetric margin instance selection algorithm. International Journal of Machine Learning and Cybernetics, doi:10.1007/s13042-014-0239-z.

[22] Cevikalp, H., Larlus, D., Douze, M. & Jurie, F. (2007). Local subspace classifiers: linear and nonlinear approaches. IEEE Workshop on Machine Learning for Signal Processing, 2007.

[23] Laguia, M. & Castro, J. L. (2008). Local distance-based classification. Knowledge-Based Systems, vol. 21, pp. 692-703.

[24] Senda, S., Minoh, M. & Ikeda, K. (1995). A fast algorithm for the minimum distance classifier and its application to kanji character recognition. Proceedings of the Third International Conference on Document Analysis and Recognition, vol. 1, pp. 283-286, 1995.

[25] Pekalska, E. & Hassdonk, B. (2009). Kernel discriminant analysis for positive definite and indefinite kernels. IEEE Transactions on Pattern and Machine Intelligence, vol. 31, no. 6.

[26] Garcı´a, S., Derrac, J., Luengo, J., Carmona, C. J. & Herrera, F. (2011). Evolutionary Selection of Hyperrectangles in Nested Generalized Exemplar Learning. Applied Soft Computing, vol. 11, pp. 3032-3045.

[27] Bartlett, P. L. & Mendelson, S. (2002). Rademacher and Gaussian Complexities: Risk Bounds and Structural Results. Journal of Machine Learning Research, vol. 3, pp. 463-482.

[28] UCI Machine Learning Repository (2013). Available: http://archive.ics.uci.edu/ml.

11

Multi-focus image fusion in DCT domain using variance and energy of laplacian and correlation coefficient for visual sensor networks

M. Amin-Naji and A. Aghagolzadeh[*]

Faculty of Electrical & Computer Engineering, Babol Noshirvani University of Technology, Babol, Iran.

Corresponding author: aghagol@nit.ac.ir (A. Aghagolzadeh).

Abstract

The purpose of multi-focus image fusion is to gather the essential information and the focused parts from the input multi-focus images into a single image. These multi-focus images are captured with different depths of focus of cameras. A lot of multi-focus image fusion techniques have been introduced using the focus measurement in the spatial domain. However, multi-focus image fusion processing is very time-saving and appropriate in discrete cosine transform (DCT) domain, especially when JPEG images are used in visual sensor networks. Thus most of the researchers are interested in focus measurement calculations and fusion processes directly in the DCT domain. Accordingly, many researchers have developed some techniques that substitute the spatial domain fusion process with the DCT domain fusion process. Previous works on the DCT domain have some shortcomings in the selection of suitable divided blocks according to their criterion for focus measurement. In this paper, calculation of two powerful focus measurements, energy of Laplacian and variance of Laplacian, are proposed directly in the DCT domain. Moreover, two other new focus measurements that work by measuring the correlation coefficient between the source blocks, and the artificial blurred blocks are developed completely in the DCT domain. However, a new consistency verification method is introduced as a post-processing, significantly improving the quality of the fused image. These proposed methods significantly reduce the drawbacks due to unsuitable block selection. The output image quality of our proposed methods is demonstrated by comparing the results of the proposed algorithms with the previous ones.

Keywords: *Image Fusion, Multi-Focus, Visual Sensor Networks, Discrete Cosine Transform, Variance and Energy of Laplacian.*

1. Introduction

The image fusion process is defined as gathering all the important information from multiple images, and their inclusion into fewer images, usually a single one. This single image is more informative and accurate than any single source image, and it consists of all the necessary information. The purpose of image fusion is not only to reduce the amount of data but also to construct images that are more appropriate and understandable for the human and machine perception [1]. The ideal image consists of all the scene components that are completely transparent but due to intrinsic limitations in the system, it may not have a single image of the scene including all the necessary information and description of the object details. The main reason is the limited depth of focus in the optical lenses of CCD/CMOS cameras [2, 3]. Therefore, those objects that are only located in the special depth of focus are clear, and the others are blurred. To solve this problem, it is recommended to record multiple images of a scene with different depths of focus. The main idea of this work is to focus all the components in multiple captured images. Fortunately, in visual sensor networks (VSNs), there is a capability to increase the different depths of focus using a large number of cameras [4, 5]. In VSN, sensors are cameras recording images and video sequences. Despite its advantages, it has some limitations such as energy consumption, power, processing time, and limited bandwidth. Due to a huge amount of data created by camera sensors compared with the other sensors e.g. pressure, temperature, and microphone, energy consumption plays an important role in the lifetime of camera sensors [6, 7]. Therefore, it is important to process the local input images. In VSN, there are many camera nodes that are able to process the captured images locally, and collect the necessary information [8]. Due to the aforementioned reasons, multi-focus image fusion is manifested. It is a process that produces an image with all the unified components of a scene by merging multiple images with different depths of focus on the scene.

1.1. Related works

Several works have been carried out on image fusion in the spatial domain [9-19]. Many of these methods are complicated and suffer from being time-consuming as they are based upon the spatial domain. Image fusion based on the multi-scale transform is the most commonly used and very promising technique. Laplacian pyramid transform [20], gradient pyramid-based transform [21], morphological pyramid transform [22] and the premier ones, discrete wavelet transform (DWT) [23], shift-invariant wavelet transform (SIDWT) [24], and discrete cosine harmonic wavelet transform (DCHWT) [25] are some examples of the image fusion methods based on the multi-scale transform. These methods are complex and have some limitations e.g. processing time and energy consumption. For example, the multi-focus image fusion methods based on DWT require a lot of convolution operations, so it takes more time and energy for processing. Therefore, most of methods used in the multi-scale transform are not suitable for performing in real-time applications [4]. Moreover, these methods are not very successful in edge places due to missing the edges of the image in the wavelet transform process. However, they create ringing artefacts in the output image and reduce its quality.

Due to the aforementioned problems in the multi-scale transform methods, researchers are interested in multi-focus image fusion in the discrete cosine transform (DCT) domain. The DCT-based methods are more efficient in terms of

transmission and archiving images coded in Joint Photographic Experts Group (JPEG) standard to the upper node in the VSN agent. A JPEG system consists of a pair of encoder and decoder. In the encoder, images are divided into non-overlapping 8×8 blocks, and the DCT coefficients are calculated for each one of them. Since the quantization of DCT coefficients is a lossy process, many of the small-valued DCT coefficients are quantized to zero, which correspond to high frequencies. The DCT-based image fusion algorithms work more properly when the multi-focus image fusion methods are applied in the compressed domain [26]. In addition, in the spatial-based methods, the input images must be decoded and then transferred to the spatial domain. After implementation of the image fusion operations, the output fused images must again be encoded [27]. Therefore, the DCT domain-based methods do not require complex and time-consuming consecutive decoding and encoding operations. Therefore, the image fusion methods based on DCT domain operate with an extremely less energy and processing time.

Recently, a lot of research works have been carried out in the DCT domain. Tang [28] has introduced the DCT+Average and DCT+Contrast methods for multi-focus image fusion in the DCT domain. In the DCT+Average method, a fused image is created by a simple average of all DCT coefficients of input images. To create the DCT coefficients of the output 8×8 block in the DCT+Contrast method, the maximum coefficient value is selected for all 63 AC coefficients of input blocks, and the average DC coefficients for all the input image block is selected for DC coefficient of the output block. These two methods suffer from undesirable side-effects like blurring and blocking effects, so the output image quality is reduced.

Most of the DCT domain methods are inspirited from the spatial domain methods. Since the implementation of all focus measurements in the spatial domain is very easy and simple, researchers try to implement the algorithms in the DCT domain after a satisfactory calculation of the focus measurements in the spatial domain. Huang and Jing have reviewed and applied several focus measurements in the spatial domain for the multi-focus image fusion process, which are suitable for real-time applications [9]. They mentioned some focus measurements including variance, energy of image gradient (EOG), Tenenbaum's algorithm (Tenengrad), energy of Laplacian of the image (EOL), sum-modified-Laplacian (SML), and spatial frequency (SF). Their conducted experiments showed that EOL of the image gave results with a better performance than the other methods like variance and spatial frequency. Haghighat et al. [27] have calculated variance in the DCT domain, and replaced the multi-focus image fusion process based on the variance in the spatial domain by multi-focus image fusion process based upon variance in the DCT domain (DCT+Variance). In this method, variance is calculated in the DCT domain for all the 8×8 blocks that constitute the input images. This algorithm creates a merged output image by selecting the corresponding blocks with the largest variance values. In some cases, unsuitable blocks are selected for the output image because their variance values are very close to each other. Phamila has proposed the DCT+AC_Max method [29]. It selects the block with more number of higher values of the AC coefficient in the DCT domain. This method cannot always choose the suitable blocks because the number of higher values of AC coefficients as a focus criterion is invalid when the majority of AC coefficients are zero. Hence, it creates an unsuitable selection of the focused block. Li et al. [10] have introduced multi-focus image fusion based on the spatial frequency in the spatial domain. However, the experiments conducted in [9] showed that the spatial frequency algorithm had a better performance than the variance algorithm. Later, DCT domain spatial frequency multi-focus image fusion (DCT+SF) was introduced by Cao et al. [30]. The spatial frequency value is used as a focus criterion in this DCT-based method. Therefore, this algorithm selects the block with a higher value of the spatial frequency that is calculated for each DCT representation of the blocks. In [31], Sum of Modified Laplacian (SML) is used in the DCT domain for fusion of multi-focus images. The higher SML value is considered as a contrast criterion, and is used for block selection in the DCT+SML algorithm. These methods (DCT+SF and DCT+SML) are similar to the aforementioned prominent methods (DCT+Variance and DCT+AC_Max) in terms of unsuitable selection of focused blocks; thus it suffers from some undesirable side-effects like blocking effects and low quality of the output image.

These DCT-based methods use a post-processing called consistency verification (CV) in order to enhance the quality of the output fused image and reduce the error of unsuitable block selection. The current CV process does not completely enhance the output fused image occasionally. Thus in very rare cases, the quality enhancing is declined. However, the existing CV processes are also associated with the blocking effects.

1.2. Contributions of this paper

Due to the problems mentioned for the earlier DCT-based methods and possibility of unsuitable focused block selection, it is recommended to use an efficient and comprehensive DCT-based focus criterion with more functionality. Hongmei et al. [12] have introduced the multi-focus image fusion using EOL for the spatial domain. Pertuz et al. [14] have conducted various tests for 36 focus measurements, and reported that the Laplacian-based functions like VOL and EOL have the best performance over all the 36 focus measurements in normal multi-focus images. However, the experiments conducted in [9] show that EOL has better results than the variance and spatial frequency methods in the spatial domain.

In this paper, four new efficient focus criteria in the DCT domain for multi-focus image fusion algorithm are developed. In these new methods, the quality of the output image is increased, and the error due to unsuitable block selection is greatly reduced. Following in this paper:

- We introduce a method for convolving a 3×3 mask over the 8×8 block directly in the DCT domain. This algorithm in the DCT domain reassembles filtering a mask with the border replication in the spatial domain. Thus the Laplacian mask and Gaussian low pass mask could be convolved easily on the 8×8 block directly in the DCT domain.

- By artificial blurring the input blocks of multi-focus images with Gaussian low-pass filter, it is possible to measure the amount of occurring changes in the blocks with the correlation coefficient relation. Therefore, we derived an efficient focus measurement in the DCT domain by calculating the correlation coefficient relation in it. Moreover, we improved this focus measurement by combining the energy in the correlation coefficient relation.

- As the Laplacian of the block was achieved easily in the DCT domain by the proposed method, we tend to calculate the two other powerful focus measurements of Laplacian-based functions directly in the DCT domain. Thus this paper introduces the EOL and VOL calculations completely in the DCT domain.

- Finally, CV as a post-processing in multi-focus image fusion algorithms is enhanced by introducing repeated consistency verification (RCV). This process greatly enhances the decision map for constructing the output fused image, and it also prevents the blocking effects in the output image.

The rest of this paper is arranged as what follows: In the second section, a complete description of the proposed methods is introduced. Then in Section 3, the proposed algorithms are assessed with the previous prominent algorithms with different experiments. Finally, we conclude the paper.

2. Proposed methods

2.1 Preliminaries

In order to abridge the description of the proposed algorithms, two images were considered for image fusion process, although these algorithms could be used for more than two multi-focus images. We assumed that the input images were aligned by an image registration method. Figures 1 and 2 show two general structures of the proposed methods for fusion of the two multi-focus images. In what follows, we explain the steps of the proposed methods.

As the general structure of the first proposed approach is shown in figure 1, after dividing the source images into 8×8 blocks, their DCT coefficients are calculated. Then the artificial blurred blocks are obtained using the DCT representation of 8×8 blocks by the proposed DCT filtering method. In this paper, a new approach with vector processing is proposed for passing the blocks through a low-pass filter in the DCT domain. Mathematical calculations of the proposed DCT filtering are described in Section 2.3. It is obvious that the difference between the sharp image and its corresponding blurred image is more than the difference between the unsharped image and its corresponding blurred image. Therefore, the block that comes from a part of the focused image and has more details is changed more when it is passed through a low-pass filter. Consequently, the correlation coefficient value between the blocks before and after passing through a low-pass filter has a lower value for the

focused block than the non-focused block. Therefore, those blocks that are changed more due to passing through a low-pass filter have lower correlation coefficient values, so they are more suitable for selection in the output fused image. Following the aforementioned reason, condition (1) (given below) is suggested. Suppose that imA and imB belong to the focused and non-focused area, respectively. Condition (2) is redefined from condition (1) using a simple mathematical action.

$$corr(imA, \overline{imA}) < corr(imB, \overline{imB}) \qquad (1)$$

$$(1 - corr(imA, \overline{imA})) > (1 - corr(imB, \overline{imB})) \qquad (2)$$

On the other hand, the block energy is a useful criterion for measurement of the image contrast in that region. The main reason could be more details of the focused image and its larger coefficient value compared with the part of the non-focused image. This criterion has a significant impact on our algorithm in two stages. In the first stage, the energy of input images for each divided block is calculated. The block that has the highest energy should be selected for the output image. This selection is done using condition (3). In the second stage, the energy criterion can be used for the artificial blurred blocks that are obtained from the input blocks using condition (4).

$$energy(imA) > energy(imB) \qquad (3)$$

$$energy(\overline{imA}) > energy(\overline{imB}) \qquad (4)$$

where, imA, $\overline{imA}$, imB, and $\overline{imB}$ are the first input image block, artificial blurred of first input image block, second input image block, and artificial blurred of second input image block, respectively. A better output image quality is achieved using the correlation coefficient criterion for both energy measurements of block given in (3) and (4). The final condition is expressed as (5) by combining conditions (2), (3), and (4).

$$energy(imA) \times (1 - corr(imA, \overline{imA})) \times$$
$$energy(\overline{imA}) > energy(imB) \times \qquad (5)$$
$$(1 - corr(imB, \overline{imB})) \times energy(\overline{imB})$$

Condition (6), a simple form of condition (5), is the condition of the proposed method displayed by the Eng_Corr symbol.

$$Eng\_Corr(imA, \overline{imA})) > Eng\_Corr(imB, \overline{imB})) \qquad (6)$$

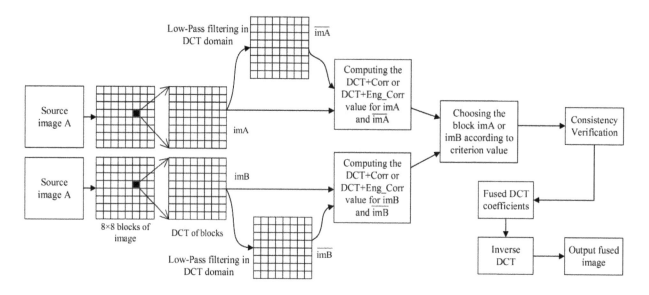

Figure 1. General structure of first approach in proposed methods.

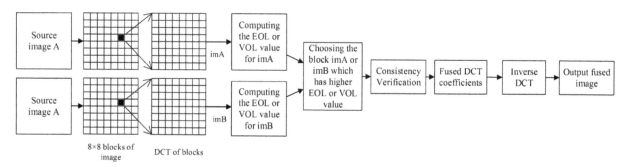

Figure 2. General structure of second approach in proposed methods.

In the second approach of the proposed methods, the focused block with two powerful focus measurements as EOL and VOL is selected. The region of the focused image has more information and high contrast. Subsequently, this region has more raised and evident edges. The amount and intensity of edges in an image are used as a criterion to specify the image quality and contrast. EOL and VOL are two appropriate measurements showing the amount of edges in an image. Therefore, the image block that comes from the focused area has higher EOL and VOL values than the block of the non-focused area. Thus the EOL and VOL values are calculated for every 8×8 block (*imA* and *imB*) in the DCT domain. The block with higher EOL or VOL values is considered as the focused area, and is selected for the output image.

2.2 Convolving a 3×3 mask on a 8×8 block in DCT domain

In order to convolve the 3×3 mask on an 8×8 block directly in the DCT domain, we have proposed a new method by defining 8×8 matrices

multiplied on the given block [32]. If the size of the mask is increased, the quality of the fused image by the proposed algorithms will be reduced for all kinds of multi-focus images in our implemented experiments. Besides this, with increase in the size of the mask, the algorithm complexity and computation time increase. In addition, for 8×8 blocks, 3×3 is very suitable. 5×5 is very large for an 8×8 block. The size of the mask is usually odd due to symmetry, which is logic in image processing. Therefore, according to the numerous conducted experiments, the 3×3 size of the mask is the best one for filtering the 8×8 blocks in terms of the output fused image quality, and also less algorithm complexity.

A 2D DCT of an $N \times N$ block of image b is given as (7):

$$B = C.b.C^t \tag{7}$$

where, C and C^t are the orthogonal matrices consisting of the DCT cosine kernel coefficients and the transpose coefficients, respectively, and B

is the DCT coefficient for the image matrix of b. For C, we have:

$$C^{-1} = C^t \qquad (8)$$

The inverse DCT of B is defined as (9):

$$b = C^t.B.C \qquad (9)$$

Usually, for still images, the correlation between pixels in both the horizontal and vertical directions is the same. Thus employing a symmetric mask is reasonable and justified. We assume that the mask has a horizontal and vertical symmetry, as (10):

$$\text{Mask} = \begin{array}{|c|c|c|} \hline X & Y & X \\ \hline Y & Z & Y \\ \hline X & Y & X \\ \hline \end{array} \qquad (10)$$

Based upon this method, some matrices are created, which are transferred to the DCT domain only one time after designing for every selected mask. They are also used in the block filtering process as constant matrices. For implementation of the first row of the mask, its first row is passed through the block; so matrix t is defined, which is multiplied by the block ($block \times t$). Since the first row of the mask is not related to the first row of the block, the first row of $block \times t$ should be zero. Thus it is necessary to multiply the lower shift matrix (l_8) by $block \times t$ (l_8 is an 8×8 matrix with one on the sub-diagonal, and zero elsewhere).

As the first and third rows of the mask are the same, for applying the third row of mask on the block, the upper shift matrix (u_8) is multiplied by $block \times t$ (u_8 is an 8×8 matrix with one on the super diagonal, and zero elsewhere). For implementation of the second row of the mask, its second row is passed through the block; thus matrix s is defined, which is multiplied by the block ($block \times s$). Finally, the result of convolution of mask and block is defined as (11):

$$output = (l_8.block.t) + (u_8.block.t)$$
$$+(block.s) = (lu.block.t) + (block.s) \qquad (11)$$

where, lu is the summation of l_8 and u_8, and matrices t and s are as follow:

$$t = \begin{pmatrix} Y & X & 0 & 0 & 0 & 0 & 0 & 0 \\ X & Y & X & 0 & 0 & 0 & 0 & 0 \\ 0 & X & Y & X & 0 & 0 & 0 & 0 \\ 0 & 0 & X & Y & X & 0 & 0 & 0 \\ 0 & 0 & 0 & X & Y & X & 0 & 0 \\ 0 & 0 & 0 & 0 & X & Y & X & 0 \\ 0 & 0 & 0 & 0 & 0 & X & Y & X \\ 0 & 0 & 0 & 0 & 0 & 0 & X & Y \end{pmatrix}_{8\times8}$$

$$s = \begin{pmatrix} Z & Y & 0 & 0 & 0 & 0 & 0 & 0 \\ Y & Z & Y & 0 & 0 & 0 & 0 & 0 \\ 0 & Y & Z & Y & 0 & 0 & 0 & 0 \\ 0 & 0 & Y & Z & Y & 0 & 0 & 0 \\ 0 & 0 & 0 & Y & Z & Y & 0 & 0 \\ 0 & 0 & 0 & 0 & Y & Z & Y & 0 \\ 0 & 0 & 0 & 0 & 0 & Y & Z & Y \\ 0 & 0 & 0 & 0 & 0 & 0 & Y & Z \end{pmatrix}_{8\times8}$$

The result of convolution satisfies the linear condition (achieving by zero padding filtering in the spatial domain). The DCT representation of s, t, lu, and block are defined as S, T, LU, and $BLOCK$, respectively. Equation (12) is redefinition of (11) in the DCT domain using (7) and (9).

$$C^t. OUTPUT_{DCT}.C = output =$$
$$(C^t.LU.C.C^t.BLOCK.C.C^t.T.C)$$
$$+(C^t.BLOCK.C.C^t.S.C) = \qquad (12)$$
$$C^t.[(LU.BLOCK.T) + BLOCK.S)].C$$

Thus equation (12) could be simplified as equation (13):

$$OUTPUT_{DCT} = (LU.BLOCK.T) + (BLOCK.S) \qquad (13)$$

Besides zero padding, a common method in signal processing for signals with a finite duration (e.g. images) is repeating the end values. Both the symmetrical and unsymmetrical replications are the same for a 3×3 mask. Generally, replication in signal border gives results better than zero padding (more continuous). Zero padding in image processing usually may lead to block effects in the border areas. In order to create the border replication condition on edges of the block, we developed some matrices resembling this operation in the DCT domain. In order to create the border replication condition in the corners of the block, matrix u is defined, which is multiplied by the block ($block \times u$). In order to select the corner elements of the matrix, the corner separator matrix (q) is multiplied by $block \times u$. The separator matrix, q, is an 8×8 matrix with one only on the $q(1,1)$ and $q(8,8)$, and zero elsewhere. However, for the lateral replication condition, matrix v is defined. Matrices u and v are given as follow:

$$u = \begin{pmatrix} X+2Y & 0 & 0 & 0 & 0 & 0 & 0 & 0 \\ 0 & 0 & 0 & 0 & 0 & 0 & 0 & 0 \\ 0 & 0 & 0 & 0 & 0 & 0 & 0 & 0 \\ 0 & 0 & 0 & 0 & 0 & 0 & 0 & 0 \\ 0 & 0 & 0 & 0 & 0 & 0 & 0 & 0 \\ 0 & 0 & 0 & 0 & 0 & 0 & 0 & 0 \\ 0 & 0 & 0 & 0 & 0 & 0 & 0 & 0 \\ 0 & 0 & 0 & 0 & 0 & 0 & 0 & X+2Y \end{pmatrix}_{8 \times 8}$$

$$v = \begin{pmatrix} 0 & X & 0 & 0 & 0 & 0 & 0 & 0 \\ X & Y & X & 0 & 0 & 0 & 0 & 0 \\ 0 & X & Y & X & 0 & 0 & 0 & 0 \\ 0 & 0 & X & Y & X & 0 & 0 & 0 \\ 0 & 0 & 0 & X & Y & X & 0 & 0 \\ 0 & 0 & 0 & 0 & X & Y & X & 0 \\ 0 & 0 & 0 & 0 & 0 & X & Y & X \\ 0 & 0 & 0 & 0 & 0 & 0 & X & 0 \end{pmatrix}_{8 \times 8}$$

The next step is to calculate the border replication condition directly in the DCT domain according to (14) using calculation of the DCT representation of u, v, and q:

$$REPLICATION_{DCT} = (Q.BLOCK.U) + (V.BLOCK.Q) + (Q.BLOCK.V) \tag{14}$$

where, matrices U, V, and Q are DCT of the matrices u, v, and q, respectively.

Finally, the convolved block with the border replication condition is achieved directly in the DCT domain by summation of (13) and (14) as (15):

$$Filtered\_Block_{DCT} = (LU.BLOCK.T) + (BLOCK.S) + (Q.BLOCK.U) + (V.BLOCK.Q) + (Q.BLOCK.V) \tag{15}$$

Although the above convolution manipulation was developed for a 3×3 mask and an 8×8 image block, it can be extended for any mask and block sizes.

• **Gaussian low-pass filtering in DCT domain**

In the first approach of the proposed methods, it is necessary to pass the 8×8 blocks through a low-pass filter, and a 3×3 Gaussian low-pass filter with σ=1 is used. We tested various low-pass filters in a lot of experiments with various kinds of multi-focus images. The Gaussian low-pass 3×3 mask with σ=1 is the best choice for blurring

8×8 blocks in case of high quality fused image in our proposed methods.

The 2D Gaussian function with σ=1 is:

$$G(x, y) = \frac{1}{2\pi} e^{-\frac{x^2 + x^2}{2}} \tag{16}$$

According to (16), $G(x,y)$ for x, y=-1, 0, and 1 are calculated. With normalizing these values by the sum of $G(x,y)$, the 3×3 Gaussian low-pass mask with σ=1 is achieved as (18):

Gaussian Mask=

0.0751	0.1238	0.0751
0.1238	0.2042	0.1238
0.0751	0.1238	0.0751

(17)

For Gaussian filtering of the block in the DCT domain, the matrices t, s, u, and v are arranged according to (10) and (17). This means that X, Y, and Z in (10) and the defined matrices (t, s, u, and v) are set to 0.0751, 0.1238, and 0.0751, respectively. In the next step, T, S, U, and V (the DCT representation of t, s, u, and v) are calculated. Finally, the filtered block in the DCT domain is calculated by (15). The DCT domain matrices of LU, Q, T, S, U, and V for the mask are demonstrated in figure 3 for 3×3 Gaussian low-pass filter with σ=1. Thus $\overline{imA}$ and $\overline{imB}$, which are the Gaussian low-pass filtered block of imA and imB, respectively, can be calculated directly in the DCT domain easily for the DCT+Corr and DCT+ENG_Corr methods according to (15).

• **Calculation of Laplacian of a block in DCT domain**

The Laplacian of the 8×8 block in spatial domain is calculated by the convolving mask (18) and the given 8×8 block.

Laplacian Mask=

-1	-4	-1
-4	+20	-4
-1	-4	-1

(18)

In order to calculate the Laplacian of the block in the DCT domain, the matrices t, s, u, and v are arranged according to (10) and (19). In the next step, matrices T, S, U, and V, the DCT representation of t, s, u, and v, respectively, are calculated. Finally, the Laplacian of the block ($Laplacian_{DCT}$) is calculated according to (15) directly in the DCT domain.

2.3. Correlation coefficient and energy-correlation coefficient calculation in DCT domain

The correlation coefficient between the two $N \times N$ image blocks, imA and $\overline{imA}$, is defined as (19) [33]:

$$corr(imA, \overline{imA}) =$$

$$\frac{\sum_{m=0}^{N-1}\sum_{n=0}^{N-1}(imA(m,n) - \overline{\overline{imA}})(imA(m,n) - \overline{\overline{imA}})}{\sqrt{\sum_{m=0}^{N-1}\sum_{n=0}^{N-1}(imA(m,n) - \overline{\overline{imA}})^2}\sqrt{\sum_{m=0}^{N-1}\sum_{n=0}^{N-1}(\overline{imA}(m,n) - \overline{\overline{imA}})^2}} \quad (19)$$

where, $imA(m,n)$ is the intensity of the $(m,n)^{th}$ pixel in image imA, $\overline{imA}$ (m,n) is the intensity of the $(m,n)^{th}$ pixel in image $\overline{imA}$, $\overline{\overline{imA}}$ is the mean intensity value of image imA, and $\overline{\overline{imA}}$ is the mean intensity value of image $\overline{imA}$.

In order to derive the correlation coefficient of the $N \times N$ image blocks of imA and $\overline{imA}$ in the DCT domain, $P_{imA}(i,j)$ and $P_{\overline{imA}}(i,j)$ are defined as below:

$$P_{imA}(i,j) = d_{imA}(i,j) - \bar{d}_{imA} \quad (20)$$

$$P_{\overline{imA}}(i,j) = d_{\overline{imA}}(i,j) - \bar{d}_{\overline{imA}} \quad (21)$$

where, $d_{imA}(i,j)$ and $d_{\overline{imA}}(i,j)$ are the DCT coefficients of $N \times N$ image blocks of imA and $\overline{imA}$, respectively. However, $\bar{d}_{imA}$ and $\bar{d}_{\overline{imA}}$ are the mean values of DCT coefficients of $N \times N$ image blocks of $\underline{imA}$ and $\overline{imA}$, respectively.

Therefore, the correlation coefficient of the two $N \times N$ image blocks of imA and $\overline{imA}$ can be obtained mathematically simply from the DCT coefficients according to (22).

$$corr_{DCT}(imA, \overline{imA}) =$$

$$\frac{\sum_{i=0}^{N-1}\sum_{j=0}^{N-1}P_{imA}(i,j) \times P_{\overline{imA}}(i,j)}{\sqrt{\sum_{i=0}^{N-1}\sum_{j=0}^{N-1}P_{imA}(i,j)^2} \times \sqrt{\sum_{i=0}^{N-1}\sum_{j=0}^{N-1}P_{\overline{imA}}(i,j)^2}} \quad (22)$$

Combining the image energy of imA and $\overline{imA}$ in the correlation coefficient relation could improve the focus measurement performance. The input image is represented by symbol imA, and the artificial blurred input image is represented by symbol $\overline{imA}$. The energies of the input images, imA and $\overline{imA}$, are defined as (23) and (24), respectively.

$$Energy_{DCT}(imA) = \sum_{i=0}^{N-1}\sum_{j=0}^{N-1}d_{imA}(i,j)^2 \quad (23)$$

$$Energy_{DCT}(\overline{imA}) = \sum_{i=0}^{N-1}\sum_{j=0}^{N-1}d_{\overline{imA}}(i,j)^2 \quad (24)$$

The second proposed focus measurement (Eng_Corr) is calculated using (25) by combining (22), (23), and (24), according to condition (5).

$$Eng\_corr_{DCT}(imA, \overline{imA}) = Energy_{DCT}(imA)$$
$$\times (1 - corr_{DCT}(imA, \overline{imA})) \times Energy_{DCT}(\overline{imA}) \quad (25)$$

2.4. EOL & VOL calculation in DCT domain

EOL measures the image border sharpness, and is calculated in the spatial domain using (26) [34].

$$EOL = \sum_{k}\sum_{l}(Laplacian(k,l))^2 \quad (26)$$

where, $Laplacian(k,l)$ is the Laplacian of the given image block.

EOL in (26), the summation of entrywise products of the elements, can be re-written as (27):

$$EOL = \sum_{k}\sum_{l}(Laplacian(k,l))^2 =$$
$$trace[Laplacian(k,l).(Laplacian(k,l))^t] \quad (27)$$

where, trace[.] is the trace of a matrix.

Since DCT is a unitary transform, if b is a matrix and B is its DCT representation, we have:

$$trace(b.b^t) = trace(B.B^t) \quad (28)$$

Using (27) and (28), the EOL in DCT domain can be written as (29):

$$EOL_{DCT} =$$
$$trace[Laplacian_{DCT}.(Laplacian_{DCT})^t] \quad (29)$$

where, the $Laplacian_{DCT}$ has been calculated using the proposed method in Section 2.2 with (18).

In this section, after EOL, the variance of image Laplacian (VOL) is calculated in the DCT domain. VOL in the spatial domain is calculated using (30).

LU=

1.7500	0	-0.3266	0	-0.2500	0	-0.1353	0
0	1.3668	0	-0.4077	0	-0.2724	0	-0.0957
-0.3266	0	0.9874	0	-0.3266	0	-0.1768	0
0	-0.4077	0	0.4197	0	-0.2310	0	-0.0811
-0.2500	0	-0.3266	0	-0.2500	0	-0.1353	0
0	-0.2724	0	-0.2310	0	-0.9197	0	-0.0542
-0.1353	0	-0.1768	0	-0.1353	0	-1.4874	0
0	-0.0957	0	-0.0811	0	-0.0542	0	-1.8668

Q=

0.2500	0	0.3266	0	0.2500	0	0.1353	0
0	0.4810	0	0.4077	0	0.2724	0	0.0957
0.3266	0	0.4268	0	0.3266	0	0.1768	0
0	0.4077	0	0.3457	0	0.2310	0	0.0811
0.2500	0	0.3266	0	0.2500	0	0.1353	0
0	0.2724	0	0.2310	0	0.1543	0	0.0542
0.1353	0	0.1768	0	0.1353	0	0.0732	0
0	0.0957	0	0.0811	0	0.0542	0	0.0190

T_Gaussian=

0.2552	0	-0.0245	0	-0.0188	0	-0.0102	0
0	0.2264	0	-0.0306	0	-0.0205	0	-0.0072
-0.0245	0	0.1980	0	-0.0245	0	-0.0133	0
0	0.0306	0	0.1553	0	-0.0173	0	-0.0061
-0.0188	0	-0.0245	0	0.1050	0	-0.0102	0
0	-0.0205	0	-0.0173	0	0.0547	0	-0.0041
-0.0102	0	-0.0133	0	-0.0102	0	0.0121	0
0	0.0072	0	-0.0061	0	-0.0041	0	-0.0164

S_Gaussian=

0.4208	0	-0.0404	0	-0.0310	0	-0.0168	0
0	0.3734	0	-0.0505	0	-0.0337	0	-0.0118
-0.0404	0	0.3264	0	-0.0404	0	-0.0219	0
0	-0.0505	0	0.2562	0	-0.0286	0	-0.0100
-0.0309	0	-0.0404	0	0.1732	0	-0.0168	0
0	-0.0337	0	-0.0286	0	0.0903	0	-0.0067
-0.0168	0	-0.0219	0	-0.0168	0	0.0201	0
0	-0.0118	0	-0.0100	0	-0.0067	0	-0.0269

U_Gaussian=

0.0806	0	0.1054	0	0.0806	0	0.0436	0
0	0.1552	0	0.1315	0	0.0879	0	0.0309
0.1054	0	0.1377	0	0.1054	0	0.0570	0
0	0.1315	0	0.1115	0	0.0745	0	0.0262
0.0806	0	0.1054	0	0.0806	0	0.0436	0
0	0.0879	0	0.0745	0	0.0498	0	0.0175
0.0436	0	0.0570	0	0.0436	0	0.0236	0
0	0.0309	0	0.0262	0	0.0175	0	0.0061

V_Gaussian=

0.2243	0	-0.0650	0	-0.0497	0	-0.0269	0
0	0.1669	0	-0.0811	0	-0.0542	0	-0.0190
-0.0650	0	0.1451	0	-0.0650	0	-0.0352	0
0	-0.0811	0	0.1125	0	-0.0459	0	-0.0161
-0.0497	0	-0.0650	0	0.0741	0	-0.0269	0
0	-0.0542	0	-0.0459	0	0.0356	0	-0.0108
-0.0269	0	-0.0352	0	-0.0269	0	0.0030	0
0	-0.0190	0	-0.0161	0	-0.0108	0	-0.0188

Figure 3. DCT representation of matrices LU, Q, T, S, U, and V for 3×3 Gaussian low-pass filter with σ=1.

$$\sigma^2 = \frac{1}{N^2}\sum_{k=0}^{N-1}\sum_{l=0}^{N-1} Laplacian^2(k,l) - \mu^2 \qquad (30)$$

where, μ is the mean value of Laplacian of the $N \times N$ block.

However, variance of the $N \times N$ block in the DCT domain is calculated using (31) [27].

$$\sigma_{DCT}^2 = \sum_{k=0}^{N-1}\sum_{l=0}^{N-1}\frac{d^2(k,l)}{N^2} - d^2(0,0) \qquad (31)$$

where, $d(k,l)$ is the DCT representation of the block.

In order to calculate the variance of image Laplacian in the DCT domain, $d(k,l)$ - used in (31) - is replaced with the calculated $Laplacian_{DCT}$ in Section 2.2. Thus the variance of image Laplacian in the DCT domain, VOL_{DCT}, is derived as (32):

$$VOL_{DCT} = \sum_{k=0}^{7}\sum_{l=0}^{7}\frac{Laplacian_{DCT}^2(k,l)}{N^2} - Laplacian_{DCT}^2(0,0) \qquad (32)$$

2.5. Block selection

After introducing the proposed DCT domain focus measurements (DCT+Corr, DCT+Eng_Corr, DCT+EOL, and DCT+VOL), it is possible to make decision map $M(i, j)$ for a suitable focused block selection in order to construct the output image.

For the DCT+Corr method:

$$M(i,j) = \begin{cases} 1 & if\ corr_{DCT}(imA, \overline{imA}) < corr_{DCT}(imB, \overline{imB}) \\ -1 & if\ corr_{DCT}(imA, \overline{imA}) > corr_{DCT}(imB, \overline{imB}) \end{cases} \qquad (33)$$

For the DCT+Eng_Corr method:

$$M(i,j) = \begin{cases} 1 & if\ Eng\_corr_{DCT}(imA, \overline{imA}) > Eng\_corr_{DCT}(imB, \overline{imB}) \\ -1 & if\ Eng\_corr_{DCT}(imA, \overline{imA}) < Eng\_corr_{DCT}(imB, \overline{imB}) \end{cases} \qquad (34)$$

For the DCT+EOL method:

$$M(i,j) = \begin{cases} 1 & if\ EOL_{DCT}(imA) > EOL_{DCT}(imB) \\ -1 & if\ EOL_{DCT}(imA) < EOL_{DCT}(imB) \end{cases} \qquad (35)$$

Finally, for the DCT+VOL method:

$$M(i,j) = \begin{cases} 1 & if\ VOL_{DCT}(imA) > VOL_{DCT}(imB) \\ -1 & if\ VOL_{DCT}(imA) < VOL_{DCT}(imB) \end{cases} \qquad (36)$$

where $i= 1, 2 \ldots \dfrac{\text{Lengh of the input image}}{8}$ and $j= 1, 2 \ldots \dfrac{\text{width of the input image}}{8}$.

For $M(i,j) = 1$, the block imA is selected for the output fused image, and for $M(i,j) = -1$, the block imB is selected.

2.6. Consistency verification (CV)

In order to improve the quality of the output image and reduce the error due to unsuitable block selection, CV is applied as a post-processing in the last step of the image fusion process. It is supposed that the central block of an area in the selected blocks for the output image come from image B but the majority of neighbouring blocks come from image A. This means that the central block should belong to image A. Li et al. have used the majority filter for the CV process [23]. The central block is replaced with the corresponding block from image A using a majority filter, which is applied on the decision map $M(i,j)$. The previous methods in the DCT domain (DCT+Variance, DCT+AC_Max, and DCT+SF) use averaging low-pass filter as the majority filter in their algorithms. For example, an averaging mask of size 5×5 is used in the simulations. Thus the new decision map is derived as below:

$$W(i,j) = \frac{1}{25} \sum_{k=-2}^{+2} \sum_{l=-2}^{+2} M(i+k, j+1) \qquad (37)$$

For $W(i,j) > 0$, the selected block for the output image is selected from imA, and for $W(i,j) < 0$, the selected block for the output image is selected from imB.

2.7. Proposed repeated consistency verification (RCV)

Although the CV process improves the decision map in most cases, it has a negative effect on outcome in some cases. This limitation can cause blocking effects on the output fused image. In order to remove this weakness and create an enhanced decision map, the RCV process is suggested. In this method, averaging masks are used to have a smooth decision map. Since the output of applying averaging mask is multi-values, it is necessary to use a thresholding process to create a desired binary decision map. Our investigation shows a two-stage successive averaging by masks with sizes of 7×7 and 5×5, thresholding with a zero dead zone with values of ±0.2 and ±0.1, respectively, and finally, applying an averaging mask of 3×3 following a soft thresholding with values ±0.2 giving better results. This method prevents any blocking effect on the output fused image, and significantly improves the quality of output image. The equations used in this method are summarized as follow:

Averaging mask with a size of 7×7:

$$M^1(i,j) = \frac{1}{49} \sum_{k=-3}^{+3} \sum_{l=-3}^{+3} M(i+k, j+1) \qquad (38)$$

Thresholding with values of ±0.2:

$$M^2(i,j) = \begin{cases} +1 & if \quad M^1(i,j) > 0.2 \\ -1 & if \quad M^1(i,j) < -0.2 \\ 0 & otherwise \end{cases} \qquad (39)$$

Averaging mask with a size of 5×5:

$$M^3(i,j) = \frac{1}{25} \sum_{k=-2}^{+2} \sum_{l=-2}^{+2} M^2(i+k, j+1) \qquad (40)$$

Thresholding with values of ±0.1:

$$M^4(i,j) = \begin{cases} +1 & if \quad M^3(i,j) > 0.1 \\ -1 & if \quad M^3(i,j) < -0.1 \\ 0 & otherwise \end{cases} \qquad (41)$$

Averaging mask of 3×3:

$$W(i,j) = \frac{1}{9} \sum_{k=-1}^{+1} \sum_{l=-1}^{+1} M^4(i+k, j+1) \qquad (42)$$

Soft thresholding with the values ±0.2 for final decision:

$$F(i,j) =$$
$$\begin{cases} imA & if \quad W(i,j) > 0.2 \\ imB & if \quad W(i,j) < -0.2 \\ (\frac{1+W}{2})imA + (\frac{1-W}{2})imB & otherwise \end{cases} \qquad (43)$$

3. Experimental results and analysis

The proposed algorithms in this paper were tested for different images. The results of the proposed methods are discussed and compared with some of the state of the art methods e.g. methods based on the multi-scale transform like DWT [23], SIDWT [24], and DCHWT [25], and the methods based on the DCT domain like DCT+Average [28], DCT+Contrast [28], DCT+Variance [27], DCT+AC_Max [29], DCT+SF [30], and DCT+SML [31].

3.1. Simulation conditions
The algorithms were coded and simulated using the MATLAB 2016b software. The simulation MATLAB code of the DCT+Variance method was taken from an online database [35], which was provided by Haghighat [27]. In the wavelet-based methods, DWT with DBSS (2,2) and the SIDWT with Haar basis, three levels of

decomposition are considered and simulated using "Image Fusion Toolbox", provided by Oliver Rockinger [36]. However, an online database was used for simulation of the DCHWT method [37]. The DCT+Average, DCT+Contrast, DCT+ AC_Max, and DCT+SF methods were simulated using MATLAB with the best performance conditions.

To evaluate the proposed methods and compare their results with the results of the previous outstanding mentioned methods, the experiments were conducted on two types of test images. The first type of test images is referenced images, and their ground-truth images are available. Typical gray-scale 512×512 test images, given in figure 4, are the referenced-images, which are obtained from an online database [38]. The 16 pair multi-focus test images were generated from eight standard test images given in figure 4. For each pair, the non-focused conditions were created by artificial blurring of images using two disk averaging filters of radii 5 and 9 pixels, separately. These images are blurred in both right and left halves of the images. The second type of test images is non-referenced images, and their ground-truth images are not available. The real multi-focus images were captured with different depths of focus in camera. Two well-known non-referenced images "Disk" 580×640 from an online database [37] and "Book" 960×1280 from an online database [36] were selected.

Figure 4. Standard gray level test images used for simulations.

3.2. Performance measurement

In order to assess the proposed algorithms and compare the given results with those of the previous algorithms, some different evaluation performance metrics of image fusion were used. The mean-squared error (MSE) [39, 40], peak signal-to-noise ratio (PSNR) [39], and structural similarity (SSIM) [41] need the ground-truth image for the referenced images. MSE calculates the total squared error between the ground-truth

image and the output fused image, as below [39, 40]:

$$MSE = \frac{1}{mn} \sum_{k=1}^{m} \sum_{l=1}^{n} [G(k,l) - O(k,l)]^2 \qquad (44)$$

where, $G(k,l)$ and $O(k,l)$ are the intensity values of the ground-truth image and the output fused image, respectively. The values for m and n are the size of the images.

MSE in the signal/image processing can be converted to PSNR as (45) but it does not have any additional information compared with MSE. Anyway, PSNR calculates the maximum available power of the signal/image over noise [39], as:

$$PSNR = 10 \log_{10}(\frac{L^2}{MSE}) \qquad (45)$$

where, L is an admissible dynamic range of image pixel values, and is equal to 2^b-1 (b=8 bits).

Structure similarity (SSIM) index is a criterion to measure the structure similarity between images x and y as [41]:

$$SSIM(x,y) = \frac{(2\mu_x\mu_x + \mu_1)(2\sigma_{xy} + c_2)}{(\mu_x^2 + \mu_y^2 + c_1)(\sigma_x^2 + \sigma_y^2 + c_2)} \qquad (46)$$

where, μ_x and μ_y are the mean values of images x and y, respectively; σ_x and σ_y are the variance of images x and y, respectively; and σ_{xy} is the covariance of images x and y. The c_1 and c_2 for 8 bit images are defined as $c_1=(k_1L)^2$ and $c_2=(k_2L)^2$, respectively, where k_1=0.01, k_2=0.03, and L=255.

$Q^{AB/F}$, $L^{AB/F}$, and $N^{AB/F}$ are used for the non-referenced images provided by Xydeas and Petrovic [42, 43]. Consider F as the fused image of the two input images A and B. The Sobel edge operator is applied for each pixel to get the edge strength $g(n,m)$ and orientation $\alpha(n,m)$, as below (e.g. for input image A):

$$g_A(n,m) = \sqrt{s_A^x(n,m)^2 + s_A^y(n,m)^2} \qquad (47)$$

$$\alpha_A(n,m) = \tan^{-1}(\frac{s_A^y(n,m)}{s_A^x(n,m)}) \qquad (48)$$

where, s_A^x and s_A^y are the horizontal and vertical Sobel templates on each pixel, respectively.

The relative edge strength and orientation are derived as:

$$G_{n,m}^{AF} = \begin{cases} \dfrac{g_{n,m}^F}{g_{n,m}^A} & if \qquad g_{n,m}^A > g_{n,m}^F \\ \dfrac{g_{n,m}^A}{g_{n,m}^F} & otherwise \end{cases} \qquad (49)$$

$$A^{AF}(n,m) = 1 - \frac{|\alpha_A(n,m) - \alpha_F(n,m)|}{\pi/2} \qquad (50)$$

Using (49) and (50), the edge strength and orientation preservation values are derived as:

$$Q_g^{AF}(n,m) = \frac{\Gamma_g}{1 + e^{K_g(G^{AF}(n,m) - \sigma_g)}} \qquad (51)$$

$$Q_\alpha^{AF}(n,m) = \frac{\Gamma_\alpha}{1 + e^{K_\alpha(A^{AF}(n,m) - \sigma_\alpha)}} \qquad (52)$$

The constants $\Gamma_g, K_g, \sigma_g, \Gamma_\alpha, K_\alpha,$ and σ_α determine the exact shape of the sigmoid functions used to form the edge strength and orientation preservation values. Thus the edge information preservation is derived as:

$$Q^{AF}(n,m) = Q_g^{AF}(n,m) Q_\alpha^{AF}(n,m) \qquad (53)$$

where, $0 \le Q^{AF}(n,m) \le 1$. The zero value indicates the complete loss of edge information, and the value 1 indicates no loss of edge information in the fusion process.

Finally, the total gradient information transferred from the source images to the fused image ($Q^{AB/F}$) is calculated as:

$$Q^{AB/F} = \frac{\sum\limits_{\forall n,m} Q_{n,m}^{AF} w_{n,m}^A + Q_{n,m}^{BF} w_{n,m}^B}{\sum\limits_{\forall n,m} w_{n,m}^A + w_{n,m}^B} \qquad (54)$$

where, $Q_{n,m}^{AF}$ and $Q_{n,m}^{BF}$ are weighted by $w_{n,m}^A$ and $w_{n,m}^B$, respectively. The constant value L is considered for $w_{n,m}^A = [g_{n,m}^A]^L$ and $w_{n,m}^B = [g_{n,m}^B]^L$.

The constant values used in this paper were taken from [41] (L=1, $\Gamma_g = 0.9994$, $K_g = -15$, $\sigma_g = 0.5$, $\Gamma_\alpha = 0.9879$, $K_\alpha = -22$, $\sigma_\alpha = 0.8$).

$L^{AB/F}$ is the fusion loss, which measures the gradient information lost during the image fusion process, and is calculated as below [43]:

$$L^{AB/F} = \frac{\sum\limits_{\forall n,m} r_{n,m}[(1 - Q_{n,m}^{AF}) w_{n,m}^A + (1 - Q_{n,m}^{BF}) w_{n,m}^B]}{\sum\limits_{\forall n,m} w_{n,m}^A + w_{n,m}^B} \qquad (55)$$

where

$$r_{n,m} = \begin{cases} 1 & if \quad g_{n,m}^F < g_{n,m}^A \ or \ g_{n,m}^F < g_{n,m}^B \\ 0 & otherwise \end{cases} \qquad (56)$$

$N^{AB/F}$ is the fusion artefacts or noise [43]. $N^{AB/F}$ measures the information that is not related to the input images but is created as artefacts during the image fusion process, and is calculated as:

$$N^{AB/F} = \frac{\sum\limits_{\forall n,m} N_{n,m}(w_{n,m}^A + w_{n,m}^B)}{\sum\limits_{\forall n,m} w_{n,m}^A + w_{n,m}^B} \qquad (57)$$

where

$$N_{n,m} = \begin{cases} 2 - Q_{n,m}^{AF} - Q_{n,m}^{BF} & if \quad g_{n,m}^F > (g_{n,m}^A \ \& \ g_{n,m}^B) \\ 0 & otherwise \end{cases} \qquad (58)$$

In addition, we used the feature mutual information (FMI) [44] as (59). The edge feature of images was considered for information representation in FMI.

$$FMI_F^{AB} = \frac{I_{FA}}{H_F + H_A} + \frac{I_{FB}}{H_F + H_B} \qquad (59)$$

where, H_A, H_B, and H_F are the information entropy of the input images A, B, and the fused image, respectively; and I_{FA} and I_{FB} are the amounts of feature information that F contains about images A and B, respectively.

These evaluation performance metrics ($Q^{AB/F}$, $L^{AB/F}$, $N^{AB/F}$, and FMI) were used for the non-reference images, i.e. their ground-truth images are not available.

3.3. Fusion result evaluation

Firstly, in order to demonstrate the advantages of the proposed methods over the other ones, the proposed methods and the previous ones were applied on the 16 pairs of artificial multi-focus images generated from the test images given in figure 4. The average values for SSIM and MSE for the proposed and other methods are listed in table 1. The results obtained show that all the four proposed methods give better results than the other methods. The DCT+Eng_Corr method shows the best results in these experiments, i.e. the MSE and SSIM values for the DCT+Eng_Corr method are 1.9594 and 0.9950, respectively, which are the lowest MSE and highest SSIM values among the other values of the other methods.

Secondly, the proposed methods and the other ones are evaluated by real multi-focus images with different depths of focus in camera. The methods were applied on the various sizes of images like "Disk" 580×640 and "Book" 960×1280, so evaluation results for the performance metrics ($Q^{AB/F}$, $L^{AB/F}$, $N^{AB/F}$, and FMI) were obtained and listed in table 2. The non-reference multi-focus image fusion metrics values for the realistic images emphasize the advantages of the proposed methods over the other ones. The output fused images of the proposed methods and the "Book" source images focusing on the left and the right are shown in figure 5. Beside this, the magnified output images of the proposed and previous methods are shown in figure 5. There are some undesirable side-effects like blurring in the DCT+Average and DCT+Contrast methods. However, the ringing artefacts in wavelet-based methods, and blocking effects/unsuitable block selection in the DCT+Variance, DCT+AC_Max, and DCT+SF methods could be concluded from the output image results. All the proposed methods could enhance the quality of output fused image and reduce unsuitable block selection significantly. Similarly, the "Disk" source multi-focus images and the results of the proposed methods (DCT+Eng_Corr and DCT+Eng_Corr+RCV) are shown in figure 6.

However, the RCV process and the CV process, as the post-processing, are applied on the DCT-based methods for fusion of "Book" images and 16 pair multi-focus images that were generated. The evaluation performance metrics of CV and RCV are listed in table 3. The results obtained showed that although CV enhanced the quality of the output fused image in most cases, the ability of RCV was more than CV in enhancing the quality of output fused image. In addition, RCV could prevent the unsuitable block selection significantly and remove the blocking effects completely in the output fused image. The visual comparison of CV and RCV of the "Book" image, shown in figure 7 demonstrate this claim.

In another experiment, the proposed methods and the pervious ones were conducted on the "Lena" and "Pepper" multi-focus images. The non-focused conditions of these multi-focus images were created by artificial blurring of images using a disk averaging filter of radius 9 pixel. The

PSNR values for the fused output image of different methods are recorded in table 4. It is understandable that the PSNR values for the results of the latest method for "Lena" is infinite (∞). Focused block recognition of "Lena" is easy because of the inherent high local correlation among pixel values and high contrast between adjacent areas, whereas the focused block recognition of "Pepper" is harder than "Lena". Thus we conducted experiments on "Pepper" as a harder quality test in order to compare the methods in fair conditions. All proposed methods have better results over the previous ones. The ground-truth image, multi-focus images of "Pepper", difference images between the ground-truth images, fused output images of the proposed methods, and other methods are depicted in figure 7. DCT+VOL+RCV and DCT+Eng_Corr+RCV have the best results in the PSNR values, and have less image differences in table 4 and figure 7, respectively.

In this paper, four new multi-focus image fusion methods are introduced. All the proposed methods have significant improvements in the quality of the output fused images. In fact, all the DCT-based fusion methods for JPEG image are less time-consuming and suitable for implementation in real-time applications. However, it is important that which one is faster in order to implement in the real-time applications. We conducted an average run-time comparison for our proposed methods in table 5. Our proposed algorithms were performed using the MATLAB 2016b software with an 8 GB RAM and Intel core i7-7500 CPU processor @ 2.7GHz & 2.9 GHz. According to table 5, DCT+Vol has the best run-time (0.110408 s) for fusion of 512×512 multi-focus images, and next, DCT+Eol, DCT+Corr, and DCT+Eng+Corr have 0.124598, 0.160410, and 0.173938 s run times, respectively. DCT+VOL has a better image quality and faster algorithm run-time than DCT+Corr & DCT+EOL. According to tables 1, 2, 3, and 4, the best quality result is for DCT+Eng_Corr, and after that is for DCT+VOL. Thus we can conclude that DCT+Eng_Corr is a better choice if the powerful hardware is available, and time-consumption has little importance. On the other side, DCT+VOL is a better choice if there is a critical need for time and energy-consumption. Anyway, all proposed methods have significant improvement in quality of the output fused images, and are appropriate for real-time applications due to implantation in the DCT domain.

4. Conclusions

In this paper, four new multi-focus image fusion methods were introduced completely in the DCT domain. By proposing an algorithm for convolving a mask on the 8×8 block directly in the DCT domain, we could calculate the image Laplacian and image low-pass filtering in DCT domain. Thus two powerful Laplacian-based focus measurements, VOL and EOL were implemented in the DCT domain. Two other powerful DCT focus measurements, DCT+Corr and DCT+Eng_Corr, were introduced. These methods measure the occurring changes in passing image blocks through the low-pass filter in the DCT domain. In addition, we substituted CV post-processing with RCV. This replacement improved the quality of the output fused image significantly and prevents unsuitable block selection and blocking effects in the output fused image. We conducted a lot of experiments on various types of multi-focus images. The accuracy of the proposed methods is assessed by applying the proposed algorithms and other well-known methods on the several referenced images and non-referenced images. However, evaluation of different methods was done using various evaluation performance metrics. The results obtained show the advantages of the proposed algorithms over some precious and the state of art algorithms in terms of quality of output image. In addition, due to a simple implementation of the proposed algorithms in the DCT domain, they are appropriate for use in real-time applications.

Table 1. MSE and SSIM comparison of various image fusion methods on reference images.

Methods	Average values for 16 pairs images created from image shown in Fig. 4	
	MSE	SSIM
DCT+Average [28]	65.1125	0.9164
DCT+Contrast [28]	23.0788	0.9647
DWT [23]	19.2411	0.9619
SIDWT [24]	15.5693	0.9641
DCHWT [25]	4.7756	0.9902
DCT+Variance [27]	17.2293	0.9720
DCT+AC_Max [29]	4.1520	0.9917
DCT+SF [30]	5.6848	0.9896
DCT+SML [31]	9.8444	0.9828
DCT+ EOL (proposed)	2.5487	0.9944
DCT+VOL (proposed)	2.5486	0.9944
DCT+Corr (proposed)	5.2722	0.9921
DCT+Eng_Corr (proposed)	1.9594	0.9950

Table 2. $Q^{AB/F}$, $L^{AB/F}$, $N^{AB/F}$, and FMI comparison of various image fusion methods on non-referenced images.

Methods	"BOOK"				"DISK"			
	$Q^{AB/F}$	$L^{AB/F}$	$N^{AB/F}$	FMI	$Q^{AB/F}$	$L^{AB/F}$	$N^{AB/F}$	FMI
DCT+Average [28]	0.4985	0.5002	0.0025	0.9075	0.5187	0.4782	0.0063	0.9013
DCT+Contrast [28]	0.6470	0.2384	0.3736	0.9074	0.6212	0.2554	0.3629	0.8981
DWT [23]	0.6621	0.2294	0.3569	0.9117	0.6302	0.2552	0.3362	0.9039
SIDWT [24]	0.6932	0.2637	0.1279	0.9122	0.6694	0.2764	0.1564	0.9049
DCHWT [25]	0.6684	0.3014	0.0705	0.9123	0.6529	0.3140	0.0789	0.9075
DCT+Variance [27]	0.7210	0.2660	0.0277	0.9135	0.7165	0.2612	0.0478	0.9070
DCT+AC_Max [29]	0.7081	0.2781	0.0294	0.9136	0.6763	0.2910	0.0696	0.9057
DCT+SF [30]	0.7151	0.2757	0.0197	0.9148	0.7213	0.2600	0.0415	0.9086
DCT+SML [31]	0.6960	0.2928	0.0241	0.9147	0.6774	0.3074	0.0324	0.9080
DCT+ EOL (proposed)	0.7283	0.2620	0.0206	0.9153	0.7280	0.2522	0.0425	0.9094
DCT+VOL (proposed)	0.7284	0.2619	0.0207	0.9153	0.7285	0.2519	0.0421	0.9094
DCT+Corr (proposed)	0.7281	0.2622	0.0207	0.9153	0.7246	0.2541	0.0456	0.9087
DCT+Eng_Corr (proposed)	0.7284	0.2622	0.0202	0.9155	0.7288	0.2530	0.0391	0.9094

Figure 5. Source images "Book" and fusion results. (a) First source image with focus on the right. (b) Second source image with focus on the left. (c) DCT + EOL (proposed) result. (d) DCT+VOL(proposed). (e) DCT+Corr(proposed). (f) DCT+Eng_Corr (proposed). (g), (h), (i), (j), (k), (l), (m), (n), (o), (p), (q), (r), and (s) are the local magnified versions of DCT+Average, DCT+Contrast, DWT, SIDWT, DCHWT, DCT+Variance, DCT+Ac_Max, DCT+SF, DCT+SML, DCT+EOL(proposed), DCT+VOL(proposed), DCT+Corr(proposed), and DCT+Eng_Corr (proposed), respectively.

Figure 6. Source images "Disk" and fusion results. (a) First source image with focus on the right. (b) Second source image with focus on the left. (c) DCT+Eng_Corr (proposed). (d) DCT+Eng_Corr+RCV (proposed).

Table 3. Comparison between CV and RCV post-processing algorithms.

Methods	Average values for 16 pair image created from image shown in Fig. 4		"BOOK"			
	MSE	SSIM	$Q^{AB/F}$	$L^{AB/F}$	$N^{AB/F}$	FMI
DCT+Variance+CV [27]	2.8536	0.9961	0.7222	0.2753	0.0056	0.9151
DCT+AC_Max+CV [29]	1.3784	0.9972	0.7180	0.2778	0.0095	0.9157
DCT+SF+CV [30]	2.1456	0.9968	0.7169	0.2796	0.0080	0.9159
DCT+SML+CV [31]	2.3901	0.9959	0.7187	0.2780	0.0072	0.9163
DCT+ EOL+CV (proposed)	1.0720	0.9976	0.7271	0.2714	0.0036	0.9162
DCT+VOL +CV(proposed)	1.0735	0.9976	0.7278	0.2708	0.0033	0.9163
DCT+Corr+CV (proposed)	1.7408	0.9974	0.7280	0.2706	0.0033	0.9163
DCT+Eng_Corr+CV (proposed)	0.8329	0.9979	0.7285	0.2701	0.0030	0.9163
DCT+VOL+RCV (proposed)	0.8491	0.9978	0.7290	0.2695	0.0024	0.9164
DCT+Eng_Corr+RCV (proposed)	0.6623	0.9980	0.7301	0.2690	0.0019	0.9165

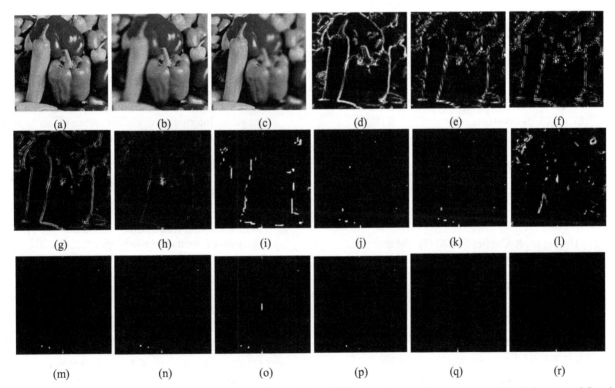

Figure 7. Source images and multi-focus images of "Pepper", and difference images between ground-truth image and fused output images of proposed methods and other methods. (a) Ground-truth image. (b) First source image with focus on the right. (c) Second source image with focus on the left. (d) DCT+Average. (e) DCT+Contrast. (f) DWT. (g) SIDWT. (h) DCHWT. (i) DCT+Variance+CV. (j) DCT+Ac_Max+CV. (k) DCT+SF+CV. (l) DCT+SML+CV. (m) DCT+EOL+CV (Proposed). (n) DCT+VOL+CV (Proposed). (o) DCT+Corr+CV (Proposed). (p) DCT+Eng_Corr+CV (Proposed). (q) DCT+VOL+RCV (Proposed). (r) DCT+Eng_Corr+RCV (Proposed).

Table 4. PSNR comparison between multi-focus image fusion methods on "Lena" and "House" images.

Methods	PSNR (dB)	
	"Lena"	"Pepper"
DCT+Average [28]	29.6283	29.6283
DCT+Contrast [28]	32.3775	33.3672
DWT [23]	34.8943	33.7156
SIDWT [24]	36.0411	34.6095
DCHWT [25]	40.8483	42.9835
DCT+Variance+CV [27]	34.3470	33.5931
DCT+AC_Max+CV [29]	∞	40.8329
DCT+SF+CV [30]	39.5646	40.4470
DCT+SML+CV [31]	∞	35.1566
DCT+ EOL+CV (proposed)	∞	44.0011
DCT+VOL+CV (proposed)	∞	44.0011
DCT+Corr+CV (proposed)	∞	40.3896
DCT+Eng_Corr+CV (proposed)	∞	48.6852
DCT+VOL+RCV (proposed)	∞	48.4816
DCT+Eng_Corr+RCV (proposed)	∞	54.3365

Table 5. Average Run-Time comparison between four proposed 512×512 multi-focus image fusion methods.

Methods	Time (s)
DCT+ EOL (proposed)	0.124598
DCT+VOL (proposed)	0.110408
DCT+Corr (proposed)	0.160410
DCT+Eng_Corr (proposed)	0.173938

References

[1] Drajic, D. & Cvejic, N. (2007). Adaptive fusion of multimodal surveillance image sequences in visual sensor networks. IEEE Transactions on Consumer Electronics, vol. 53, no. 4, pp. 1456-1462.

[2] Wu, W., Yang, X., Pang, Y., Peng, J. & Jeon, G. (2013). A multifocus image fusion method by using hidden Markov model. Optics Communication, vol. 287, January, pp. 63-72.

[3] Kumar, B., Swamy, M. & Ahmad, M. O. (2013). Multiresolution DCT decomposition for multifocus image fusion. In 26th Annual IEEE Canadian Conference on Electrical and Computer Engineering (CCECE), pp. 1-4.

[4] Haghighat, M. B. A, Aghagolzadeh, A. & Seyedarabi, H. (2010). Real-time fusion of multi-focus images for visual sensor networks. In 6th Iranian Machine Vision and Image Processing (MVIP), pp. 1-6.

[5] Naji, M. A., & Aghagolzadeh, A. (2015). A new multi-focus image fusion technique based on variance in DCT domain. In 2nd International Conference on Knowledge-Based Engineering and Innovation (KBEI), pp. 478-484.

[6] Castanedo, F., García, J., Patricio, M., & Molina, J.M. (2008). Analysis of distributed fusion alternatives in coordinated vision agents. In 11th International Conference on Information Fusion, pp. 1-6.

[7] Kazemi, V., Seyedarabi, H. & Aghagolzadeh, A. (2014). Multifocus image fusion based on compressive sensing for visual sensor networks. In 22nd Iranian Conference on Electrical Engineering (ICEE), pp. 1668-1672.

[8] Soro, S., & Heinzelman, W. (2009). A Survey of Visual Sensor Networks. Advances in Multimedia. vol. 2009, Article ID 640386, 21 pages, May.

[9] Huang, W. & Jing, Z. (2007). Evaluation of focus measures in multi-focus image fusion. Pattern Recognition Letters, vol. 28, no. 4, pp. 493-500.

[10] Li, S., Kwok, J. T., & Wang, Y. (2001). Combination of images with diverse focuses using the spatial frequency, Information fusion, vol. 2, no. 3, pp. 169-176.

[11] Li, S., & Yang, B. (2008). Multifocus Image Fusion Using Region Segmentation and Spatial Frequency. Image and Vision Computing, vol. 26, no. 7, pp. 971-979.

[12] Hongmei, W., Cong, N., Yanjun, L., & Lihua, C. (2011). A Novel Fusion Algorithm for Multi-focus Image. International Conference on Applied Informatics and Communication (ICAIC), pp. 641-647.

[13] Mahajan, S., & Singh, A. (2014). A Comparative Analysis of Different Image Fusion Techniques. IPASJ International Journal of Computer Science (IIJCS), vol. 2, no. 1, pp. 634-642.

[14] Pertuz, S., Puig, S. D., & Garcia, M. A. (2013). Analysis of focus measure operators for shape-from-focus. Pattern Recognition. Vol. 46, no. 5, pp.1415-1432.

[15] Kaur, P., & Kaur, M. (2015). A Comparative Study of Various Digital Image Fusion Techniques: A Review. International Journal of Computer Applications, vol. 114, no. 4.

[16] Zhao, H., Li, Q., & Feng, H. (2008). Multi-focus color image fusion in the HSI space using the sum-modified-Laplacian and a coarse edge map. Image and Vision Computing, vol. 26, no.9, pp. 1285-1295.

[17] Zaveri, T., Zaveri, M., Shah, V., & Patel, N. (2009). A Novel Region Based Multifocus Image Fusion Method. Proceeding of IEEE International Conference on Digital Image Processing (ICDIP), pp. 50-54.

[18] Eltoukhy, H. A., & Kavusi, S. (2003). Computationally efficient algorithm for multifocus

image reconstruction. Proceedings SPIE Electronic Imaging, vol. 5017, pp. 332–341.

[19] Zhan, K., Teng, J., Li, Q., & Shi, J. (2015). A Novel Explicit Multi-focus Image Fusion Method. Journal of Information Hiding and Multimedia Signal Processing, vol. 6, no. 3, pp. 600-612.

[20] Burt P. J., & Adelson, E. H. (1983). The Laplacian pyramid as a compact image code. IEEE Transactions Communications. Vol. 31, no. 4, pp. 532-540.

[21] Petrovic V. S., & Xydeas, C. S. (2004). Gradient-based multiresolution image fusion. IEEE Transactions Image Processing. vol. 13, no. 2, pp. 228-237.

[22] De, I., & Chanda, B. (2006). A simple and efficient algorithm for multifocus image fusion using morphological wavelets. Signal Processing. vol. 86, no. 5, pp. 924-936.

[23] Li, H., Manjunath, B., & Mitra, S. K. (1995). Multisensor image fusion using the wavelet transform. Graphical models and image processing. vol. 57, no.3, pp. 235-245.

[24] Rockinger, O. (1997). Image sequence fusion using a shift-invariant wavelet transform. Proceedings of the IEEE International Conference on Image Processing, pp. 288–291.

[25] Kumar, B. K. S. (2013). Multifocus and multispectral image fusion based on pixel significance using discrete cosine harmonic wavelet transform. Signal, Image and Video Processing, vol. 7, no. 6, pp.1125-1143.

[26] Tang, J., Peli, E., & Acton, S. (2003). Image enhancement using a contrast measure in the compressed domain. IEEE Signal Processing Letters, vol. 10, no.10, pp. 289-292.

[27] Haghighat, M. B. A, Aghagolzadeh, A., & Seyedarabi, H. (2011). Multi-focus image fusion for visual sensor networks in DCT domain. Computers & Electrical Engineering, vol. 37, no. 5, pp. 789-797.

[28] Tang, J. (2004). A contrast based image fusion technique in the DCT domain. Digital Signal Processing, vol. 14, no. 3, pp. 218-226.

[29] Phamila Y. A. V., & Amutha, R. (2014). Discrete Cosine Transform based fusion of multi-focus images for visual sensor networks. Signal Processing, vol. 95, pp. 161-170.

[30] Cao, L., Jin, L., Tao, H., Li, G., Zhuang, Z., & Zhang, Y. (2015). Multi-focus image fusion based on spatial frequency in discrete cosine transform domain. IEEE Signal Processing Letters, vol. 22, no. 2, pp. 220-224.

[31] Abdollahzadeh, M., Malekzadeh, M., & Seyedarabi, H. (2016). Multi-focus image fusion for visual sensor networks. In 24th Iranian Conference on Electrical Engineering (ICEE), pp. 1673-1677.

[32] Amin-Naji, M., & Aghagolzadeh, A. (2016). Block DCT filtering using vector processing. In 2016 1st International Conference on New Research Achievements in Electrical and Computer Engineering (ICNRAECE), pp. 722-727.

[33] Naji, M. A., & Aghagolzadeh, A. (2015). Multi-focus image fusion in DCT domain based on correlation coefficient. In 2nd International Conference on Knowledge-Based Engineering and Innovation (KBEI), pp. 632-639.

[34] Amin-Naji, M., & Aghagolzadeh, A. (2016). Multi-focus image fusion using VOL and EOL in DCT domain. In 2016 1st International Conference on New Research Achievements in Electrical and Computer Engineering (ICNRAECE), pp. 728-733.

[35] Haghighat, M. B. A. Multi-Focus Image Fusion in DCT Domain, (2016), Available: https://github.com/mhaghighat/dctVarFusion

[36] Rockinger, O. image fusion toolbox, (1999). Available: http://www.metapix.de/toolbox.htm

[37] Kumar, B. K. S., Multifocus and multispectral image fusion based on pixel significance using dchwt, (2013), Available: http://www.mathworks.com/matlabcentral/fileexchange/43051-multifocus-and-multispectral-image-fusion-based-on-pixel-significance-using-dchwt

[38] Image processing place, Available: http://www.imageprocessingplace.com/root_files_V3/image_databases.htm

[39] Wang, Z., & Bovik, A. (2009). Mean squared error: Love it or leave it? A new look at Signal Fidelity Measures. IEEE Signal Processing Magazine, vol. 26, no. 1, pp. 98-117.

[40] Esmilizaini, A. M, Latif, A. M., & Loghmani, Gh. B. (2017). Tuning Shape Parameter of Radial Basis Functions in Zooming Images using Genetic Algorithm. Journal of AI & Data Mining, Articles in Press.

[41] Wang, Z., Bovik, A. C., Sheikh, H. R., & Simoncelli, E. P. (2004). Image quality assessment: from error visibility to structural similarity. IEEE Transactions on Image Processing, vol. 13, no.4, pp. 600-612.

[42] Xydeas, C., & Petrovic, V. (2000). Objective image fusion performance measure. Electronics Letters, vol. 36, no.4, pp. 308-309.

[43] Petrovic, V., & Xydeas, C. (2005). Objective image fusion performance characterization. In Tenth IEEE International Conference on Computer Vision (ICCV), pp. 1866-1871.

[44] Haghighat, M. B. A, Aghagolzadeh, A., & Seyedarabi, H. (2011). A non-reference image fusion metric based on mutual information of image features. Computers & Electrical Engineering, vol. 37, no. 5, pp. 744-756.

12

A time-frequency approach for EEG signal segmentation

M. Azarbad[1], H. Azami[2*], S. Sanei[3], A. Ebrahimzadeh[1]

1. Department of Electrical and Computer Engineering, Babol University of Technology, Babol, Iran
2. Department of Electrical Engineering, Iran University of Science and Technology, Tehran, Iran
3. Faculty of Engineering and Physical Sciences, University of Surrey, Guildford, United Kingdom

*Corresponding author: hmd.azami@yahoo.com (H. Azami)

Abstract

The record of human brain neural activities, namely electroencephalogram (EEG), is known to be non-stationary in general. In addition, the human head is a non-linear medium for such signals. In many applications, it is useful to divide the EEGs into segments in which the signals can be considered stationary. Here, Hilbert-Huang Transform (HHT), as an effective tool in signal processing is applied since unlike the traditional time-frequency approaches, it exploits the non-linearity of the medium and nonstationarity of the EEG signals. In addition, we use Singular Spectrum Analysis (SSA) in the pre-processing step as an effective noise removal approach. By using synthetic and real EEG signals, the proposed method is compared with Wavelet Generalized Likelihood Ratio (WGLR) algorithm as a well-known signal segmentation method. The simulation results indicate the performance superiority of the proposed method.

Keywords: *EEG Signal Segmentation, Time-Frequency Approach, Empirical Mode Decomposition (EMD), Singular Spectrum Analysis (SSA), and Hilbert-Huang Transform (HHT).*

1. Introduction

Nonstationarity of the signals can be quantified by measuring some statistics of the signals, such as mean and variance, at different time lags. The signals can be deemed stationary if there is no considerable variation in such statistics. In general, the signals are stationary if their distributions do not vary with time. Often it is necessary to label the electroencephalogram (EEG) signals by segments of similar characteristics that are particularly meaningful to clinicians and for evaluation by neurophysiologists. Within each segment, the signals are considered statistically stationary, usually with similar time or frequency distributions. For example, an EEG recorded from an epileptic patient may be divided into three segments of preictal, ictal, and postictal with variable durations [1].

The segmentation may be fixed or adaptive. Dividing the signals into fixed (rather small) size segments is easy and fast. However, it cannot precisely follow the epoch boundaries [2,3]. On the other hand, in adaptive segmentation the boundaries are accurately and automatically followed [2]. Many adaptive segmentation methods have been suggested by researchers in the field such as those in [4-10].

In order to increase the accuracy of the classification in EEG signals, Kosar et al. [6] have proposed to use the segmentation method as a pre-processing step. It was done by a dividing signal to segments of different lengths that are stationary. In this method two characteristics were used that are based on estimation of average frequency in the segment and the value of mean amplitude in the window.

Azami et al. have proposed a method to segment a signal in general and real EEG signal in particular using the standard deviation, integral operation, Discrete Wavelet Transform (DWT), and variable threshold [2]. In this paper we have illustrated that the standard deviation can indicate the changes in amplitude and/or frequency [2]. To remove the effect of shifting and smooth the signal, the integral operation has been used as a pre-processing step.

However, the performance of the method is entirely dependent on the level of noise components.

In Generalized Likelihood Ratio (GLR) method to obtain the boundaries of signal segments, it has been suggested to use two windows that slide along the signal. The signal within each window of this method is modelled by an autoregressive (AR) process. For the signals within such windows the statistical properties don't change; in other words AR coefficients remain approximately constant and equal. However, when the sliding windows fall in the different segments, the AR coefficients change and the boundaries are detected [11]. In [12] Lv et al. have suggested using wavelet transform for decreasing the number of false segments and reducing the computation load. This method has been named Wavelet GLR (WGLR) [12].

Azami et al. for the first time have proposed an adaptive signal segmentation approach using DWT and Higuchi's Fractal Dimension (FD) [5]. In order to obtain a better multi-resolution representation of a signal which is very valuable in detection of abrupt changes within that signal, the DWT has been used. The changes in the Higuchi's FD refer to the underlying statistical variations of the signals and time series including the transients and sharp changes in both amplitude and frequency. The performance of the method is still dependent on the noise components.

Since Time-Frequency Signal Analysis and Processing (TFSAP) exploits variations in both time and frequency, most of the brain signals are decomposed in the time-frequency domain. Because the instantaneous energy depends on the frequency of the signal, in this article, using Time-Frequency Distribution (TFD) for signal segmentation has been proposed [13].

A recent contribution to signal processing is named Hilbert-Huang Transform (HHT) that is combination of the Empirical Mode Decomposition (EMD) and the Hilbert Transform (HT) [14,15]. Fourier transform, wavelet transform, and HHT can be used to discuss the frequency characteristics of stationary signals and system linearity, the time-frequency features of non-stationary signals and outputs of non-linear systems, respectively. Since EEG signals are non-stationary, HHT is most suitable process for analyzing them [14].

Moreover, since noise can significantly decrease the performance of the segmentation methods, first we use Singular Spectrum Analysis (SSA) as a filter. SSA is becoming an effective and powerful tool for time series analysis in meteorology, hydrology, geophysics, climatology, economics, biology, physics, medicine, and other sciences where short and long, one-dimensional and multi-dimensional, stationary and non-stationary, almost deterministic and noisy time series are to be analyzed [16].

The rest of the paper is organized as follows: The proposed adaptive method as well as brief explanations of SSA and HHT is explained in Section 2. The performance of the proposed method is evaluated in Section 3. The last section concludes the paper.

2. Proposed Adaptive Segmentation

First, we use a powerful tool, SSA, to reduce the noise sources. The SSA is much faster than previous widely used filters or smoothers like the DWT. A brief description of the two SSA stages together with the corresponding mathematics is given. At the first stage, the series is decomposed and at the second stage we reconstruct the original series and use the reconstructed series (which is without noise) to predict new data points [17,18].

1) Decomposition: This stage is composed of two sequential steps including embedding and SVD. In the embedding step, the time series $\mathbf{s}$ is mapped to k multidimensional lagged vectors of length l as follows:

$$\mathbf{x}_i = [s_{i-1}, s_i, ..., s_{i+l-2}]^T, \quad 1 \le i \le k \quad (1)$$

where $k = r - l + 1$, l is the window length ($1 \le l \le r$), and $[]^T$ denotes the transpose of a matrix. An appropriate window length totally depends on the application and the prior information about the signals of interest. The trajectory matrix of the series $\mathbf{s}$ is constructed by inserting each $\mathbf{x}_i$ as the ith column of an $l \times k$ matrix, i.e.

$$\mathbf{X} = [\mathbf{x}_1, \mathbf{x}_2, ..., \mathbf{x}_k] = \begin{bmatrix} s_0 & s_1 & s_2 & \cdots & s_{k-1} \\ s_1 & s_2 & s_3 & \cdots & s_k \\ s_2 & s_3 & s_4 & \cdots & s_{k+1} \\ \vdots & \vdots & \vdots & \ddots & \vdots \\ s_{l-1} & s_l & s_{l+1} & \cdots & s_{r-1} \end{bmatrix} \quad (2)$$

Note that the trajectory matrix $\mathbf{X}$ is a Hankel matrix, i.e. for all the elements along its diagonals $i+j$=constant.

In the SVD sub-stage, the SVD of the trajectory matrix is computed and represented as the sum of rank-one biorthogonal elementary matrices. Consider the eigenvalues and corresponding eigenvectors of $\mathbf{S} = \mathbf{X}\mathbf{X}^T$ are $\lambda_1, \lambda_2, ..., \lambda_l$ and

$\mathbf{e}_1, \mathbf{e}_2, ..., \mathbf{e}_l$, respectively. If $\mathbf{v}_i = \mathbf{X}^T \mathbf{e}_i / \sqrt{\lambda_i}$, then the SVD of the trajectory matrix can be written as

$$\mathbf{X} = \mathbf{X}_1 + \mathbf{X}_2 + ... + \mathbf{X}_d \qquad (3)$$

where $d = \arg\max_i \{\lambda_i > 0\}$ and $\mathbf{X}_i = \sqrt{\lambda_i} \, \mathbf{e}_i \mathbf{v}_i^T$. The ith eigentriple of the SVD decomposition comprises of $\mathbf{v}_i$, $\mathbf{e}_i$, and λ_i. Projecting the time series onto the direction of each eigenvector yields the corresponding temporal principal component [17,18].

2) Reconstruction: This stage has two steps: grouping and diagonal averaging. The grouping step divides the set of indices $\{1, 2, ..., d\}$ to m disjoint subsets I_1, I_2, ..., I_m. For every group $I_j = \{i_{j1}, i_{j2}, ..., i_{jp}\}$, we have $\mathbf{X}_{I_j} = \{X_{i_{j1}}, X_{i_{j2}}, ..., X_{i_{jp}}\}$. Grouping the eigentriples and expanding all matrices $\mathbf{X}_{I_j}$, (3) can be written as

$$\mathbf{X} = \{\mathbf{X}_{I_1}, \mathbf{X}_{I_2}, ..., \mathbf{X}_{I_m}\} \qquad (4)$$

There is no general rule for grouping. For each application, the grouping rule depends on the special requirements of the problem and the type of the contributing signals and noise.

b) Diagonal averaging: In the final stage of analysis, each group is transformed into a series of length r. For a typical $l \times k$ matrix $\mathbf{Y}$, the qth element of the resulted time series, g_q is calculated by averaging the matrix elements over the diagonal $i + j = q + 2$, where i and j are the row and column indices of $\mathbf{Y}$, respectively [17,18].

The concept of separability is an important part of the SSA methodology. Assume that $\mathbf{s}$ is the sum of two series $\mathbf{s}_1$ and $\mathbf{s}_2$, i.e., $\mathbf{s} = \mathbf{s}_1 + \mathbf{s}_2$. Separability means that the matrix terms of the SVD of the trajectory matrix of X can be divided into two disjoint groups, such that the sums of the terms within the groups result in the trajectory matrices $\mathbf{X}_1$ and $\mathbf{X}_2$ of the time series $\mathbf{s}_1$ and $\mathbf{s}_2$, respectively [17,18]. A necessary condition for separability of the sources is disjointedness of their frequency spectrum. It is also worth mentioning that exact separability cannot be achieved for real-world signals; hence, only approximate separability can be considered.

The eigentriples resulting from the SSA also contain information about the frequency content of the data. If there is a periodic component in the data, it will be reflected in the output of the SSA as a pair of (almost) equal eigenvalues [17,18]. Moreover, the highest peaks in the Fourier transform of the corresponding eigenvectors are related to the frequency of the periodic component. These features of the SSA are used to construct data-driven filters.

After employing the SSA, we use the combination of EMD and Hilbert transform, namely HHT. EMD is a powerful and new method applied to decompose the Intrinsic Mode Functions (IMFs) from a complex time series. This decomposition, sifting process, uses the mean of the upper and lower envelopes [19-22]. The sifting process must be repeated until every component satisfies two conditions:

1. The number of extrema and the number of zero-crossings must either be equal or differ at most by one.
2. At any point, the mean value of the two envelopes defined respectively by local maxima and local minima must be zero.

For an arbitrary time series $x(t)$, the sifting process can be summarized as follows:

1) Identify all the local extrema (maxima or minima) of signal $x(t)$, and then connect all the local maxima by a cubic spline line (upper envelope)

2) Repeat similarly all the local minima (lower envelope).

3) The mean of the upper and lower envelopes is designated as $m(t)$. The difference between the data and $m(t)$ is the first component as follows:
$$h_1(t) = x(t) - m(t) \qquad (5)$$

4) Suppose $h_1(t)$ as the new original signal and repeat above steps.

Generally, this process must be repeated until the last $h_1(t)$ has at most one extrema or becomes constant. However in many cases, it is not a suitable criterion. In this paper we use the criterion applied in [19].

The second step of HHT, definition of instantaneous frequency, is to compute the instantaneous frequency by using the Hilbert transform [20-22]. Hilbert transform of a given time series $x(t)$ can be computed as:

$$y(t) = HT[x(t)] = \frac{1}{\pi} PV \int_{-\infty}^{+\infty} \frac{x(\tau)}{t - \tau} d\tau \qquad (6)$$

which PV illustrates the principal value of the singular integral [20-22]. $x(t)$ and $y(t)$ can be represented as a complex number $z(t)$ as follows:

$$z(t) = x(t) + iy(t) = a(t)e^{i\theta(t)} \qquad (7)$$

where i is the imaginary unit, $a(t) = [x(t)^2 + y(t)^2]^{0.5}$ and $\theta(t) = arctg\left\{\dfrac{y(t)}{x(t)}\right\}$.

In other words, $a(t)$ and $\theta(t)$ are the instantaneous amplitude and phase, respectively [20-22]. Moreover, instantaneous frequency can be defined as follows:

$$f(t) = \frac{1}{2\pi}\frac{d\theta}{dt} \qquad (8)$$

3. Simulation Results

In order to assess the performance of the suggested method, two kind signals including the synthetic data and a real EEG signal are utilized. The synthetic signal includes the following seven epochs:

Epoch 1: 3.5cos(2πt) + 4.5cos(6πt),
Epoch 2: 3.5cos(3πt) + 5.5cos(10πt),
Epoch 3: 4.5cos(2πt) + 5.5cos(8πt),
Epoch 4: 3cos(2πt) + 7cos(6πt) + 2cos(7πt),
Epoch 5: 4cos(2πt) + 5cos(10πt),
Epoch 6: 4cos(3πt) + 7.5cos(9πt),
Epoch 7: 2cos(4πt) + 7cos(8πt) + 3cos(3πt).

In Figures 1.a and 1.b the synthetic data described above and the filtered signal by SSA with window length 2 are shown, respectively. As can be seen, the filtered signal is smoother than the original signal. After filtering the signal by SSA to decompose the IMFS of the signal EMD is employed. In Figure 2, the result of decomposition performed by EMD of the filtered synthetic signal is depicted. This figure illustrates that the first mode has a higher frequency than the second mode where modes are ordered from the highest frequency to the lowest.

As mentioned previously, the reason for using EMD is that HT can be better computed. HHT of the synthetic signal is shown in Figure 3. As we can see in this figure, all seven segments boundaries are shown accurately.

To demonstrate the emphasis of this algorithm, in Figure 4, the output of the WGLR method is shown. Figure 4.a and Figure 4.b show respectively the original signal the same as Figure1.a and the decomposed signal using wavelet transform. Here, the DWT with Daubechies wavelet of order 8 is used. Note that the WGLR parameters for this paper are attained by considering many trials. In a general manner, the decomposed signal indicates the slowly and rapidly changing features of the signal in the lower frequency and higher frequency bands, respectively. As can be seen in Figure 4.c, there are some false boundaries selected by the WGLR. Comparing the last two figures, it has been shown that the proposed method has a superior performance compared with WGLR for signal segmentation. Although, as mentioned before, there are several advantages in combining HHT and SSA, the computation time for the proposed method is not as intensive as that of the WGLR method.

As described before, signal segmentation is a pre-processing step for EEG signal analysis. In this part one epoch of a real newborn is shown in Figure 5.a. Firstly, for smoothing the EEG signal, we use SSA as a fast and powerful pre-processing step. The result of using SSA is shown in Figure 5.b. The SSA used for this real signal has window length equal to 20 that is selected with trial and error. After using SSA, the combination of EMD and HT named HHT is applied on the filtered signal in Figure 6 and Figure 7, respectively. We can see the influence of this method on the achieved outputs in the both synthetic signals and real EEG signals.

As can be seen in the result of the proposed method all three segments can be accurately segmented. In order to represent efficiency of the proposed method, in Figure 8, WGLR is used for real newborn EEG signal the same as Figure 5.a. Output of WGLR method is shown in Figure 8.b. It should be mentioned that the DWT with Daubechies wavelet of order 8 is used. As can be seen in this figure, there are some false boundaries and one missed boundary. Therefore, for this application, WGLR is not a reliable method for signal segmentation.

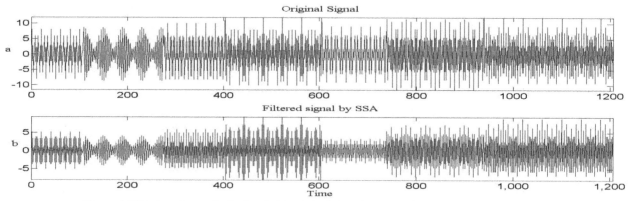

Figure 1. Filtering the synthetic signal; (a) original signal, and (b) filtered signal by SSA.

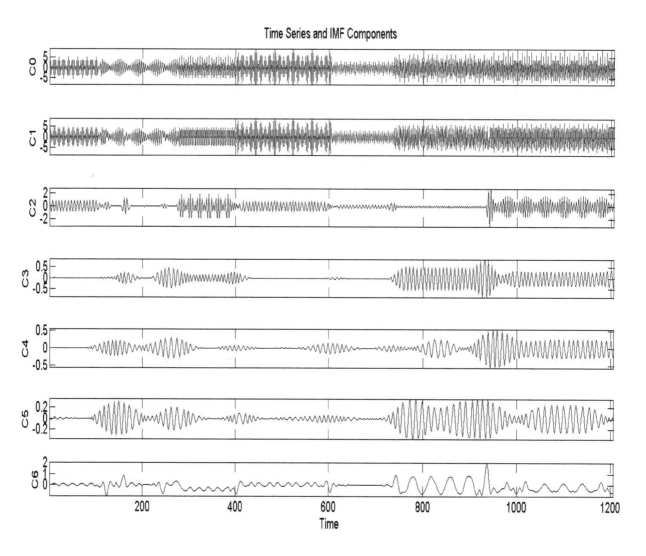

Figure 2. Components of the filtered synthetic signal by EMD. The first time series is the filtered signal by SSA. The decomposition yields 5 IMF and a residual. The IMFs are the time-frequency constituents or components of the synthetic signal.

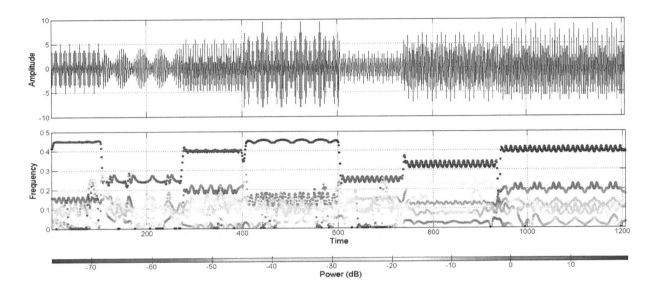

Figure 3. Hilbert transform of the synthetic signal gather prepared using EMD(i.e. HHT of the synthetic signal); (a) the time series analyzed, and b) signal power plotted in time-frequency.

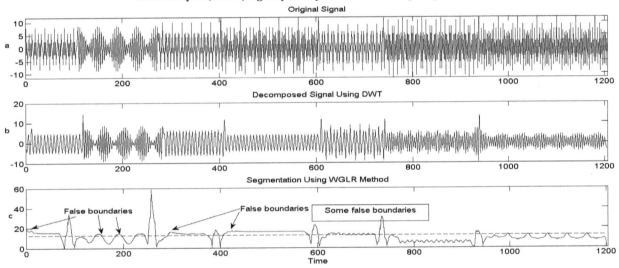

Figure 4. Signal segmentation in synthetic signal, (a) original signal, (b) decomposed signal by DWT, and (c) output of the WGLR method.

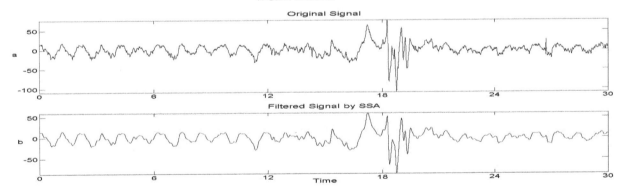

Figure 5. Filtering the real EEG signal; (a) original signal, and (b) filtered signal by SSA.

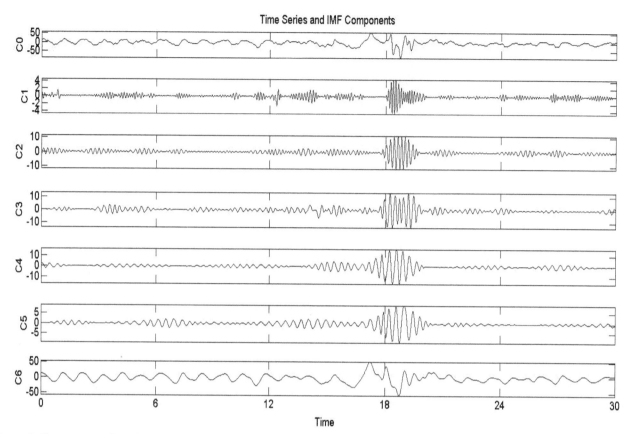

Figure 6. Components of the filtered real EEG signal by EMD. The first time series is the filtered signal. The decomposition yields 5 IMF and a residual. The IMFs are the time-frequency constituents or components of the EEG signal.

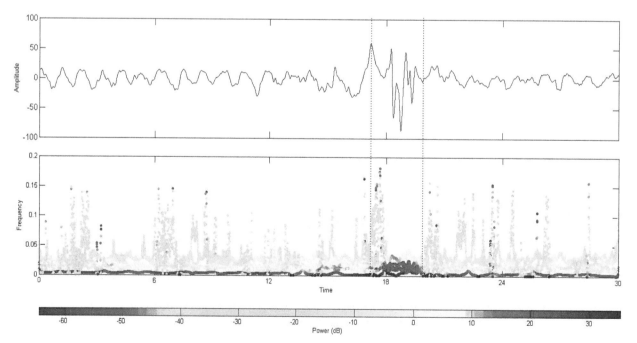

Figure 7. Hilbert transform of the real filtered EEG signal gather prepared using EMD(i.e. HHT of the filtered EEG signal); (a) the time series analyzed, and b) signal power plotted in time-frequency domain.

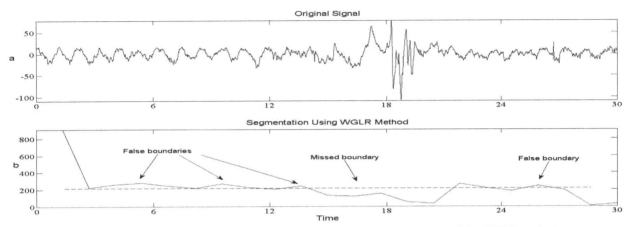

Figure 8. Signal segmentation in real EEG signal, (a) original signal, and (b) output of the WGLR method.

4. Conclusion

The objective of this work has been to investigate and demonstrate the ability of combination of the SSA, EMD and HT in segmenting the non-stationary signals such as EEG. Unlike commonly used segmentation methods, the proposed time-frequency approach has effectively exploited the nonstationarity of the signals and non-linearity of the medium. Since noise can significantly affect the performance of the segmentation methods, the SSA as a fast and powerful tool for mitigation of noise has been employed. After filtering the signal by SSA, HHT has been used for segmenting the signals. The integrity of the EMD is crucial to the ability of the HHT to outperform traditional Fourier-based techniques. The results have indicated superiority of the proposed method comparing with a well-known method, WGLR, for EEG signal segmentation.

References

[1] Sanei, S. and Chambers, J. (2007). EEG signal processing. John Wiley and Sons.

[2] Azami, H., Sanei, S. and Mohammadi, K. (2011). A novel signal segmentation method based on standard deviation and variable threshold. Journal of Computer Applications, vol. 34, no. 2, 27-34.

[3] Agarwal, R. and Gotman, J. (1999). Adaptive segmentation of electroencephalographic data using a non-linear energy operator. IEEE International Symposium on Circuits and Systems, vol. 4, 199-202.

[4] Azami, H. and Sanei, S. (2012). Automatic Signal Segmentation based on singular spectrum analysis and imperialist competitive algorithm. 2nd International eConference on Computer and Knowledge Engineering, 50-55, 2012.

[5] Azami, H., Khosravi, A., Malekzadeh, M. and Sanei, S. (2012). A new adaptive signal segmentation approach based on Higuchi's fractal dimension.

Computer and Information Science, Springer-Verlag, vol. 304, 152-159.

[6] Kosar, K., Lhotska, L. and V. Krajca, (2004). Classification of long-term EEG recordings. Lecture Notes in Computer Science, vol. 3337, 322-332.

[7] Azami, H., Sanei, S., Mohammadi, K. and Hassanpour, H. (2013). A hybrid evolutionary approach to segmentation of non-stationary signals. Digital Signal Processing, 1-12, DOI: 10.1016/j.dsp.2013.02.019.

[8] Azami, H., Mohammadi, K. and Bozorgtabar, B. (2012). An improved signal segmentation using moving average and Savitzky-Golay filter. Journal of Signal and Information Processing, vol. 3, no. 1, 39-44.

[9] Azami, H., Mohammadi, K. and Hassanpour, H. (2011). An improved signal segmentation method using genetic algorithm. Journal of Computer Applications, vol. 29, no. 8, 5-9.

[10] Hassanpour, H. and Anisheh, S. M. (2010). An improved adaptive signal segmentation method using fractal dimension. International Symposium on Signal Processing and Its Applications, 720-723.

[11] Wang, D., Vogt, R., Mason, M. and Sridharan, S. (2008). Automatic audio segmentation using the generalized likelihood ratio. 2nd IEEE International Conference on Signal Processing and Communication Systems, 1-5.

[12] Lv, J., Li, X. and Li, T. (2007). Web-based application for traffic anomaly detection algorithm. Second IEEE International Conference on Internet and Web Applications and Services, 44-60.

[13] Boashash, B. (2003). Introduction to the concepts of time–frequency signal analysis and processing. Time–Frequency Signal Analysis and Processing: A Comprehensive Reference part I, Oxford: Elsevier.

[14] Lin, C. F. and Zhu, J. D. (2011). HHT-based time-frequency analysis method for biomedical signal applications. Proceedings of the 5th WSEAS

international conference on Circuits, systems, signal and telecommunications, 65-68.

[15] Huang, N. E., Shen, Z., Long, S. R., Wu, M. C., Shih, H. H., Zheng, Q., Yen, N. C., Tung, C. C. and Liu, H. H. (1998). The empirical mode decomposition and the Hilbert spectrum for non-linear and non-stationary time series analysis. in Proceedings of the Royal Society A: Mathematical, Physical and Engineering Sciences, vol. 454, no. 1971, 903-995.

[16] Sanei, S., Lee, T. K. M. and Abolghasemi, V. (2012) A new adaptive line enhancer based on singular spectrum analysis. IEEE Transaction on Biomedical Engineering, vol. 59, no. 2. 428-434.

[17] Hassani, H. (2007). Singular spectrum analysis: methodology and comparison. Journal of Data Science, vol. 5, no. 2, 239-257.

[18] Ghaderi, F., Mohseni, H. and Sanei, S., (2011). Localizing heart sounds in respiratory signals using singular spectrum analysis. IEEE Transactions on Biomedical Engineering, vol. 59, no. 12, 3360-3367.

[19] Battista, B. M., Knapp, C., McGee, T. and Goebel, V. (2007). Application of the empirical mode decomposition and Hilbert-Huang transform to seismic reflection data. Geophysics, vol. 72, no. 2.

[20] Xiaoming, N., Jian, Z. and Xingwu, L. (2012). Application of Hilbert-Huang transform to laser Doppler velocimeter. Optics & Laser Technology, vol. 44, no. 7, 2197-2201.

[21] Fana, S. Z., Wei, Q., Shi, P. F., Chenc, Y. J., Liub, Q. and Shieh, J. S. (2012). A comparison of patients' heart rate variability and blood flow variability during surgery based on the Hilbert–Huang Transform. Biomedical Signal Processing and Control, vol. 7, no. 5, 465-473.

[22] Peng, J. and Zhang, G. (2012). Analysis of signal characteristics of swirlmeter in oscillatory flow based on Hilbert–Huang Transform (HHT). Measurement, vol. 45, no. 7, 1765-1781.

13

Overlap-based feature weighting: The feature extraction of Hyperspectral remote sensing imagery

M. Imani and H. Ghassemian[*]

Faculty of Electrical & Computer Engineering, Tarbiat Modares University, Tehran, Iran.

Corresponding author: ghassemi@modares.ac.ir (H. Ghassemian).

Abstract
Hyperspectral sensors provide a large number of spectral bands. This massive and complex data structure of hyperspectral images presents a challenge to traditional data processing techniques. Therefore, reducing the dimensionality of hyperspectral images without losing important information is a very important issue for the remote sensing community. We propose to use overlap-based feature weighting (OFW) for supervised feature extraction of hyperspectral data. In the OFW method, the feature vector of each pixel of hyperspectral image is divided to some segments. The weighted mean of adjacent spectral bands in each segment is calculated as an extracted feature. The less the overlap between classes is, the more the class discrimination ability will be. Therefore, the inverse of overlap between classes in each band (feature) is considered as a weight for that band. The superiority of OFW, in terms of classification accuracy and computation time, over other supervised feature extraction methods is established on three real hyperspectral images in the small sample size situation.

Keywords: *Class Discrimination, Overlap, Feature Weighting, Feature Extraction, Hyperspectral.*

1. Introduction

The high spectral resolution hyperspectral images allow the characterization, identification, and classification of the land covers with improved accuracy, robustness, and more details. A large number of training samples is required for achieving satisfactory accuracy in classification problems. However, the collection of ground reference data (training samples) in real world applications is an expensive and time consuming task and so the number of available training samples might be very limited.

There are different solutions to cope with the small training sample size. Semi-supervised approaches use the ability of unlabeled samples in addition to labeled samples to improve the classification accuracy [1,2]. Advanced classifiers such as kernel-based classifiers are distribution free and do not make assumptions about the density functions of the data [3,4]. Feature reduction is one of the most important solutions for small sample size problem [5-9]. In addition to improving the classification accuracy, feature reduction techniques reduce the computational

complexity and also simple the visualization of data. Feature reduction methods are divided into two general groups: feature selection and feature extraction. Feature selection methods select an appropriate subset of features from the original candidate features and maintain the physical meaning of data. Feature extraction methods transform the feature space of data usually with using a projection matrix. Feature reduction techniques can be done supervised [10,11], unsupervised [12,13] or semi-supervised [14]. We assess the supervised feature extraction methods in this paper.

Multiple features such as spectral, texture, and shape features are employed to represent pixels from different perspectives in hyperspectral image classification. The properly combining multiple features results in good classification performance. A patch alignment framework to linearly combine multiple features in the optimal way, which obtains a unified low-dimensional representation of these multiple features for subsequent classification, is introduced in [15]. A pixel in a hyperspectral image can be represented by both spatial and spectral features. Each view of a feature summarizes a specific characteristic of the studied object from different feature spaces, and also features for different views are complementary to each other. An ensemble manifold regularized sparse low-rank approximation algorithm for multi-view feature dimensionality reduction is proposed in [16].

Linear discriminant analysis (LDA) is a simple and popular method for feature extraction in different pattern recognition applications [17]. LDA maximizes the between-class scatter matrix and minimizes the within-class scatter matrix to increase the class discrimination. Because of singularity of within-class scatter matrix, LDA has weak efficiency when the number of training samples is limited. Generalized discriminant analysis (GDA) is the nonlinear version of LDA, which works in the kernel space [18]. Because of the limitation of rank of between-class scatter matrix, LDA and GDA can extract maximum $c - 1$ features where c is the number of classes. Nonparametric weighted feature extraction (NWFE) uses the nonparametric form and weighted mean for calculation of scatter matrices [19]. Thus, NWFE can extract more than $c - 1$ features and, moreover, it has good efficiency with small training set. Median-mean line discriminant analysis (MMLDA), which is recently proposed, copes with the negative effect of the class mean caused by outliers with introduction of median–mean line as an adaptive class-prototype [20].

We propose a supervised feature extraction method in this paper that is simple, fast and efficient in small sample size situation. The proposed method is named overlap-based feature weighting (OFW). In a hyperspectral image, the adjacent spectral bands contain redundant information. Thus, we divide the feature vector of each sample of data to some segments in such a way that each segment contains adjacent spectral bands. We consider the weighted mean of spectral bands (original features) in each segment as an extracted feature. If classes have more overlap in a spectral band, then, the discrimination of classes in that band is harder. Thus, the class discrimination ability in each band has reverse relationship with the overlap value between classes in that band.

Therefore, we assign the inverse of overlap between classes in each feature, as a weight for that feature in the weighted mean. Feature extraction methods such as LDA, GDA, NWFE, and MMLDA need to estimate the mean vectors (the first order statistics) and the scatter matrices

(the second order statistics). The accurate estimate of statistics needs large enough training set. When the number of training samples is limited, the accurate estimate of mean vectors and covariance matrices cannot be provided, and so, the accuracy of LDA-based methods such as conventional LDA, GDA, NWFE, and MMLDA is decreased. The proposed method, OFW, just uses the original training samples and does not need to estimate the statistics of data. Therefore, it can have good efficiency in small sample size situations compared to LDA-based methods. Moreover, OFW has simple calculations, so, it is fast. The efficiency of OFW is investigated by three real hyperspectral images. The current paper focuses on the following sections: section 2 introduction of proposed method, section 3 the experimental results, and section 4 conclusions.

2. Proposed method

The adjacent spectral bands (features) in each pixel of hyperspectral image contain high redundant information. Then, for extraction of m features from d original spectral bands, we divide the feature vector of each sample of data to m segments containing $K = \left\lfloor \frac{d}{m} \right\rfloor$ adjacent spectral bands. Then, the weighted mean of spectral bands in each segment, is considered as an extracted feature for that segment. Let, $\boldsymbol{x} = [x_1 \quad x_2 \cdots \quad x_d]^T$ be the feature vector of a pixel of hyperspectral image and $\boldsymbol{y} = [y_1 \quad y_2 \cdots \quad y_m]^T$ be the extracted feature vector of $\boldsymbol{x}$ where $m < d$. The elements of $\boldsymbol{y}$ are calculated as follows:

$$y_l = \sum_{j=(l-1)K+1}^{lK} w_j x_j , \qquad 1 \le l \le m - 1 \qquad (1)$$

$$y_m = \begin{cases} \sum_{j=(m-1)K+1}^{d} w_j x_j \; ; \; mK < d \; (m < \frac{d}{K}) \\ \sum_{j=(m-1)K+1}^{mK} w_j x_j \; ; \; mK = d \; (m = \frac{d}{K}) \end{cases} \qquad (2)$$

where, w_j is the weight of jth spectral band in the above weighted mean. How to decompose the whole spectral signature has been searched in some literatures such as [21].

To this end, we implemented the simplest possible approach for segmentation of spectral signature of pixels. The calculation of weights is the novelty of our proposed method. In some spectral bands, the difference between classes is more than other bands.

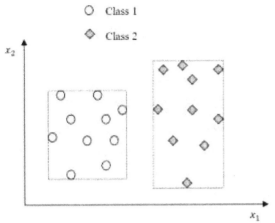

The more the overlap between classes is in a

Figure 1. Samples of two classes in a two-dimensional feature space.

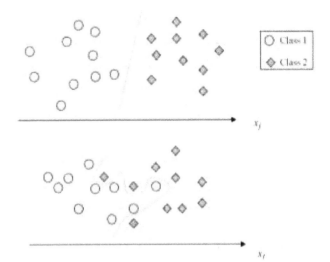

Figure 2. There is not overlap between classes in band x_j, and so two classes are easily separated from each other in x_j while there is overlap between classes in band x_l, and so two classes are hardly separated from each other in x_l.

spectral band (feature), the harder the class discrimination will be in that spectral band. In other words, the class discrimination ability, in each feature, has reverse relationship with the overlap between classes in that feature.

Figure 1 shows the samples of two classes in a two-dimensional feature space. In band x_1, two classes have not overlap and thus are discriminable from each other, while in the band x_2, classes are overlapped and discrimination between them is hard. To better understanding, see figure 2.

Two classes in band x_j, have no overlap; thus, they are easily separated from each other using a simple line; while these two classes have overlap in band x_l, and so, a complex nonlinear curve is needed to separate them from each other. Therefore, it is obvious that the ability of each spectral band in discrimination between classes has a reverse relationship with the overlap between classes in that band.

Let, $x_{jq}^i (j = 1, ..., d; q = 1, ..., n_i; i = 1, ..., c)$ be the jth feature of qth sample of class i where d, c, and n_i are the number of spectral bands (features), the number of classes, and the number of training samples in class i, respectively. The minimum and maximum values of each spectral band in each class are given by:

$$f_{min,ji} = \min_{q=1,...,n_i} x_{jq}^i \; ; i = 1, ..., c \; ; j = 1, ..., d \quad (3)$$

$$f_{max,ji} = \max_{q=1,...,n_i} x_{jq}^i \; ; i = 1, ..., c \; ; j = 1, ..., d \quad (4)$$

where, $f_{min,ji}$ is the minimum value of feature j in class i and $f_{max,ji}$ is the maximum value of feature j in class i.

Two classes i and k $(i, k = 1, ..., c)$ are not overlapped and are completely separate from each other in band j if:

$$\left(f_{min,ji} < f_{min,jk}\right) \& \left(f_{min,ji} < f_{max,jk}\right) \\ \& \left(f_{max,ji} < f_{min,jk}\right) \& \left(f_{max,ji} < f_{max,jk}\right) \quad (5)$$

or

$$\left(f_{min,ji} > f_{min,jk}\right) \& \left(f_{min,ji} > f_{max,jk}\right) \& \\ \left(f_{max,ji} > f_{min,jk}\right) \& \left(f_{max,ji} > f_{max,jk}\right) \quad (6)$$

Otherwise, two classes i and k have overlap and the value of overlap between them in feature j is calculated as follows:

$$(OV_{ik})_j = \left|\max\left(f_{min,ji}, f_{min,jk}\right) \\ - \min\left(f_{max,ji}, f_{max,jk}\right)\right| \; ; \\ i = 1, ..., c; k = 1, ..., c; j = 1, ..., d \quad (7)$$

where, $(OV_{ik})_j$ is the overlap value of class i and class k in feature j. The overlap between all pairs of classes is calculated as follows:

$$OV_j = \frac{1}{2}\sum_{k=1}^{c}\sum_{i=1}^{c}(OV_{ik})_j \; ; j = 1, ..., d \quad (8)$$

The class discrimination ability has reverse relationship with the overlap value between classes. Thus, the weight associated with each feature in the weighted mean in (1) and (2) is calculated by:

$$w_j = \frac{1}{OV_j}; j = 1, ..., d \quad (9)$$

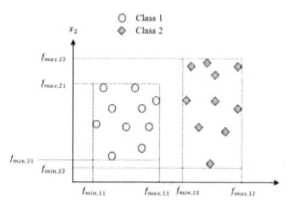

Figure 3. An example of determination of overlap between two classes.

Figure 3 shows an example of determination of overlap between two classes. In band x_1, we have:

$$\left(f_{min,11} < f_{min,12}\right) \& \left(f_{min,11} < f_{max,12}\right)$$

$$\& \left(f_{max,11} < f_{min,12}\right) \& \left(f_{max,11} < f_{max,12}\right)$$

Thus, in band x_1, classes are not overlapped while in band x_2, classes are overlapped and the overlap value between them is given by:

$$(OV_{12})_2 = \left|max\left(f_{min,21}, f_{min,22}\right) - min\left(f_{max,21}, f_{max,22}\right)\right|$$

$$= \left|f_{min,21} - f_{max,21}\right|$$

3. Experiments and discussion

In this section, we assessed the performance of proposed method, OFW, compared to some supervised feature extraction methods such as LDA, NWFE, GDA, and MMLDA using three real hyperspectral images: Indian, university of Pavia, and KSC datasets. The Indian Pines is provided by Airborne Visible/Infrared Imaging Spectrometer (AVIRIS) over Northwestern Indiana. Indian image comprises 224 spectral bands, which are initially reduced to 200 by removing water absorption bands. This image has 145×145 pixels and 16 classes which 10 interesting classes of it are chosen for our experiments. The university of Pavia dataset is collected by the Reflective Optics System Imaging Spectrometer (ROSIS). The number of spectral bands in the original recorded image is 115 from which 103 bands are selected for analysis of data after the removal of noisy bands. This urban image has nine classes and 610×340 pixels. The KSC dataset is provided by AVIRIS over the Kennedy Space Center, Florida. After removing water absorption and low SNR bands,

176 bands are used for the analysis of data. The KSC image has 512×614 pixels and 13 classes.

Support vector machine (SVM) and Gaussian maximum likelihood (ML) are used as classifier to assess the performance of feature extraction methods. The polynomial with degree 3 with default parameters defined in LIBSVM [22] is used as kernel function in SVM classifier. We used some measures for assessment of classification accuracy: Average accuracy, average reliability, and kappa coefficient [23]. The reliability in a class is the number of testing samples that are correctly classified divided to the overall samples, which are classified in that class. We used the McNemars test [24] for assessment of statistical significance of differences in the classification results. The sign of Z_{12} indicates whether classifier 1 is more accurate than classifier 2 ($Z_{12} > 0$) or vice versa ($Z_{12} < 0$). The difference in classification accuracy between two classifiers is statistically significant if $|Z_{12}| > 1.96$. We used 16 training samples per class in our experiments to investigate the performance of feature extraction methods in small sample size situation. The training samples are chosen randomly from entire scene. We used the reminded samples as testing samples. We did each experiment 10 times and the average results are reported here.

Figures 4, 5, 6 show the average classification accuracy versus the number of extracted features with 16 training samples by a) SVM, b) ML classifiers for Indian, Pavia, and KSC datasets respectively. The accuracy and reliability of classes obtained by 16 training sample and SVM classifier for Indian (with 9 extracted features), Pavia (with 8 extracted features), and KSC (with 10 extracted features) are represented in tables 1, 2, and 3. The ground truth map (GTM) and classification maps for Indian and Pavia datasets are shown in figures 7, and 8 respectively. The highest classification accuracies achieved by 16 training samples for all feature extraction methods and hyperspectral images are shown in table 4. Table 5 shows the McNemars test results for different cases. The comparison of computation time of feature extraction processes is done in table 6.

We can see from the obtained results that OFW works better than other methods almost in all cases (only for Pavia urban image with ML classifier, GDA has better performance than other feature extraction methods). Popular feature extraction methods such as LDA, NWFE, GDA, and MMLDA calculate the scatter matrices and maximum the between-class scatter matrix and minimum the within-class scatter matrix. The proposed method, OFW, calculates the weighted mean of adjacent spectral bands and considers the inverse of overlap between classes in each feature as a weight for that feature. LDA, NWFE, GDA, and MMLDA methods need to calculate the first and second order statistics of data (mean vectors and covariance matrices) while OFW does not need to estimate theses statistics. Therefore, when a limited number of training samples is available, the accurate estimations of mean vectors and scatter matrices cannot be provided. In these conditions, OFW is superior to LDA-based methods. However, with increasing the number of training samples, the accurate estimations of scatter matrices are obtained and the performance of LDA-based methods is improved.

The performance of OFW is compared with LDA in different training sample size for Indian dataset by SVM classifier and 9 extracted features and the results are shown in figure 9.

Moreover, the OFW method uses the simple calculations to obtain weight for each feature and calculates the weighted mean. Thus, it is faster than LDA, NWFE, GDA, and MMLDA methods which need to calculate scatter matrices. After OFW, LDA is faster than others. MMLDA, because of calculation of median-mean line, and GDA, because of calculations in kernel space, are slower than LDA. NWFE is the slowest method because it needs to calculate the weighted mean of all training samples to estimate the nonparametric scatter matrices.

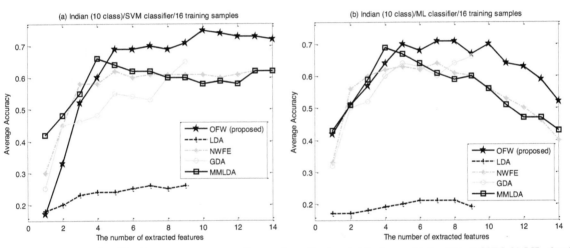

Figure 4. Average classification accuracy versus the number of extracted features obtained by a) SVM, b) ML classifiers for Indian dataset.

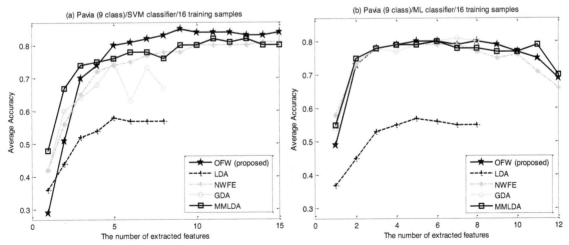

Figure 5. Average classification accuracy versus the number of extracted features obtained by a) SVM, b) ML classifiers for Pavia dataset.

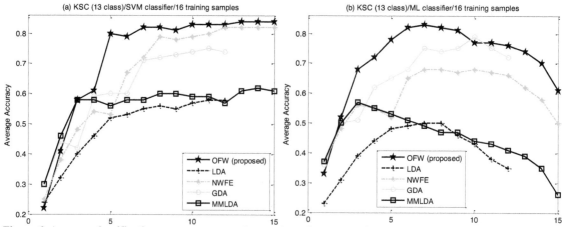

Figure 6. Average classification accuracy versus the number of extracted features obtained by a) SVM, b) ML classifiers for KSC dataset.

Table 1. Accuracy and reliability of classes of Indian dataset obtained by SVM classifier and 9 extracted features.

class			OFW (proposed)		LDA		NWFE		GDA		MMLDA	
No	Name of class	# samples	Acc.	Rel.	Acc.	Rel.	Acc.	Rel.	Acc.	Rel.	Acc.	Rel.
1	Corn-no till	1434	0.64	0.68	0.19	0.32	0.60	0.56	0.59	0.39	0.49	0.43
2	Corn-min till	834	0.64	0.40	0.24	0.18	0.55	0.40	0.58	0.51	0.63	0.38
3	Grass/pasture	497	0.93	0.67	0.32	0.14	0.50	0.40	0.83	0.58	0.74	0.50
4	Grass/trees	747	0.74	0.81	0.31	0.28	0.78	0.83	0.72	0.83	0.59	0.75
5	Hay-windrowed	489	0.99	1.00	0.20	0.31	0.95	1.00	0.99	0.99	0.97	0.98
6	Soybeans-no till	968	0.72	0.52	0.09	0.21	0.48	0.39	0.38	0.43	0.45	0.49
7	Soybeans-min till	2468	0.50	0.80	0.31	0.42	0.49	0.68	0.50	0.72	0.48	0.63
8	Soybeans-clean till	614	0.57	0.52	0.23	0.11	0.46	0.47	0.44	0.48	0.30	0.38
9	Woods	1294	0.89	0.95	0.28	0.61	0.68	0.83	0.89	0.92	0.90	0.90
10	Bldg-Grass-Tree-Drives	380	0.53	0.48	0.40	0.11	0.64	0.39	0.56	0.57	0.51	0.50
	Average Acc. and Average Rel.		**0.71**	**0.68**	**0.26**	**0.27**	**0.61**	**0.59**	**0.65**	**0.64**	**0.60**	**0.59**
	Kappa coefficient		0.63		0.16		0.53		0.56		0.52	

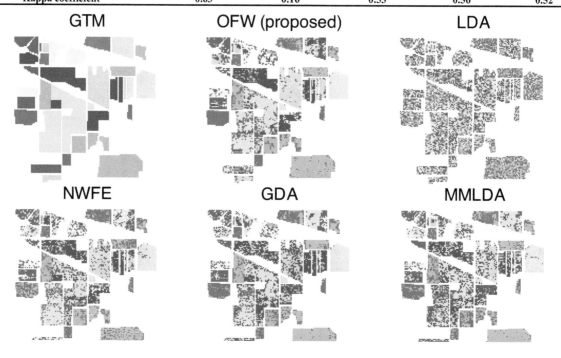

Figure 7. GTM and classification maps for Indian dataset obtained by SVM classifier and 9 extracted features.

Table 1. Accuracy and reliability of classes of Indian dataset obtained by SVM classifier and 9 extracted features.

No	Name of class	# samples	OFW (proposed) Acc.	Rel.	LDA Acc.	Rel.	NWFE Acc.	Rel.	GDA Acc.	Rel.	MMLDA Acc.	Rel.
1	Corn-no till	1434	0.64	0.68	0.19	0.32	0.60	0.56	0.59	0.39	0.49	0.43
2	Corn-min till	834	0.64	0.40	0.24	0.18	0.55	0.40	0.58	0.51	0.63	0.38
3	Grass/pasture	497	0.93	0.67	0.32	0.14	0.50	0.40	0.83	0.58	0.74	0.50
4	Grass/trees	747	0.74	0.81	0.31	0.28	0.78	0.83	0.72	0.83	0.59	0.75
5	Hay-windrowed	489	0.99	1.00	0.20	0.31	0.95	1.00	0.99	0.99	0.97	0.98
6	Soybeans-no till	968	0.72	0.52	0.09	0.21	0.48	0.39	0.38	0.43	0.45	0.49
7	Soybeans-min till	2468	0.50	0.80	0.31	0.42	0.49	0.68	0.50	0.72	0.48	0.63
8	Soybeans-clean till	614	0.57	0.52	0.23	0.11	0.46	0.47	0.44	0.48	0.30	0.38
9	Woods	1294	0.89	0.95	0.28	0.61	0.68	0.83	0.89	0.92	0.90	0.90
10	Bldg-Grass-Tree-Drives	380	0.53	0.48	0.40	0.11	0.64	0.39	0.56	0.57	0.51	0.50
	Average Acc. and Average Rel.		**0.71**	**0.68**	**0.26**	**0.27**	**0.61**	**0.59**	**0.65**	**0.64**	**0.60**	**0.59**
	Kappa coefficient		**0.63**		**0.16**		**0.53**		**0.56**		**0.52**	

Table 2. Accuracy and reliability of classes of Pavia dataset obtained by SVM classifier and 8 extracted features.

No	Name of class	# samples	OFW (proposed) Acc.	Rel.	LDA Acc.	Rel.	NWFE Acc.	Rel.	GDA Acc.	Rel.	MMLDA Acc.	Rel.
1	Asphalt	6631	0.90	0.87	0.37	0.70	0.78	0.86	0.18	0.53	0.73	0.80
2	Meadows	18649	0.67	0.91	0.33	0.91	0.48	0.85	0.63	0.79	0.54	0.86
3	Gravel	2099	0.71	0.63	0.44	0.30	0.73	0.53	0.80	0.45	0.65	0.48
4	Trees	3064	0.87	0.61	0.78	0.75	0.83	0.63	0.86	0.64	0.92	0.64
5	Painted metal sheets	1345	0.99	0.98	0.90	1.00	0.98	0.98	0.97	0.99	0.99	1.00
6	Bare Soil	5029	0.77	0.46	0.78	0.22	0.75	0.31	0.47	0.30	0.66	0.33
7	Bitumen	1330	0.80	0.80	0.37	0.22	0.81	0.64	0.46	0.13	0.65	0.43
8	Self-Blocking Bricks	3682	0.73	0.80	0.35	0.32	0.67	0.80	0.62	0.82	0.70	0.76
9	Shadows	947	1.00	0.97	0.78	0.71	1.00	0.99	1.00	1.00	1.00	1.00
	Average Acc. and Average Rel.		**0.83**	**0.78**	**0.57**	**0.57**	**0.78**	**0.73**	**0.67**	**0.63**	**0.76**	**0.70**
	Kappa coefficient		**0.70**		**0.36**		**0.57**		**0.47**		**0.58**	

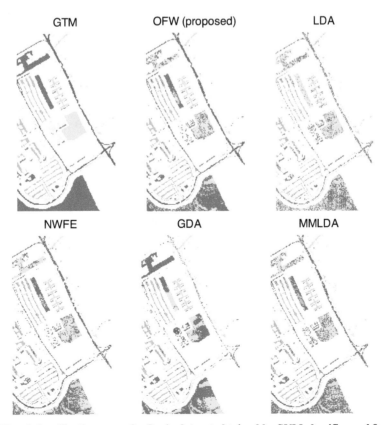

Figure 8. GTM and classification maps for Pavia dataset obtained by SVM classifier and 8 extracted features.

Table 3. Accuracy and reliability of classes of KSC dataset obtained by SVM classifier and 10 extracted features.

	lass		OFW (proposed)		LDA		NWFE		GDA		MMLDA	
No	Name of class	# samples	Acc.	Rel.	Acc.	Rel.	Acc.	Rel.	Acc.	Rel.	Acc.	Rel.
1	Scrub	761	0.95	0.91	0.51	0.84	0.92	0.90	0.77	0.91	0.71	0.86
2	Willow swamp	243	0.89	0.92	0.51	0.54	0.92	0.86	0.84	0.84	0.65	0.50
3	Cabbage palm hammock	256	0.90	0.79	0.62	0.34	0.89	0.75	0.80	0.76	0.74	0.68
4	Cabbage palm/oak hammock	252	0.54	0.59	0.29	0.17	0.31	0.35	0.40	0.45	0.24	0.36
5	Slash pine	161	0.68	0.59	0.33	0.22	0.65	0.44	0.66	0.44	0.45	0.33
6	Oak/broadleaf hammock	229	0.56	0.75	0.36	0.33	0.43	0.73	0.42	0.35	0.48	0.32
7	Hardwood swamp	105	0.90	0.85	0.70	0.37	0.87	0.85	0.85	0.84	0.50	0.41
8	Graminoid marsh	431	0.80	0.83	0.58	0.58	0.82	0.77	0.43	0.74	0.45	0.38
9	Spartina marsh	520	0.94	0.87	0.55	0.53	0.88	0.85	0.89	0.83	0.86	0.73
10	Cattail marsh	404	0.87	0.99	0.75	0.96	0.76	0.89	0.75	0.84	0.23	0.39
11	Salt marsh	419	0.98	0.90	0.74	0.86	0.98	0.93	0.97	0.84	0.94	0.96
12	Mud flats	503	0.83	0.86	0.54	0.71	0.83	0.95	0.81	0.62	0.52	0.56
13	Water	927	0.98	0.98	0.99	0.99	0.99	0.98	0.97	1.00	0.94	0.96
	Average Acc. and Average Rel.		0.83	0.83	0.57	0.57	0.79	0.79	0.74	0.73	0.59	0.57
	Kappa coefficient		0.86		0.59		0.83		0.75		0.62	

Table 4. Highest classification accuracies achieved by 16 training samples (numbers in parentheses represent the number of features which obtain the highest average accuracies in experiments).

Dataset	Classifier	OFW (proposed)	LDA	NWFE	GDA	MMLDA
Indian	SVM	**0.75** **(10)**	0.26 (7)	0.62 (5)	0.65 (9)	0.66 (4)
	ML	**0.71** (7)	0.21 (6)	0.64 (7)	0.66 (9)	0.69 (4)
Pavia	SVM	**0.85** **(9)**	0.58 (5)	0.81 (14)	0.75 (5)	0.82 (11)
	ML	0.80 (5)	0.57 (5)	0.79 (4)	**0.81** **(7)**	0.80 (6)
KSC	SVM	**0.84** **(13)**	0.58 (11)	0.82 (12)	0.75 (11)	0.62 (14)
	ML	**0.83** (7)	0.50 (7)	0.68 (7)	0.79 (10)	0.57 (3)

Table 5. McNemars test results (Z_{rc} denotes each case of table where r is the row and c is the column).

Indian/SVM classifier/16 training samples/ 9 extracted features

	OFW (proposed)	LDA	NWFE	GDA	MMLDA
OFW (proposed)	0	55.64	16.28	11.26	16.91
LDA	-55.64	0	-45.62	-49.19	-45.35
NWFE	-16.28	45.62	0	-5.90	0.54
GDA	-11.26	49.19	5.90	0	6.88
MMLDA	-16.91	45.35	-0.54	-6.88	0

Indian/ML classifier/16 training samples/ 7 extracted features

	OFW (proposed)	LDA	NWFE	GDA	MMLDA
OFW (proposed)	0	62.41	15.16	19.60	15.08
LDA	-62.41	0	-54.47	-51.39	-54.19
NWFE	-15.16	54.47	0	6.15	0.10
GDA	-19.60	51.39	-6.15	0	-6.08
MMLDA	-15.08	54.19	-0.10	6.08	0

Pavia /SVM classifier/16 training samples/ 8 extracted features

	OFW (proposed)	LDA	NWFE	GDA	MMLDA
OFW (proposed)	0	93.00	46.11	56.76	41.14
LDA	-93.00	0	-60.79	-36.21	-61.98
NWFE	-46.11	60.79	0	23.90	-2.65
GDA	-56.76	36.21	-23.90	0	-24.25
MMLDA	-41.14	61.98	2.65	24.25	0

Pavia /ML classifier/16 training samples/ 5 extracted features

	OFW (proposed)	LDA	NWFE	GDA	MMLDA
OFW (proposed)	0	73.49	7.93	-9.72	2.47
LDA	-73.49	0	-69.13	-82.25	-72.50
NWFE	-7.93	69.13	0	-17.80	-5.64
GDA	9.72	82.25	17.80	0	11.91
MMLDA	-2.47	72.50	5.64	-11.91	0

KSC / SVM classifier/16 training samples/ 10 extracted features					
	OFW (proposed)	LDA	NWFE	GDA	MMLDA
OFW (proposed)	0	30.71	6.03	17.66	29.21
LDA	-30.71	0	-26.81	-17.83	-3.54
NWFE	-6.03	26.81	0	11.53	25.19
GDA	-17.66	17.83	-11.53	0	16.57
MMLDA	-29.21	3.54	-25.19	-16.57	0

KSC / ML classifier/16 training samples/ 7 extracted features					
	OFW (proposed)	LDA	NWFE	GDA	MMLDA
OFW (proposed)	0	36.83	24.02	16.09	37.01
LDA	-36.83	0	-18.83	-27.59	0.02
NWFE	-24.02	18.83	0	-12.91	22.60
GDA	-16.09	27.59	12.91	0	30.03
MMLDA	-37.01	-0.02	-22.60	-30.03	0

Table 6. Comparison of computation time of feature extraction process obtained by 16 training samples and 6 extracted features for Indian dataset.

Indian, 16 training samples, 6 extracted features The comparison of computation time in feature extraction processes					
	OFW (proposed)	LDA	NWFE	GDA	MMLDA
Computation time (seconds)	0.24	0.56	88.34	0.67	0.66

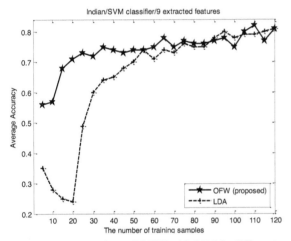

Figure 9. Comparison of OFW with LDA in different training sample size for Indian dataset obtained by SVM classifier and 9 extracted features.

4. Conclusion

The overlap-based feature weighting (OFW) is proposed for feature extraction of hyperspectral images in this paper. In the proposed method, the feature vector of each pixel is divided into some segments and the weighted mean of features in each segment is calculated as an extracted feature. The weight for each feature is obtained by calculation of overlap between classes in that feature. In the OFW method, there is no need to calculate the statistics of data. As a result, OFW is a simple, fast, and efficient for feature extraction of high dimensional data in small sample size situations. The superiority of OFW compared to some popular feature extraction methods is shown for Indian, Pavia, and KSC datasets using limited training samples.

References

[1] Dobigeon, N., Tourneret, J.-Y. & Chang, C.-I (2008). Semi-Supervised Linear Spectral Unmixing Using a Hierarchical Bayesian Model for Hyperspectral Imagery. IEEE Transactions on Signal Processing, vol. 56, no. 7, pp. 2684-2695.

[2] Yang, L., et al. (2014). Semi-Supervised Hyperspectral Image Classification Using Spatio-Spectral Laplacian Support Vector Machine. IEEE Geoscience and Remote Sensing Letters, vol. 11, no. 3, pp. 651-655.

[3] Camps-Valls, G., & Bruzzone, L. (2005). Kernel-based methods for hyperspectral image classification. IEEE Transactions on Geoscience and Remote Sensing, vol. 43, no. 6, pp.1351–1362.

[4] Cortes, C., & Vapnik, V. (1995). Support vector networks. Machine Learning, vol. 20, no. 3, pp. 273–297.

[5] Imani, M. & Ghassemian, H. (2015). Feature space discriminant analysis for hyperspectral data feature reduction. ISPRS Journal of Photogrammetry and Remote Sensing, vol. 102, pp. 1-13.

[6] Ghamary Asl, M., Mobasheri, M. R. & Mojaradi, B. (2014). Unsupervised Feature Selection Using Geometrical Measures in Prototype Space for Hyperspectral Imagery. IEEE Transactions on Geoscience and Remote Sensing, vol. 52, no. 7, pp. 3774-3787.

[7] Imani, M. & Ghassemian, H. (2015). Feature Extraction Using Weighted Training Samples. IEEE Geoscience and Remote Sensing Letters, vol. 12, no. 7, pp. 1387-1391.

[8] Kamandar, M. & Ghassemian, H. (2013). Linear Feature Extraction for Hyperspectral Images Based on Information Theoretic Learning. IEEE Geoscience and Remote Sensing Letters, vol. 10, no. 4, pp. 702 - 706.

[9] Kuncheva, L. I. & Faithfull, W. J. (2014). PCA Feature Extraction for Change Detection in Multidimensional Unlabeled Data. IEEE Transactions on Neural Networks and Learning Systems, vol. 25, no. 1, pp. 69-80.

[10] Wen, J., et al. (2013). Neighborhood Preserving Orthogonal PNMF Feature Extraction for Hyperspectral Image Classification. IEEE Journal of Selected Topics in Applied Earth Observations and Remote Sensing, vol. 6, no. 2, pp. 759-768.

[11] Imani, M. & Ghassemian, H. (2014). Band Clustering-Based Feature Extraction for Classification of Hyperspectral Images Using Limited Training Samples. IEEE Geoscience and Remote Sensing Letters, vol. 11, no. 8, pp. 1325 - 1329.

[12] Cariou, C., Chehdi, K. & Le Moan, S. (2011). BandClust: An Unsupervised Band Reduction Method for Hyperspectral Remote Sensing. IEEE Geoscience and Remote Sensing Letters, vol. 8, no. 3, pp. 565-569.

[13] Fan, W., Bouguila, N. & Ziou, D. (2013). Unsupervised Hybrid Feature Extraction Selection for High-Dimensional Non Gaussian Data Clustering with Variational Inference. IEEE Transactions on Knowledge and Data Engineering, vol. 25, no. 7, pp. 1670-1685.

[14] Izquierdo-Verdiguier, E., et al. (2014). Semisupervised Kernel Feature Extraction for Remote Sensing Image Analysis. IEEE Transactions on Geoscience and Remote Sensing, vol. 52, no. 9, pp. 5567-5578.

[15] Zhang, L., et al. (2012). On Combining Multiple Features for Hyperspectral Remote Sensing Image Classification. IEEE Transactions on Geoscience and Remote Sensing, vol. 50, no. 3, pp. 879-893.

[16] Zhang, L., et al. (2015). Ensemble Manifold Regularized Sparse Low-Rank Approximation for Multiview Feature Embedding. Pattern Recognition, vol. 48, pp. 3102–3112.

[17] Fukunaga, K. (1990). Introduction to Statistical Pattern Recognition. California, USA. San Diego: Academic Press Inc.

[18] Baudat, G. & Anouar, F. (2000). Generalized discriminant analysis using a kernel approach. Neural Computation, vol. 12, no. 10, pp. 2385–2404.

[19] Kuo, B. C. & Landgrebe, D. A. (2004). Nonparametric weighted feature extraction for classification. IEEE Transactions on Geoscience and Remote Sensing, vol. 42, no. 5, pp. 1096-1105.

[20] Xu, J., et al. (2014). Median–mean line based discriminant analysis. Neurocomputing, vol. 123, pp. 233–246.

[21] Zortea, M., Haertel, V. & Clarke, R. (2007). Feature Extraction in Remote Sensing High-Dimensional Image Data. IEEE Geoscience and Remote Sensing Letters, vol. 4, no. 1, pp. 107-111.

[22] Chang, C. & Linin, C. (2008). LIBSVM—A Library for Support Vector Machines. Available: http://www.csie.ntu.edu.tw/~cjlin/libsvm.

[23] Cohen, J. (1960). A coefficient of agreement from nominal scales. Educational and Psychological Measurement, vol. 20, no. 1, pp. 37–46.

[24] Foody, G. M. (2004). Thematic map comparison: Evaluating the statistical significance of differences in classification accuracy. Photogrammetric Engineering and Remote Sensing, vol. 70, no. 5, pp. 627–633.

14

Image authentication using LBP-based perceptual image hashing

R. Davarzani[1*], S. Mozaffari[2] and Kh.Yaghmaie[2]

1. Department of Electrical & Computer Engineering, College of Engineering, Shahrood Branch, Islamic Azad University, Shahrood, Iran.
2. Faculty of Electrical and Computer Engineering, Semnan University, Semnan, Iran.

*Corresponding author:re.davarzani@gmail.com (R.Davarzani).

Abstract

Feature extraction is a main step in all perceptual image hashing schemes in which robust features will lead to better results in perceptual robustness. Simplicity, discriminative power, computational efficiency and robustness to illumination changes are counted as distinguished properties of Local Binary Pattern features. In this paper, we investigate the use of local binary patterns for perceptual image hashing. In feature extraction, we propose to use both sign and magnitude information of local differences. So, the algorithm utilizes a combination of gradient-based and LBP-based descriptors for feature extraction. To provide security needs, two secret keys are incorporated in feature extraction and hash generation steps. Performance of the proposed hashing method is evaluated with an important application in perceptual image hashing scheme: image authentication. Experiments are conducted to show that the present method has acceptable robustness against perceptual content-preserving manipulations. Moreover, the proposed method has this capability to localize the tampering area, which is not possible in all hashing schemes.

Keywords: *Center-symmetric Local Binary Patterns, Perceptual Image Hashing, Image Authentication, Tamper Detection.*

1. Introduction

In recent years, we have witnessed the development of multimedia information in many aspects of our daily lives. Multimedia finds its application in various areas including, but not limited to, advertisements, art, entertainment, engineering, medicine, business, scientific research and spatial temporal applications. Many of the advantages of digital multimedia have led to the fast progress on media acquisition tools, powerful hardware, sophisticated editing software and network technologies that provide various media sharing and streaming services. However, digital multimedia data have suffered from illegal access and unauthorized distributions. Professional forgers with advanced technology can alter multimedia data without any trail on forged information. Therefore, it is necessary to create new tools and techniques to discover the authenticity and integrity of digital media [1]. In recent decade, several methods have been extensively studied for intellectual property protection of digital images and image forgeries

detection including image watermarking-based schemes [2], digital image forensic-based schemes [3] and perceptual image hashing- based schemes [4, 5].

For security/authentication of multimedia data, perceptual image hashing is introduced based on traditional cryptosystems. Traditional cryptographic hash functions have been used in applications involving data integrity issues and data retrieval [6]. However, it should be noted that the purpose of a cryptographic hash function and a perceptual image hash function are totally different. Hash functions in traditional cryptosystems are very secure, but they are very sensitive, i.e. changing even one bit of the input will change the output considerably. However, digital images should undergo content-preserving manipulations such as compression, enhancement, cropping, and scaling. An image hash function should tolerate such changes and produce hash values similar to the original image hash values with the same visual appearance [7]. On the other hand, the perceptual hashing system should be sensitive to content-changing distortions and reject malicious manipulations and attacks. Perceptual image hash functions generally consist of two steps, as illustrated in figure 1 [8]. The first step extracts a feature vector from the image which is depending on the image content or characteristics itself. In the second step, this feature vector is compressed and quantized into a binary or real number sequence to form the final hash value. Since an image hash also serves as a secure tag of the image, a secret key is incorporated into either feature extraction or hash generation or both to guarantee that the hash is hardly obtained by unauthorized adversaries without the secret key.

This paper is organized as follows. Section 2 and 3 review the background literature of perceptual image hashing methods and center-symmetric local binary patterns, respectively. Section 4 presents the proposed new image hashing scheme. Experimental results are given in section 5. Finally, conclusion is drawn in section 6.

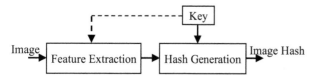

Figure 1. Two main stages of the general image hashing scheme.

2. Related works

Feature extraction is the key step in the image hashing which differentiates perceptual hashing methods. The aim of feature extraction is to present a compact and robust representation of the image content. The extracted features are quantized into a binary or real numbers sequence to form the final hash value.

By reviewing the literature, the existing hash generation algorithms can be roughly classified into three categories based on their feature extraction method: transform based schemes, matrix factorization based schemes, and local feature pattern based schemes.

2.1. Transform based schemes

Many approaches are utilized classic image transforms to extract image features. Various properties of the DCT can be utilized to create perceptual image hash functions.

For example, low-frequency DCT coefficients of an image are mostly stable under image manipulations. Fridrich and Goljan [9] proposed a robust hashing algorithm based on the stability of low-frequency DCT coefficients. Another method

using scale- and rotation-invariant property of Fourier-Mellin transform (FMT) was proposed in [10]. The authors presented a robust image hashing method using the magnitudes of the Fourier transform coefficients which were randomly weighted and summed. Their method is robust to various content-preserving manipulations such as geometric distortions, filtering operations, and etc. In a more recent development, several methods have been proposed by Radon transform.

To provide robustness against geometric distortions in image hashing, the Radon transform was first used in [11]. An expanded method was proposed in [12]. The method uses Radon transform to divide an image into radial projections and build a RAdial Variance (RAV) vector of image pixels. Then, the first 40 DCT coefficients of the RAV vectors are converted into the robust image hash called RASH. The method is computationally simple and is resilient to scaling and rotation but its discriminative capability needs to be strengthened. Venkatesan et al. [13] proposed a perceptual image hashing technique based on quantized statistics of randomized rectangles in the discrete wavelet domain (DWT). In their method, averages or variances of the random blocks in wavelet image are computed and then quantized with randomized rounding to form a secure binary hash. This method is sensitive to contrast adjustment and gamma correction and robust against a limited range of geometric attacks.

2.2. Matrix factorization based schemes

In the second type of image hashing schemes, the advantage of matrix factorization or decomposition are used to extract the image features. In this category singular value decomposition (SVD) and non negative matrix factorization (NMF) are the most popular decomposition tools for image matrixes. Kozat et al. [14] proposed a hashing algorithm in two steps using SVD.

The method is robust against some small variations in rotation and scaling. In another work in [15], Non-negative Matrix Factorization (NMF) is used as a dimensionality reduction technique to generate image hashing. Although, the method is resilient to a large class of perceptually insignificant attacks but it is vulnerable to brightness changes and large hashing methods using dimension reduction techniques, a new robust and secure image hash algorithm was also proposed based on Fast Johnson-Lindenstrauss transform (FJLT) [16].

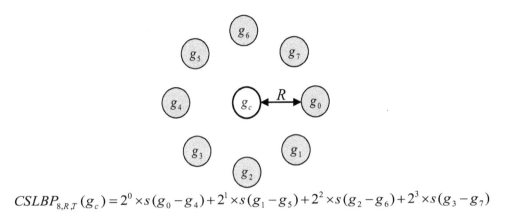

$$CSLBP_{8,R,T}(g_c) = 2^0 \times s(g_0 - g_4) + 2^1 \times s(g_1 - g_5) + 2^2 \times s(g_2 - g_6) + 2^3 \times s(g_3 - g_7)$$

Figure 2. Circularly symmetric neighborhoods and CSLBP feature for radius R and P=8 neighborhood pixels.

2.3. Local feature pattern based schemes

Finally, the methods like [17], [18] and [19] can be included in the third group of image hashing algorithms called local feature patterns-based hashing schemes. In [18] and [19] SIFT keypoints are used as most significant and robust local features for image hashing.

In this work we propose a novel and robust perceptual image hashing method based on Center-Symmetric Local Binary Pattern (CSLBP) features. CSLBP features are extracted from each non-overlapping block of the original gray-scale image. For each block, the final hash code is obtained by inner product of its CSLBP feature vector and a pseudorandom weight vector. To provide security needs, two secret keys are incorporated in feature extraction and hash generation steps. Many experiments are conducted and the results show that our algorithm can reach a good balance between robustness and discrimination and outperforms some well-known algorithms. High robustness against luminance changes, applicability in image tampering detection, acceptable hash length and running time can be also counted as the advantage of our proposed hashing method.

3. Center-symmetric local binary patterns (CSLBP)

Among the feature descriptors, Local Binary Patterns (LBP) is one of the most famous and powerful ones. The idea of LBP is originally proposed by Ojala et al. [20, 21] for texture classification. Then, it has gained increasing attention in many image analyses applications due to its low computational complexity, invariance to monotonic gray-scale changes and texture description ability [20]. LBP has been utilized in various image analyses applications such as dynamic texture recognition [22], face recognition

forgery [25], image region descriptors [26] and so on.

In the original LBP, signed gray level differences of each pixel with its neighboring pixels are described as a binary form. However, the LBP operator produces rather long histograms and it is therefore difficult to use in the context of a region descriptor. Furthermore, the original LBP feature is not robust on flat images. To address the problems, center-symmetric local binary patterns, CSLBP, as a modified version of LBP was proposed in [26].

Let $I(x,y)$ be a gray level image and g_c indicates the gray level of an arbitrary pixel positioned at (x_c, y_c), i.e. $g_c = I(x_c, y_c)$. Gray values of P equally spaced circular neighborhood pixels on a circle of radius $R(R > 0)$, around g_c are shown by $g_p, p = 0,1,...,P-1$, (See Figure 2). The CSLBP form shown by $CS\_LBP_{P,R,T}(x_c, y_c)$ is obtained as follows:

$$g_p = I(x_p, y_p), \quad p = 0,...,P-1 \qquad (1)$$

$$x_p = x_c + R\cos(2\pi p / P)$$

$$y_p = y_c - R\sin(2\pi p / P)$$

$$CSLBP_{P,R,T}(x_c, y_c) = \sum_{p=0}^{P/2-1} s(g_p - g_{p+(P/2)})2^p,$$

$$s(x) = \begin{cases} 1, & x > T \\ 0, & \text{otherwise} \end{cases}$$

where, T is a small value used to threshold the gray-level difference to increase the robustness of the CSLBP feature on flat image regions. CSLBP captures better gradient information than the basic LBP, because instead of comparing the gray-level of each pixel with the center pixel, gray-level differences between center-symmetric pairs of opposite pixels in a neighborhood are compared.

4. Proposed algorithm for perceptual image hashing

In this section, we propose image hashes generation based on block feature extraction using center-symmetric local binary patterns (CSLBP).

As shown in figure 3, the proposed technique consists of three steps: pre-processing, feature extraction, and hash generation. To guarantee the security requirements, two secret keys, *K1* and *K2*, are also incorporated in feature extraction and hash generation steps. The following section describes details of our hashing algorithms.

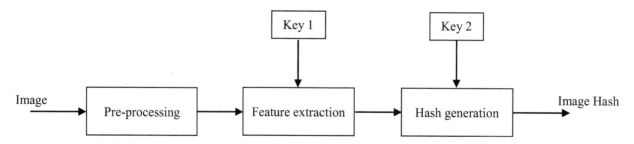

Figure 3. Block diagram of the proposed hashing algorithms.

4.1. Pre-processing

In this work, we are dealing with gray-level images, so RGB images are first converted to grayscale images using standard color space conversion.

Since real images may have different size, to ensure that the final generated hash has a fixed length, all input images are first rescaled into a standard resolution of $M \times N$ by bi-linear interpolation. Then, the resized input image is divided into non-overlapping blocks of $B \times B$ pixels and feature extraction is applied to each image block. We need to keep a trade-off between the hash length, the discriminative capability and perceptual robustness in choosing the size of blocks. This is because a large block size means few features which will inevitably reduce discriminative capability. When the size of block is decreased, discrimination can be improved but perceptual robustness is easily affected by minor modification. In addition, a smaller block size will increase the hash size. In experiments, we find that $B = 32$ is an acceptable moderate size for 256×256 images.

In this scheme, before feature extraction, we first filter each block with an edge-preserving adaptive low-pass filter. The adaptive filter is more selective than a comparable linear filter, because of preserving edges and other high-frequency parts of an image. For this purpose, we use a pixel-wise adaptive Wiener method based on statistics estimated from a local neighborhood of each pixel. Our experiments have shown that this filtering has considerably improvements on robustness of image hash. The consecutive operations in the pre-processing step are drawn in figure 4.

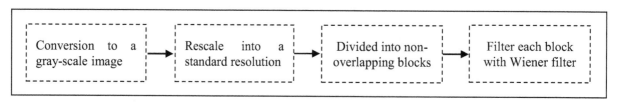

Figure 4. Pre-processing steps in our algorithm.

4.2. Feature extraction

In CSLBP-based image hashing, CSLBP features are extracted to represent the main content of the image compactly. Then, in hash generation step, the extracted features are converted into a real number sequence to form the final hash value. The details of these feature extraction method is presented as follows.

Given a central pixel g_c and its P equally spaced circular neighborhood pixels $g_p, p = 0, 1, ..., P-1$, we can simply calculate gray-level differences between center-symmetric pairs of opposite pixels in a neighborhood as (2):

$$d_{p,q} = g_p - g_q, \qquad (2)$$

$$q = p + (P/2), p = 0, 1, ..., (P/2 - 1)$$

$d_{p,q}$ can be further decomposed into two components:

$$d_{p,q} = s_{p,q} \times m_{p,q} \qquad (3)$$

$$s_{p,q} = \text{sign}(g_p - g_q), \quad \text{sign}(x) = \begin{cases} 1, & x \geq 0 \\ -1, & x < 0 \end{cases}$$

$$m_{p,q} = |g_p - g_q|$$

Where $s_{p,q}$ and $m_{p,q}$ are the sign and the magnitude of $d_{p,q}$, respectively. The original CSLBP operator discards the magnitude information of the difference between the center-symmetric pairs of pixels and uses only the sign information (see (1)). In other words, for a given $M \times N$ image, after identifying the CSLBP pattern of each pixel (i,j), the normalized histogram of CSLBP codes is computed over the image and it is used as a feature vector, (4):

$$H(b) = \left(\frac{1}{M \times N}\right) \sum_{i=1}^{M} \sum_{j=1}^{N} f(CSLBP_{P,R,T}(i,j),b), \qquad (4)$$

$$b \in [0,B]$$

$$f(x,y) = \begin{cases} 1, & x = y \\ 0, & \text{otherwise} \end{cases}$$

where, B is the maximal CSLBP pattern value.

In a gradient-based descriptor, image gradients are used to obtain magnitude and orientation for each image pixel. Since, definition of magnitude in CSLBP operator, $m_{p,q}$, is similar to image gradient, it contains useful information for image description [27].

In our proposed CSLBP-based image hashing, the motivation behind proposed feature descriptor is an efficient combination of CSLBP-based descriptor and gradient-based descriptor using sign and magnitude information of local differences. We extract two features for each pixel of the image by using the CSLBP operator.

The sign feature is the same as the original CSLBP code defined by (1) and the magnitude feature vector corresponds to gradient information which is achieved by the magnitude of local differences.

The CSLBP operator has three parameters: radius R, number of neighboring pixels P, and threshold on the gray level difference T. In our experiments best results are achieved by $R=1$, $P=8$, and $T=0.01$. Using 8 neighboring samples, for each pixel (i,j), the sign feature (CSLBP code) can get 16 decimal numbers from 0 to 15, and the magnitude feature vector, MV, is defined by (5):

$$CS\_LBP_{8,1,0.01}(i,j) = \sum_{p=0}^{3} s(g_p - g_{p+4})2^p \qquad (5)$$

$$MV(i,j) = [m_{0,4}, m_{1,5}, m_{2,6}, m_{3,7}]$$

where, $m_{p,q}$, $q = p+4$, $p = 0,1,2,3$ is defined by (2) and (3).

Four histograms are built considering four components of magnitude vector. Each pixel of the image with a given CSLBP code is assigned to a bin in the histogram according to its magnitude. In other words, the magnitude feature, MV, is used as an adaptive weight in histogram calculation of CSLBP codes, (6).

$$H_p(b) = \sum_{i=1}^{B} \sum_{j=1}^{B} m_{p,q}(i,j) \times f(CSLBP(i,j),b), \qquad (6)$$

$b \in [0,15]$, $p = 0,1,2,3$ and $q = p+4$.

Finally, the obtained histograms are joined together to create the feature vector of an image block, FV, which is used for hash generation, (7). Each FV has 64 elements and to enhance the security of the scheme, all the elements in each FV are randomly scrambled according to a secret key $K1$.

$$FV = [H_0, H_1, H_2, H_3] \qquad \cdots$$

where, $\langle U, V \rangle$ indicates the inner product of two vectors U and V.

4.3. Hash generation

In the previous step, a feature vector was constructed for each non-overlapping block of input image. We generate pseudorandom weights $\omega = \{\alpha_i\}, i = 1,...,64$ from the normal distribution $N(u, \sigma^2)$ using a secret key, $K2$. ω is a random vector with 64 dimensions, with the same size of FV. Let $H = \{h_b\}, b = 1,...,N$ be the hash vector of input image where N is the total number of non-overlapping image blocks; we define FV_b as feature vector of bth block and its corresponding h_b component by (8):

$$h_b = \langle FV_b, \omega \rangle \qquad \cdots$$

where, $\langle U, V \rangle$ indicates the inner product of two vectors U and V.

5. Experiments

In this section, we provide a comprehensive evaluation of the proposed algorithm in image authentication [19]. Furthermore, some experiments are also included to analyze the performances of the proposed hashing scheme with respect to forged region detection.

5.1. Evaluation of image authentication

Image authentication experiment is designed to measure the sensitivity of our method to distinguish malicious attacks from content-preserving distortions. Figure 5 illustrates this usage mode for perceptual image hashing. In image authentication, the hash of an original image, H_{org}, is available and called the reference hash. The hash of a test image, H_{test}, is extracted using the same perceptual image hashing algorithm. Then, these two hashes are compared. Now, the image in question is declared to be authentic if $d\left(H_{test}, H_{org}\right) < T$, where $d(.)$ is a distance measure and T is a predefined threshold.

In our method, since hash values are approximately linearly changed, the correlation coefficient is used as a distance measure.

We considered the problem of image authentication as a hypothesis testing problem with two hypotheses: (H_0: *Image is authentic*) and (H_1: *Image is not authentic*). Each test image is classified into one of the hypothesis states. We use the receiver operating characteristics (ROC) curve to examine the discriminative capabilities of various hashing schemes in image authentication. True positive rate (TPR) and false positive rate (FPR) are two axes of ROC curve, which are defined by (9) and (10), respectively.

$$TPR(T) = \frac{\text{Number of true images detected as authentic images}}{\text{Total number of authentic images}} \quad \cdots$$

$$FPR(T) = \frac{\text{Number of forged images detected as authentic images}}{\text{Total number of forged images}} \quad \cdots\cdot$$

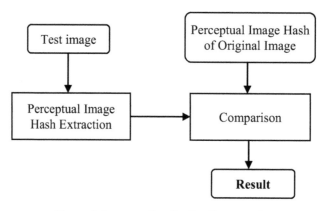

Figure 5. Image authentication framework.

Based on a given threshold (T), TPR gives us an estimate of the probability of true detection and FPR obtains the percentage of images that are falsely classified as original image.

To implement authentication experiment, we construct three databases: an *original images database*, a *similar images database* and a *forged images database*. The original images database is constructed by a collection of 1000 color images from two databases: The Corel database [28] and Columbia photographic images and photorealistic computer graphics dataset [29]. All the color images are resized to 256×256 and converted as gray-scale images in the experiments. Similar images are obtained by applying several content-preserving operations on each original image. The operations are listed in table 1. Our forged image database is constructed by splicing image forgery. Image splicing is a simple form of photomontage

technology where is defined by simple combining image fragments from two or more different images without further post-processing. A total of 1000 tampered images are created with perform splicing forgery on each original image. In each forged image the pasted area is 10% of the host image.

Figure 6 compares the ROC curves of the proposed method and those of [30] and two methods in [19]. Refer to (9) and (10), it is clear that TPR and FPR indicate robustness and discrimination, respectively. It can be observed from figure 6 (f) that the proposed method has shown stronger ability than the other four methods to distinguish content-preserving distortions from malicious attack. For example with the same probability of false detection in FPR = 0.2, CSLBP achieves higher probability of correct detection (TPR = 0.77) than other hashing methods. In the same FPR, the TPR for RSCH [19], ASCH [19] and FP [30] hashing methods are 0.46, 0.58 and 0.022 respectively.

Table1. Content-preserving manipulations with some details in parameters description and setting.

Manipulation	Parameter description	Parameter setting
Gaussian noise	Mean (m), Variance (v)	$m = 0, \; v = 0.0005$
Gaussian blurring	Standard deviation (σ), window size (F_s)	$F_s = 3, \sigma = 0.5$
Gamma correction	Gamma (γ)	$\gamma = 1.1$
Scaling	Scaling factor (s)	$s = 1.5$
JPEG Compression	Quality factor (Q)	$Q = 70$
A combination of attacks		$(\gamma = 1.1), (Q = 70), (\sigma = 0.5, F_s = 3)$ and $(s = 1.5)$.

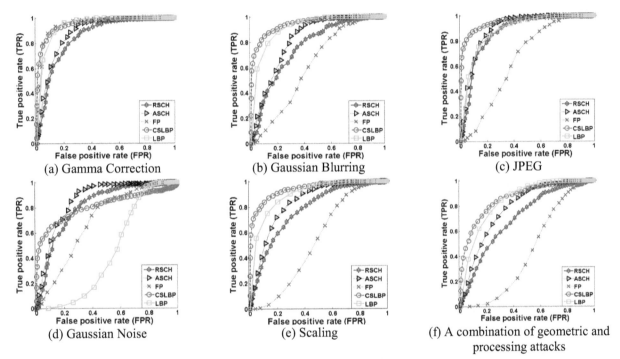

(a) Gamma Correction   (b) Gaussian Blurring   (c) JPEG

(d) Gaussian Noise   (e) Scaling   (f) A combination of geometric and processing attacks

Figure 6. ROC curve comparisons between our hashing and other methods in image authentication test.

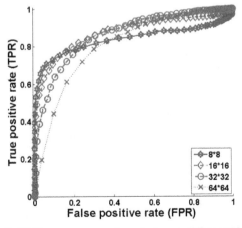

Figure 7. ROC curve comparisons between different block sizes.

5.2. Effect of block size

To show effect of block size on hash performances of our methods, we change the block size and conduct the experiment under a combination of geometric and processing attacks, (in the last row of Table 1). The used block sizes are: 8 × 8, 16 × 16, 32 × 32 and 64 × 64. The ROC graphs are shown in figure 7. We can observe that all block sizes have similar ROC curves. However, based on the hash length and the area of under ROC curves, block size 32 × 32 is an acceptable compromise for 256 × 256 images.

5.3. Tampering localization

A forger can easily modify local regions of an image and alter its original content by available photo-editing software. In digital image forensics, many techniques have been proposed to address the problem of forged region detection [3, 31]. Block-based matching is one of the main methods in forged region localization. In the method, first, the image is divided into overlapping or non-overlapping blocks. Then, the perceptual hash function generates a hash value for each block of the original image. During forensic analysis, hashing codes are extracted from the

corresponding blocks of the suspect image and a block-wise comparison can reveal potential tampered regions. For tampering localization, the choice of block size controls the trade-off between hash length and detection performance. Larger block size gives a smaller hash length but can introduce higher false detection than a smaller block size. An illustration of tampering localization functionality of the proposed method is provided by the following experiment. We used a database of 100 image pairs, which includes the original image and tampered copy. Tampered images are generated by splicing technique where some regions of the original image are replaced with foreign blocks. We assess the accuracy of tampering localization by ROC analysis. In the results, the receiver operating curve is a plot of the probability of true positive rate versus the false positive rate as the system threshold is varied. The two probabilities are defined as follows:

$$TPR(T) = \frac{\text{Number of tampered blocks detected as tampered}}{\text{Total number of tampered blocks}} \qquad \cdots$$

$$FPR(T) = \frac{\text{Number of genuine blocks detected as tampered}}{\text{Total number of genuine blocks}} \qquad \cdots$$

where, T is the variant threshold parameter.

The result of ROC analysis is presented in figure 8, in which the true positive rates and false positive rates are averaged based on the results from 100 image pairs. The figure compares the sensitivity of forged region detection in our method and the method in [18]. Roy et al. uses quantized edge direction histogram features to localize tempered blocks. We can observe from figure 8 that the proposed method attain better accuracy than [18]. Because our method for hash generation utilize combine LBP-based descriptors and gradient-based descriptors. It is worth noting that FP [30] is not applicable for tampering detection. In this sense, the proposed hashing scheme is more generally applicable.

An example of forged region detection, using CSLBP-based hashing method, is also illustrated in figure 9. From left to right, columns 1 to 3 are original images, tampered images and detection results, respectively.

5.4. Hash length and CPU running time

Clearly, hash length in the methods based on the block feature extraction is proportional to the number of image blocks. In the local feature point-based schemes, the number of keypoints

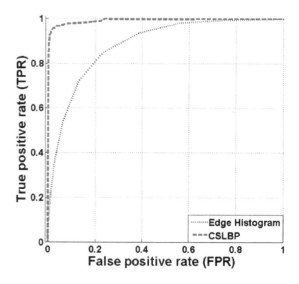

Figure 8. The ROC curve for tampering localization.

determines the hash length. According to the parameters used in the experiment, the hash length of different methods is listed in table 2.

The hash length of our method is 64 decimal digits. Table 2 also compares the average time of producing each image hash in different methods. In implementation we used a Sony Vaio laptop, Intel Core 2 Duo Processor P8800 (2.66 GHz), memory 4 GB and software of MATLAB 7.7.0.

(a)   (b)   (c)

Figure 9. Visualized forged detection results using CSLBP-based hashing method. From the left, columns 1 to 3 are original images, tampered images and detection results, respectively.

An example of forged region detection, using CSLBP-based hashing method, is also illustrated in figure 9. From left to right, columns 1 to 3 are original images, tampered images and detection results, respectively.

5.4. Hash length and CPU running time
Clearly, hash length in the methods based on the block feature extraction is proportional to the number of image blocks. In the local feature point-based schemes, the number of keypoints determines the hash length. According to the parameters used in the experiment, the hash length of different methods is listed in table 2. The hash length of our method is 64 decimal digits. Table 2 also compares the average time of producing each image hash in different methods. In implementation we used a Sony Vaio laptop, Intel Core 2 Duo Processor P8800 (2.66 GHz), memory 4 GB and software of MATLAB 7.7.0. The processing time of hash generation is computed through the average time on 100 images of size 256×256. Since the algorithms in [19] spent a computation time on the robust local keypoint detection, the average time in ASCH and RSCH is higher than the other methods. Our fast hashing method can be attributed to the low computational complexity of LBP features.

Table 2. Time and hash length comparisons among different algorithms

Method	Hash length	Average time (sec)
SCH	20 decimal digits	3.55
CSLBP	64 decimal digits	0.1

6. Conclusion
In this paper we proposed a new perceptual image hashing method based on local binary patterns (LBP). In this algorithm a simple and efficient version of LBP feature, called center-symmetric LBP (CSLBP), was used for feature extraction.

The original CSLBP descriptor uses only the sign information of local differences. In this paper, however, both sign and magnitude information are utilized for image hashing to make benefit of gradient-based and LBP-based descriptor simultaneously. To increase security of our hashing method, two secret keys were used in feature extraction and hash generation steps. To evaluate our proposed method, an experiment was conducted for image authentication. The results demonstrated that our proposed scheme could distinguish legal distortions from malicious manipulations. Finally, applicability in image tampering detection, acceptable hash length and running time can be also counted as the advantage of our proposed hashing method.

References
[1] Haouzia, A. & Noumeir, R. (2008). Methods for image authentication: a survey, Multimedia Tools and Applications, vol. 39, no. 1, pp. 1-46.

[2] Cox, I., M. Fridrich, J. & Kalker, T. (2008). Digital Watermarking and Steganography: Morgan Kaufmann Publishers Inc.

[3] Birajdar, G. K. & Mankar, V. H. (2013). Digital image forgery detection using passive techniques: A survey, Digital Investigation, vol. 10, no. 3, pp. 226-245.

[4] Shuo-zhong W. & Xin-peng, Z. (2007). Recent development of perceptual image hashing, Journal of Shanghai University (English Edition), vol. 11, no. 4, pp. 323-331.

[5] Weng, L. (2012). Perceptual Multimedia Hashing (Ph.D. thesis), Department of Electrical Engineering (ESAT), Katholieke Universiteit Leuven, Heverlee (Belgium).

[6] Rivest, R. (1992). The MD5 Message-Digest Algorithm: RFC Editor.

[7] Wu, M., Mao, Y. & Swaminathan, A. (2007). A Signal Processing and Randomization Perspective of

Robust and Secure Image Hashing, 14th IEEE Workshop on Statistical Signal Processing, SSP '07., pp. 166-170.

[8] Monga, V. (2005). Perceptually based methods for robust image hashing (Ph.D. thesis), in Electrical Engineering, Electrical and Computer Engineering, The University of Texas at Austin.

[9] Fridrich J. & Goljan, M. (2000). Robust hash functions for digital watermarking, International Conference on Information Technology: Coding and Computing, 2000, pp. 178-183.

[10] Swaminathan, A. Mao, Y. & Wu, M. (2006). Robust and secure image hashing, IEEE Transactions on Information Forensics and Security, vol. 1, no. 2, pp. 215-230.

[11] Lefbvre, F., Macq, B. & Legat, J. D. (2002). RASH: RAdon Soft Hash algorithm, 11th European IEEE Signal Processing Conference, 2002, pp. 1-4.

[12] De Roover, C., De Vleeschouwer, C., Lefebvre, F. & Macq, B. (2005). Robust image hashing based on radial variance of pixels, IEEE International Conference on Image Processing, ICIP, pp. 77-80.

[13] Venkatesan, R., Koon, S., Jakubowski, H. & Moulin, P. (2000). Robust image hashing, International Conference on Image Processing, 2000, pp. 664-666.

[14] Kozat, S., Venkatesan, R. & Mihcak, M. K. (2004). Robust perceptual image hashing via matrix invariants, International Conference on Image Processing, ICIP 2004, pp. 3443-3446.

[15] Monga, V. & M. K. Michkak, (2007). Robust and Secure Image Hashing via Non-Negative Matrix Factorizations, IEEE Transactions on Information Forensics and Security, , vol. 2, no. 3, pp. 376-390.

[16] Xudong, L. & Wang, J. (2008). Fast Johnson-Lindenstrauss Transform for robust and secure image hashing, 10th IEEE Workshop on Multimedia Signal Processing, pp. 725-729.

[17] Monga, V. & Evans, B. L. (2006). Perceptual Image Hashing Via Feature Points: Performance Evaluation and Tradeoffs, IEEE Transactions on Image Processing, , vol. 15, no. 11, pp. 3452-3465.

[18] Roy, S. & Sun, Q. (2007). Robust Hash for Detecting and Localizing Image Tampering, IEEE International Conference on Image Processing, ICIP 2007, pp. VI - 117-VI - 120.

[19] Xudong, L. & Wang, Z. J. (2012). Perceptual Image Hashing Based on Shape Contexts and Local Feature Points, IEEE Transactions on Information Forensics and Security, , vol. 7, no. 3, pp. 1081-1093.

[20] Ojala, T., Pietikäinen, M. & Harwood, D. (1996), A comparative study of texture measures with classification based on featured distributions, Pattern Recognition, vol. 29, no. 1, pp. 51-59.

[21] Ojala, T., Pietikäinen, M. & Mäenpää, T. (2002). Multiresolution gray-scale and rotation invariant texture classification with local binary patterns," IEEE Transactions on Pattern Analysis and Machine Intelligence, vol. 24, no. 7, pp. 971-987.

[22] Zhao, G. & Pietikäinen, M. (2007). Dynamic texture recognition using local binary patterns with an application to facial expressions, IEEE Transactions on Pattern Analysis and Machine Intelligence, vol. 29, no. 6, pp. 915-928.

[23] Ahonen, T., Hadid, A. & Pietikainen, M. (2006). Face Description with Local Binary Patterns: Application to Face Recognition, IEEE Transactions on Pattern Analysis and Machine Intelligence, , vol. 28, no. 12, pp. 2037-2041, Dec 2006.

[24] Heikkila, M. & Pietikainen, M. (2006). A texture-based method for modeling the background and detecting moving objects," IEEE Transactions on Pattern Analysis and Machine Intelligence, vol. 28, no. 4, pp. 657-662.

[25] Davarzani, R., Yaghmaie, K. Mozaffari, S. & Tapak, M. (2013). Copy-move forgery detection using multiresolution local binary patterns, Forensic Science International, vol. 231, no. 1-3, pp. 61-72.

[26] Heikkilä, M., Pietikäinen, M. & Schmid, C. (2009). Description of interest regions with local binary patterns, Pattern Recognition, vol. 42, no. 3, pp. 425-436.

[27] Guo, Z. & Zhang, D. (2010). A Completed Modeling of Local Binary Pattern Operator for Texture Classification, IEEE Transactions on Image Processing, vol. 19, no. 6, pp. 1657-1663, 2010.

[28] Corel, test set. [Online]. http://wang.ist.psu.edu/~jwang/test1.tar , (2001).

[29] Ng, T., Chang, S., Hsu, Y. & Pepeljugoski, M. (2005). Columbia Photographic Images and Photorealistic Computer Graphics Dataset.

[30] Monga, V., Vats, D. & Evans, B. L. (2005). Image Authentication Under Geometric Attacks Via Structure Matching, IEEE International Conference on Multimedia and Expo, ICME 2005, pp. 229-232.

[31] Stamm, M. C., Wu, M., & Liu, K. J. R., (2013). Information Forensics: An Overview of the First Decade, IEEE Access, vol. 1, no. 1, pp. 167-200.

15

Discrete-time repetitive optimal control:
Robotic manipulators

M. M. Fateh[*] and M. Baluchzadeh

Department of Electrical and Robotic Engineering, University of Shahrood, Shahrood, Iran.

Corresponding author: mmfateh@shahroodut.ac.ir (M.M. Fateh).

Abstract

This paper proposes a discrete-time repetitive optimal control of electrically driven robotic manipulators using an uncertainty estimator. The proposed control method can be used for performing repetitive motion, which covers many industrial applications of robotic manipulators. This kind of control law is in the class of torque-based control in which the joint torques are generated by permanent magnet dc motors in the current mode. The motor current is regulated using a proportional-integral controller. The novelty of this paper is a modification in using the discrete-time linear quadratic control for the robot manipulator, which is a nonlinear uncertain system. For this purpose, a novel discrete linear time-variant model is introduced for the robotic system. Then, a time-delay uncertainty estimator is added to the discrete-time linear quadratic control to compensate the nonlinearity and uncertainty associated with the model. The proposed control approach is verified by stability analysis. Simulation results show the superiority of the proposed discrete-time repetitive optimal control over the discrete-time linear quadratic control.

Keywords: *Discrete-Time Linear Quadratic Control, Optimal Control, Repetitive Control, Electrically Driven Robotic Manipulators, Uncertainty Estimator.*

1. Introduction

Discrete-time control is a favorite approach since the digital processors and computers have been used as common controllers. Digital control systems have more capabilities over the traditional control systems such as flexibility to changes, immunity to noises, and less number of computations [1]. The digital control was originally developed for linear systems using the famous z transform. Considering literature confirms that the discrete-time control has been developed to cover the nonlinear systems, as well. The discrete-time control of robotic manipulators was presented in various types such as sliding mode control [2], learning control [3], adaptive control [4] and [5]. In this paper, a discrete-time repetitive optimal control (DROC) is developed.

A promising control approach to track periodic signals is repetitive control. This type of control method can be used for performing repetitive motion, which covers many industrial applications of robotic manipulators. Repetitive control has gained a great deal of research interest in various forms of control approaches applied on the robot manipulators. The control performance is related to how well the uncertainty is compensated. A discrete-time repetitive control scheme was presented using the computed-torque control link to overcome a part of uncertainty model [5]. The repetitive model reference adaptive control [6] and the adaptive repetitive learning control [7] can overcome the parametric uncertainty and the periodic external disturbance. A Lyapunov-based repetitive learning control was presented to have a good tracking performance in the presence of unknown nonlinear dynamics with a known period [8]. A robust repetitive control was developed and can compensate uncertainties including the structured uncertainty and unstructured uncertainty [9]. Time delay method [10] and uncertainty estimation [11] can be used to control the robot manipulator by estimating the unknown dynamics and disturbances. Uncertainty can be well estimated by a time-delay estimator [12] or an adaptive fuzzy system [13]. The time-delay method was effectively applied to compensate uncertainty in the robust impedance control of a suspension system [12], robust repetitive control of rigid robots [9] and robust control of flexible-joint robots [14].

The repetitive adaptive control and repetitive robust control are appreciated to overcome the structured uncertainties and unstructured uncertainties, respectively. However, they may not provide an optimal control performance. The optimal control performance is a desired control goal for repetitive control, which can be achieved by Discrete-time Linear Quadratic Control (DLQC) in linear systems with no uncertainties. However, a model of robotic system is nonlinear and uncertain. Therefore, the nonlinearity and uncertainty should be compensated.

This paper introduces a novel discrete-time linear time-variant model for the robotic system to apply the DLQC. The difference between the model and actual system is considered as a lumped uncertainty. A two-term control law is proposed in which the first term is a DLQC. The second term is a robust time-delay estimator to compensate the uncertainty and nonlinearity. The obtained control is called as the discrete-time repetitive optimal control. The permanent magnet dc motor in the current mode generates the control command as the joint torque. The motor current is regulated using a proportional-integral controller.

The rest of the paper is organized as follows: Section 2 presents the discrete-time linear time-variant model for the robot manipulator. Section 3 develops the discrete-time linear quadratic control. Section 4 presents stability analysis. Section 5 illustrates simulation results. Finally, Section 6 concludes the paper.

2. Discrete-time linear time-variant model

In order to define a model-based control, some discrete-time models were presented for the robot manipulators. However, some models such as [15] are too complex and some models such as [16] are too simple. In order to apply the DLQC, a novel discrete-time linear time-variant model is introduced as follows.

Dynamics of a robotic manipulator [17] is given by

$$\mathbf{D(q)\ddot{q}} + \mathbf{C(q,\dot{q})\dot{q}} + \mathbf{g(q)} = \mathbf{T} \tag{1}$$

where, $\mathbf{q} \in R^n$ is the vector of generalized joint positions, $\mathbf{D(q)}$ is the complete inertia matrix, $\mathbf{C(q,\dot{q})\dot{q}}$ is the centrifugal and Coriolis torque vector, $\mathbf{g(q)}$ is the gravitational torque vector.

In the proposed approach, a permanent magnet dc motor drives each joint of the manipulator in the control system. The inserted torque on the joint to drive the manipulator is the load torque of motor, which is considered as

$$\mathbf{T_m} = \mathbf{J_m\ddot{\theta}_m} + \mathbf{B_m\dot{\theta}_m} + \mathbf{rT} + \mathbf{r\xi} \tag{2}$$

where, $\dot{\boldsymbol{\theta}}_\mathbf{m} \in R^n$ is the vector of motor velocities, $\mathbf{T} \in R^n$ is the load torque, $\mathbf{T_m} \in R^n$ is the motors torque. The $n \times n$ positive diagonal coefficient matrices $\mathbf{J_m}$, $\mathbf{B_m}$ and $\mathbf{r}$ are the inertia, damping and reduction gear ratio, respectively. $\boldsymbol{\xi} \in R^n$ presents the external disturbances.

Substituting (1) into (2) and using $\dot{\boldsymbol{\theta}}_\mathbf{m} = \mathbf{r}^{-1}\dot{\mathbf{q}}$ yields

$$\begin{aligned}\mathbf{T_m} &= \mathbf{J_m r^{-1}\ddot{q}} + \mathbf{B_m r^{-1}\dot{q}} \\ &+ \mathbf{r}\left(\mathbf{D(q)\ddot{q}} + \mathbf{C(q,\dot{q})\dot{q}} + \mathbf{g(q)}\right) + \mathbf{r\xi}\end{aligned} \tag{3}$$

Equation (3) can be written as

$$\mathbf{T_m} = \mathbf{M(q)\ddot{q}} + \mathbf{N(q,\dot{q})\dot{q}} + \mathbf{W(q)} + \mathbf{r\xi} \tag{4}$$

Where

$$\mathbf{M(q)} = \left(\mathbf{J_m r^{-1}} + \mathbf{rD(q)}\right) \tag{5}$$

$$\mathbf{N(q,\dot{q})} = \left(\mathbf{B_m r^{-1}} + \mathbf{rC(q,\dot{q})}\right) \tag{6}$$

$$\mathbf{W(q)} = \mathbf{rg(q)} \tag{7}$$

Then, it is easy to show that

$$\begin{aligned}\mathbf{\ddot{q}} &= -\mathbf{M^{-1}(q)N(q,\dot{q})\dot{q}} - \mathbf{M^{-1}(q)W(q)} - \mathbf{M^{-1}(q)r\xi} \\ &+ \mathbf{M^{-1}(q)T_m}(t)\end{aligned} \tag{8}$$

Using nominal terms in (8) obtains that

$$\begin{aligned}\mathbf{\ddot{q}} &= -\mathbf{\hat{M}^{-1}(q)\hat{N}(q,\dot{q})\dot{q}} - \mathbf{\hat{M}^{-1}(q)\hat{W}(q)} + \\ &\mathbf{\hat{M}^{-1}(q)T_m}(t) + \boldsymbol{\varphi}\end{aligned} \tag{9}$$

where, $\mathbf{\hat{M}(q)}$, $\mathbf{\hat{N}(q,\dot{q})}$ and $\mathbf{\hat{W}(q)}$ are the nominal terms for the real terms $\mathbf{M(q)}$, $\mathbf{N(q,\dot{q})}$ and $\mathbf{W(q)}$, respectively, and $\boldsymbol{\varphi}$ is the uncertainty.

The nominal terms have the same dynamics as the real terms with parametric errors. The uncertainty $\boldsymbol{\varphi}$ is expressed by substituting (8) into (9) as

$$\begin{aligned}\boldsymbol{\varphi} &= (\mathbf{\hat{M}^{-1}(q)\hat{N}(q,\dot{q})} - \mathbf{M^{-1}(q)N(q,\dot{q})})\mathbf{\dot{q}} \\ &+ \mathbf{\hat{M}^{-1}(q)\hat{W}(q)} - \mathbf{M^{-1}(q)W(q)} \\ &- \mathbf{M^{-1}(q)r\xi} + (\mathbf{M^{-1}(q)} - \mathbf{\hat{M}^{-1}(q)})\mathbf{T_m}(t)\end{aligned} \tag{10}$$

Assume that there exists a $\mathbf{T_m}(t) = \mathbf{T_{md}}(t)$ that satisfies

$$\ddot{\mathbf{q}}_{\mathbf{d}} = -\hat{\mathbf{M}}^{-1}(\mathbf{q_d})\hat{\mathbf{N}}(\mathbf{q_d},\dot{\mathbf{q}}_{\mathbf{d}})\dot{\mathbf{q}}_{\mathbf{d}}$$
$$-\hat{\mathbf{M}}^{-1}(\mathbf{q_d})\hat{\mathbf{W}}(\mathbf{q_d}) + \hat{\mathbf{M}}^{-1}(\mathbf{q_d})\mathbf{T_{md}}(t) \tag{11}$$

where, $\mathbf{q_d}$ is the desired trajectory. Subtracting (9) from (11) yields

$$\ddot{\mathbf{q}}_{\mathbf{d}} - \ddot{\mathbf{q}} = \hat{\mathbf{M}}^{-1}(\mathbf{q})\hat{\mathbf{N}}(\mathbf{q},\dot{\mathbf{q}})\dot{\mathbf{q}} - \hat{\mathbf{M}}^{-1}(\mathbf{q_d})\hat{\mathbf{N}}(\mathbf{q_d},\dot{\mathbf{q}}_{\mathbf{d}})\dot{\mathbf{q}}_{\mathbf{d}}$$
$$-\boldsymbol{\varphi} + \hat{\mathbf{M}}^{-1}(\mathbf{q_d})\mathbf{T_{md}}(t) - \hat{\mathbf{M}}^{-1}(\mathbf{q})\mathbf{T_m}(t) \tag{12}$$
$$+ \hat{\mathbf{M}}^{-1}(\mathbf{q})\hat{\mathbf{W}}(\mathbf{q}) - \hat{\mathbf{M}}^{-1}(\mathbf{q_d})\hat{\mathbf{W}}(\mathbf{q_d})$$

Or, writing it out,

$$\ddot{\mathbf{q}}_{\mathbf{d}} - \ddot{\mathbf{q}} = -\hat{\mathbf{M}}^{-1}(\mathbf{q_d})\hat{\mathbf{N}}(\mathbf{q_d},\dot{\mathbf{q}}_{\mathbf{d}})(\dot{\mathbf{q}}_{\mathbf{d}} - \dot{\mathbf{q}}) + \tag{13}$$
$$\hat{\mathbf{M}}^{-1}(\mathbf{q_d})(\mathbf{T_{md}}(t) - \mathbf{T_m}(t)) + \hat{\mathbf{M}}^{-1}(\mathbf{q_d})\boldsymbol{\psi}$$

where, the uncertainty $\boldsymbol{\psi}$ is expressed as

$$\boldsymbol{\psi} = (\hat{\mathbf{M}}(\mathbf{q_d})\hat{\mathbf{M}}^{-1}(\mathbf{q})\hat{\mathbf{N}}(\mathbf{q},\dot{\mathbf{q}}) - \hat{\mathbf{W}}(\mathbf{q_d})$$
$$-\hat{\mathbf{N}}(\mathbf{q_d},\dot{\mathbf{q}}_{\mathbf{d}}))\dot{\mathbf{q}} - (\hat{\mathbf{M}}(\mathbf{q_d})\hat{\mathbf{M}}^{-1}(\mathbf{q}) - \mathbf{I})\mathbf{T_m} \tag{14}$$
$$-\hat{\mathbf{M}}(\mathbf{q_d})\boldsymbol{\varphi} + \hat{\mathbf{M}}(\mathbf{q_d})\hat{\mathbf{M}}^{-1}(\mathbf{q})\hat{\mathbf{W}}(\mathbf{q})$$

where, $\mathbf{I}$ is the identify matrix. The lumped uncertainty $\boldsymbol{\psi}$ includes the parametric uncertainty, unmodelled dynamics and external disturbances. The state space form of (13) is given by

$$\dot{\mathbf{E}} = \mathbf{A}(\mathbf{q_d},\dot{\mathbf{q}}_{\mathbf{d}})\mathbf{E} + \mathbf{B}(\mathbf{q_d})\mathbf{U} + \mathbf{B}(\mathbf{q_d})\boldsymbol{\psi} \tag{15}$$

where, $\mathbf{E}$ is the state vector, $\mathbf{U}$ the input vector, $\mathbf{A}(\mathbf{q_d},\dot{\mathbf{q}}_{\mathbf{d}})$ the state matrix and $\mathbf{B}(\mathbf{q_d})$ a gain matrix. The details are

$$\mathbf{A}(\mathbf{q_d},\dot{\mathbf{q}}_{\mathbf{d}}) = \begin{bmatrix} \mathbf{0} & \mathbf{I} \\ \mathbf{0} & -\hat{\mathbf{M}}^{-1}(\mathbf{q_d})\hat{\mathbf{N}}(\mathbf{q_d},\dot{\mathbf{q}}_{\mathbf{d}}) \end{bmatrix} \mathbf{E} = \begin{bmatrix} \mathbf{q_d} - \mathbf{q} \\ \dot{\mathbf{q}}_{\mathbf{d}} - \dot{\mathbf{q}} \end{bmatrix}$$

$$\mathbf{B}(\mathbf{q_d}) = \begin{bmatrix} \mathbf{0} \\ \hat{\mathbf{M}}^{-1}(\mathbf{q_d}) \end{bmatrix} \quad \mathbf{U} = \mathbf{T_{md}}(t) - \mathbf{T_m}(t) \tag{16}$$

The proposed model (15) has an advantage that $\mathbf{A}(\mathbf{q_d},\dot{\mathbf{q}}_{\mathbf{d}})$ and $\mathbf{B}(\mathbf{q_d})$ are known in advance, however, this model includes the uncertainty $\boldsymbol{\psi}$. The proposed model is an uncertain linear time-variant system with periodical coefficients. I obtain from (15) a linear discrete-time time-variant system using a sampling period σ that is a small positive constant. Substituting $k\sigma$ into t for $k = 1, 2, \ldots$ and then approximating $\dot{\mathbf{E}}$ as $\dot{\mathbf{E}} = (\mathbf{E}(t+\sigma) - \mathbf{E}(t))/\sigma$ provides a discrete-time model in the form of

$$\mathbf{E}_{k+1} = \mathbf{A}_k\mathbf{E}_k + \mathbf{B}_k\mathbf{U}_k + \mathbf{B}_k\boldsymbol{\psi}_k \tag{17}$$

where, $\mathbf{E}_k = \mathbf{E}(k\sigma)$, $\mathbf{A}_k = \mathbf{I} + \sigma\mathbf{A}(\sigma k)$, $\mathbf{B}_k = \sigma\mathbf{B}(\sigma k)$, $\mathbf{U}_k = \mathbf{U}(\sigma k)$ and $\boldsymbol{\psi}_k$ denotes the uncertainty. Since $\mathbf{A}_k$ and $\mathbf{B}_k$ are available, they can be computed in advance.

3. Discrete-time repetitive optimal control

A two-term control law is proposed to track the desired trajectory. The first term is DLQC and the second term is a robust time-delay controller. Thus, system (17) is presented as

$$\mathbf{E}_{k+1} = \mathbf{A}_k\mathbf{E}_k + \mathbf{B}_k\mathbf{U}_{1,k} + \mathbf{B}_k\mathbf{U}_{2,k} + \mathbf{B}_k\boldsymbol{\psi}_k \tag{18}$$

where, $\mathbf{U}_{1,k}$ and $\mathbf{U}_{2,k}$ are the first and second terms of control input. The control performance is improved if the lumped uncertainty $\boldsymbol{\psi}_k$ is compensated. The uncertainty is perfectly compensated if

$$\mathbf{B}\mathbf{U}_{2,k} = -\mathbf{B}\boldsymbol{\psi}_k \tag{19}$$

Since $\boldsymbol{\psi}_k$ is not known, control law (19) cannot be defined. To estimate the uncertainty, I obtain from (18)

$$\mathbf{B}\boldsymbol{\psi}_k = \mathbf{E}_{k+1} - \mathbf{A}\mathbf{E}_k - \mathbf{B}\mathbf{U}_{1,k} - \mathbf{B}\mathbf{U}_{2,k} \tag{20}$$

Since $\mathbf{E}_{k+1}$ is not available in the kth step, $\mathbf{B}\boldsymbol{\psi}_k$ cannot be calculated. Instead, the previous value of $\mathbf{B}\boldsymbol{\psi}_k$ is used as

$$\mathbf{B}\boldsymbol{\psi}_{k-1} = \mathbf{E}_k - \mathbf{A}\mathbf{E}_{k-1} - \mathbf{B}\mathbf{U}_{1,k-1} - \mathbf{B}\mathbf{U}_{2,k-1} \tag{21}$$

The term $\mathbf{B}\boldsymbol{\psi}_{k-1}$ can be calculated since all terms in the RHS of (21) are known and available. Thus, a robust control law is proposed as

$$\mathbf{B}\mathbf{U}_{2,k} = -\mathbf{B}\boldsymbol{\psi}_{k-1} \tag{22}$$

The second term in the control law is expressed by substituting (21) into (22) to yield the robust time-delay controller [9]

$$\mathbf{B}\mathbf{U}_{2,k} = -\mathbf{E}_k + \mathbf{A}\mathbf{E}_{k-1} + \mathbf{B}\mathbf{U}_{1,k-1} + \mathbf{B}\mathbf{U}_{2,k-1} \tag{23}$$

Substituting (22) into (18) yields

$$\mathbf{E}_{k+1} = \mathbf{A}\mathbf{E}_k + \mathbf{B}\mathbf{U}_{1,k} + \mathbf{B}(\boldsymbol{\psi}_k - \boldsymbol{\psi}_{k-1}) \tag{24}$$

In order to apply the DLQC, a nominal model in the form of discrete-time linear system is suggested from (24) as

$$\mathbf{E}_{k+1} = \mathbf{A}\mathbf{E}_k + \mathbf{B}\mathbf{U}_{1,k} \tag{25}$$

Then, the DLQC is given by

$$\mathbf{U}_{1,k} = -\mathbf{K}_k\mathbf{E}_k \tag{26}$$

The gain matrix $\mathbf{K}_k$ is calculated by minimizing a cost function of [1]

$$L = 0.5\mathbf{E}_N^*\mathbf{S}\mathbf{E}_N +$$
$$\frac{1}{2}\sum_{k=0}^{N-1}\begin{Bmatrix}\left(\mathbf{E}_k^*\mathbf{Q}\mathbf{E}_k + \mathbf{U}_{1,k}^*\mathbf{R}\mathbf{U}_{1,k}\right) + \lambda_{k+1}^*\left(\mathbf{A}_k\mathbf{E}_k + \mathbf{B}_k\mathbf{U}_{1,k} - \mathbf{E}_{k+1}\right) \\ +\left(\mathbf{A}_k\mathbf{E}_k + \mathbf{B}_k\mathbf{U}_{1,k} - \mathbf{E}_{k+1}\right)^*\lambda_{k+1}\end{Bmatrix}$$

(27)

With respect to $\mathbf{E}_k$, $\mathbf{U}_{1,k}$ and λ_k, where λ_k is the Lagrange multiplier, $\mathbf{Q}$, $\mathbf{R}$ and $\mathbf{S}$ are symmetric positive definite matrices. As a result,

$$\mathbf{K}_k = [\mathbf{R} + \mathbf{B}_k^*\mathbf{p}_k\mathbf{B}_k]^{-1}\mathbf{B}_k^*\mathbf{p}_k\mathbf{A}_k \qquad (28)$$

Where $\mathbf{p}_k$ is calculated as

$$\mathbf{p}_k = \mathbf{Q} + \mathbf{A}_k^*\mathbf{p}_{k-1}\mathbf{A}_k - \mathbf{A}_k^*\mathbf{p}_{k-1}\mathbf{B}_k[\mathbf{R} + \mathbf{B}_k^*\mathbf{p}_{k-1}\mathbf{B}_k]^{-1}\mathbf{B}_k^*\mathbf{p}_{k-1}\mathbf{A}_k$$

(29)

The algorithm starts from $k = 0$ in (29), where $\mathbf{p}_{-1} = \mathbf{0}$. Then, $\mathbf{K}_k$ is calculated as (28). Next, $\mathbf{U}_{1,k}$ is computed from (26).

The discrete-time repetitive optimal control (DROC) is formed using (23) and (26) as

$$\mathbf{U}_k = \left(\mathbf{B}^T\mathbf{B}\right)^{-1}\mathbf{B}^T.$$
$$\left(-(\mathbf{I} + \mathbf{B}\mathbf{K}_k)\mathbf{E}_k + \mathbf{A}\mathbf{E}_{k-1} + \mathbf{B}\left(\mathbf{U}_{1,k-1} + \mathbf{U}_{2,k-1}\right)\right)$$

(30)

In which from (16) $\left(\mathbf{B}^T\mathbf{B}\right)^{-1} = \hat{\mathbf{M}}^2(\mathbf{q_d})$ and

$$\mathbf{U}_k = \mathbf{T}_{\mathbf{md}k} - \mathbf{T}_{\mathbf{m}k}^* \qquad (31)$$

Calculating $\mathbf{T}_{\mathbf{md}k}$ from (11), $\mathbf{T}_{\mathbf{m}k}^*$ is obtained from (31) as

$$\mathbf{T}_{\mathbf{m}k}^* = \hat{\mathbf{M}}(\mathbf{q}_{\mathbf{d}k})\ddot{\mathbf{q}}_{\mathbf{d}k} + \hat{\mathbf{N}}(\mathbf{q}_{\mathbf{d}k},\dot{\mathbf{q}}_{\mathbf{d}k})\dot{\mathbf{q}}_{\mathbf{d}k} + \hat{\mathbf{W}}(\mathbf{q}_{\mathbf{d}k}) - \mathbf{U}_k$$

(32)

where, $\mathbf{U}_k$ is computed by (30).

The vector of motor torques $\mathbf{T}_{\mathbf{m}k}$ is proportional to the vector of motor currents $\mathbf{I}_k$ as

$$\mathbf{T}_{\mathbf{m}k} = \mathbf{K_m}\mathbf{I}_k \qquad (33)$$

where, $\mathbf{K_m}$ is the torque coefficient matrix. Thus

$$\mathbf{T}_{\mathbf{m}k}^* = \mathbf{K_m}\mathbf{I}_{\mathbf{d},k} \qquad (34)$$

Then, it is easy to show

$$\mathbf{I}_{\mathbf{d},k} = \mathbf{K_m}^{-1}\mathbf{T}_{\mathbf{m}k}^* \qquad (35)$$

where, $\mathbf{I}_{\mathbf{d},k}$ is the desired armature current.

A proportional integral controller is proposed to control the electric motors for generating the desired torque (34) as

$$\mathbf{V}_k = \mathbf{K_p}\left(\mathbf{e}_k - \mathbf{e}_{k-1}\right) + \sigma\mathbf{K_I}\mathbf{e}_k + \mathbf{V}_{k-1} \qquad (36)$$

where, $\mathbf{e}_k = \mathbf{I}_{d,k} - \mathbf{I}_k$, $\mathbf{V} \in R^n$ represents a vector of motor voltages as the input of robotic system.

4. Stability analysis

To make the dynamics of tracking error well-defined in such a way that the robot can track the desired trajectory, the following assumptions are made:

Assumption 1: The desired trajectory $\mathbf{q_d}$ must be smooth in the sense that $\mathbf{q_d}$ and its derivatives up to a necessary order are available and all uniformly bounded.

Smoothness of the desired trajectory can be guaranteed by proper trajectory planning.

As a necessary condition to design a robust controller, the matching condition must be satisfied:

Matching condition: the uncertainty must be entered into the system the same channel as the control input. Then, the uncertainty is said to satisfy the matching condition [18] or equivalently it is said to be matched. I ensure the matching condition since in the system (15), the lumped uncertainty ψ enters the system the same channel as the control input $\mathbf{U}$.

As a necessary condition to design a robust control, the external disturbance ξ in (2) must be bounded.

Assumption 2: The external disturbance ξ is bounded as

$$\|\xi\| \le \xi_{\max} \qquad (37)$$

where, $\xi_{\max}$ is a positive constant.

The voltage of every motor should be limited to protect the motor against over voltages. For this purpose, every motor is equipped with a voltage limiter. Therefore, the following assumption is made:

Assumption 3: The voltages of motors are constrained as

$$\|\mathbf{V}\| \le V_{\max} \qquad (38)$$

where, $V_{\max}$ is the template value of motor voltage.

The robust discrete-time linear quadratic is formed using (23) and (26) as

$$\mathbf{B}_k\mathbf{U}_k = -\left(\mathbf{I} + \mathbf{B}_k\mathbf{K}_k\right)\mathbf{E}_k + \mathbf{A}_k\mathbf{E}_{k-1} + \mathbf{B}_k\left(\mathbf{U}_{1,k-1} + \mathbf{U}_{2,k-1}\right)$$

(39)

Applying the control law (39) on the system (17) and using (21) results in the closed-loop system

$$\mathbf{E}_{k+1} = \left(\mathbf{A}_k - \mathbf{B}_k \mathbf{K}_k\right)\mathbf{E}_k + \mathbf{B}_k\left(\mathbf{\psi}_k - \mathbf{\psi}_{k-1}\right) \qquad (40)$$

The lumped uncertainty $\mathbf{\psi}$ is bounded as

$$\|\mathbf{\psi}\| \le \psi_{max} \qquad (41)$$

where, ψ_{max} is a positive scalar.

Proof: Under assumptions 1-3 and the matching condition, it is proven in [14] that for electrically driven robot manipulators, the vector of motor velocities $\dot{\mathbf{\theta}}_\mathbf{m}$ and the vector of motor currents $\mathbf{I}_\mathbf{a}$ are bounded. Since $\dot{\mathbf{q}} = \mathbf{r}\dot{\mathbf{\theta}}_\mathbf{m}$, the vector of joint velocities $\dot{\mathbf{q}}$ is bounded. Since $\mathbf{T}_\mathbf{m} = \mathbf{K}_\mathbf{m}\mathbf{I}_\mathbf{a}$, The vector of motor torques $\mathbf{T}_\mathbf{m}$ is bounded. For $\forall t$, $0 \le t \le T$ where T is the operating time of the desired trajectory $\mathbf{q}_\mathbf{d}$, it can be written that $\mathbf{q} = \int_0^t \dot{\mathbf{q}}dt + \mathbf{q}(0)$. Since $\dot{\mathbf{q}}$ is bounded, the vector of joint positions $\mathbf{q}$ is bounded.

According to the properties of robot manipulator [19], $\mathbf{D}(\mathbf{q})$, $\mathbf{C}(\mathbf{q},\dot{\mathbf{q}})\dot{\mathbf{q}}$ and $\mathbf{g}(\mathbf{q})$ in (1) are bounded as $m_1\mathbf{I} \le \mathbf{D}(\mathbf{q}) \le m_2(\mathbf{q})\mathbf{I}$, $\|\mathbf{C}(\mathbf{q},\dot{\mathbf{q}})\dot{\mathbf{q}}\| \le m_3(\mathbf{q})\|\dot{\mathbf{q}}\|$ and $\|\mathbf{g}(\mathbf{q})\| \le m_4(\mathbf{q})$. The matrix $\mathbf{D}(\mathbf{q})$ is a positive definite symmetric matrix which is invertible, m_1 is a positive constant, $m_2(\mathbf{q})$, $m_3(\mathbf{q})$, $m_4(\mathbf{q})$ are positive definite functions of $\mathbf{q}$, and $\mathbf{I}$ is an identity matrix. Since $\mathbf{r}$, $\mathbf{J}_\mathbf{m}$ and $\mathbf{B}_\mathbf{m}$ are constant diagonal matrices and $\mathbf{D}(\mathbf{q})$, $\mathbf{C}(\mathbf{q},\dot{\mathbf{q}})\dot{\mathbf{q}}$ and $\mathbf{g}(\mathbf{q})$ are bounded, thus $\mathbf{M}(\mathbf{q})$, $\mathbf{N}(\mathbf{q},\dot{\mathbf{q}})$ and $\mathbf{W}(\mathbf{q})$ expressed in (5), (6), and (7) are bounded. The $\hat{\mathbf{M}}(\mathbf{q})$, $\hat{\mathbf{N}}(\mathbf{q},\dot{\mathbf{q}})$ and $\hat{\mathbf{W}}(\mathbf{q})$ are the nominal terms with the same structure with $\mathbf{M}(\mathbf{q})$, $\mathbf{N}(\mathbf{q},\dot{\mathbf{q}})$ and $\mathbf{W}(\mathbf{q})$. Thus, they are bounded as well. It was implied that $\dot{\mathbf{q}}$, $\mathbf{q}$ and $\mathbf{T}_\mathbf{m}$ are bounded. The external disturbance $\mathbf{\xi}$ is bounded in assumption 2. Therefore, the boundedness of all terms in (10) implies that $\mathbf{\phi}$ is bounded. Thus, the boundedness of all terms in the right hand side of (14) proves that $\mathbf{\psi}$ is bounded.

Since the DLQC provides $\mathbf{K}_k$ such that $\mathbf{A}_k - \mathbf{B}_k \mathbf{K}_k$ is Hurwitz, thus system (40) is stable. In addition, the term $\mathbf{B}_k\left(\mathbf{\psi}_k - \mathbf{\psi}_{k-1}\right)$ is a bounded input to system (40) because the lumped uncertainty $\mathbf{\psi}$ is bounded in (41) and $\mathbf{B}_k$ is a gain matrix. Therefore, the discrete-time linear system (40) provides a bounded output $\mathbf{E}_{k+1}$ under the bounded input $\mathbf{B}_k\left(\mathbf{\psi}_k - \mathbf{\psi}_{k-1}\right)$.

The robust time-delay control law (23) plays a main role in compensating the uncertainty. If there exists a much difference between the nominal model (25) and the actual system (24), the closed-loop system (40) is subject to a large uncertainty. The residual uncertainty in the closed-loop system (40) is reduced from a large value of $\mathbf{B}_k\mathbf{\psi}_k$ to a small value of $\mathbf{B}_k\left(\mathbf{\psi}_k - \mathbf{\psi}_{k-1}\right)$ due to using the robust time-delay control law (23). As a result, the performance of control system is improved by reducing the residual uncertainty. The residual uncertainty $\mathbf{B}_k\left(\mathbf{\psi}_k - \mathbf{\psi}_{k-1}\right)$ will be very small when the uncertainty is smooth and sampling time is very short.

5. Simulation results

The proposed control algorithms, namely DROC in (30) are applied on an articulated robot manipulator given by [14]. The motor parameters are given in table 1, while the three motors are the same.

Table 1. Parameters of dc servomotors.

K_m	J_m	B_m	$1/r$	R_a	L_a
0.26	0.002	0.001	100	1.26	0.001

The desired repetitive trajectory is given by

$$\mathbf{q}_\mathbf{d} = \begin{bmatrix} \cos(0.1\pi t) & \cos(0.1\pi t) & \cos(0.1\pi t) \end{bmatrix}^T \qquad (42)$$

where, $\mathbf{q}_\mathbf{d}$ is a vector of desired joint angles with a period of $20\,\sec$.

Simulations are presented to show the performance of proposed control laws DROC in (39) and DLQC in (26).

The desired trajectory is sufficiently smooth and the motors are sufficiently strong such that the robot can track the desired trajectory. I run the simulations for two periods to illustrate the repetitive motion.

The uncertainty may include the external disturbances, unmodelled dynamics, and parametric uncertainty. To consider the parametric uncertainty, all parameters of the nominal model used in the control law are given as 95% of the real one. The external disturbance is given to load torque of the third joint by $100\,N.m$. The uncertainty is unknown; however, I have to use an example of a bounded uncertainty to check the performance of the control system. The matrices $\mathbf{Q}$ and $\mathbf{R}$ in (28) and (29) are given by trial and error method to have a good performance through using $\mathbf{Q} = 10^8 \mathbf{I}_{6\times6}$ and $\mathbf{R} = 10\mathbf{I}_{3\times3}$ where $\mathbf{I}_{n\times n}$ is the

$n \times n$ identity matrix. The matrices $\mathbf{K_p}$ and $\mathbf{K_I}$ in (36) are given by

$$\mathbf{K_p} = \begin{bmatrix} 0.1 & 0 & 0 \\ 0 & 1 & 0 \\ 0 & 0 & 1 \end{bmatrix}, \quad \mathbf{K_I} = \begin{bmatrix} 1 & 0 & 0 \\ 0 & 10 & 0 \\ 0 & 0 & 10 \end{bmatrix}.$$

Simulation 1: The DROC in (30) for tracking control with the zero initial error is simulated. Using the sampling time of 0.001s, the tracking performance is very well such that the tracking error is under $9 \times 10^{-5} rad$ shown in figure 1. The sampling time of 0.001s may be too short in real-time control. Thus, the sampling time is set to 0.01s. As a result, the tracking error is under $7 \times 10^{-4} rad$ shown in figure 2. Compared with figure 1, the tracking error is increased if used longer sampling time. The real-time control needs a sufficient time for computation and implementation. The control efforts behave well under the permitted values shown in figure 3.

To see the effect of initial error, it is set to

$$\mathbf{e}(0) = \mathbf{q_d}(0) - \mathbf{q}(0) = \begin{bmatrix} 0.5 & 1.5 & 2 \end{bmatrix}^T rad.$$

The tracking error is reduced well from initial value to be under $2.7 \times 10^{-5} rad$ at the end shown in figure 4.

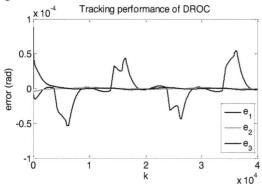

Figure 1. Tracking performance of DROC in the sampling time of 0.001s .

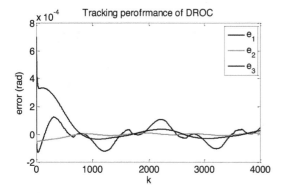

Figure 2. Tracking performance of DROC in the sampling time of 0.01s .

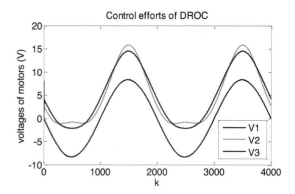

Figure 3. Control efforts of DROC.

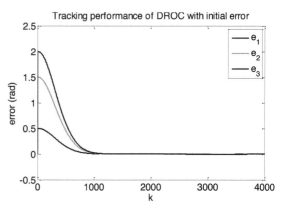

Figure 4. Tracking performance of DROC with initial error.

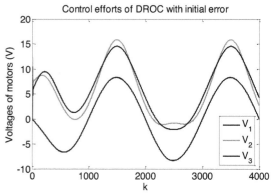

Figure 5. Control efforts of DROC with Initial error.

The control efforts behave well under the permitted values shown in figure 5.

Simulation 2: I apply the DROC in (30) for the set point control in the sampling time of 0.01s. The initial positions of the joint angles are set to $\mathbf{q}(0) = \begin{bmatrix} 0 & 0.5 & 2 \end{bmatrix}^T rad$ while the position of the desired trajectory is given by $\mathbf{q_d} = \begin{bmatrix} 1 & 1 & 1 \end{bmatrix}^T rad$. The initial error is calculated as

$$\mathbf{e}(0) = \mathbf{q_d}(0) - \mathbf{q}(0) = \begin{bmatrix} 1 & 0.5 & -1 \end{bmatrix}^T rad.$$

The motor voltages are practically limited to the maximum value of $40V$ to protect the motors from over voltages. The set point performance is very well such that the norm of errors is vanished well after $10\,\mathrm{s}$ and comes under the $2.2\times10^{-7}\,rad$ in the end shown in figure 6. The motor voltages are under the permitted value of 40V and behave well without any problems shown in figure 7.

The control efforts behave well under the permitted values. As a result, the uncertainties are compensated well.

Simulation 3: I apply the DLQC in (23) for tracking control with zero initial error and the sampling time of $0.01\,\mathrm{s}$.

The tracking errors are under the $0.085\,rad$ shown in figure 8 and the control efforts behave well under the permitted value of $40\,V$ shown in figure 9. The maximum value of errors for the DLQC is about 121 times larger than one for the DROC.

Simulation 4: The set point performance of the DLQC is simulated with the sampling time of $0.01\,\mathrm{s}$. The initial errors and desired trajectories are given the same as the DROC for comparing the results. The tracking errors are vanished after $10\,\mathrm{s}$ and come under $0.033\,rad$ in the end shown in figure 10.

The motor voltages are under the permitted value of 40V and behave well without any problems shown in figure 11. The maximum value of errors for the DLQC is about 1.5×10^{5} times larger than one for the DROC at the end.

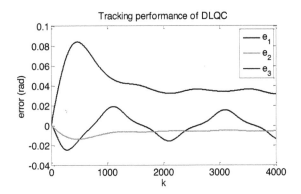

Figure 8. Tracking performance of DLQC.

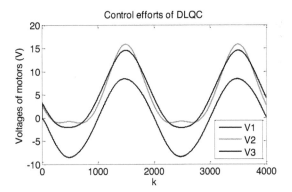

Figure 9. Control efforts of DLQC.

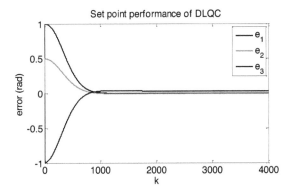

Figure 10. Set point performance of DLQC.

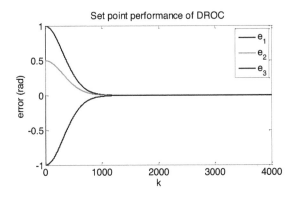

Figure 6. Set point performance of DROC.

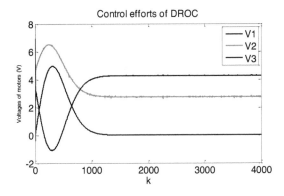

Figure 7. Control efforts of Set point DROC.

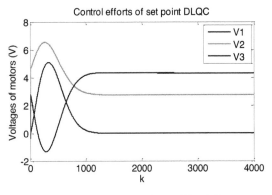

Figure 11. Control efforts of DLQC.

6. Conclusion

A novel discrete-time repetitive optimal control of electrically driven robot manipulators has been developed by a modification on the discrete linear quadratic control. The proposed control law includes two terms: The discrete linear quadratic controller and the robust time-delay controller. In order to apply the discrete linear quadratic control, a control-oriented discrete-time linear time-variant model has been proposed for the robotic system. The control-oriented model highly differs from the actual system. To compensate the model imprecision, I have used the time-delay controller. The proposed control approach has been verified by stability analysis. Simulation results have shown the superiority of the proposed control method over the discrete linear quadratic control. The time-delay controller efficiently compensates the uncertainty and nonlinearity.

References

[1] Ogata, K. (1987). Discrete Time Control Systems, Prentice-Hall.

[2] Corradini, M. L., Fossi, V., Giantomassi, A., Ippoliti, G., Longhi, S. & Orlando, G. (2012). Discrete Time Sliding Mode Control of Robotic Manipulators: Development and Experimental Validation. Control Engineering Practice, vol. 20, no. 8, pp. 816-822.

[3] Poo, A. N., Lim, K. B. & Ma, Y. X. (1996). Application of Discrete Learning Control to a Robotic Manipulator. Robotics and Computer-Integrated Manufacturing, vol. 12, no. 1, pp. 55-64.

[4] Mahmoud, M. S. & Bahnasawi, A. A. (1993). Indirect Discrete-Time Adaptive Algorithm for Manipulator Control. Applied Mathematical Modelling, vol. 17, no. 8, pp. 423-429.

[5] Tsai, M. C., Anwar, G. & Tomizuka, M. (1988) Discrete Time Repetitive Control for Robot Manipulators. IEEE International Conference on Robotics and Automation, Philadelphia, PA, 1988.

[6] Tsai, M. C. & Tomizuka, M. (1989). Model Reference Adaptive Control and Repetitive Control for Robot Manipulators. IEEE International Conference on Robotics and Automation, Scottsdale, AZ, 1989.

[7] Sun, M., Ge, S. S. & Moreels, I. M. Y. (2006). Adaptive Repetitive Learning Control of Robotic Manipulators without the Requirement for Initial Repositioning. IEEE Transactions on Robotics, vol. 22, no. 3, pp. 563-568.

[8] Dixon, W. E., Zergeroglu, E., Dawson, D. M. & Costic, B. T. (2002). Repetitive Learning Control: A Lyapunov-based Approach. IEEE Transactions on Systems, Man, and Cybernetics, Part B: Cybernetics, vol. 32, no. 4, pp. 538-545.

[9] Fateh, M. M., Ahsani Tehrani, H. & Karbassi, S.M. (2013). Repetitive Control of Electrically Driven Robot Manipulators. International Journal of Systems Science, vol. 44, no. 4, pp. 775-785.

[10] Youcef-Toumi, K. & Shortlidge, C. (1991). Control of Robot Manipulators Using Time Delay, Proc. IEEE International Conference on Robotics and Automation, Sacramento, CA, 1991.

[11] Talole, S. E. & Phadke, S. B. (2008). Model Following Sliding Mode Control Based on Uncertainty and Disturbance Estimator. ASME Journal of Dynamic, Systems, Measurement and Control, vol. 130, no. 3, pp. 034501 (5 pages).

[12] Fateh, M. M. (2009). Robust Impedance Control of a Hydraulic Suspension System. International Journal of Robust and Nonlinear Control, vol. 2, no. 8, pp. 858-872.

[13] Fateh, M. M. & Khorashadizadeh S. (2012). Robust Control of Electrically Driven Robots by Adaptive Fuzzy Estimation of Uncertainty. Nonlinear Dynamics, vol. 69, no. 3, pp. 1465-1477.

[14] Fateh, M. M. (2012). Robust Control of Flexible-Joint Robots Using Voltage Control Strategy. Nonlinear Dynamics, vol. 6, no. 2, pp. 1525–1537.

[15] Neuman, C. P. & Tourassis, V. D. (1985). Discrete dynamic robot models. IEEE Transactions on Systems Man and Cybernetics, vol. 15, no. 2, pp.193–204.

[16] Mareels, I. M. Y., Penfold, H. B. & Evans, R. J. (1992). Controlling Nonlinear Time-Varying Systems via Euler Approximations. Autotomatica, vol. 28, no. 4, pp. 681–696.

[17] Spong, M. W., Hutchinson, S. & Vidyasagar, M. (2006). Robot Modelling and Control. John Wiley & Sons, Inc..

[18] Corless, M. & Leitmann, G. (1981). Continuous State Feedback Guaranteeing Uniform Ultimate Boundedness for Uncertain Dynamics Systems. IEEE Transactions on Automatic Control, vol. 26, no. 5, pp. 1139-1144.

[19] Qu, Z. & Dawson, D. M. (1996). Robust tracking control of robot manipulators. IEEE Press, Inc., New York.

16

A block-wise random sampling approach: Compressed sensing problem

V. Abolghasemi[1*], S. Ferdowsi[1] and S. Sanei[2]

1. Department of Electrical Engineering & Robotics, University of Shahrood, Shahrood, Iran.
2. Faculty of Engineering and Physical Sciences, University of Surrey, Guildford, UK.

*Corresponding author: vabolghasemi@shahroodut.ac.ir (V. Abolghasemi).

Abstract
The focus of this paper is to consider the compressed sensing problem. It is stated that the compressed sensing theory, under certain conditions, helps relax the Nyquist sampling theory and takes smaller samples. One of the important tasks in this theory is to carefully design measurement matrix (sampling operator). Most existing methods in the literature attempt to optimize a randomly initialized matrix with the aim of decreasing the amount of required measurements. However, these approaches mainly lead to sophisticated structure of measurement matrix which makes it very difficult to implement. In this paper we propose an intermediate structure for the measurement matrix based on random sampling. The main advantage of block-based proposed technique is simplicity and yet achieving acceptable performance obtained through using conventional techniques. The experimental results clearly confirm that in spite of simplicity of the proposed approach it can be competitive to the existing methods in terms of reconstruction quality. It also outperforms existing methods in terms of computation time.

Keywords: *Compressed Sensing, Sparse Recovery, Signal Processing, Random Sampling, Matching Pursuit, Measurement Matrix.*

1. Introduction

Recently, the new theory of compressed sensing (CS) [1, 2] has emerged and brings on new findings regarding signal sampling. This theory states that for certain type of signals one can recover the original samples from fewer measurements than those required by Nyquist-Shannon theory [3, 4]. Compressed sensing is valid for signals with underlying sparse structure. A sparse signal has merely few non-zeros. The CS experts originally showed that random measurement matrices are suitable for compressed sensing problem. However, later it shows that a carefully designed measurement matrix improves the performance. Generally, the maturity of a sampling strategy for CS can be judged in the following aspects:

- *Optimality of the sampling process:* the required number of measurements for exact recovery is desired to be as small as possible. Although random sampling can lead to an exact recovery, the required number of measurements is not optimal yet;

- *Low complexity and simplicity for hardware implementation:* the complexity and required memory space in sampling techniques should be minimized to become suitable for large-scale problems ;

- *Universality:* the random measurement matrices are universal and can be obtained non-adaptively. This means that their performance does not vary with changing the sparsifying matrices. Any designed (or optimized) measurement matrix should also have this property.

Two categories of algorithms have been proposed for improving the signal sampling in CS framework; First, the family of algorithms which attempts to propose a particular structure (e.g. by exploiting prior knowledge about the signal of interest) for sampling the signals. Second, those approaches which attempt to improve the structure of an initially random measurement matrix using optimization techniques [5-10]. In this paper, the first family of approaches is addressed.

In [11], which is an application to magnetic resonance imaging (MRI), the authors define an incoherence criterion based on point spread function (PSF) and propose a Monte Carlo scheme for random incoherent sampling of this type of data. They believe that a pure random sampling of k-space in all dimensions is not generally practical due to hardware implementation issues.

In short, k-space is a special representation of data points in Fourier transform of the MR images. Hence, they design an incoherent sampling technique (still by following the existing incoherence properties of random undersampling) to allow rapid data collection. Based on their observations, a better performance is achieved by less undersampling near the k-space origin and more in the periphery of k-space. Other related techniques for MRI acquisitions can be found in [12, 13].

Wang et al. [14] proposed a variable density sampling strategy by exploiting the prior information about the statistical distributions of natural images in the wavelet domain. Their proposed method is computationally efficient and can be applied to several transforming domains. In another work [15], Wang et al. show that if the spectral characteristics of the underlying signal are not expected to be uniform, then, the less number of measurements is required compared with when using conventional compressed sensing. They first propose to generate colored random projections using a bandpass filter when the spectral profile of the signal to be sampled is known, and then propose an adaptive scheme to generate colored random projections when such a priori is not available.

In this paper, a novel random sampling scheme for compressed sensing framework is proposed. The aim is to propose a technique which can offer at least the same reconstruction performance as that exists for the conventional compressed sensing, but allows a simpler implementation and less required storage for the measurement matrix.

The rest of this paper is as follows. Next section describes the basics of compressed sensing theory. Section 3 gives an example of the advantages of random undersampling and applying CS recovery methods over linear recovery. The proposed method is then described in section 4. The simulation results and concluding remarks are drawn in sections 5 and 6, respectively.

2. Compressed sensing

The basic compressed sensing scenario can be expressed as follows. Assume a one-dimensional signal $x \in \mathbb{R}^n$ which can be represented sparsely in a known transform domain (e.g. Fourier, or wavelet). Although x can be sparse in the current domain (e.g. time, or pixel), we always assume that x is sparse in a known transform domain, unless otherwise stated. The sparsifying transform can be expressed in matrix form denoted by $\Psi \in \mathbb{R}^{n \times m}$, with Ψ containing m columns vectors $\{\psi_i\}_{i=1}^m$ of length $n \leq m$. The case of $n < m$ is treated as overcomplete sparse representation. Considering the above notations, the signal x can be expressed as:

$$x = \sum_{i=1}^{m} s_i \psi_i = \Psi s \tag{1}$$

where, $s \in \mathbb{R}^m$ is a column vector of sparse coefficients, having merely $k \ll m$ non-zero samples. Clearly, x is the representation of the signal in non-sparse domain (e.g. time, space) and s is the representation in sparse domain (e.g. wavelet, frequency). The signal x is called k-sparse since it can be generated as a linear combination of only k vectors from Ψ. Here, the signal s is called exact-sparse since it has k non-zeros and the rest of the elements are exactly equal to zero. However, there might be some cases where the coefficient vector s includes only few large components and many small coefficients. In this case, x is treated as a compressible signal and sparse approximation methods are applied.

Now the acquisition process is defined as follows, where the measurements $y \in \mathbb{R}^p$ with $p < n$ are computed as a set of linear measurements from x. This process is mathematically expressed as:

$$y = \Phi x = \Phi \Psi s = \Theta s \tag{2}$$

where, $\Phi \in \mathbb{R}^{p \times n}$ is called the measurement matrix (or sensing matrix) and y is treated as measurements.

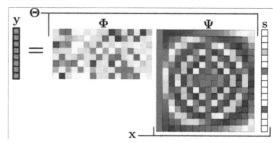

Figure 1. Graphical schematic of the basic compressed sensing model.

Figure 1 depicts a graphical representation of the basic CS model, which clearly implies that y of length $p < n$ is a compressed version of x. It is important to note that CS model is non-adaptive.

It means that the measurement matrix does not basically depend on the signal x. This has the advantage of universality of this sampling method. However, the minimum possible number of measurements p and the structure of Φ are two critical factors which should be determined based upon some specific criteria [1, 2].

Assume sampling of a signal using the above scheme and then transmitting the measurements y via an available media. The second crucial task (at the receiver) is to recover (decode) the original samples x with the knowledge about the measurements y and the measurement matrix Φ. The recovery problem is ill-conditioned since the number of available measurements p is less than the number of unknown samples n. However, several methods have been proposed to tackle this problem.

3. Random undersampling
In order to demonstrate the effectiveness of random undersampling (sub-Nyquist–Shannon) for compressed sensing problem here, we present a simple example. Consider the following periodic signal comprised of three harmonics:

$$x(t) = \cos(2\pi t) + \cos(10\pi t) \tag{3}$$

$$+ \cos(40\pi t),$$

The aim is to downsample the above signal using a random scheme, and then reconstructing it using CS techniques. The maximum frequency in the above signal, related to $\cos(40\pi t)$, is $f_{max} = 20$ Hz. Based on the Nyquist–Shannon rule the sampling frequency must obey $f_s \geq 2f_{max} = 40$ Hz. However, we do not follow the Nyquist–Shannon rule and undersample the above signal by taking only p = 50 (equivalent to $f_s = 10$ Hz) random samples in the time interval of $t \in [0\ 5]$ seconds. Note that p is called the number of measurements (equivalent to length of vector y). The random sampling is carried out simply by taking samples from x(t) at random locations which follow a Gaussian distribution. Note that this way of random sampling differs from the conventional CS where a set of linear measurements should be taken rather than the actual samples. However, for illustrative purposes and to show the strength of CS, we use such a simple scheme.

Consider DCT transform of x(t) where only three major components exist (Figure 2 (a)). Three different methods are applied to the undersampled vector of length p to approximate the components of the original signal. The first method is (nonlinear) OMP, the second is linear interpolation and the third method is a simple zero padding. The linear interpolation is applied as the concatenation of linear interpolants between each pair of data points of y(t). Zero padding is simply carried out by inserting zero at random locations within the components of y(t) until its length gets equal to x(t). The corresponding resulted signals in DCT domain are shown in figure 2 (b), (c) and (d), respectively. It is clearly illustrated that OMP can successfully recover the major components from the random undersampled signal, while linear interpolation and zero padding fail to do so. This shows the influence of random undersampling and using CS techniques to recover the original signal. Next, we propose a new sampling technique with less required storage for the measurement matrix.

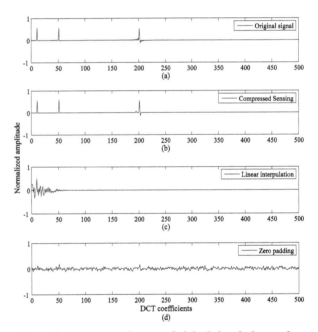

Figure 2. From top to bottom: Original signal, the result of compressed sensing reconstruction, the result of linear interpolation, and simple zero padding. All the signals are shown in the DCT domain and the amplitudes are normalized.

4. The proposed method
In conventional compressed sensing, the measurement matrix Φ of size $p \times n$ is normally selected randomly. However, dealing with this matrix in large scale problems is challenge and requires large size memory. In order to alleviate this problem, we propose a different random sampling scheme which requires less memory for storing the measurement matrix.

In spite of conventional random samplers in CS framework which takes p linear measurements from the input signal x, we propose to break x into M segments of length L, and then take $p_i <$

L, (for $i = 1,2,...M$) random projections from each segment, independently. This can be equivalently defined as:

$$y_i = \Phi_i x_i \text{ for } i = 1,...M, \qquad (4)$$

where Φ_i's are measurement matrices of size $p_i \times L$. Now, if we concatenate all y_i's, which are of length p_i, and create vector y of length $M(p_1 + p_2 + \cdots + p_M)$, the following equation can be obtained:

$$y = \Phi x: \begin{bmatrix} y_1 \\ y_2 \\ \vdots \\ y_M \end{bmatrix} = \begin{bmatrix} \Phi_1 x_1 \\ \Phi_2 x_2 \\ \vdots \\ \Phi_M x_M \end{bmatrix} \qquad (5)$$
$$= \begin{bmatrix} \Phi_1 & 0 & \cdots & 0 \\ 0 & \Phi_2 & \cdots & 0 \\ \vdots & \vdots & \ddots & \vdots \\ 0 & 0 & \cdots & \Phi_M \end{bmatrix} \begin{bmatrix} x_1 \\ x_2 \\ \vdots \\ x_M \end{bmatrix}.$$

Equation (5) is the mathematical representation of a sampling strategy proposed above. In fact, taking random projections from segments of input signal can be mathematically illustrated as multiplying a block-diagonal matrix Φ by full-length input signal x.

The main advantage of this scheme is that the measurement matrix Φ, comparing with the measurement matrix in conventional CS, is block-diagonal and thus requires less memory for storage and lower transmission band. In addition, this block-wise strategy gives more flexibility so that one can use different measurements $p_1 \neq \cdots \neq p_M$, per segment--a kind of variable density sampling.

The above block-wise procedure can be seen as sliding a rectangular window across the signal and taking few random projections at each slide. However, in many applications we prefer to use overlapping windows to avoid any possible loss of information at the segment boundaries. Therefore, we introduce τ as the number of overlapped components and use such overlapping scheme in practice. Figure 3 demonstrates a random measurement matrix with overlapping blocks. It is obvious that such measurement matrix has many zero elements and can be stored with less effort. Due to such a special shape of the obtained measurement matrix, we choose the term "block-wise" for the proposed approach.

After applying the proposed sampling method, the projection vectors $\{y_i\}_{i=1}^M$ and the measurement matrices $\{\Phi_i\}_{i=1}^M$ should be transmitted to the receiver. At the receiver side, the actual measurement matrix, i.e. Φ, should be formed using small sub-matrices $\{\Phi_i\}_{i=1}^M$.

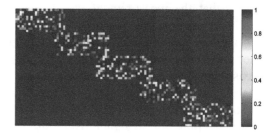

Figure 3. Illustration of a block diagonal Φ resulted from applying the proposed segmented sampling. Notice the overlapping between the blocks for avoiding information loss.

The knowledge about overlapping parameter τ is also required at this step. Then, the original sparse signal can be reconstructed by applying one of the common sparse recovery techniques [16-18]. Indeed, the recovery process should be carried out jointly over the entire random projections. Figure 4 represents an illustrative block diagram of a send-receive paradigm using the proposed method.

One important point which should be noted here is how one can choose M and L. One feasible approach is based on characteristics of the input signal/image. For instance, depending on the amplitude/energy of the signal at specific intervals, appropriate M, L, and corresponding p are chosen. Based on this adaptive strategy, more emphasis is applied to parts of the signal which contain important information and vice versa. Such decision can also be made based on any other *a priori* about the signal.

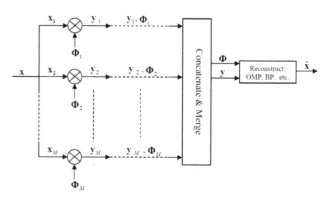

Figure 4. Block diagram of the proposed sampling method in a send-receive paradigm.

5. Experimental results

The first experiment was carried out by making a synthetic sparse signal x of length n = 100 and s = 15 non-zeros with random locations. In this experiment, we treated x as a sparse signal in the current domain and not with respect to a sparsifying matrix, i.e. $\Psi = I$. The proposed algorithm was then applied to x, with the following parameters; the number of segments: $M = 5$, overlapping each segment: $\tau = 6$, and measurements number per segment: $p_i = 10$, for $i = 1,2, \ldots M$. We then reconstructed this signal by solving ℓ_1-norm minimization problem, i.e. BP. The corresponding algorithm was taken from ℓ_1-magic [19], which is a well-designed and simple MATLAB toolbox available online for solving the convex optimization problems mainly based on standard interior-point methods. Figure 5 displays the recovery results along with SNR as the quality measure.

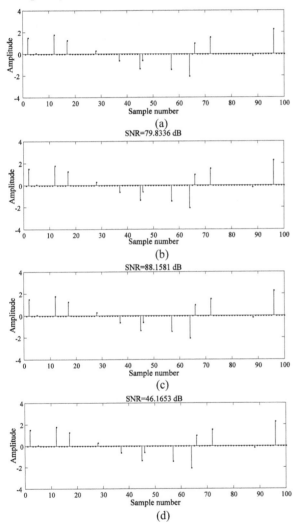

Figure 5. The reconstruction results with corresponding SNRs when the proposed sampling method is used; (a) original signal, and those recovered using (b) BP, (c) OMP, and (d) SL0.

Signal to noise ratio (SNR) is the measure of the ratio between signal power and the power of reconstruction error. It is mathematically defined as $\text{SNR}_{dB} = 20 \log_{10} \frac{\|x\|_2}{\|\hat{x}-x\|_2}$, where x and $\hat{x}$ are the original and estimated signals, respectively. We have also applied two other methods named OMP, taken from "SparseLab" toolbox [20], and SL0

(smoothed ℓ_0) [21], taken from [17], for reconstruction. SL0 is a fast optimization method which attempts to solve ℓ_1-norm minimization problem by approximating the ℓ_0-norm reconstruction using a smoothing function $F_\sigma(.)$, where σ determines the quality of approximation [21]. As it is seen from figure 5, the common recovery algorithms could successfully recover the underlying sparse signal when the proposed sampling strategy is applied.

Due to block-diagonal structure of the obtained measurement matrix in the proposed method, we expected the reconstruction algorithm to perform faster. In order to verify this expectation, we set up an experiment in which the response times of three reconstruction methods (i.e. BP, OMP and SL0) were recorded. This experiment was repeated for different signal dimensions, 5 segments, and total of 50 measurements. Table 1 demonstrates the corresponding results. Table 1 shows that the common recovery algorithms perform faster when the proposed measurement matrix is used compared with the conventional random measurement matrices. This is more noticeable at higher dimensions, especially for BP which is a more complicated algorithm among others. However, the computation times of different methods do not change significantly when the proposed scheme is used in low dimensions (e.g. the signal length of 100 in table 1). In the second experiment, a fixed number of measurements $p = 30$ was selected for signals of length $n = 120$.

Then, we varied the non-zeros of 10000 sparse signal ensembles from 1 to 10 and applied the proposed method. In this experiment the proposed method was used with $M = 5$, $p_i = 6$ for $i = 1,2, \ldots M$ and the segments had 50% overlap. Finally, we applied several recovery methods to reconstruct the sparse signals and evaluated the recovery performance. The results of this experiment are depicted in figure 6. As expected, the recovery error increases with increasing the number of non-zeros. In addition, figure 6 demonstrates that the degradation in the reconstruction performance is negligible, when the proposed sampling scheme has been used. Also, less recovery error of the proposed method, observed in figure 6 (a) and (c) for large number of non-zeros, cannot be fairly explained since the performance of recovery techniques are not reliable at these dimensions.

In the third experiment, we evaluated the performance of the proposed algorithm against variations in the number of measurements.

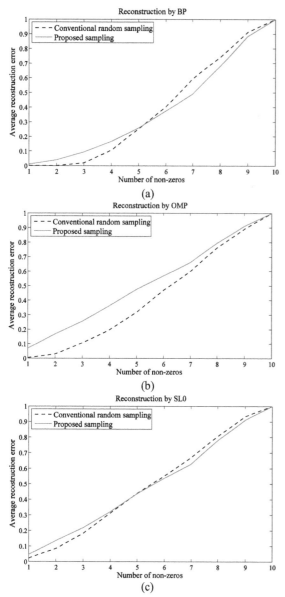

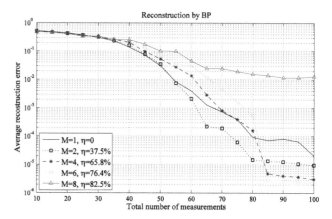

Figure 7. Average recovery error versus number of measurements. *M* denotes the number of segments and η indicates the percentage of zero components in Φ.

measurement matrix (based on the model in (5) and in Figure 3). This means the overall block-diagonal measurement matrix requires less memory which is desired.

However, figure 7 shows that choosing very large number of segments causes degradation in performance, which is a disadvantage. This behavior can be because of the fact that choosing large number of segments (for a signal of fixed length) leads to very small segment-size, and consequently, the segments cannot convey much information about the signal. In fact, there is a trade-off between the number of segments and the recovery performance and the number of segments and their sizes (compared with the total length of signal) should be obtained empirically.

Figure 6. The reconstruction error against number of non-zeros when (a) BP, (b) OMP and (c) SL0 used as the recovery method.

In order to do this, we computed the average recovery error for 1000 signal ensembles of length 120 and 15 non-zeros. This experiment was carried out while we varied the total number of measurements from 10 to 80. The results are given in figure 7 when different numbers of segments were chosen in the sampling stage. The parameter η in the graphs, represents the percentage of free space (zeros) in the measurement matrix.

As the graphs in figure 7 show, increasing the number of measurements leads to smaller recovery error in all curves. However, the resulting curves behave slightly different for different segment numbers (i.e. M). Obviously, more segments mean more percentage of zero components (η) in the corresponding

Like the last experiment, we used the proposed method for compression and reconstruction of an MR image of size 230×180. Conventionally, we first applied Haar wavelet transform to the image in figure 8 (a). Then, detailed coefficients (horizontal, vertical and diagonal) were rearranged into a single sparse vector x of length 7830. This vector was then multiplied by the measurement matrix Φ, leading to the measurements $y = \Phi x$. Two types of measurement matrices were chosen for this experiment; traditional random Gaussian Φ of size 2100×7830, and proposed block-diagonal Φ where M = 30, $p_i = 70$ and $\tau = 100$.

The results of reconstruction using BP are given in figure 8. These results were obtained after reconstruction of sparse vector and taking inverse wavelet transform.

Figure 8 shows that the achieved SNR using the proposed method is higher than that obtained using traditional CS.

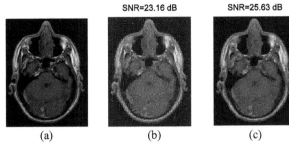

Figure 8. MRI reconstruction results: (a) input image. The reconstructed image using (b) traditional CS, and (c) the proposed method.

6. Conclusions

A new and simple method to design the measurement matrix in compressed sensing has been presented in this paper. The proposed method obtains random linear measurements by dividing the input signal into several overlapping segments.

The resulting measurement matrix has a block-diagonal structure which is more efficient in terms of required memory storage and transmission costs. In addition, the overlapped segments avoid possible loss of information at the segment boundaries. Our simulation results revealed that by using the proposed method, one can achieve similar recovery performance as that obtained when conventional random sampling is used. Furthermore, the recovery time is reduced when the proposed scheme is used due to simpler structure of the proposed measurement matrix. However, more investigation is required to improve the recovery performance as well as optimizing the sampling process.

Another important aspect of the proposed approach is its applicability for real-world scenarios. There exist numerous applications which can benefit from this approach. For example, in compressed sensing based MRI, generating a fully random measurement matrix is a challenging issue.

Therefore, the proposed mitigated technique could be practical. Also, in terahertz imaging systems [22] achieving a simple acquisition operator is of interest. All these applications and other related problems can be further investigated and studied.

Table 1. Computation time (in second) per iteration for different methods for M=5 segments.

		Signal length				
		100	1000	4000	7000	10000
Random Sampling	BP	0.0077	3.0271	10.0603	20.7773	41.1924
	OMP	0.0031	0.0043	0.0060	0.0102	0.0113
	SL0	0.0021	0.0189	0.0353	0.0521	0.747
Proposed Sampling	BP	0.0076	1.2730	4.8648	12.9129	21.3821
	OMP	0.0032	0.0039	0.0057	0.0082	0.0107
	SL0	0.0022	0.0154	0.0252	0.0418	0.0575

References

[1] Donoho, D. L. (2006). Compressed sensing. IEEE Transactions on Information Theory, vol. 52, no. 4, pp. 1289–1306.

[2] Candes, E. J., Romberg, J. & Tao, T. (2006). Robust uncertainty principles: exact signal reconstruction from highly incomplete frequency information. IEEE Transactions on Information Theory, vol. 52, no. 2, pp. 489 – 509.

[3] Shannon, C. E. (1949). Communication in the presence of noise. Proceedings of the IRE, vol. 37, no. 1, pp. 10–21.

[4] Nyquist, H. (1928). Certain topics in telegraph transmission theory. Transactions of the American Institute of Electrical Engineers, vol. 47, no. 2, pp. 617–644.

[5] Elad, M. (2007). Optimized projections for compressed sensing. IEEE Transactions on Signal Processing, vol. 55, no. 12, pp. 5695–5702.

[6] Abolghasemi, V., Ferdowsi, S. & Sanei, S. (2010). On optimization of the measurement matrix for compressive sensing. 18th European Signal Processing Conference, EUSIPCO, pp. 427–431, Aalborg, Denmark, 2010.

[7] Duarte-Carvajalino, J. M. & Sapiro, G. (2009). Learning to sense sparse signals: Simultaneous sensing matrix and sparsifying dictionary optimization. IEEE Transactions on Image Processing, vol. 18, no. 7, pp. 1395-1408.

[8] Abolghasemi, V., Jarchi, D., & Sanei, S. (2010). A robust approach for optimization of the measurement matrix in compressed sensing. 2nd International Workshop on Cognitive Information Processing, CIP, pp. 388–392, Elba, Italy, 2010.

[9] Cleju, N. (2014). Optimized projections for compressed sensing via rank-constrained nearest correlation matrix. Applied and Computational Harmonic Analysis, vol. 36, no. 3, pp. 495-507.

[10] Krahmer, F. & Rauhut, H. (2014). Structured random measurements in signal processing, GAMM-Mitteilungen, vol. 37, no. 2, pp. 217–238.

[11] Lustig, M., Donoho, D. L. & Pauly, J. M. (2007). Sparse MRI: The application of compressed sensing for rapid MR imaging. Magnetic Resonance in Medicine, vol. 58, no. 6, pp. 1182–1195.

[12] Wang, H., Liang, D. & Ying, L. (2009). Pseudo 2D random sampling for compressed sensing MRI, Annual International Conference of the IEEE Engineering in Medicine and Biology Society, EMBC, pp. 2672-2675, Minneapolis, USA, 2009.

[13] Liu, D., Liang, D., Liu, X. & Zhang, Y. (2012). Under-sampling trajectory design for compressed sensing MRI. In Annual International Conference of the IEEE Engineering in Medicine and Biology Society EMBC, pp. 73-76, San Diego, USA, 2012.

[14] Wang, Z. & Arce, G. R. (2010). Variable density compressed image sampling. IEEE Transactions on Image Processing, vol. 19, no. 1, pp. 264 –270.

[15] Wang, Z., Arce, G. R. & Paredes, J. L. (2007). Colored random projections for compressed sensing. IEEE International Conference on Acoustics, Speech and Signal Processing, ICASSP, pp. III–873 –III–876, Hawaii, USA, 2007.

[16] Tropp, J. A. & Gilbert, A. C. (2007). Signal recovery from random measurements via orthogonal matching pursuit. IEEE Transactions on Information Theory, vol. 53, no. 12, pp. 4655–4666.

[17] Smoothed L0 Algorithm for Sparse Decomposition, Sharif University. http://ee.sharif.ir/SLzero/.

[18] Blumensath, T. & Davies, M. E. (2008). Iterative thresholding for sparse approximations. Journal of Fourier analysis and Applications, vol. 14, no. 5, pp. 629–654.

[19] Candes, E. J., L1-Magic: recovery of sparse signals. http://www.acm.caltech.edu/l1magic/.

[20] Donoho, D. L., Drori, I., Stodden, V., & Tsaig, Y. Sparselab. https://sparselab.stanford.edu/.

[21] Mohimani, H., Babaie-Zadeh, M. & Jutten, C. (2009). A fast approach for overcomplete sparse decomposition based on smoothed L0 norm. IEEE Transactions on Signal Processing, vol. 57, no. 1, pp. 289-301.

[22] Abolghasemi, V., Ferdowsi, S., Shen, H., & Shen, Y. (2014). Spatio-spectral data reconstruction in terahertz imaging. IEEE 7th International Symposium on Telecommunications (IST), pp. 129-133, Tehran, Iran, 2014.

17

An emotion recognition approach based on wavelet transform and second-order difference plot of ECG

A. Goshvarpour, A. Abbasi* and A. Goshvarpour

Department of Biomedical Engineering, Faculty of Electrical Engineering, Sahand University of Technology, Tabriz, Iran.

Corresponding author: ata.abbasi@sut.ac.ir (A. Abbasi).

Abstract

Emotion, as a psychophysiological state, plays an important role in the human communications and daily life. Emotion studies related to the physiological signals have recently been the subject of many research works. In this work, a hybrid feature-based approach is proposed to examine the affective states. To this effect, the electrocardiogram (ECG) signals of 47 students are recorded using the pictorial emotion elicitation paradigm. Affective pictures are selected from the International Affective Picture System and assigned to four different emotion classes. After extracting the approximate and detailed coefficients of Wavelet Transform (WT/Daubechies 4 at level 8), two measures of the second-order difference plot (CTM and D) are calculated for each wavelet coefficient. Subsequently, Least Squares Support Vector Machine (LS-SVM) is applied to discriminate between the affective states and the rest. The statistical analysis results indicate that the CTM density in the rest is distinctive from the emotional categories. In addition, the second-order difference plot measurements at the last level of WT coefficients show significant differences between the rest and the emotion categories. Applying LS-SVM, a maximum classification rate of 80.24% was reached for discrimination between the rest and the fear. The results of this study indicate the usefulness of WT in combination with the non-linear technique in characterizing the emotional states.

Keywords: *Combining Features, Electrocardiogram, Emotion, Second-Order Difference Plot, Wavelet Transform.*

1. Introduction

Electrocardiogram (ECG) signals are a valuable tool used to study the physiological changes of the heart in different situations. These signals have been used for the detection of various ailments such as heart diseases, arrhythmia, and epilepsy [1-6]. Cardiac fluctuations somehow represent the performance of the autonomic nervous system (ANS), particularly the sympathetic and parasympathetic functions [7-9]. As a result, ECG signals have also been applied to evaluate various mental and psychological conditions [10-11]. Emotion is known as a psychophysiological state. Various theories have shown that ANS and, in particular, the heart functions play a major role in the presentation of emotional states (for a brief review, see [12]). In addition, there are several attempts to evaluate and classify the emotional modes using the heart measures [13-15]. There are several emotion recognition applications in the

human life. Human-computer interfaces, interaction between patient and doctor in some diseases such as schizophrenia and autism, and computer games and entertainments are some examples [16-19]. This crucial role has resulted in the advent of a new discipline called "affective computing". In this field of research, there have been many attempts to develop some automatic devices that can deal with the problem of human affect recognition and interpretation.

In the past, different analytical methodologies have been presented using ECG signals. Over the past decades, Wavelet Transform (WT) has become an interesting tool for evaluating the biomedical signals [20]. It has been extensively employed for feature extraction and classification of heart beats in different conditions. WT is able to demonstrate the temporal and spatial information of the signals, simultaneously. Owing to the use of window with variable width, it is more flexible than a short-time Fourier transform. In this sense, long-term information with low-frequency and short-term information with high-frequency can be displayed concurrently. The procedure is very useful for analyzing the non-stationary signals owing to the outstanding of the subtle changes in the morphology of the desired scale of a signal.

On the other hand, due to the chaotic behavior of biological systems including the heart, the application of non-linear methods has been suggested [21]. Up to the present time, several non-linear approaches have been studied. One of the most common non-linear approaches is based upon the graphical representation of the signals. The Poincare plots, recurrent-based analysis, and Central Tendency Measure (CTM) are some examples. CTM is defined as a chaotic modeling approach [22]. It is usually applied to quantify the degree of variability in a time-series. In the current work, this non-linear technique was combined with the wavelet coefficients to evaluate the heart functions in different affective states. We believe that by combining the wavelet-based methods with non-linear approaches, a

detailed information can be obtained from the signals that cannot be recognized with each one of the methods separately. As a result, this combination may improve the recognition rates.

The structure of the remaining parts of the article is as what follows. First the signal acquisition procedure is introduced. Then the proposed methodology is described in detail. Next, the results are presented. Finally, the article is concluded.

2. Methods

In the current work, a six-step procedure was adopted. First ECG signals were recorded during affective visual stimuli. Secondly, the preprocessing stage was performed, which involved line noise removal and signal segmentation according to the blocks of emotion classes. Thirdly, the WT coefficients (db4 at level 8) were extracted. Fourthly, the second-order difference plot measurements were implemented to the WT coefficients. Next, the statistical Mann-Whitney U-test was performed. Finally, the classification accuracy was evaluated based on the extracted features. Figure 1 summarizes the adopted steps of this work.

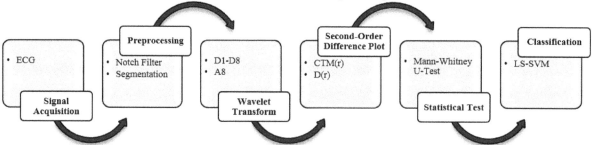

Figure 1. Block-diagram of proposed methodology applied in current study.

2.1. Data collection

In order to recognize emotions based on ECG signals, images gathered from the International Affective Picture System (IAPS) were employed [23]. Based on the dimensional structure, four emotion classes including happy, sad, relaxed, and afraid were chosen.

By combining the two scores arousal and valence, the designation of four different emotional states can be provided. Exactly, employing empirical thresholds on arousal and valence scores, each picture was assigned to one of the mentioned emotional categories. Figure 2 demonstrates the emotional load of the stimuli on a 2D emotion space using the valence and arousal axis. 47 college students including 31 females (age range: 19-25 years; mean age: 21.90±1.7 years) and 16 males (age range: 19-23 years; mean age: 21.1±1.48 years) participated in this study; they

were naive to the purpose of the experiment. All the participants were asked to read an agreement form and sign it if they agreed to take part in the study. They were also requested to determine if they were in a very relaxed or very aroused state. Filling out a preliminary questionnaire, it was indicated that they were all healthy subjects. In addition, no history of any epileptic, cardiovascular, neurological, and hypertension ailments was reported. They were instructed not to consume salty and fatty foods or caffeine two hours before the test.During the experiment, the participants were asked to sit in front of a laptop screen, particularly avoid movements of their fingers, hands, and legs, and watch the images. Her/his ECG signals (Lead I) were measured simultaneously [24]. Totally, the ECG signals of 47 students were acquired in Computational Neuroscience Laboratory (CNLab) using a 16-

channel PowerLab (manufactured by ADInstruments). All signals were recorded at a 400 Hz sampling rate. A digital notch filter was applied to remove power line noise. After 2 minutes of rest, in which the subjects were asked to keep their eyes open and watch a blank screen, 28 blocks of emotional stimuli were brought to the screen.

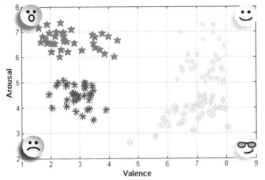

Figure 2. Valence and arousal distributions of pictorial stimuli. Fear: Red pentagrams; Happy: Yellow circles; Relaxed: Blue hexagram; and Sad: Dark blue asterisk.

Constructing a random sequence of the emotional blocks, a similar protocol was applied for all the volunteers. Each block contained 5 pictures from the same emotional class, and was displayed by random to prevent habituation in subjects. Each image was presented for 3 s on the screen leading a total of 15 s per block. 10 s of a blank screen period was applied at the end of each block to allow the return of physiological fluctuations to the baseline. The blank screen was followed by a white plus (for 3 s) in the middle of the screen to attract the subject attention to the center of the screen and prepare for the next block. The whole data acquisition took about 15 min.

After data recording, the subjects watched the same stimuli and their feelings were rated using self-assessment questionnaires. In other words, similar stimuli were brought to the screen, and each subject selected the best-matched emotion for each emotion block on a paper sheet in terms of sad, fear, happy or relaxed. Figure 3 demonstrates the protocol description.

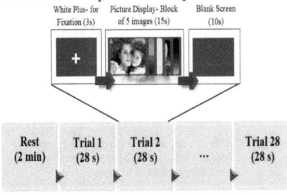

Figure 3. Proposed protocol.

2.2. Feature extraction
2.2.1. Discrete wavelet transform (DWT)
Applying DWT, the signal was transformed from the time domain to the wavelet domain, and different coefficient values were obtained [25].

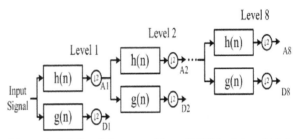

Figure 4. Sub-band decomposition of DWT. g[n] and h[n] are high-pass filter and low-pass filter, respectively.

In DWT, a given ECG signal was passed through two kinds of filters: a high-pass filter and a low-pass one. Employing the first filtering, as it is sub-sampled by a factor of two, half of the samples was excluded. This process resulted in the first level of decomposition. In the next stage, the extracted coefficients from the low-pass filter were subjected to other low-pass and high-pass filters. In order to have different decomposition levels, this procedure was repeated. The frequency band and the number of samples were divided into two equal parts at each level [26]. Therefore, a signal was converted into the approximate (low-pass) and detailed (high-pass) coefficients. It was important to select an appropriate wavelet function and the number of decomposition levels. In the current protocol, the Daubechies mother wavelet function (db4) with eight levels was used. Consequently, A8 corresponded to the eighth level of the approximate coefficients. D1 and D8 were the first to the eighth level of the detailed coefficients. Figure 4 depicts the schematic representation of this.

2.2.2. CTM
Central Tendency Measure (CTM(r)) is an index used to calculate the degree of variability in the second-order difference plot $(x(i+2)-x(i+1)$, $x(i+1)-x(i))$. To compute CTM, at first, a circular region of radius r was selected. Around the origin (0,0), the number of points existing within the radius was counted. Dividing the achieved number by the total number of points, CTM was calculated. Considering the time series with n points, the quantity of the points on the graphic was n-2:

$$CTM(r) = \frac{\left[\sum_{i=1}^{n-2} \delta(d(i))\right]}{n-2}, \quad (1)$$

where

$$\delta(d(i)) = \qquad\qquad\qquad\qquad\qquad (2)$$

$$\begin{cases} 1 & if \ \left(\left[x(i+2)-x(i+1)\right]^2 + \left[x(i+1)-x(i)\right]^2\right)^{0.5} < r \\ 0 & Otherwise \end{cases}$$

where, n and r are the total number of points and the radius of the central area, respectively.

The average distance of the points within a certain radius is characterized by D(r); these distances were calculated by (3):

$$d(i) = \left(\left[x(i+2)-x(i+1)\right]^2 + \left[x(i+1)-x(i)\right]^2\right)^{0.5} \qquad (3)$$

2.3. Classification

Support Vector Machine (SVM) is a popular binary classifier, which uses an ideal separating hyper-plane in the feature space. The system results in robust classification rates. More explanation about SVM has been presented by Hu and Hwang [27]. Least Squares Support Vector Machine (LS-SVM) Classifier is a least square version of traditional SVM, which keeps the characteristics and the benefits of SVM [28]. In addition to the good generalization performances and low computational costs [29], it also provides a simpler training compared to SVM [30].

3. Results

Figure 5 demonstrates three different time series with a constant, periodic, and random configuration. The capability of this approach in the discrimination of these time series was evaluated by means of the second-order difference plots.

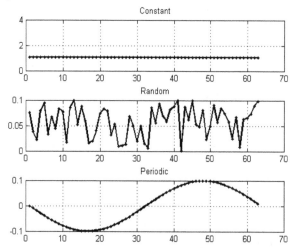

Figure 5. Different time series with 63 points: (top) constant, (middle) random, and (bottom) periodic time series. Vertical axis represents Xi, where i is number of samples, presented by horizontal axis.

Figure 6 exemplifies the arrangement of the points in a typical graphical representation.

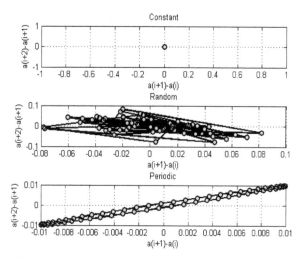

Figure 6. Second-order difference plot: (top) constant, (middle) random, and (bottom) periodic time series. Vertical axis represents X(i+2)-X(i+1), whereas horizontal axis demonstrates X(i+1)-X(i).

As shown in figure 6, a constant time series is converged into a single point in the center of the coordinates; whereas a periodic signal (like sinusoid) exhibits a circular pattern. In contrast, for a random data, there is no specific pattern of the points, and they just scatter in the space accidently. The CTM parameter with different radius was also evaluated for the above-mentioned time series. Figure 7 demonstrates the results.

As expected, the CTM values for different radii remain persistent in a constant data; whereas increasing the radius of the circle surrounding random points result in a gradual increment in the CTM values. Higher CTM values denote the focus of the points adjacent to the center, while the spreading points in the plot can be demonstrated by lower CTM values. A combined pattern is demonstrated for a periodic one.

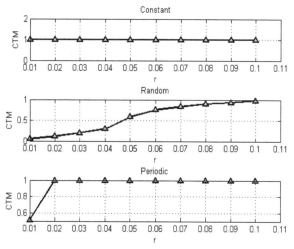

Figure 7. Considering different radii, CTM values for (top) constant, (middle) random, and (bottom) periodic time series are presented.

In the current work, this approach was employed on the WT coefficients of ECGs. A typical second-order difference plot for approximate coefficients at the level of eight is displayed in figure 8a. Considering different radii (r = 1-15), the corresponding CTMs are plotted in figure 8b. These findings are more similar to the random time series than those of the others.

For all the emotion categories, CTM and the corresponding D values were calculated. The mean density of the CTM values of all the emotion categories is presented in figure 9.

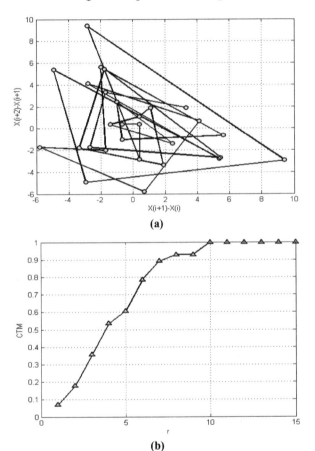

(a)

(b)

Figure 8. (a) Second-order difference plot for A8 of ECG during rest. (b) Corresponding CTMs for different radii.

For some emotion classes (happy-relax and sad-fear), the CTM distributions were the same (Figure 9). In addition, the density of the CTM values for the rest was different from those of the affective states. Significant differences between the emotions and the rest were evaluated by means of the Mann-Whitney U-test.

To investigate the efficiency of the proposed second-order difference plot indices, some statistical measures of the wavelet coefficients were also extracted. The statistical measures were

mean, standard deviation, maximum, minimum, median, mode, and second-, third-, and fourth-moments. Table 1 demonstrates the results obtained.

As shown in table 1, there were no significant differences between the rest and the emotional states for the statistical measures. However, the second-order difference plot measures for the last level of wavelet coefficients (level 8; A8 and D8) could successfully differentiate between the emotional states and the rest. In addition, significant differences between the CTM values in the rest and the affective states were observed in D3.

Next, the LS-SVM classifier was employed to measure the classification performance based on the extracted features. 75% of the feature vector was randomly considered as the training set, and the remaining 25% of the vector was chosen as the test.

To evaluate the classifier performance, the accuracy, sensitivity (true positive rate), and specificity (true negative rate) were calculated. The classification accuracy was measured using (4):

$$Accuracy = \frac{TP + TN}{TP + FP + FN + TN} \tag{4}$$

where, TP designates true positives, TN shows true negatives, FP denotes false positives, and FN represents false negatives.

The sensitivity and specificity of the classifier were also verified based on (5) and (6), respectively:

$$Sensitivity = \frac{TP}{TP + FN} \tag{5}$$

$$Specificity = \frac{TN}{TN + FP} \tag{6}$$

In addition, a Receiver Operating Characteristic (ROC) curve was provided to graphically evaluate the classifier performance.

Figure 10 represents the ROC curves for the proposed methodology. In addition, the classification accuracy, sensitivity, and specificity are provided in figure 10.

The classification results reveal that CTM in combination with the wavelet coefficients outperformed the other index in the classification of each emotional state and the rest. Higher performances (~80%) were achieved for the fear and relaxed affective states.

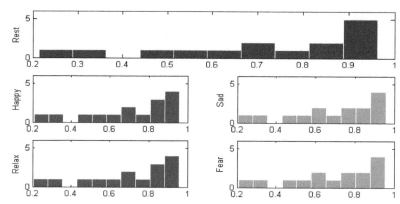

Figure 9. Histogram of mean CTM values for all emotion classes.

Table 1. Comparison between different linear and non-linear indices in emotions and rest for different DWT coefficients.

Feature	DWT Coefficients	Rest vs. Happy	Rest vs. Relax	Rest vs. Sad	Rest vs. Fear
Mean	A8	0.4896	0.4676	0.0638	0.2124
	D8	0.6565	0.4441	0.4426	0.9244
	D7	0.8852	0.6848	0.5437	0.7357
	D6	0.4418	0.3427	0.136	0.9603
	D5	0.1365	0.2685	0.0585	0.0666
	D4	0.5922	0.7633	0.49	0.9979
	D3	0.8237	0.3598	0.7582	0.732
	D2	0.752	0.5396	0.5823	0.7633
	D1	0.9596	0.7773	0.3258	0.8538
STD	A8	0.4282	0.4188	0.2346	0.3035
	D8	0.5266	0.6771	0.3162	0.4888
	D7	0.4432	0.4611	0.3466	0.4324
	D6	0.6697	0.6056	0.5919	0.7349
	D5	0.7586	0.5501	0.6551	0.5475
	D4	0.6655	0.6056	0.4897	0.5659
	D3	0.4279	0.2297	0.339	0.3702
	D2	0.3964	0.3543	0.3197	0.3174
	D1	0.4347	0.3535	0.2635	0.2181
Maximum	A8	0.1546	0.0966	0.0829	0.1605
	D8	0.1204	0.0415*	0.0073*	0.0978
	D7	0.166	0.1856	0.114	0.1168
	D6	0.1642	0.3116	0.1657	0.3268
	D5	0.249	0.3199	0.4979	0.1834
	D4	0.3782	0.3618	0.3088	0.2295
	D3	0.2695	0.0216*	0.1336	0.1415
	D2	0.3879	0.1854	0.4149	0.2962
	D1	0.3906	0.1658	0.1137	0.1629
Minimum	A8	0.053	0.0101*	0.0007*	0.0013*
	D8	0.1759	0.152	0.064	0.2261
	D7	0.2492	0.0838	0.1135	0.2249
	D6	0.835	0.1406	0.3483	0.5692
	D5	0.731	0.545	0.397	0.2763
	D4	0.9596	0.5046	0.5909	0.5833
	D3	0.0502	0.0263*	0.0616	0.0399*
	D2	0.0359*	0.0148*	0.0935	0.0378*
	D1	0.1832	0.01*	0.0858	0.0207*
Median	A8	0.9512	0.5192	0.3472	0.6978
	D8	0.271	0.1038	0.1408	0.2162
	D7	0.981	0.3383	0.6722	0.9691
	D6	0.788	0.6248	0.1818	0.6191
	D5	0.4504	0.1793	0.1612	0.1226
	D4	0.3666	0.3093	0.3393	0.7958
	D3	0.3176	0.1348	0.2439	0.4021
	D2	0.2407	0.7194	0.8312	0.7205
	D1	0.6365	0.8125	0.1977	0.986
Mode	A8	0.053	0.0101*	0.0007*	0.0013*
	D8	0.1759	0.152	0.064	0.2261
	D7	0.2492	0.0838	0.1135	0.2249
	D6	0.835	0.1406	0.3483	0.5692
	D5	0.731	0.545	0.397	0.2763
	D4	0.9596	0.5046	0.5909	0.5833
	D3	0.0502	0.0263*	0.0616	0.0399*
	D2	0.0359*	0.0148*	0.0935	0.0378*
	D1	0.1832	0.01*	0.0858	0.0207*

(Continued Table 1). Comparison between different linear and non-linear indices in emotions and rest for different DWT coefficients.

Feature	DWT Coefficients	Rest *vs.* Happy	Rest *vs.* Relax	Rest *vs.* Sad	Rest *vs.* Fear
1st Moment	A8	0.429	0.4152	0.2344	0.3008
	D8	0.5157	0.6645	0.3088	0.4836
	D7	0.4404	0.4446	0.3436	0.4285
	D6	0.6708	0.6086	0.5916	0.7331
	D5	0.7622	0.5565	0.6558	0.544
	D4	0.6631	0.6016	0.4851	0.5585
	D3	0.4237	0.2269	0.3383	0.3628
	D2	0.3946	0.351	0.3167	0.3158
	D1	0.4316	0.3441	0.2592	0.2149
2nd Moment	A8	0.5026	0.6957	0.3795	0.4511
	D8	0.4903	0.0671	0.5204	0.1304
	D7	0.4579	0.1434	0.8163	0.0259*
	D6	0.2192	0.8681	0.8219	0.6729
	D5	0.8662	0.7212	0.9046	0.4467
	D4	0.8871	0.8237	0.3528	0.4305
	D3	0.5135	0.8159	0.5741	0.5111
	D2	0.6722	0.8196	0.2284	0.5285
	D1	0.4951	0.9979	0.2007	0.9309
3rd Moment	A8	0.2714	0.2316	0.1296	0.1553
	D8	0.4204	0.4848	0.1635	0.3155
	D7	0.3991	0.3414	0.2542	0.3628
	D6	0.5272	0.5074	0.3959	0.6464
	D5	0.6873	0.5731	0.6187	0.4421
	D4	0.5569	0.4435	0.4097	0.3954
	D3	0.2708	0.1099	0.1939	0.2131
	D2	0.3118	0.2276	0.2656	0.2748
	D1	0.3588	0.2091	0.1706	0.1318
CTM	A8	0.3016	0.0282*	0.0092*	0.0084*
	D8	0.0273*	0.0036*	0.0006*	0.0088*
	D7	0.3428	0.1541	0.139	0.0265*
	D6	0.0678	0.1769	0.0071*	0.1415
	D5	0.0185*	0.063	0.1057	0.0769
	D4	0.2007	0.253	0.0768	0.137
	D3	0.0391*	0.0448*	0.0429*	0.0401*
	D2	0.0215*	0.0067*	0.0512	0.0207*
	D1	0.381	0.0361*	0.0757	0.0927
D	A8	0.0222*	0.0069*	0.0135*	0.0105*
	D8	0.045*	0.0505*	0.0095*	0.0094*
	D7	0.0849	0.1676	0.0155*	0.1007
	D6	0.1881	0.2234	0.1138	0.0968
	D5	0.0327*	0.1489	0.0779	0.0623
	D4	0.1033	0.0956	0.2095	0.0519
	D3	0.0749	0.199	0.0883	0.174
	D2	0.0634	0.083	0.0128*	0.0707
	D1	0.043*	0.11	0.0226*	0.052

*$p<0.05$

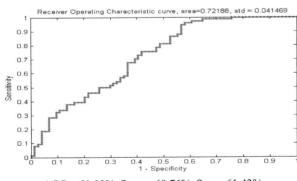

ACC = 61.09%, Spec = 60.76%, Sen = 61.43%

(a)

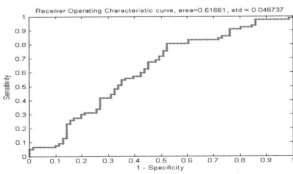

ACC = 55.83%, Spec = 55.73%, Sen = 55.93%

(b)

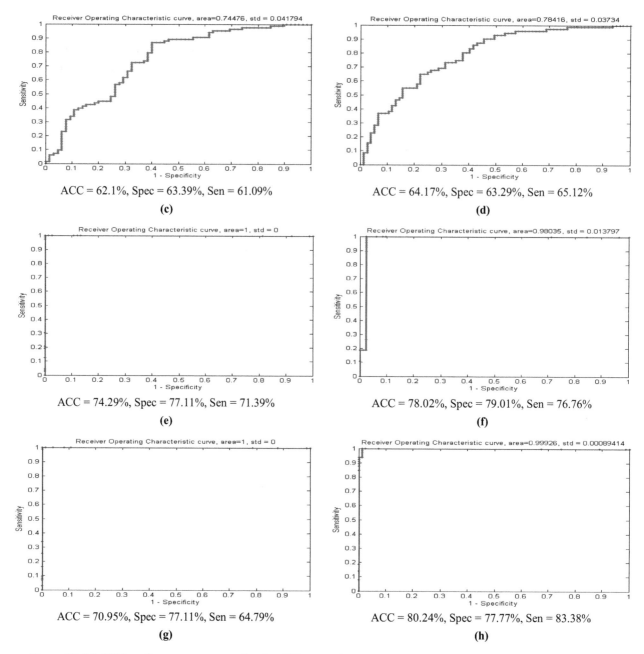

ACC = 62.1%, Spec = 63.39%, Sen = 61.09%

(c)

ACC = 64.17%, Spec = 63.29%, Sen = 65.12%

(d)

ACC = 74.29%, Spec = 77.11%, Sen = 71.39%

(e)

ACC = 78.02%, Spec = 79.01%, Sen = 76.76%

(f)

ACC = 70.95%, Spec = 77.11%, Sen = 64.79%

(g)

ACC = 80.24%, Spec = 77.77%, Sen = 83.38%

(h)

Figure 10. LS-SVM performance on: second-order difference plot measure (D) of last level of wavelet coefficient (A8) in discrimination between rest and (a) happy, (b) relax, (c) sad, (d) fear; CTM of last level of wavelet coefficient (A8) in discrimination between rest and (e) happy, (f) relax, (g) sad, (h) fear; Note- ACC: Accuracy; Spec: Specificity; Sen: Sensitivity.

4. Discussion

In the past, both the WT and non-linear approaches have been used in the problem of affect interpretation and recognition [14,15,24,31-37]. In the current study, a methodology was presented based on the WT and non-linear indices to evaluate the emotional ECGs. The non-linear technique was carried out using a second-order difference plot. The ECG signals were pre-processed to eliminate the line noise power and segmented according to the emotional loads. For each segment, the WT coefficients (db4 at level 8) were extracted. Then two features of a second-order difference plot were calculated for each WT coefficient. These indices were D and CTM. The Mann-Whitney U-Test was performed to show the significant differences between classes. Finally, LS-SVM was implemented to differentiate between each emotional class and the rest.

The higher variability of the signal (random) results in a higher dispersion of the points in the second-order difference plot (Figure 6). In contrast, the low variable signal (constant) makes the points congregated toward the center of the plot. Comparing figure 8 with figures 7 and 6, it was revealed that the ECG signals tended to have a random pattern.

The results obtained (Figure 8) also showed that the CTM density was comparable in happy/relax and sad-/fear, which was not the same for the rest. It can be concluded that this pattern can be interpreted based on the valence dimension of emotion. For affective states assigned to the positive valence, the CTM distributions were equivalent. Similar results were achieved for the negative valence. However, this scheme is distinctive for the positive and negative emotions, and also the rest. In addition, the second-order difference plot indices extracted from the last level of the WT coefficients show significant differences between the rest and the emotion classes (Table 1). The p-value results also indicate that there is no significant difference between the categories for linear indices of DWT. In contrast, the non-linear indices including CTM and D show significant differences between the rest and each emotion class. Therefore, a combination of non-linear analysis and DWT is more useful to apprehend the emotional changes than that of linear indices.

Classification rates also designate the superiority of CTM over D in discrimination between the rest and the emotional states. Among the affective states, higher recognition rates were assigned to fear and relax (Figure 10).

In the past, different ECG analyses have been performed in the problem of emotion recognition. Bong et al. [38] have extracted time-based features of ECG and have mapped them into K-nearest neighbor (KNN) and SVM to emotional stress classification. The best recognition rate of 77.69% was reported. In the study performed by Basu et al. [39], six time domain features have been calculated from physiological signals. By evaluating different classification algorithms including Quadratic Discriminant Classifier (QDC), kNN, Naive Bayes, and Linear Discriminant Analysis (LDA), a maximum accuracy of 75% was realized. Time, frequency, and statistical analysis of ECG were recruited to offer a wearable emotion detection device [40]. However, the correct rate of 50% was provided by the proposed system. By employing the empirical mode decomposition, as a non-linear signal processing approach, and discrete Fourier transform, no improvement on accuracy rates (~52%) was achieved with linear discriminant analysis and KNN [33]. However, combining information from standard and non-linear ECG analysis estimated through lagged Poincare plots improved the recognition rates up to 84% [41]. Their results confirm that the ECG signals are a powerful tool for emotion recognition, especially with the use of non-linear dynamics. Although the reported rates are slightly higher than the results of the current study, there are two major differences between the studies. First, their experiment was performed on fewer number of subjects. Secondly, they only focused on the arousal dimension [41], while in this study, both the arousal and valence-based emotion dimensions were considered. In conclusion, the current study emphasizes the importance of non-linear dynamics for affect recognition. The efficiency of non-linear techniques has attracted many researchers in the field of emotion recognition. However, they applied other bio-signals rather than ECG.

Dynamical evaluation of ECG, respiration, skin conductance, and temperature were combined with some traditional linear approaches to monitor five affective states [42]. An accuracy of about 60% was reported for classifying 5 discrete emotion categories. Recently, Valencia et al. [43] have incorporated recurrence quantification measures (RQA) as a non-linear approach to classify two valence categories and three arousal categories using the multimodal emotion recognition scheme. Other examples can be found in [14-15,34,35,44-48].

In the future studies, improvements in the classification rates will be evaluated using the feature selection approaches.

5. Acknowledgment

We gratefully acknowledge Computational Neuroscience Laboratory, where the data was collected, and all the subjects volunteered for the study.

References

[1] Jansen, K., Varon, C., Van Huffel, S., & Lagae, L. (2013). Peri-ictal ECG changes in childhood epilepsy: Implications for detection systems. Epilepsy & Behavior, vol. 29, no. 1, pp. 72-76.

[2] Khalaf, A. F., Owis, M. I., & Yassine, I. A. (2015). A novel technique for cardiac arrhythmia classification using spectral correlation and support vector machines. Expert Systems with Applications, vol. 42, no. 21, pp. 8361-8368.

[3] Thomas, M., Kr Das, M., & Ari, S. (2015). Automatic ECG arrhythmia classification using dual tree complex wavelet based features. AEU - International Journal of Electronics and Communications, vol. 69, no. 4, pp. 715-721.

[4] Vafaie, M. H., Ataei, M., & Koofigar, H. R. (2014). Heart diseases prediction based on ECG signals' classification using a genetic-fuzzy system and

dynamical model of ECG signals; Biomedical Signal Processing and Control, vol. 14, pp. 291-296.

[5] Varon, C., Jansen, K., Lagae, L., & Van Huffel, S. (2015). Can ECG monitoring identify seizures? Journal of Electrocardiology, vol. 48, no. 6, pp. 1069-1074.

[6] Ebrahimzadeh, A., Ahmadi M., & Safarnejad, M. (2016). Classification of ECG signals using Hermit functions and MLP neural networks. Journal of AI and Data Mining, vol. 4, no. 1, pp. 55-65.

[7] Akselrod, S., Gordon, D., Ubel, F. A., Shannon, D.C., Berger, A. C., & Cohen, R. J. (1981). Power spectrum analysis of heart rate fluctuation: A quantitative probe of beat-to-beat cardiovascular control. Science, vol. 213, no. 4504, pp. 220-222.

[8] Grasso, R., Schena, F., Gulli, G, & Cevese, A. (1997). Does low-frequency variability of heart period reflect a specific parasympathetic mechanism? J Auton Nerv Syst, vol. 63, no. 1-2, pp. 30-38.

[9] Pagani, M., Lombardi, F., Guzzetti, S., Rimoldi, O., Furlan, R., Pizzinelli, P., Sandrone, G., Malfatto, G., Dell'Orto, S., Piccaluga, E., et al. (1986). Power spectral analysis of heart rate and arterial pressure variabilities as a marker of sympatho-vagal interaction in man and conscious dog. Circ Res, vol. 59, no. 2, pp. 178-193.

[10] Goshvarpour, A., Goshvarpour, A., & Rahati, S. (2011). Analysis of lagged Poincaré plots in heart rate signals during meditation. Digital Signal Processing, vol. 21, no. 2, pp. 208-214.

[11] Ranganathan, G., Rangarajan, R., & Bindhu, V. (2012). Estimation of heart rate signals for mental stress assessment using neuro fuzzy technique. Applied Soft Computing, vol. 12, no. 8, pp. 1978-1984.

[12] Kreibig, S. (2010). Autonomic nervous system activity in emotion: a review. Biological Psychology, vol. 84, no. 3, pp. 394-421.

[13] Costa, T., Galati, D., & Rognoni, E. (2009). The Hurst exponent of cardiac response to positive and negative emotional film stimuli using wavelet. Autonomic Neuroscience: Basic and Clinical, vol. 151, no. 2, pp. 183–185.

[14] Valenza, G., Lanata, A., & Scilingo, E. (2012). The role of nonlinear dynamics in affective valence and arousal recognition. IEEE Transactions on Affective Computing, vol. 3, no. 2, pp. 237-249.

[15] Valenza, G., Allegrini, P., Lanata, A., & Scilingo, E. (2012). Dominant Lyapunov exponent and approximate entropy in heart rate variability during emotional visual elicitation. Frontiers in Neuroengineering, vol. 5, no. 3, pp. 1-7.

[16] Park, S., & Kim, K. (2011). Physiological reactivity and facial expression to emotion-inducing films in patients with schizophrenia. Archives of Psychiatric Nursing, vol. 25, no. 6, pp. e37-e47.

[17] Drusch, K., Stroth, S., Kamp, D., Frommann, N., & Wolwer, W. (2014). Effects of training of affect recognition on the recognition and visual exploration of emotional faces in schizophrenia. Schizophrenia Research, vol. 159, no. 2-3, pp. 485-490.

[18] Hazlett, R. (2006). Measuring emotional valence during interactive experiences: Boys at video game play, CHI '06: Proceedings of the SIGCHI Conference on Human Factors in Computing Systems. ACM Press, New York, NY, USA. pp. 1023-1026.

[19] Yannakakisa, G., & Hallam, J. (2008). Entertainment modeling through physiology in physical play. International Journal of Human-Computer Studies, vol. 66, no. 10, pp. 741-755.

[20] Rafiee, J., Rafiee, M. A., Prause, N., & Schoen, M.P. (2011). Wavelet basis functions in biomedical signal processing. Expert System with Applications, vol. 38, no. 5, pp. 6190–6201.

[21] Henry, B. I., Lovell, N. H., & Camacho, F. (2001). Nonlinear dynamics time series analysis. In M. Akay (Ed.), Nonlinear Biomedical Signal Processing (pp. 1–39). Institute of Electrical and Electronics Engineers, Inc.

[22] Cohen, M.E., Hudson, D. L., & Deedwania, P. C. (1996). Applying continuous chaoticmodeling to cardiac signal analysis. IEEE Engineering in Medicine and Biology Magazine, vol. 15, no. 5, pp. 97–102.

[23] Lang, P. J., Bradley, M. M., & Cuthbert, B. N. (2005). International affective picture system (IAPS): Digitized photographs, instruction manual and affective ratings (Technical Report A-6). University of Florida: Gainesville, FL.

[24] Goshvarpour, A., Abbasi, A., & Goshvarpour, A. (2015). Affective visual stimuli: Characterization of the picture sequences impacts by means of nonlinear approaches. Basic and Clinical Neuroscience, vol. 6, no. 4, pp. 209-221.

[25] Daubechies, I. (1990). The wavelet transform, time frequency localization and signal analysis. IEEE Transactions on Information Theory, vol. 36, no. 5, pp. 961-1005.

[26] Ratnakar, M., Sunil, K. S., & Nitisha, J. (2009). Signal filtering using discrete wavelet transform, International Journal of Recent Trends in Engineering, vol. 2, no. 3, pp. 96-98.

[27] Hu, Y. H., & Hwang, J. N. (Eds.) (2002). Handbook of neural network signal processing. Electrical engineering and applied signal processing (Series), CRC PRESS, pp 384.

[28] Suykens, J. A. K., Van Gestel, T., De Brabanter, J., De Moor, B., & Vandewalle, J. (2002). Least squares support vector machines. World Scientific, Singapore.

[29] Suykens, J. A. K., & Vandewalle, J. (1999). Least squares support vector machine classifiers. Neural Processing Letters, vol. 9, no. 3, pp. 293–300.

[30] Zhou, J., Shi, J., & Li, G. (2011). Fine tuning support vector machines for short-term wind speed forecasting. Energy Conversion and Management, vol. 52, no. 4, pp. 1990–1998.

[31] Jerritta, S., Murugappan, M., Wan, K., & Yaacob, S. (2013). Emotion detection from QRS complex of ECG signals using hurst exponent for different age groups, Humaine Association Conference on Affective Computing and Intelligent Interaction (ACII), Geneva, Switzerland. pp. 849-854.

[32] Jerritta, S., Murugappan, M., Wan, K., & Yaacob, S. (2013). Classification of emotional states from electrocardiogram signals: a non-linear approach based on hurst. BioMedical Engineering OnLine, vol. 12, 44.

[33] Jerritta, S., Murugappan, M., Wan, K., & Yaacob, S. (2014). Electrocardiogram-based emotion recognition system using empirical mode decomposition and discrete Fourier transform. Expert Systems, vol. 31, no. 2, pp. 110-120.

[34] Nardelli, M., Valenza, G., Greco, A., Lanata, A., & Scilingo, E. (2015). Recognizing emotions induced by affective sounds through heart rate variability. IEEE Transactions on Affective Computing, vol. 6, no. 4, pp. 385-394.

[35] Valenza, G., Citi, L., Lanata, A., Scilingi, E., & Barbieri, R. (2014). Revealing real-time emotional responses: a personalized assessment based on heartbeat dynamics. Scientific Reports, vol. 4, 4998.

[36] Xu, Y., Liu, G., Hao, M., Wen, W., & Huang, X. (2010). Analysis of affective ECG signals toward emotion recognition. Journal of Electronics (China), vol. 27, no. 1, pp. 8-14.

[37] Xu, Y., & Liu, G.-Y. (2009). A method of emotion recognition based on ECG signal, International Conference on Computational Intelligence and Natural Computing. IEEE. pp. 202-205.

[38] Bong, S. Z., Murugappan, M., & Yaacob, S. (2012). Analysis of Electrocardiogram (ECG) Signals for human emotional stress classification, First International Conference on Trends in Intelligent Robotics, Automation, and Manufacturing. Kuala Lumpur, Malaysia, 28-30Nov., pp. 198-205.

[39] Basu, S., Bag, A., Mahadevappa, M., Mukherjee, J., & Guha, R. (2015). Affect detection in normal groups with the help of biological markers. India Conference (INDICON). 17-20 Dec. IEEE.

[40] Guo, H. W., Huang, Y. S., Chien J. C., & Shieh, J. S. (2015). Short-term analysis of heart rate variability for emotion recognition via a wearable ECG device. International Conference on Intelligent Informatics and Biomedical Sciences (ICIIBMS). 28-30 Nov., IEEE.

[41] Nardelli, M., Valenza, G., & Greco, A. (2015). Arousal recognition system based on heartbeat dynamics during auditory elicitation. 37th Annual International Conference of the Engineering in Medicine and Biology Society (EMBC). 25-29 Aug., IEEE.

[42] Kukolja, D., Popović, S., Horvat, M., Kovač, B., & Ćosić, K. (2014). Comparative analysis of emotion estimation methods based on physiological measurements for real-time applications. International Journal of Human-Computer Studies, vol. 72, no. 10-11, pp. 717-727.

[43] Valencia, C. T., Lopez, M. A., & Gutierrez, A. O. (2017). SVM-based feature selection methods for emotion recognition from multimodal data. Journal on Multimodal User Interfaces, vol. 11, no. 1, pp. 9-23.

[44] Kim, J., & Andre, E. (2008). Emotion recognition based on physiological changes in music listening. IEEE Transactions on Pattern Analysis and Machine Intelligence. vol. 30, no. 12, pp. 2067-2083.

[45] Goshvarpour, A., Abbasi, A., & Goshvarpour, A. (2016). Dynamical analysis of emotional states from electroencephalogram signals. Biomedical Engineering Applications, Basis and Communications, vol. 28, no. 2, pp. 1650015 [12 pages].

[46] Roque, A., Valenti, V., Guida, H., Campos, M., Knap, A., Vanderlei, L., Ferreira, L., Ferreira, C., & Abreu, L. (2013). The effects of auditory stimulation with music on heart rate variability in healthy women. Clinics, vol. 68, no. 7, pp. 960-967.

[47] Silva, S., Guida, H., Santos, A., Vanderlei, L., Ferreira, L., de Abreu, L., Sousa, F., & Valenti, V. (2014). Auditory stimulation with music influences the geometric indices of heart rate variability in men. International Archives of Medicine, vol. 7, no. 27, pp. 1-7.

[48] Wang, L., Liu, G., & Yang, Z. (2014). The emotion recognition for grief based on nonlinear features of GSR. Journal of Computational Information Systems, vol. 10, no. 4, pp.1639-1649.

18

A sensor-based scheme for activity recognition in smart homes using dempster-shafer theory of evidence

V. Ghasemi[1*], A. A. Pouyan[1], and M. Sharifi[2]

1. Department of Computer and IT Engineering, Shahrood University of Technology, Shahrood, Iran.
2. Department of Computer Engineering, Iran University of Science and Technology, Tehran, Iran.

*Corresponding author: vghasemi@shahroodut.ac.ir (V. Ghasemi).

Abstract

This paper proposes a scheme for daily activity recognition in sensor-based smart homes using Dempster-Shafer theory of evidence. For this purpose, opinion owners and their belief masses are constructed from sensors and employed in a single-layered inference architecture. The belief masses are calculated using the beta probability distribution function. The frames of opinion owners are derived automatically for activities to achieve more flexibility and extensibility. Our method is verified via two experiments. In the first experiment, it is compared with a naïve Bayes approach and three ontology-based methods. In this experiment, our method outperforms the naïve Bayes classifier, having 88.9% accuracy. However, it is comparable and similar to the ontology-based schemes. Since no manual ontology definition is needed, our method is more flexible and extensible than the previous ones. In the second experiment, a larger dataset is used, and our method is compared with three approaches that are based on naïve Bayes classifiers, hidden Markov models, and hidden semi-Markov models. Three features are extracted from the sensors' data and incorporated in the benchmark methods, making nine implementations. In this experiment, our method shows an accuracy of 94.2% that, in most cases, outperforms the benchmark methods or is comparable to them.

Keywords: *Activity Recognition, Dempster-Shafer Theory of Evidence, Smart Homes.*

1. Introduction

With the rapid population ageing that is currently occurring across the world, the need for aged health care, and social and technology services will increase [1]. Studies show that elderly people would prefer to stay at home until it is impossible for them to do so, rather than move into a residential care [2], and that the benefits of home care are enormous, both to the individuals and to the state. Therefore, they must be able to do so safely at a reasonable cost. One possible solution is through the use of remote monitoring technologies, which can increase the level of security. Through automatically inferring human activities, care-givers can monitor the health and behavioral status of elderly people and provide them with essential services.

A sensor network is an efficient tool for remote monitoring. Currently, a wide range of sensors including contact sensors, accelerometers, audio and motion detectors, to name but a few, are available for activity monitoring. Based on the way the sensors are deployed, the task of senor-based activity recognition can be classified in two main categories: wearable sensor-based, and dense sensing-based activity recognition. Wearable sensors are positioned on human body and monitor features that depict the person's state such as body position and movement, while in dense sensing-based activity recognition, sensors are attached to objects, and activities are monitored by detecting user-object interactions. In this work, we focus on the dense sensing-based activity recognition.

The accuracy of an activity recognition process is affected by different levels and sources of uncertainty [3]. For instance, in [4-6], the uncertainty is considered to stem from both the sensor hardware failures and the probabilistic nature of human activities. However, uncertainty may be due to other sources such as misplacement of sensors or modeling inefficacies [3]. Sensor data fusion techniques such as Dempster-Shafer theory provide a promising solution to mitigate the effect of uncertainty, especially when the inconsistency between sensor data is not very high [7]. Fusion techniques are required to combine data from multiple sensors in order to achieve more accurate inferences since data from a single sensor does not provide sufficient evidence to infer an activity [8].

Several classification methods have been proposed for human activity recognition (HAR). They are categorized into three casts: data-driven, knowledge-driven, and hybrid methods based on their modeling schemes [9]. Among these, the Dempster-Shafer theory (DST) is known as an effective approach to deal with uncertainty and to fuse sensor data. DST can show better results in a reasoning scheme under unknown probability circumstances [10]. Approaches described in [4-6], and [11-15] are instances in which DST is incorporated for HAR. They will be discussed in more detail in the next section. However, in these approaches, static ontology definitions for activities are made available manually, and activity recognition schemes are implemented accordingly. Manual ontology definition for activities might be a complicated and error-prone task in environments with unknown human activity patterns.

In this paper, we introduce a novel method to extract the ontology definitions of activities of daily life (ADLs) automatically with the aim of using DST for HAR as a data fusion formalism. We propose a method to extract the frame of opinion owners (i.e. objects that have a degree of uncertainty, belief, and disbelief about an activity) for each activity automatically in order to accomplish this task. Opinion-owners are created from sensor nodes, and their belief masses for activities are calculated based on the beta probability distribution function, as represented in subjective logic [16,17]. The frame of opinion-owners for each activity is determined based on their uncertainty, belief, and disbelief about that activity. Having a sequence of sensor activations, a set of triggered opinion owners is calculated, and their belief masses for possible activities are fused using the Dempster's combination rule. Eventually, based on the fusion results, a decision is made about the happening activity. Two experiments are implemented to evaluate the performance of the proposed method. The

proposed method is used to detect several activities within single resident environments.

The remainder of the paper is organized as what follows. In section 2, we provide an analytic survey on the literature of the subject. The Dempster-Shafer theory of evidence is introduced in section 3. Section 4 and its sub-sections address the proposed activity recognition method. A work through example is illustrated in section 5. In section 6, simulation results are shown, and finally section 7 concludes the paper.

2. Related works

There is an intense research literature on the human activity recognition. Generally speaking, they can be classified into two main categories based on their activity modeling schemes. They are *data-driven* versus *knowledge-driven* activity recognition. A third emerging category, namely *hybrid-methods* has been introduced by researchers, which uses the characteristics of both previous methods [18,19].

Data-driven activity recognition is based on learning activity models from pre-existent datasets of resident's behaviors using data mining and machine learning techniques. Probabilistic graphical models, frequent pattern mining-based approaches, and some other machine learning techniques such as the nearest neighbor classifiers (NN), decision trees, and support vector machines (SVM) are common instances of data-driven activity recognition methods.

Probabilistic graphical models provide formal mechanisms for learning activity models, and inference. These models use a template graph structure to represent the dependencies among the observed random variables (sensor readings) and the unknown variables (activity labels). Given a sequence of observations, the template graph is unrolled, and the most likely sequence of unknown variables will be estimated using a formal inference method (e.g. Viterbi algorithm) [20,21]. Various types of such graphical models exist based on the characteristics of the template graph and the unrolling rules. Naive Bayes classifiers (NBCs)[22,23], Dynamic Bayesian networks (DBNs) [24,25], hidden Markov models (HMMs) [26-28], hidden semi-Markov models (HSMMs) [28,29], coupled HMMs (CHMMs) [30,31], conditional random fields (CRFs) [26,28,32,33], skip-chain CRFs (SCCRFs) [26,34], factorial CRFs (FCRFs) [31], latent dynamic CRFs (LDCRFs) [35], and some other variants of such models are common instances that have been used for HAR. For instance, in NBCs, only the dependency of the current sensor observation with the hidden variables (activity labels) is modeled and temporal information is weakly supported; in HMMs and its variants, a directed acyclic graph (DAG) represents the temporal dependency of the current activity label (hidden variable) with the previous ones; in HSMMs, the duration of an activity (hidden state) is modeled explicitly by a duration variable; in CRFs and its variants, the unrolled graph is an undirected graph that captures the joint dependency of the activities; in SCCRF, skip chains are added to the unrolled graph based on some heuristics to model long range dependencies; and in FCRFs and CHMMs, there are more than one channel of inter-connected CRFs and HMMs, respectively, to infer concurrent activities.

Frequent pattern mining approaches show promising performances when applied to HAR. Generally, such methods try to find frequent patterns throughout the sensor data stream for further interpretation as activities. The approaches of [36-38] are instances of such works, in which the concepts of emerging patterns [36] and compression [37,38] are used to unearth the frequent patterns.

Among the other data-driven techniques, the K-nearest neighbor (KNN), decision trees, and support vector machines (SVMs) are the common approaches that have been used for HAR. In KNNs, a new sequence of observations (e.g. sensor firings) is compared with a set of training sequences, and the k most closely matching sequences vote for the activity label [39]. In [39], it is also shown that the simple KNN approach is outperformed by decision trees. In [40] (and similarly, in [41]), a support vector machine (SVM) is used to classify the features that have been computed for fixed-length time frames/windows into daily activities. In [42], a one-class SVM is hired to recognize abnormal activities. Also in [43], SVM is used to classify the sensor events based on the features calculated out of a dynamic sliding window.

In knowledge-driven activity recognition, activity models are directly acquired by exploiting a rich prior knowledge in the domain of interest using knowledge engineering and management technologies. This usually involves knowledge acquisition, formal modeling, and representation. Inference can also be done using the formal reasoning or statistical analysis. Approaches of [44] and [45] are instances in which the sensor activations in a period of time are mapped to pre-defined static activity ontologies, and then a formal logical reasoning scheme is hired to infer

the associated activities. The approaches of [46] and [47] are other instances of knowledge-driven methods, in which static ontologies are hired for HAR. However, in addition to static manual ontology definition, which can be an error-prone task due to insufficient or inefficient domain specific knowledge, another criticism about these approaches is that they manage uncertainty poorly [9,46].

There are also some hybrid approaches that try to benefit from the features of both data- and knowledge-driven HAR processes by fusing them in a single modeling approach. The works of [18, 19] are instances of such methods. In [18], an ontology-based hybrid approach for activity modeling is proposed, where learning techniques are also developed to learn specific user profiles. The presented scheme is capable of learning descriptive properties of activities. In [19], an approach is proposed to use the data-driven techniques to evolve the knowledge-driven activity models with a user's behavioral data. In these schemes, the ontologies will have a dynamic nature, although they do not consider uncertainty as a main concern.

The above-mentioned activity recognition approaches do not consider the uncertainty as a key point in their procedures. Therefore, we aim at using DST, which can mitigate the uncertainty of sensor data by its data fusion facilities. Among HAR methods, the knowledge-driven approaches of [4-6], and [11-15] are instances that deal with uncertainty. In these methods, DST is hired for inference under uncertainty as follows. However, these approaches are also based on manual ontology definitions.

In [4] and [5], the uncertainty is supposed to stem from sensor hardware errors and human activity variations. In [4], the belief masses of sensors about activities are calculated statistically and discounted by fixed rates. The sensors are mapped to activity ontologies, and then the discounted belief masses of temporally correlated triggered sensors are fused using DST to decide about the happening activity. This approach is named BDS throughout the paper, and is compared with our proposed method. In [5], a hierarchal lattice structure is proposed for activity inference. In this approach, the hierarchical lattice structure of the activity models is composed of three types of layers, namely object, context, and activity layers. The elements of each layer are connected to those of the next layer based on the ontology definition of the activity, and a weight factor is assigned to each connection, representing the uncertainty associated with their relation. Sensors are mapped to the lattice structure, and the belief masses are propagated from the first to the last layer and combined using the Dempster's combination rule. In this work, two variations of the architecture with two and three layers are implemented, which are called 2LDS and 3LDS, respectively, throughout the paper. Our proposed method is also compared with 2LDS and 3LDS in the experiments. In [6], the approach of [5] is improved by introducing a new weight factor method for the lattice-based evidential fusion. The approach of [14] is similar to that of [6], in that they are both based on layered lattice structures of activities that have been introduced in [5]. The difference is that in [14], an alternative weighting scheme is introduced, and the results are comparable to those provided in [5] and [6]. In [12], an approach similar to that of [5] is implemented. In this work, it is shown that by incorporating the Dempster's combination rule, the more the evidences are available, the more confident decisions can be made.

In [11], the activity model is represented using situation directed acyclic graphs (DAGs), which include temporal information as well. In this structure, the nodes in DAG are labeled with sensor IDs, context values, and activities. They are inter-connected in a layered style, and a weight factor is dedicated to each connection, representing the uncertainty of the relation. The activity duration and the absolute time (e.g. morning, afternoon) at which the activity usually takes place are also accommodated into DAG. To infer an activity, evidences are accumulated along the duration time of the activities, and their belief masses are fused using the Dempster's combination rule.

In [13], the Dempster-Shafer rules are changed to include temporal information in belief mass assignment and combination to recognize activities. However, this work makes use of contexts of activities in the form of directed acyclic graph as a prior knowledge. In [14], a mapping technique for converting the raw sensors' data into a high-level activity knowledge is proposed, and a conflict resolution technique for the Dempster-Shafer theory is introduced to optimize decision-making. This work hires prior knowledge of activities in the form of directed acyclic graphs for belief propagation as well.

As it can be seen, knowledge-driven methods that incorporate DST hire a static structure for each activity based on the activity ontology, map the installed sensors into that structure, and then use a fusion technique, i.e. the Dempster's combination rule, to fuse the beliefs of pre-determined activity

evidences, and decide about the happening activity. A criticism about these procedures is the generality of the ontology definitions and the complexities of deriving them, especially in situations with unknown activity patterns. Thus we propose a method to derive the evidences of activities in an automatic way, i.e. not based on predefined ontologies, fuse their beliefs via DST, and decide about the happening activity.

3. Dempster-Shafer theory of evidence

The Dempster-Shafer theory (DST) is a mathematical theory of evidence [10]. DST can combine evidences from different sources and arrive at a degree of belief (represented by a belief function) that takes into account all available evidences.

In DST, a frame of discernment, called Θ, is a domain of all possible elements of interest. Each proposition pertains to a subset of Θ. A piece of evidence that supports one or more propositions can be expressed by a basic probability assignment (BPA) function $m: 2^{\Theta} \rightarrow [0,1]$ such that $m(\emptyset) = 0$ and $\sum_{A \subseteq \Theta} m(A) = 1$, where $\emptyset$ is the empty set. The belief function can be expressed as follows:

$$Bel(X) = \sum_{A \subseteq X, X \subseteq \Theta} m(A) \qquad (1)$$

where, $Bel(X)$ represents the total degree of support for proposition X. Two BPAs, namely m_1 and m_2, from two sources of evidence can be combined using the Dempster's combination rule as:

$$m_1 \oplus m_2 = \begin{cases} \dfrac{1}{1-K} \sum_{A_i \cap A_j}^{i,j} m_1(A_i) m_2(A_j) \; if \; A \neq 0 \\ 0 \; if \; A = 0 \end{cases} \qquad (2)$$

where, K is the inconsistency factor, which can be calculated as follows:

$$K = \sum_{A_i \cap A_j = \phi}^{i,j} m_1(A_i) m_2(A_j). \qquad (3)$$

The more K is closer to 1, the more the evidences are conflicting. Equation (2) can also be used to combine more than two pieces of evidence, as in (4). The obtained result represents the effect of all pieces of evidence.

$$m_1 \oplus \cdots \oplus m_n = ((m_1 \oplus m_2) \oplus \cdots \oplus m_n). \qquad (4)$$

4. Proposed activity inference structure

The proposed method has two phases, namely the training phase and the inference phase. In the training phase, two tasks are accomplished using the training set: 1- opinion-owners are made out of sensors and their BPAs are calculated, as described in sub-section 4.1, 2- based on BPAs, the frame of opinion-owners for each activity is extracted automatically, as explained in sub-section 4.2. In the inference phase, two tasks are carried out as well: 1- having a sequence of triggered sensors, temporally-correlated sensors are extracted, as presented in sub-section 4.3, 2- the corresponding activity for each sequence of temporally-correlated sensors is inferred, as described in sub-section 4.4.

In this work, we used the binary switch sensors. Whenever an activity happens, different sensors would be triggered from the start to the end of the activity. The sensors record and send their data to a base station for further processing. Their data is simply their IDs along with their activation and deactivation times.

4.1. Opinion owners and their BPAs

Opinion-owners are the evidences that have a degree of uncertainty, belief, and disbelief about an activity. In the case of sensor-based smart homes, since the resident triggers a specific pattern of consecutive sensors for each activity, the sequences of sensors can testify about the activities. Therefore, ordered n-tuples ($n = 1, ..., d$) of sensors are considered as opinion-owners, and are shown within $< \cdots >$ signs, i.e. an n-tuple is composed of n triggered sensors from the input sensor stream, ordered by their occurrence time. The sensor triggers are due to the resident's activities. Given an input sensor stream, all n-tuples with lengths $n = 1, ..., d$ are extracted as opinion-owners, where $d \in \mathbb{N}$ is a constant that is determined as a system design parameter. The belief, disbelief, and uncertainty of opinion-owners can be calculated by beta distribution, as illustrated in [16]. These calculations are taken in the following for more clarification (i.e. Equations (5)-(11)).

The posterior probabilities of binary events can be represented by the beta distribution [16]. The beta-family of density functions is a continuous family of functions indexed by the two parameters α and β. The beta distribution can be expressed using the gamma function, as follows:

$$\begin{cases} f(p \mid \alpha, \beta) = \dfrac{\Gamma(\alpha+\beta)}{\Gamma(\alpha)\Gamma(\beta)} p^{\alpha-1}(1-p)^{\beta-1} \\ \Gamma(t) = \int\limits_0^\infty x^{t-1}e^{-x}dx \end{cases} \tag{5}$$

where, $\Gamma(.)$ is the gamma function, $0 \le p \le 1$, and $\alpha, \beta \ge 0$, with the restriction that probability value $p \ne 0$ if $\alpha < 1$ and $p \ne 1$ if $\beta < 1$. The

expectation value of the beta distribution is given by:

$$E(p) = \frac{\alpha}{\beta+\alpha}. \tag{6}$$

For a binary event space, namely $\{x, \sim x\}$, let r and s denote the number of positive and negative past observations that support x and $\sim x$, respectively. Let p denote the probability of x and f be a probability density function over the probability variable p. Having a prior uniform distribution over $\{x, \sim x\}$, f is characterized by r and s, as follows in (7) [16].

$$f(p \mid r,s) = \frac{(r+s+2)}{(r+1)(s+1)} p^r (1-p)^s. \tag{7}$$

Equation (7) is a beta distribution with $\alpha = r + 1$ and $\beta = s + 1$. Therefore, the expectation of p, named $E(p)$, can be obtained by substituting α and β in (6), as follows:

$$E(p) = \frac{r+1}{r+s+2}. \tag{8}$$

For a binary event space, namely $\{x, \sim x\}$, let b, d, and u represent the belief, disbelief, and uncertainty about proposition x such that $b + d + u = 1$. The expectation of probability of x, named E_x, can also be obtained by (9) [16], [17].

$$E_x = b + \frac{1}{2}u. \tag{9}$$

The values for b, d, and u are derived by applying an equality between (8) and (9), i.e. E_x and $E(p)$, with the restriction that $b + d + u = 1$, as:

$$\begin{cases} E_x = E(p) \\ b+d+u=1 \end{cases} \Rightarrow \begin{cases} b + \dfrac{1}{2}u = \dfrac{r+1}{r+s+2}. \\ b+d+u=1 \end{cases} \tag{10}$$

The solution of (10) is required to make b an increasing function of r, and d an increasing function of s, so that there is an affinity between b and r, and between d and s [16]. Also u is required to be a decreasing function of r and s [16]. By applying this affinity requirement, the solution of (10) will be:

$$\begin{cases} b = \dfrac{r}{r+s+2} \\ d = \dfrac{s}{r+s+2}. \\ u = \dfrac{2}{r+s+2} \end{cases} \tag{11}$$

Regarding the DST notations from the previous section, let $m_O(E)$ denote the BPA of opinion owner O about event $E \subseteq \{x, \sim x\}$ for a binary event space $\{x, \sim x\}$. Sub-set $E = \{x\}$ denotes "event x is happening", $E = \{\sim x\}$ denotes "event x is not happening", $E = \{x, \sim x\}$ stands for "we are uncertain on whether x or $\sim x$ is happening", and $E = \phi$ is considered as an impossible event, i.e. $m_O(\phi) = 0$. Furthermore, let r_x^o and s_x^o denote the number of past positive and negative observations of O that support x and $\sim x$, respectively. If b_x^o, d_x^o, and u_x^o represent the belief, disbelief, and uncertainty of opinion-owner O about happening of x, then the BPAs of O are defined by substituting r and s in (11) for r_x^o and s_x^o, as follows:

$$\begin{cases} m_O\left(\{x\}\right) = b_x^o = \dfrac{r_x^o}{r_x^o + s_x^o + 2} \\[3mm] m_O\left(\{\sim x\}\right) = d_x^o = \dfrac{s_x^o}{r_x^o + s_x^o + 2} \\[3mm] m_O\left(\{x, \sim x\}\right) = u_x^o = \dfrac{2}{r_x^o + s_x^o + 2} \end{cases} \quad (12)$$

It is clear that the equations in (12) are derived by substituting positive and negative observations (r_x^o and s_x^o) in the equations in (11), respectively. In the case of HAR, the frame of discernment for an activity, namely a, will be $\{a, \sim a\}$, where a represents the occurrence of the activity and $\sim a$ represents that the activity is not taking place. Consider $m_O(A)$ as the belief mass of opinion-owner $O = <s_1, s_2, \dots, s_n>$ for event $A \subseteq \{a, \sim a\}$. Also let $N(O, a)$ represent the number of times that the n-tuple of opinion-owner $O = <s_1, s_2, \dots, s_n>$ has been a subsequence of the ordered triggered sensors for activity a in the training set. If the happening of a is considered as a positive and $\sim a$ as a negative observation, then the numbers of positive and negative observations of opinion-owner O for activity a are considered as $r_a^O = N(O, a)$ and $s_a^O = N(O, \sim a)$, respectively. Thus the BPAs of opinion-owner O for activity a will be obtained directly by substituting r_x^O, s_x^O, and x in (12) for r_a^O, s_a^O, and a, respectively. The result obtained is shown in (13).

$$\begin{cases} m_O\left(\{a\}\right) = b_a^o = \dfrac{N(O, a)}{N(O, a) + N(O, \sim a) + 2} \\[3mm] m_O\left(\{\sim a\}\right) = d_a^o = \dfrac{N(O, \sim a)}{N(O, a) + N(O, \sim a) + 2} \\[3mm] m_O\left(\{a, \sim a\}\right) = u_a^o = \dfrac{2}{N(O, a) + N(O, \sim a) + 2} \end{cases} \quad (13)$$

4.2. Frame of opinion-owners

Let S denote an opinion-owner and a denote an activity label. With the notations of (12) and (13), an opinion about activity a can be represented by a triple (b_a^S, d_a^S, u_a^S). Since $b_a^S + d_a^S + u_a^S = 1$, the domain of all opinions for a can be shown by the equilateral triangle of figure 1. This triangle is introduced as opinion triangle or opinion space in [17]. Axes u, b, and d correspond to uncertainty, belief, and disbelief, respectively. These axes run from one edge to the opposite vertex. Coordination of a point can be calculated by drawing perpendicular lines from the point to the corresponding axes and calculating the distance of the intersection point from the origin.

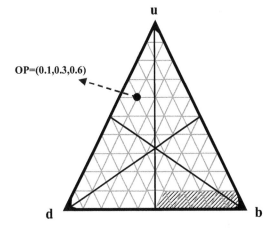

Figure. 1. Opinion triangle for an activity, namely a. Point OP shows an opinion with $b_a^S = 0.1, d_a^S = 0.3$, and $u_a^S = 0.6$, where s is an opinion-owner. The dashed area shows an accept area for activity a [17].

The frame of opinion-owners for an activity is comprised of the opinion-owners that have been triggered frequently whenever the activity has taken place. Therefore, the beliefs of these opinion-owners for that activity should be high, and their disbeliefs and uncertainties for that activity should be low. Therefore, the frame of opinion-owners for activity a will include the opinion-owners whose opinions about a fall within an area of the opinion triangle with a high belief, low disbelief, and low uncertainty level. This area is named accept area in our approach. The dashed area in figure 1 shows an accept area for activity a with uncertainty degrees less than or equal to 0.1, beliefs of more than or equal to 0.5, and disbeliefs of less than or equal to 0.5. Each activity would have its specific accept area. The accept area is one of the input parameters of our scheme.

4.3. Temporal correlation in a sequence of sensors

Let $S = s_1, s_2, ..., s_n$ represent a sequence of n sensor triggers that corresponds to a number of activities in a period of time. Suppose that we want to infer the activities associated with S. A prerequisite task for inference is to find the subsequences of S that have been triggered for an identical activity, although the activity is not known yet. To extract such subsequences, the temporal correlation of sensors' activations is considered, i.e. sensors with close activation times are possibly triggered due to the same activity. We name such sensors temporally correlated. Therefore, to decide which sensors are temporally correlated, a clustering algorithm can be used. To do this, the k-means clustering algorithm is used to cluster the sensors based on their activation times. After clustering, the sensors in each cluster are considered as temporally correlated and an activity is inferred for each cluster. Note that in k-means, the number of clusters must be known beforehand. In this case, since we do not know the number of clusters, we assume the maximum number of possible clusters, and finally, ignore the clusters with no instance. The maximum number of clusters will be equal to the number of sensors in S, i.e. n, because in the worst case, every single sensor would be in a separate cluster. As an example, consider a part of data in one day of sensor activations from a dataset by VanKasteren et al. [28], as shown in table 1. We want to infer the activities for this day. In the first step, the sensors are clustered. The sequences of sensors for each cluster are shown in table 2. Table 2 is called relation matrix throughout the paper. In the second step, activities will be inferred for the sequences of sensors in each row of the relation matrix. Sensors in each row are in the ascending activation time order. After inferring an activity for each row, the time interval from the activation of the first sensor to

the last one in the row will be labeled with the inferred activity. If a real world activity is inferred correctly within its real time interval, a true positive, and otherwise, a false negative will be recorded for it. A complete activity inference example is illustrated in section 5.

Table 1. Sensor activations for a single day.

Activation Time	Sensor ID	Activation Time	Sensor ID
3/7/2008 6:59	24	3/7/2008 8:49	7
3/7/2008 6:59	24	3/7/2008 8:49	8
3/7/2008 6:59	6	3/7/2008 8:50	9
3/7/2008 7:00	6	3/7/2008 8:50	23
3/7/2008 8:38	24	3/7/2008 8:50	8
3/7/2008 8:38	24	3/7/2008 8:51	8
3/7/2008 8:44	6	3/7/2008 9:07	5
3/7/2008 8:45	14	3/7/2008 9:15	5
3/7/2008 8:45	8	3/7/2008 9:29	12
3/7/2008 8:49	8	3/7/2008 9:29	12

Table 2. Relation matrix for a single day.

	Sensor1	Sensor2	Sensor3	Sensor4
cluster1	24	24	6	6
cluster2	24	24	----	----
cluster3	6	14	8	----
cluster4	8	7	8	----
cluster5	9	23	8	8
cluster6	5	----	----	----
cluster7	5	----	----	----
cluster8	12	12	----	----

4.4. Inference Architecture

After the training phase, to infer the activities for a sequence of triggered sensors, firstly, the temporally correlated sensors are extracted, as illustrated in the previous sub-section (sub-section 4.3). Then, for each sequence of temporally correlated sensors, a single activity is inferred. Let $S = s_1, s_2, s_3, ..., s_l$ represent a temporally correlated sequence of sensors in the ascending activation time order, for which a single activity should be inferred. The proposed architecture of figure 2 is used to infer the activity that corresponds to S. In this architecture, at first, all triggered opinion-owners, i.e. n-tuples with $n =$

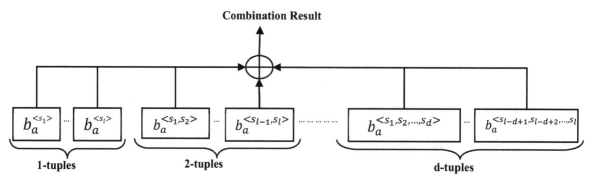

Figure 2. Belief mass combination for activity a. Belief masses of triggered opinion-owners that belong to a's frame of opinion-owners are combined using Dempster's combination rule.

$1,2,3,...,d$ are extracted from S. Parameter d determines the number of n-tuple categories in the architecture. For example, for $S' = s_1, s_2, s_3$ and $d = 3$, three 1-tuples ($< s_1 >, < s_2 >, < s_3 >$), three 2-tuples ($< s_1, s_2 >, < s_1, s_3 >, < s_1, s_2 >$), and one 3-tuple ($< s_1, s_2, s_3 >$) can be extracted as opinion-owners. Note that in S', $< s_2, s_1 >$ is not considered as a triggered opinion-owner because sensor s_1 is activated before s_2 in S. This temporal order can take the activation time order into consideration. For example, suppose that a switch sensor, namely s_1, is installed for the bedroom lamp, and is triggered whenever the lamp turns on or off, and switch sensor s_2 is installed for the bedroom door, and is triggered whenever the door is opened. Consider that someone opens the door and then turns on the lights whenever enters the bedroom, and vice versa when exiting. Thus, the sequence $< s_2, s_1 >$ shows an entrance activity, while the sequence $< s_1, s_2 >$ shows an exit activity. In fact, different sensor activation orders are evidences for different actions. Thus, different sensor orders are considered as different opinion-owners.

After the first step, for each individual activity, namely a, the belief masses of the triggered opinion-owners that belong to a's frame of opinion-owners are fused via the Dempster's combination rule, as shown in figure 2. Finally, the activity with the maximum combined belief result is considered as the corresponding one.

5. Work through example
In this section, the inference scheme is illustrated through an example. The training dataset used in the following sub-sections consists of the sensors' activation data and annotated activities of table 3 and table 4, respectively.

Table 3. Sensor data.

Activation Time	Sensor ID	Activation Time	Sensor ID
3/6/2008 4:38:06	6	3/6/2008 9:04:51	6
3/6/2008 4:38:30	8	3/6/2008 9:04:54	8
3/6/2008 4:38:48	14	3/6/2008 9:38:53	6
3/6/2008 8:39:37	6	3/6/2008 9:40:02	14
3/6/2008 8:40:11	14	3/6/2008 9:42:31	6
3/6/2008 9:04:35	8		

Table 4. Activity annotations.

Index	Start Time	End Time	Activity
1	3/6/2008 4:38:02	3/6/2008 4:38:56	Use Toilet
2	3/6/2008 8:39:35	3/6/2008 8:40:18	Use Toilet
3	3/6/2008 9:04:05	3/6/2008 9:09:56	Prepare Breakfast
4	3/6/2008 9:38:48	3/6/2008 9:43:12	Use Toilet

There are three sensors, i.e. 6, 8, and 14, and two activities, i.e. "Use Toilet" and "Prepare Breakfast", in the dataset. It is supposed that one

activity can take place at any time. The training and inference phases are exemplified in the following sub-sections.

5.1. Training
In the training phase, the first step is to make the set of opinion-owners and calculate their BPAs. As already illustrated, opinion-owners are the set of n-tuples with $n = 1, 2, ..., d$, that are made out of sensors. We consider $d = 2$ and obtain the set of all 1-tuples and 2-tuples from sensor IDs. It can be seen that there are 3 sensors in the training set. Thus there will be 9 opinion-owners, as shown in the first column of table 6.

To calculate the BPAs of opinion-owners for activities, the sequence of sensors that are triggered for each annotated activity is obtained, and then (13) is applied. A sensor with an activation time greater than the start and less than the end time of an activity belongs to that activity's sequence of triggered sensors. The start and end of an activity are annotated in table 4, which shows the triggered sensors for each activity of the training set.

Now let's calculate the BPAs of the opinion-owner $< 6 >$ for "Use Toilet" activity. In order to incorporate (13), the number of times where the activity "Use Toilet" has happened along with the opinion-owner $< 6 >$, i.e. $N(6, "Use\ Toilet")$, and the number of times where the activity "Use Toilet" has not happened along with opinion-owner $< 6 >$, i.e. $N(6, \sim "Use\ Toilet")$ must be calculated. As it can be seen in table 5, opinion-owner $< 6 >$ has been triggered in three "Use Toilet" activities and also in one "Prepare Breakfast" activity (repeated triggers for the same activity are counted once). Thus $N(< 6 >, "Use\ Toilet") = 3$ and $N(6, \sim "Use\ Toilet") = 1$. Therefore, by applying (13) for "Use Toilet" activity, we will have (14) as in the following:

$$
\begin{cases}
m_{\langle 6 \rangle}\left(\{"Use\ Toilet"\}\right) = \\
\dfrac{N\left(\langle 6 \rangle, "Use\ Toilet"\right)}{N\left(\langle 6 \rangle, "Use\ Toilet"\right)+N\left(\langle 6 \rangle, \sim "Use\ Toilet"\right)+2} = \dfrac{3}{6}, \\[4mm]
m_{\langle 6 \rangle}\left(\{\sim "Use\ Toilet"\}\right) = \\
\dfrac{N\left(\langle 6 \rangle, \sim "Use\ Toilet"\right)}{N\left(\langle 6 \rangle, "Use\ Toilet"\right)+N\left(\langle 6 \rangle, \sim "Use\ Toilet"\right)+2} = \dfrac{1}{6}, \\[4mm]
m_{\langle 6 \rangle}\left(\{"Use\ Toilet", \sim "Use\ Toilet"\}\right) = \\
\dfrac{2}{N\left(\langle 6 \rangle, "Use\ Toilet"\right)+N\left(\langle 6 \rangle, \sim "Use\ Toilet"\right)+2} = \dfrac{2}{6}.
\end{cases} \quad (14)
$$

As another instance, let's calculate BPAs of opinion-owner $<6,14>$ for "Use Toilet" activity. This opinion-owner has been triggered in 3 "Use Toilet" activities, i.e. the opinion-owner $< 6,14 >$ is a subsequence of three sensor sequences of "Use Toilet" activities in table 5 (note that in the first "Use Toilet" activity in table 5, sensors 6 and 14 are not consecutive but their activation order is preserved). We can see that $< 6,14 >$ has not been triggered for "Prepare Breakfast". Therefore, $N(< 6,14 >, "Use\,Toilet") = 3$, and $N(< 6,14 >, \sim"Use\,Toilet") = 0$. By applying (13), we will have (15) as in the following.

$$
\begin{cases}
m_{\langle 6,14\rangle}\big(\{"Use\,Toilet"\}\big) = \\
\qquad \dfrac{N\big(\langle 6,14\rangle,"Use\,Toilet"\big)}{N\big(\langle 6,14\rangle,"Use\,Toilet"\big)+N\big(\langle 6,14\rangle,\sim"Use\,Toilet"\big)+2} = \dfrac{3}{5}, \\[2em]
m_{\langle 6,14\rangle}\big(\{\sim"Use\,Toilet"\}\big) = \\
\qquad \dfrac{N\big(\langle 6,14\rangle,\sim"Use\,Toilet"\big)}{N\big(\langle 6,14\rangle,"Use\,Toilet"\big)+N\big(\langle 6,14\rangle,\sim"Use\,Toilet"\big)+2} = 0, \\[2em]
m_{\langle 6,14\rangle}\big(\{"Use\,Toilet",\sim"Use\,Toilet"\}\big) = \\
\qquad \dfrac{2}{N\big(\langle 6,14\rangle,"Use\,Toilet"\big)+N\big(\langle 6,14\rangle,\sim"Use\,Toilet"\big)+2} = \dfrac{2}{5}.
\end{cases} \qquad (15)
$$

The process will be the same for the other opinion-owners and activities. All the opinion-owners and their BPAs for "Use Toilet" and "Prepare Breakfast" are depicted in table 6.

Table 6. Opinion owners and their BPAs for activities.

OW	"Use Toilet" Activity			"Prepare Breakfast" Activity		
	B	D	U	B	D	U
<6>	0.5	0.17	0.33	0.17	0.5	0.33
<8>	0.25	0.25	0.5	0.25	0.25	0.5
<14>	0.6	0	0.4	0	0.6	0.4
<6,8>	0.25	0.25	0.5	0.25	0.25	0.5
<6,14>	0.6	0	0.4	0	0.6	0.4
<8,6>	0	0.33	0.67	0.33	0	0.67
<8,14>	0.33	0	0.67	0	0.33	0.67
<14,6>	0.33	0	0.67	0	0.33	0.67
<14,8>	0	0	1	0	0	1

OW= opinion owner, B= belief, D= disbelief, U= uncertainty.

In the second step, the frame of opinion-owners for each activity should be calculated. To do this, an accept area must be defined for the activities. The opinion-owners whose opinions for an activity fall within the accept area of that activity are added to the activity's frame of opinion-owners. In this example, let's define the same area for all the activities with an uncertainty less than or equal to 0.5 and a belief greater than 0. Thus for "USE Toilet", the set of opinion owners will be $\{< 6 >, < 8 >, < 14 >, < 6,8 >, < 6,14 >\}$.

Table 5. Sequence of sensors in ascending activation time order for each activity.

Index	Activity	Sequence of sensors
1	Use Toilet	6, 8, 14
2	Use Toilet	6, 14
3	Prepare Breakfast	8, 6, 8
4	Use Toilet	6, 14, 6

Similarly, it will be $\{< 6 >, < 8 >, < 6,8 >\}$ for "Prepare Breakfast" activity.

In this example, we used a simple and relatively large accept area for the sake of simplicity and expressiveness. But indeed, the opinion-owners of an activity must have a low uncertainty and high belief (low disbelief) about the activity. Therefore, in practice, a more confined accept area with such characteristics must be defined to get more reliable results.

5.2. Inference

Consider the sequence of sensor activations of table 1. The first step to infer the activities for this sequence is to find the temporal correlation of sensors and obtain the relation matrix. The temporal correlation of these sensors has already been calculated in table 2.

In the second step, an activity is inferred for each cluster, i.e. each row of the relation matrix. To do this, the triggered opinion-owners for each row are extracted. Then the belief masses of the triggered opinion-owners that belong to an activity's frame of opinion-owners are combined for it using the Dempster's combination rule. The activity with the maximum combination result is inferred for the row.

Let's infer the activity pertaining to cluster 3, i.e. the sequence $S = 6,14,8$ in table 2. With $d = 2$, as determined in the training phase, the triggered opinion-owners for S will be $\{< 6 >, < 14 >, < 8 >, < 6,14 >, < 6,8 >, < 14,8 >\}$. Note that the triggered opinion-owners are ordered n-tuples whose sensors appear in S with the same order. For example, opinion-owners $<8,6>$ or $<14,6>$ have not been triggered because sensors 8 or 14 had not been triggered before 6 in S.

Next, the belief masses of the triggered opinion-owners that belong to the frame of "Use Toilet" and "Prepare Breakfast" will be combined for their corresponding activity. We can see that all opinion-owners in the frame of "Use Toilet" and "Prepare Breakfast" activities are triggered in S. The combination results are shown in (16) and (17).

$$m_{\langle 6 \rangle}\left(\text{"Use Toilet"}\right) \oplus m_{\langle 8 \rangle}\left(\text{"Use Toilet"}\right) \oplus$$
$$m_{\langle 14 \rangle}\left(\text{"Use Toilet"}\right) \oplus m_{\langle 6,8 \rangle}\left(\text{"Use Toilet"}\right) \oplus \qquad (16)$$
$$m_{\langle 6,14 \rangle}\left(\text{"Use Toilet"}\right) = 0.91.$$

$$m_{\langle 6 \rangle}\left(\text{"Prepare Breakfast"}\right) \oplus$$
$$m_{<8>}\left(\text{"Prepare Breakfast"}\right) \oplus \qquad (17)$$
$$m_{\langle 6,8 \rangle}\left(\text{"Prepare Breakfast"}\right) = 0.30.$$

As it can be seen, the combination results for "Use Toilet" and "Prepare Breakfast" are 0.91 and 0.30, respectively. Thus "Use Toilet" is the inferred activity for the sequence S.

6. Simulations and results

We run two experiments to evaluate the performance of the proposed method. In the first experiment, a comparison between the proposed method and three knowledge-driven approaches, i.e. BDS, 2LDS, and 3LDS is provided. Also a comparison with a naïve Bayes method is made available. In this experiment, an activity of daily life (ADL) dataset from MIT lab [22] is used.

In the second experiment, we compare the proposed method with three data-driven activity recognition approaches. These approaches are based on NBCs, HMMs, and HSMMs, as implemented in [28]. In the second experiment, a larger dataset consisting of several frequent daily activities is used.

In both experiments, the input parameter d (that determines categories of n-tuples with $n = 1, ..., d$) is considered to be 2, and the accept area is considered as a region in the opinion space with an uncertainty less than 0.1, a belief greater than 0.5 and a disbelief less than 0.5 for all activities.

6.1 Experiment 1

In this experiment, the proposed method is compared with the naïve Bayes activity recognition method of [22], and the approaches of BDS [4], 2LDS [5], and 3LDS [5]. An ADL dataset from MIT lab [22] is used to verify the proposed method. Subject one from the dataset is used for this simulation. In this case, 77 switch sensors are installed in a single-person apartment to collect data about the resident's activities. The sensors are installed on different appliances such as drawers, cabinets, and taps to collect resident's data. More details on the topology and data acquisition scheme are illustrated in [22].

The dataset includes two weeks of daily activities, in which a single person has done his/her daily activities. Leave-one-out cross-validation strategy,

i.e. 13 days activity information for training and 1 day information for testing, is used to measure the performance of the proposed method. In this experiment, we compare our method with the others for detecting the toileting activities because this activity is the most frequent one in the dataset that happens several times a day and adequate numbers of sensors are triggered for it. Thus the training data will be sufficient. Also the ontologies based on the sensors in the state of the art approaches can be well-defined. The three

Table 7. Results of Proposed Method for Activity Recognition.

Date	TP	FP	FN	TN	PR	RC
27/3/2003	1	1	1	12	50%	50%
28/3/2003	3	0	1	11	100%	75%
29/3/2003	5	1	3	11	83.3%	62.5%
30/3/2003	4	1	2	7	80%	66.67%
31/3/2003	2	0	1	9	100%	66.67%
1/4/2003	5	0	0	9	100%	100%
2/4/2003	3	0	2	17	100%	60%
3/4/2003	2	1	1	12	66.67%	66.67%
4/4/2003	4	1	0	13	80%	100%
5/4/2003	5	0	0	8	100%	100%
6/4/2003	7	0	2	11	100%	77.78%
7/4/2003	5	0	2	8	100%	71.42%
8/4/2003	5	1	0	7	83.3%	100%
9/4/2003	7	1	0	10	87.5%	100%
10/4/2003	6	3	1	16	66.67%	85.7%
11/4/2003	4	3	1	12	57.1%	80%
Total	**68**	**13**	**17**	**173**	**84%**	**80%**

TP= true positive, FP= false positive, FN= false negative, TN= true negative, PR= precision, RC= recall.

Table 8. Comparison of BDS, 2LDS, 3LDS, and the proposed method.

Method	PR	RC	FM	ACC
BDS	69.4%	88.3%	77.7%	81.4%
2LDS	84.7%	93.5%	88.9%	92.34%
3LDS	88.2%	80%	84.2%	86.6%
proposed method	84%	80%	82%	88.9%

PR= precision, RC= recall, FM= F-measure, ACC= accuracy.

ontology-based approaches, i.e. BDS, 2LDS, and 3LDS, have incorporated this activity to verify their methods, and reported their results for it as well [5].

Table 7 shows the simulation results for our method. The naïve Bayes method has provided 61.2% precision and 83.5% recall, as reported in [22]. It can be seen that the proposed method has a precision of 84%, and outperforms the naïve Bayes approach. The recall resulted from our scheme is comparable, and approximately similar to the 83.5% recall from the naïve Bayes algorithm. However, the 82% F-measure of our method is also better than that of naïve Bayes algorithm.

Table 8 provides a comparison between our algorithm and those of BDS, 2LDS, and 3LDS, as reported in [5]. It can be seen that our method is better than BDS in terms of classification accuracy, precision, and F-measure. Also it can be seen that our method is slightly different from 3LDS, having the same recall and a little difference in precision, F-measure, and accuracy. In comparison with 2LDS, the proposed method, BDS, and 3LDS have worse recall and F-measure, although the precision of the proposed method is the same as 2LDS, and its accuracy is similar to

Table 9. T-test comparison of the proposed method with 2LDS, and 3LDS.

	Proposed method	Comparison with 2LDS	Comparison with 3LDS
mean	0.890	0.896	0.854
variance	0.0048	0.0151	0.0186
observations	16	16	16
pearson correlation		0.2371	0.2278
hypothesized mean difference		0	0
df		15	15
t-Stat		-0.1908	1.0371
P(T<=t) one-tail		0.4256	0.1580
t-critical one-tail		1.7530	1.7530
P(T<=t) two-tail		0.8512	0.3161
t-critical two-tail		2.1314	2.1314

2LDS. It can be seen that the proposed method is comparable to 2LDS and 3LDS, and is slightly different from them.

A statistical analysis, i.e. paired t-test, is also performed to show that there is no significant difference between our method, 2LDS, and 3LDS. To do this, the accuracies of activity recognition schemes are calculated for each day. The average accuracy of the proposed method, 2LDS, and 3LDS were 89, 89.6, and 85.4 percent, respectively, and it seemed that they had no significant difference. To prove this, the paired t-test was carried out to compare the accuracy means at a significance level of $\alpha = 0.05$, and the null hypothesis was considered as equal accuracy means. As the results are shown in table 9, since the absolute of t-values (t-Stat) is less than the t-critical values, we fail to reject the null hypothesis, i.e. equal means. Thus the t-test testifies that there is no significant difference between the accuracies of the proposed method and those of 2LDS and 3LDS.

The main difference between 2LDS, 3LDS, and our method is the way through which the ontology definitions for the activities are derived. In the proposed method, this task is done in an automatic manner, while it is done manually in 2LDS and 3LDS. Therefore, our method is more extensible and flexible than the previous ones. It also preserves the previous method classification criteria, as the statistical analysis showed.

6.2 Experiment 2

In this experiment, the proposed method is compared to three benchmark activity recognition schemes, which are based on NBC, HMM, and HSMM classifiers, as implemented in [28] using a larger dataset than that of experiment 1. An ADL dataset by VanKasteren et. al. [28] is used for this experiment. The dataset consists of several weeks of data recorded in a real world setting. The wireless network nodes are equipped with various kinds of sensors that give binary outputs. A "0" indicates that the sensor is not in use, and a "1" indicates that the sensor is fired. The House A from dataset is selected for this experiment. In this case, 14 state change digital sensors are installed indoors, kitchen appliances, etc. Annotations are carried out by the resident using a headset and a voice-recognition software over 25 days. More details on the datasets can be found in [28].

We compared our method with the others to recognize several frequent daily activities from the dataset that happen in different places of the house consisting of "leave the house", "use toilet", "go to bed", and "prepare breakfast". Sufficient numbers of sensors are triggered for these activities, and a convenient training set will be available.

As it is stated in [28], 3 features can be extracted from sensor activations/deactivations, and employed in the three above-mentioned activity recognition processes, i.e. raw data, change-point data, and last-fired data. The definitions of these features are as follow. For more details on the features and the way they are incorporated in the benchmark methods, the reader is referred to [28].

Raw: The raw sensor representation uses the sensor data directly as it was received from the sensors. It gives a 1 when the sensor is firing and a 0 otherwise.

Change-point: The change point representation indicates when a sensor event takes place. More formally, it gives a 1 when a sensor changes state (i.e. goes from zero to one or vice versa) and a 0 otherwise.

Last-fired: The last-fired sensor representation indicates which sensor fired last. The sensor that changed state last, continues to give 1 and changes to 0 when another sensor changes state.

We incorporated these features in the benchmark methods, as demonstrated in [28]. The classification criteria were calculated using the leave-one-out cross-validation strategy for each activity, and then averaged for each method.

The results of experiment 2 are presented in table 10. It can be seen that the proposed method outperforms all of the three methods that use raw data in terms of precision, recall, f-measure, and accuracy. Also our method outperforms the naïve Bayes approach that uses change-point feature. It can be seen that the proposed method is slightly different from the other approaches, and in most of the cases, it has a better performance.

Table 10. The results of experiment 2.

Method	Feature	PR	RC	FM	ACC
naïve Bayes	raw data	74.4%	58.4%	64.9%	77.6%
	change-point	73.5%	53.3%	61.3%	56.3%
	last-Fired	86.8%	74.6%	80.0%	95.9%
HMM	raw data	56.7%	66.3%	60.0%	61.0%
	change-point	81.5%	84.2%	82.6%	90.1%
	last-Fired	76.4%	84.0%	79.6%	93.0%
HSMM	raw data	57.3%	67.7%	60.8%	62.0%
	change-point	82.1%	84.9%	83.2%	91.5%
	last-Fired	81.1%	86.8%	83.5%	95.0%
proposed method	-----	86.7%	84.4%	85.5%	94.2%

PR= precision, RC= recall, FM= F-measure, ACC= accuracy.

7. Conclusion and future work

In this paper, a single layered architecture for human activity inference within smart homes was proposed. In this work, n-tuples (with $n = 1,2,3,...,d$) of sensor IDs formed the set of opinion-owners. The belief masses were calculated using Beta probability distribution function through the training data. Having a sequence of triggered switch sensors, the Dempster's combination rule was employed to combine the belief masses of triggered opinion-owners, and finally an activity could be inferred via a decision-making scheme.

We implemented two experiments to evaluate the performance of our method. In the first experiment, we used an ADL dataset from MIT lab. The proposed method was compared to a naïve Bayes approach [22] and three other ontology-based approaches, namely BDS, 2LDS, and 3LDS [5]. The results obtained showed that the proposed method outperforms the naïve Bayes and BDS schemes, having a precision of 84% and an accuracy of 88.9%. However, it had a similar performance, compared to 2LDS and 3LDS. But the proposed method is more extensible and flexible since no manual ontology definition is required. In the second experiment, a larger dataset by VanKasteren et. al. [28] was used, and the proposed method was compared with three approaches based on NBCs, HMMs, and HSMMs. Three features were extracted from the sensors' data and incorporated in the benchmark methods, which made 9 implementations. The simulations showed that our method outperformed the benchmark methods in most of the cases or was

comparable to them, having a precision of 86.7% and an accuracy of 94.2%.

The proposed method has two input parameters. The first one is parameter d that determines the number of n-tuple categories, as depicted in sub-section 4.4. This parameter can affect the classification efficiency and complexity. By increasing d, the number of opinion-owners will increase. Thus the beliefs of more opinion-owners are likely to be fused in the inference scheme. This will influence the classification efficiency and time/space complexity of the proposed method. However, we showed that with $d = 2$, the classification performance of the proposed method was comparable to the others through the experiments. The second input parameter is the accept area that determines the frame of opinion-owners for activities. The larger the accept area is, the more opinion-owners are likely to fall within the frame of opinion-owners of an activity. Thus more evidences, though contradicting, would be available for it. On the other hand, if the accept area is strictly confined, then the frame of opinion-owners may become empty, and no evidence may exist for an activity. This will also affect the efficiency of the activity inference scheme. The study of the impact of input parameters on the performance of the proposed method is left as a future work.

References

[1] Morris, M., Ozanne, E., Miller, K., Santamaria, N., Pearce, A., Said, C., & Adair, B. (2012). Smart technologies for older people: A systematic literature review of smart technologies that promote health and wellbeing of older people living at home. IBES, The University of Melbourne, Australia.

[2] Clough, R., Leamy, M., Miller, V., & Bright, L. (2005). Housing decisions in later life. In: Housing Decisions in Later Life. Springer pubs., Palgrave Macmillan UK, pp. 45-67.

[3] Kim, E., Helal, S., Nugent, C., & Beattie, M. (2015). Analyzing activity recognition uncertainties in smart home environments. ACM Transactions on Intelligent Systems and Technology (TIST), vol. 6, no. 4, p. 52.

[4] Liao, J., Bi, Y., & Nugent, C. (2009). Evidence fusion for activity recognition using the Dempster-Shafer theory of evidence. 9th International Conference on Information Technology and Applications in Biomedicine, Larnaca, Cyprus, 2009.

[5] Liao, J., Bi, Y., & Nugent, C. (2011). Using the Dempster–Shafer theory of evidence with a revised lattice structure for activity recognition. IEEE Transactions on Information Technology in Biomedicine, vol. 15, no. 1, pp. 74-82.

[6] Liao, J., Bi, Y., & Nugent, C. (2011). A weight factor algorithm for activity recognition utilizing a lattice-based reasoning structure. IEEE 23rd International Conference on Tools with Artificial Intelligence, Florida, USA, 2011.

[7] Khaleghi, B., Khamis, A., Karray, F. O., & Razavi, S. N. (2013). Multisensor data fusion: A review of the state-of-the-art. Information Fusion, vol. 14, no. 1, pp. 28-44.

[8] Hall, D. L., & Llinas, J. (1997). An introduction to multisensor data fusion. Proceedings of the IEEE, vol. 85, no. 1, pp. 6-23.

[9] Chen, L., Hoey, J., Nugent, C. D., Cook, D. J., & Yu, Z. (2012). Sensor-based activity recognition. IEEE Transactions on Systems, Man, and Cybernetics, Part C (Applications and Reviews), vol. 42, no. 6, pp. 790-808.

[10] Shafer, G. (1976). A mathematical theory of evidence. Princeton: Princeton university press.

[11] Mckeever, S., Ye, J., Coyle, L., Bleakley, C., & Dobson, S. (2010). Activity recognition using temporal evidence theory. Journal of Ambient Intelligence and Smart Environments, vol. 2, no. 3, pp. 253-269.

[12] Lee, H., Choi, J. S., & Elmasri, R. (2009). Sensor data fusion using dsm theory for activity recognition under uncertainty in home-based care. 23rd IEEE International Conference on Advanced Information Networking and Applications, Bradford, UK, 2009.

[13] Kushwah, A., Kumar, S., & Hegde, R. M. (2015). Multi-sensor data fusion methods for indoor activity recognition using temporal evidence theory. Pervasive and Mobile Computing, vol. 21, pp. 19-29.

[14] Javadi, E., Moshiri, B., & Yazdi, H. S. (2013). Activity Recognition In Smart Home Using Weighted Dempster-Shafer Theory. International journal of smart homes, vol. 7, no. 6, pp. 23-34.

[15] Sebbak, F., Benhammadi, F., Chibani, A., Amirat, Y., & Mokhtari, A. (2014). Dempster–shafer theory-based human activity recognition in smart home environments. Annals of telecommunications-annales des télécommunications, vol. 69, no. (3-4), pp. 171-184.

[16] Jøsang, A. (2001). A logic for uncertain probabilities. International Journal of Uncertainty, Fuzziness and Knowledge-Based Systems, vol. 9, no. 3, pp. 279-311.

[17] Pope, S., & Josang, A. (2005). Analysis of competing hypotheses using subjective logic. Queensland University, Brisbane, Australia.

[18] Chen, L., Nugent, C., & Okeyo, G. (2014). An ontology-based hybrid approach to activity modeling for smart homes. IEEE Transactions on human-machine systems, vol. 44, no. 1, pp. 92-105.

[19] Azkune, G., Almeida, A., López-de-Ipiña, D., & Chen, L. (2015). Extending knowledge-driven activity models through data-driven learning techniques. Expert Systems with Applications, vol. 42, no. 6, pp. 3115-3128.

[20] Bilmes, J. (2010). Dynamic graphical models. IEEE Signal Processing Magazine, vol. 27, no. 6, pp. 29-42.

[21] Koller, D., & Friedman, N. (2009). Probabilistic graphical models: principles and techniques. MIT press.

[22] Tapia, E. M., Intille, S. S., & Larson, K. (2004). Activity recognition in the home using simple and ubiquitous sensors. International Conference on Pervasive Computing. Springer Berlin Heidelberg, 2004.

[23] van Kasteren, T., & Krose, B. (2007). Bayesian activity recognition in residence for elders. 3rd IET International conference on intelligent environments, Ulm, Germany, 2007.

[24] Wang, X., & Ji, Q. (2012, November). Learning dynamic bayesian network discriminatively for human activity recognition. IEEE 21st International conference on pattern recognition, Japan, 2012.

[25] Wilson, D. H., & Atkeson, C. (2005). Simultaneous tracking and activity recognition (STAR) using many anonymous, binary sensors. 23rd International conference on pervasive computing, Munich, Germany, 2005.

[26] Kim, E., Helal, S., & Cook, D. (2010). Human activity recognition and pattern discovery. IEEE Pervasive Computing, vol. 9, no. 1, 48-53.

[27] Singla, G., Cook, D. J., & Schmitter-Edgecombe, M. (2009). Tracking activities in complex settings using smart environment technologies. International journal of biosciences, psychiatry, and technology (IJBSPT), vol. 1, no.1, p. 25.

[28] van Kasteren, T. L., Englebienne, G., & Kröse, B. J. (2011). Human activity recognition from wireless sensor network data: Benchmark and software. In: Chen, L., Nugent, C. D., Biswas, J., & Hoey, J. (Eds.). Atlantis Press, pp. 165-186.

[29] Van Kasteren, T. L. M., Englebienne, G., & Kröse, B. J. (2010). Activity recognition using semi-markov models on real world smart home datasets. Journal of ambient intelligence and smart environments, vol 2, no. 3, pp. 311-325.

[30] Natarajan, P., & Nevatia, R. (2007). Coupled hidden semi-markov models for activity recognition. IEEE Workshop on Motion and Video Computing, Austin, Texas, USA, 2007.

[31] Wang, L., Gu, T., Tao, X., Chen, H., & Lu, J. (2011). Recognizing multi-user activities using wearable sensors in a smart home. Pervasive and Mobile Computing, vol. 7, no. 3, pp. 287-298.

[32] Cook, D. J. (2010). Learning setting-generalized activity models for smart spaces. IEEE intelligent systems, vol. 27, pp. 32-38.

[33] Ghasemi, V., & Pouyan, A. A. (2015, May). Activity recognition in smart homes using absolute temporal information in dynamic graphical models. 10th Asian control conference (ASCC), Malaysia, 2015.

[34] Hu, D. H., & Yang, Q. (2008, July). CIGAR: concurrent and interleaving goal and activity recognition. 23rd AAAI conference on artificial intelligence, Chicago, USA, 2008.

[35] Tong, Y., & Chen, R. (2014). Latent-Dynamic conditional random fields for recognizing activities in smart homes. Journal of ambient intelligence and smart environments, vol. 6, no. 1, pp. 39-55.

[36] Gu, T., Wu, Z., Tao, X., Pung, H. K., & Lu, J. (2009). epsicar: An emerging patterns based approach to sequential, interleaved and concurrent activity recognition. IEEE International conference on pervasive computing and communications, Texas, USA, 2009.

[37] Cook, D. J., Krishnan, N. C., & Rashidi, P. (2013). Activity discovery and activity recognition: A new partnership. IEEE transactions on cybernetics, vol. 43, no. 3, pp. 820-828.

[38] Chua, S. L., Marsland, S., & Guesgen, H. W. (2011). Unsupervised Learning of Human Behaviours. In 25th AAAI Conference on artificial intelligence, California, USA, 2011.

[39] Bao, L., & Intille, S. S. (2004). Activity recognition from user-annotated acceleration data. 2nd International Conference on Pervasive Computing, Munich, Germany, 2004.

[40] Fleury, A., Vacher, M., & Noury, N. (2010). SVM-based multimodal classification of activities of daily living in health smart homes: sensors, algorithms, and first experimental results. IEEE transactions on information technology in biomedicine, vol. 14, no. 2, pp. 274-283.

[41] Fatima, I., Fahim, M., Lee, Y. K., & Lee, S. (2013). A unified framework for activity recognition-based behavior analysis and action prediction in smart homes. Sensors, vol 13, no. 2, pp. 2682-2699.

[42] Yin, J., Yang, Q., & Pan, J. J. (2008). Sensor-based abnormal human-activity detection. IEEE Transactions on Knowledge and Data Engineering, vol. 20, no. 8, pp. 1082-1090.

[43] Krishnan, N. C., & Cook, D. J. (2014). Activity recognition on streaming sensor data. Pervasive and mobile computing, vol. 10, pp. 138-154.

[44] Chen, L., & Nugent, C. (2009). Ontology-based activity recognition in intelligent pervasive environments. International Journal of Web Information Systems, vol. 5, no. 4, pp. 410-430.

[45] Chen, L., Nugent, C. D., & Wang, H. (2012). A knowledge-driven approach to activity recognition in smart homes. IEEE Transactions on Knowledge and Data Engineering, vol. 24, no. 6, pp. 961-974.

[46] Okeyo, G., Chen, L., Wang, H., & Sterritt, R. (2014). Dynamic sensor data segmentation for real-time knowledge-driven activity recognition. Pervasive and Mobile Computing, vol. 10, pp. 155-172.

[47] Ye, J., Stevenson, G., & Dobson, S. (2015). KCAR: A knowledge-driven approach for concurrent activity recognition. Pervasive and Mobile Computing, vol. 19, pp. 47-70.

19

A novel hybrid method for vocal fold pathology diagnosis based on russian language

V. Majidnezhad

United Institute of Informatics Problems, National Academy of Science of Belarus, Minsk, Belarus.

*Corresponding author: vahidmn@yahoo.com (V. Majidnezhad).

Abstract

In this paper, first, an initial feature vector for vocal fold pathology diagnosis is proposed. Then, for optimizing the initial feature vector, a genetic algorithm is proposed. Some experiments are carried out for evaluating and comparing the classification accuracies, which are obtained by the use of the different classifiers (ensemble of decision tree, discriminant analysis and K-nearest neighbours) and the different feature vectors (the initial and the optimized ones). Finally, a hybrid of the ensemble of decision tree and the genetic algorithm is proposed for vocal fold pathology diagnosis based on Russian Language. The experimental results show a better performance (the higher classification accuracy and the lower response time) of the proposed method in comparison with the others. While the usage of pure decision tree leads to the classification accuracy of 85.4% for vocal fold pathology diagnosis based on Russian language, the proposed method leads to the 8.5% improvement (the accuracy of 93.9%).

Keywords: *Ensemble of Decision Tree, Genetic Algorithm (GA), Mel Frequency Cepstral Coefficients (MFCC), Wavelet Packet Decomposition (WPD), Vocal Fold Pathology Diagnosis.*

1. Introduction

Early detection of vocal fold pathology by the use of non invasive methods and employing different techniques of speech processing has recently attracted scientists' attention. Their aim is to develop new techniques for processing the speech signals of patients in order to decrease the treatments expenses and to increase the accuracy of diagnosis.

Nowadays, medical specialists use different medical techniques based on the direct examination of vocal folds. But these methods have two main drawbacks. Firstly, they are invasive. They may cause patients to feel uncomfortable and to distort the actual signal. Secondly, they are expensive to buy and their maintenance fees are high. The best option, for overcoming the disadvantages related to the medical instruments is to employ acoustic analysis techniques. They let medical specialists examine vocal fold in short time with minimal discomfort. They also allow to reveal the pathologies on early stages. In recent years, a number of methods based on acoustic analysis were developed for vocal fold pathology classification [1-3]. These methods usually have two phases, which are the feature extraction phase and the classification phase. The feature extraction phase involves the transformation of speech signal into some parameters or features. The second phase implies a choice including a variety of machine learning methods.

Traditionally, for the feature extraction phase, one deals with such parameters like as jitter [4-5], shimmer [6-7], signal to noise ratio [8-9], formants [10-11]. Also some of the well-known classifiers for the classification phase in the previous works were such as Support Vector Machine (SVM) [12-15], Gaussian Mixture Model (GMM) [16-18], Artificial Neural Network (ANN) [19-21], Hidden Markov Model (HMM) [22-24].

In [25], it is proved that the classification accuracy of vocal fold pathology detection systems extremely depends on the dataset and its characteristics such as volume of dataset. So, it is obvious that the reported accuracies of the pervious works are not comparable due to the lack of the same conditions such as dataset. Even it is possible that they use the same dataset but their train and test sets would be different and consequently their reported accuracies cannot be compared.

In fact the acoustic characteristics of vowels differ in different languages. There are some researches such as [26,27] in which the differences of vowels in the different languages have been investigated. That is why; each language needs its special technique for vocal fold pathology detection system. So, the existing methods for the other languages such as English or Arabic or Korean cannot be used for Russian language. Of course, our main aim is to develop a high efficient method for vocal fold pathology detection based on Russian language.

The rest of the paper is organized as follows: In the second section, the initial feature vector based on the combination of the MFCC and the WPD is presented. In the third section, optimizing of the initial feature vector by the use of feature reduction methods is investigated. Experimental results are summarized in the fourth section. The last section concludes the paper.

2. Initial feature vector

First, using cepstral representation of input signal, the 13 Mel Frequency Cepstral Coefficients (MFCCs) are extracted. Then, the wavelet packet decomposition in 5 levels is applied on the input signal to make the wavelet packet tree with the 63 nodes. Next, from the nodes of the obtained wavelet packet tree, the 63 energy features as well as the 63 Shannon entropy features are extracted. Finally, by the combination of these features, the initial feature vector with the length of 139 features is constructed.

2.1. Mel frequency cepstral coefficients (MFCCs)

MFCCs are widely used features to characterize a voice signal and can be estimated by using a parametric approach derived from linear prediction coefficients (LPC), or by the non-parametric discrete fast Fourier transform (FFT), which typically encodes more information than the LPC method.

The Matlab code to calculate the MFCC features was adapted from the Auditory Toolbox (Malcolm Slaney).

2.2. Wavelet packet decomposition (WPD)

The most important property of WPD is that it reveals more information than DWT or CWT due to its detailed sub-bands information. The hierarchical wavelet packet (WP) transform uses a family of wavelet functions and their associated scaling functions to decompose the original signal into subsequent sub-bands. The decomposition process is recursively applied to both the low and high frequency sub-bands to generate the next level of the hierarchy. WPs can be described by the following collection of basic functions [28]:

$$W_{2n}(2^{p-1}x-1)=\sqrt{2^{1-p}}\sum_m h(m-2l)\sqrt{2^p}W_n(2^p x-m) \quad (1)$$

$$W_{2n+1}(2^{p-1}x-1)=\sqrt{2^{1-p}}\sum_m g(m-2l)\sqrt{2^p}W_n(2^p x-m) \quad (2)$$

Where p is scale index, l the translation index, h the low-pass filter and g the high-pass filter with

$$g(k)=(-1)^k h(1-k) \quad (3)$$

The WP coefficients at different scales and positions of a discrete signal can be computed as follows:

$$C_{n,k}^p = \sqrt{2^p}\sum_{m=-\infty}^{\infty} f(m)W_n(2^p m-k) \quad (4)$$

$$C_{2n,l}^{p-1} = \sum_m h(m-2l)C_{n,m}^p \quad (5)$$

$$C_{2n+1,l}^{p-1} = \sum_m g(m-2l)C_{n,m}^p \quad (6)$$

For a group of wavelet packet coefficients, energy feature in its corresponding sub-band is computed as [28]

$$Energy_n = \frac{1}{N^2}\sum_{k=1}^{n}\left|C_{n,k}^p\right|^2 \quad (7)$$

The entropy evaluates the rate of information, which is produced by the pathogens factors as a measure of abnormality in pathological speech. Also, the measure of Shannon entropy can be computed using the extracted wavelet packet coefficients, through the following formula [28]

$$Entropy_n = -\sum_{k=1}^{n}\left|C_{n,k}^p\right|^2 \log\left|C_{n,k}^p\right|^2 \quad (8)$$

In this study, the mother wavelet function of the tenth order Daubechies has been used. It is reported to be effective in voice signal analysis [29,30].

3. Optimized feature vector

The discrimination power of the initial features can be evaluated by the use of T-test. It can be used to investigate whether the means of two groups are statistically different from each other or not. For this purpose, it calculates a ratio between the difference of two group means and the variability of two groups. The T-test is applied on each feature in our dataset to compare p-value for each feature as a measure of how effective it is at separating groups. The result is shown in figure 1.

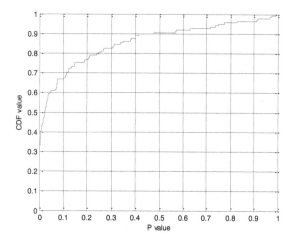

Figure 1. The P-value for the features.

There are about 40% of features having p-values close to zero and 60% of features having p-values smaller than 0.05, means that there are about 83 features among the original 139 features, which have strong discrimination power. Also, 40% of initial features (56 features) are not strong for the classification purpose. Therefore, feature reduction phase is necessary and important for our task.

Using every feature for the classification process is not good idea and it may cause to increase the misclassification error rate. Therefore, it is better to select proper features from the whole features. This process is called "Feature Reduction" or "Feature Selection". In other words, the goal is to reduce the dimension of the data by finding a small set of important features, which can give good classification performance.

It is possible to categorize the feature reduction approaches into two categories: filter methods and wrapper methods. Filter methods focus on the general characteristics of the data to evaluate and to select the feature subsets without involving the chosen learning algorithm or the classifier. However, wrapper methods use the performance feedbacks of the chosen learning algorithm or the classifier to evaluate each candidate feature subset. Wrapper methods search for a subset of features, which has better fitted for the chosen learning algorithm or the classifier, but they can be significantly slower than filter methods if the learning algorithm takes a long time to learn. The concepts of "filters" and "wrappers" are described in [31].

In this section, a well-known approach of the filter methods, which is called the Principal Component Analysis (PCA), is introduced. It is used frequently in the previous works such as [32-35]. Also a novel approach, the GA-based method, is proposed for the feature reduction phase. This method belongs to the wrapper methods.

3.1. Principal component analysis (PCA)

This method searches a mapping to find the best representation for distribution of data [36]. Therefore, it uses a signal-representation criterion to perform dimension reduction while preserving much of the randomness or variance in the high-dimensional space as possible [37]. The first principal component accounts for as much of the variability in the data as possible, and each succeeding component accounts for as much of the remaining variability as possible. PCA involves the calculation of the eigenvalues decomposition of a data covariance matrix or singular value decomposition of a data matrix, usually after mean centering the data for each attribute.

In PCA, the optimal approximation of a random vector $X \in R^N$ in N-dimensional space by a linear combination of M $(M < N)$ independent vectors is obtained by projecting the random vector X into the eigenvectors corresponding to the largest eigenvalues of the covariance matrix of vector X [37]. The main limitation of PCA is that it does not consider class separately, since it does not take into account the class label of the feature vectors.

3.2. GA-based feature reduction

GA is a heuristic optimization method, which acts on the basis of evaluation in nature and search for the final solution among a population of potential solutions. At the beginning of algorithm, a number of individuals (initial population) are created randomly and the fitness function is evaluated for all of them. If we do not reach to the optimal answer, the next generation is produced with selection of parents based on their fitness and the children mutates with a fixed probability and then the new children fitness is calculated and new population is formed by substitution of children with parents and this process is repeated until the final condition is established.

In the proposed GA-based method, a fitness function f is defined which shows the misclassification error rate of the ensemble classifier for the train set.

$$f = \frac{\sum_{i=1}^{n} |a_i - r_i|}{n} \qquad (9)$$

The a_i is the result of classifier and the r_i is the real class for i^{th} sample. The n is the number of samples in the train set. The aim of the proposed GA-based method is to find the subset of the initial features so that they minimize the f.

In the proposed method, the length of each chromosome is 139 (the length of the initial feature vector). Each gene in the chromosomes is related to one feature and can choose one of binary values (zero or one). These values show that whether the respective feature participates in the classification's process or not.

4. Experiments and results

Specialists from the Belarusian Republican Center of Speech, Voice and Hearing Pathologies created the dataset. The 75 pathological (vocal fold paralysis) samples and the 55 healthy samples, which are related to sustained vowel "a" have randomly been selected. All of the samples are the wave files in the PCM format and in a mono mode and the sample rate of 44100 Hertz and the bit-depth of 16 bit.

In this section, three experiments have been designed. These experiments are simulated in the Matlab. In all of the experiments, the 10 folds cross-validation scheme has been adapted to assess the generalization capabilities of the system and the obtained results [38]. The general scheme of the proposed method for the classification is illustrated in the figure 2.

In the first experiment, the classification has been done based on the initial feature vector, which contains all the 139 features. The results are shown in the table 1.

In the second experiment, the classification has been done based on the optimized feature vectors, which are obtained by the use of the PCA-based or the GA-based methods. The different feature vectors with different length are evaluated. The final optimized feature vector lengths and the obtained classification accuracies are shown in the table 2.

As it is obvious in the tables 1-2, both the PCA-based and the GA-based methods can lead to the increasing of the classification accuracies. Of course, in terms of classification accuracy, the proposed GA-based method has a better performance in comparison with the PCA-based method. The main limitation of the PCA is that it does not take into account the class labels and it just focuses on the sample's value. In other words, the PCA searches for the features which their values have bigger variance in comparison with others and it does not collaborate with the classifier. But the proposed GA-based method uses a genetic algorithm in order to overcome this limitation of PCA. The GA-based method considers the misclassification error rate of the classifier in its fitness function and tries to minimize it.

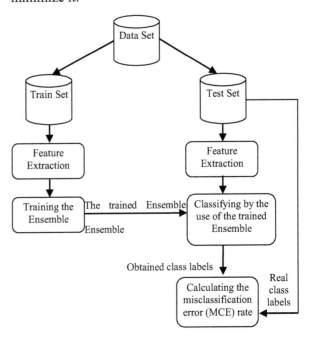

Figure 2. The general scheme of the proposed method for the classification.

Table 1. The obtained classification accuracies.

The classifiers	Ensemble of KNN	Ensemble of Discriminant Analysis	Ensemble of Binary Decision Tree
Classification Accuracy (%)	64.7	77	85.4

Table 2. The final feature vector lengths and the obtained classification accuracies.

The Classifiers/ Feature Reduction Methods	Ensemble of KNN	Ensemble of Discriminant Analysis	Ensemble of Binary Decision Tree
PCA-Based	77.7% (Feature vector length=22)	75.4% (Feature vector length=19)	86.2% (Feature vector length=11)
GA-Based	84.6% (Feature vector length=29)	78.5% (Feature vector length=3)	93.9% (Feature vector length=14)

Also, from the classifier point of view, the binary decision tree shows better results than the others. Finally, the experiment results show a better performance of the proposed method, which is based on the hybrid of the ensemble of decision tree as the classifier and the GA-based method as the feature reduction approach. It provides the best classification accuracy (93.9% of accuracy) in comparison with the others. It also leads to reduce the length of feature vector from 139 to 14 features. Therefore, the response time of the vocal fold pathology classification system based on the initial feature vector (with the length of 139) and the reduced feature vector (with the length of 14) should be different.

The third experiment is carried out to compare the response time of the vocal fold pathology classification system based on the initial feature vector and the reduced feature vectors. This experiment has carried out on a personal computer, which is equipped by the processor of Intel dual-core 2.13 Giga Hertz and the memory of 2 Giga Bytes. The response time in the case of the initial feature vector (139 features), 9.7 milliseconds is reported. The response time in the case of the reduced feature vector (11 features), which is obtained by the PCA-based method, 3.3 milliseconds is reported. Also, the response time in the case of the final reduced feature vector (14 features), which is obtained by the GA-based method, 3.6 milliseconds is reported. Therefore, using the reduced feature vectors leads to the decreasing of the response time of the program of vocal fold pathology classification in comparison with the non-reduced feature vector.

5. Conclusion

In this article, an initial feature vector based on the combination of the Wavelet Packet Decomposition (WPD) and the Mel Frequency Cepstral Coefficients (MFCCs) is proposed. The performances of the ensembles of three kinds of learners (KNN, discriminant analysis and binary decision tree) in the task of vocal fold pathology diagnosis are investigated. The experiments' results show the priority of the ensemble of decision tree in comparison with the others.

Also, the performance of three kinds of feature vector (the initial feature vector, the optimized feature vector by the means of the PCA-based method and the optimized feature vector by the means of the proposed GA-based method) is evaluated. The experiments' results show the priority of the optimized feature vector by the means of the proposed GA-based method in

comparison with the others. This better performance is due to taking into consideration of the ensemble classifier in the feature reduction phase. In other words, the proposed GA-based method tries to optimize the initial feature vector with the aim of decreasing the misclassification error rate of the ensemble classifier. But the PCA-based method just focuses on the data without any attention on the misclassification error rate of the ensemble classifier.

Finally, the proposed method is proposed based on the hybrid of the ensemble of decision tree as the classifier and the proposed GA-based method as the feature reduction approach. It is concluded that the proposed method has the higher accuracy (93.9% of accuracy) and the lower response time in comparison with the other ones.

Acknowledgment

This work was supported by the speech laboratory of the United Institute of Informatics Problems of NASB in Belarus. The authors wish to thank the Belarusian Republican Center of Speech, Voice and Hearing Pathologies by its support in the speech database.

References

[1] Manfredi, C. (2000). Adaptive Noise Energy Estimation in Pathological Speech Signals. IEEE Trans. Biomedical Engineering, vol. 47, no. 11, pp. 1538-1543.

[2] Alonso, J. B., Leon, J. D., Alonso, I. & Ferrer, M. A. (2001). Automatic Detection of Pathologies in the Voice by HOS Based Parameters. EURASIP Journal on Applied Signal Processing. 2001(4), pp. 275-284.

[3] Rosa, M. D. O., Pereira, J. C. & Grellet, M. (2000). Adaptive Estimation of Residue Signal for Voice Pathology Diagnosis. IEEE Trans. Biomedical Engineering, vol. 47, no. 1, pp. 96-104.

[4] Jo, C., Li, T. & Wang, J. (2005). Estimation of Harmonic and Noise Components from Pathological Voice using Iterative Method. 27th Annual Conference on IEEE Engineering in Medicine and Biology, Shanghai, China, pp. 4678-4681.

[5] Gomez, P., Diaz, F., Lazaro, C., Murphy, K., Martinez, R., Rodellar, V. & Alvarez, A. (2005). Spectral Perturbation Parameters for Voice Pathology Detection. in the International Symposium on Signals, Circuits and Systems (ISSCS), Iasi, Romania, pp. 299-302.

[6] Xu, W., Zhiyan, H. & Jian, W. (2008). Pathological Speech Deformation Degree Assessment Based on Integrating Feature and Neural Network. 27th Chinese Control, Kunming, Yunnan, China, pp. 441-444.

[7] Wei, Y., GholamHosseini, H., Cameron, A., Harrison, M. J. & Al-Jumaily, A. (2009). Voice Analysis for Detection of Hoarseness Due to a Local Anesthetic Procedure. 3rd International Conference on Signal Processing and Communication Systems (ICSPCS 2009), Omaha, NE, pp. 1-7.

[8] Sarria-Paja, M., Castellanos-Domínguez, G. & Delgado-Trejos, E. (2010). A new approach to discriminative HMM training for pathological voice classification. 32nd Annual International Conference of the IEEE EMBS, Buenos Aires, Argentina, pp. 4674-4677.

[9] Li, T. & Jo, C. (2004). Discrimination of Severely Noisy Pathological Voice with Spectral Slope and HNR. 7th International Conference on Signal Processing, (ICSP '04), Beijing, China, pp. 2218-2221.

[10] Hansen, J. H. L., Gavidia-Ceballos, L. & Kaiser, J. F. (1998). A Nonlinear Operator-Based Speech Feature Analysis Method with Application to Vocal Fold Pathology Assessment. IEEE Transactions On Biomedical Engineering, vol. 45, no. 3, pp. 300- 313.

[11] Fetisova, O. G., Lamtyugin, D. V., Makukha, V. K. & Voronin, E. M. (2007). Spectrum analysis of vocalization application for voice pathology detection. International Conference on Computer as a Tool (EUROCON2007), Warsaw, Poland, pp. 2725-2728.

[12] Majidnezhad, V. & Kheidorov, I. (2013). A Hybrid of Genetic Algorithm and Support Vector Machine for Feature Reduction and Detection of Vocal Fold Pathology. International Journal of Image, Graphics and Signal Processing, vol. 5, no. 9, pp. 1-7.

[13] Markaki, M. & Stylianou, Y. (2011). Voice Pathology Detection and Discrimination Based on Modulation Spectral Features. IEEE Transactions on Audio, Speech, and Language Processing, vol. 19, no. 7, pp. 1938-1948.

[14] Majidnezhad, V. & Kheidorov, I. (2012). A Novel Method for Feature Extraction in Vocal Fold Pathology Diagnosis. 3rd International Conference MobiHealth2012, Paris, France, pp. 96-105.

[15] Majidnezhad, V. & Kheidorov, I. (2013). The SVM-Based Feature Reduction in Vocal Fold Pathology Diagnosis. International Journal of Future Generation Communication and Networking, vol. 6, no. 1, pp. 45-55.

[16] Godino-Llorente, J. I., Gomez-Vilda, P. & Blanco-Velasco, M. (2006). Dimensionality Reduction of a Pathological Voice Quality Assessment System Based on Gaussian Mixture Models and Short-Term Cepstral Parameters. IEEE Transactions on Biomedical Engineering, vol. 53, no. 10, pp. 1943-1953.

[17] Arias-Londono, J. D., Godino-Llorente, J. I., Sa□enz-Lecho□n, N., Osma-Ruiz, V. & Castellanos-Domi□nguez, G. (2011). Automatic Detection of Pathological Voices Using Complexity Measures, Noise Parameters, and Mel-Cepstral Coefficients. IEEE Transactions on Biomedical Engineering, vol. 58, no. 2, pp. 370-379.

[18] Majidnezhad, V. & Kheidorov, I. (2013). A Novel GMM-Based Feature Reduction for Vocal Fold Pathology Diagnosis. Research Journal of Applied Sciences, Engineering and Technology, vol. 5, no. 6, pp. 2245-2254.

[19] Carvalho, R. T. S., Cavalcante, C. C. & Cortez, P. C. (2011). Wavelet Transform and Artificial Neural Networks Applied to Voice Disorders Identification. 3rd World Congress on Nature and Biologically Inspired Computing (NaBIC), Salamanca, Spain, pp. 371 – 376.

[20] Drugman, T., Dubuisson, T. & Dutoit, T. (2011). Phase-based information for voice pathology detection. International Conference on Acoustics, Speech and Signal Processing (ICASSP), Prague, Czech Republic, pp. 4612-4615.

[21] Majidnezhad, V. & Kheidorov, I. (2013). An ANN-Based Method for Detecting Vocal Fold Pathology. International Journal of Computer Applications, vol. 62, no. 7, pp. 1-4.

[22] Gavidia-Ceballos, L. & Hansen, J. H. L. (1996). Direct Speech Feature Estimation Using an Iterative EM Algorithm for Vocal Fold Pathology Detection. IEEE Transactions on Biomedical Engineering, vol. 43, no. 4, pp. 373-383.

[23] Arias-Londono, J. D., Godino-Llorente, J. I., Castellanos-Dominguez, G., Saenz-Lechon, N. & Osma-Ruiz, V. (2009). Complexity Analysis of Pathological Voices by means of Hidden Markov Entropy measurements. 31st Annual International Conference of the IEEE Engineering in Medicine and Biology Society, Minneapolis, Minnesota, USA, pp. 2248-2251.

[24] Majidnezhad, V. & Kheidorov, I. (2012). A HMM-Based Method for Vocal Fold Pathology Diagnosis. International Journal of Computer Science Issues, vol. 9, no. 6, pp. 135-138.

[25] Markaki, M., Stylianou, Y., Arias-Londono, J. D. & Godino-Llorente, J. I. (2010). Dysphonia detection based on modulation spectral features and cepstral coefficients. International Conference on Acoustics Speech and Signal Processing (ICASSP 2010), Dallas, 14-19 March 2010, pp. 5162-5165.

[26] Tsukada, K. (2009). An acoustic comparison of vowel length contrasts in Arabic, Japanese and Thai: Durational and spectral data. International Journal of Asian Language Processing, vol. 19, no. 4, pp. 127-138.

[27] Vaissiere, J. (2011). On the acoustic and perceptual characterization of reference vowels in a cross-language perspective. International Congress of

Phonetic Sciences (ICPhS XVII), Hong Kong, August 2011, pp. 52-59.

[28] Aghazadeh, B. S. (2012). Traumatic Brain Injury Assessment Using the Integration of Pattern Recognition Methods and Finite Element Analysis. Ph.D. dissertation, Virginia Commonwealth University, Richmond, Virginia, USA.

[29] Guido, R. C., Pereira, J. C., Fonseca, E., Sanchez, F. L. & Vierira, L. S. (2005). Trying different wavelets on the search for voice disorders sorting. 37th IEEE International Southeastern Symposium on System Theory, Tuskegee, AL, USA, pp. 495-499.

[30] Umapathy, K. & Krishnan, S. (2005). Feature analysis of pathological speech signals using local discriminant bases technique. Medical and Biological Engineering and Computing, vol. 43, no. 4, pp. 457-464.

[31] Kohavi, R. & John, G. (1997). Wrappers for feature subset selection. Artificial Intelligence, vol. 97, no. 1-2, pp. 273-324.

[32] Chen, W., Peng, C., Zhu, X., Wan, B. & Wei, D. (2007). SVM-based identification of pathological voices. 29th Annual International Conference of the IEEE Engineering in Medicine and Biology Society, Lyon, France, pp. 3786-3789.

[33] Go´mez, P., Dı´az, F., A´lvarez, A., Murphy, K., Lazaro, C., Martinez, R. & Rodellar, V. (2005). Principal component analysis of spectral perturbation parameters for voice pathology detection. 18th IEEE Symposium on Computer-Based Medical Systems, Dublin, Ireland, pp. 41-46.

[34] Michaelis, D., Frohlich, M. & Strube, H. W. (1998). Selection and combination of acoustic features for the description of pathologic voices. Journal of the Acoustical Society of America, vol. 103, no. 3, pp. 1628–1639.

[35] Marinaki, M., Kotropoulos, C., Pitas, I. & Maglaveras, N. (2004). Automatic detection of vocal fold paralysis and edema. 8th International Conference on Spoken Language Processing (ICSLP), Jeju Island, South Korea, pp. 537-540.

[36] Bashashati, A. (2007). Towards Development of a 3-State Self-Paced Brain Computer Interface System. Ph.D. dissertation, the faculty of graduate studies (electrical And Computer Engineering), the university of British Columbia, Vancouver, Canada.

[37] Jolliffe, I. T. (2002). Principal Component Analysis. Second edition, New York, USA. Springer.

[38] Michie, D., Spiegelhalter, D. J. & Taylor, C. C. (1994). Machine Learning, Neural and Statistical Classification. Englewood, USA. Prentice Hall.

20

An enhanced median filter for removing noise from MR images

S. Arastehfar[1], A. A. Pouyan[2*], A. Jalalian[1]

1. National University of Singapore (NUS)
2. School of Computer Engineering, Shahrood University of Technology, Iran

*Corresponding author: apouyan@shahroodut.ac.ir (A.A. Pouyan)

Abstract

In this paper, a novel decision based median (DBM) filter for enhancing MR images has been proposed. The method is based on eliminating impulse noise from MR images. A median-based method to remove impulse noise from digital MR images has been developed. Each pixel is leveled from black to white like gray-level. The method is adjusted in order to decide whether the median operation can be applied on a pixel. The main deficiency in conventional median filter approaches is that all pixels are filtered with no concern about healthy pixels. In this research, to suppress this deficiency, noisy pixels are initially detected, and then the filtering operation is applied on them. The proposed decision method (DM) is simple and leads to fast filtering. The results are more accurate than other conventional filters. Moreover, DM adjusts itself based on the conditions of local detections. In other words, DM operation on detecting a pixel as a noise depends on the previous decision. As a considerable advantage, some unnecessary median operations are eliminated and the number of median operations reduces drastically by using DM. Decision method leads to more acceptable results in scenarios with high noise density. Furthermore, the proposed method reduces the probability of detecting noise-free pixels as noisy pixels and *vice versa*.

Keywords: *Median filter, Impulse noise, Magnetic Resonance Image.*

1. Introduction

Digital images play an important role in some medical issues especially in detecting cancers, internal organs' diseases and injuries. Some medical images are acquired based on Magnetic Resonance (MR) phenomenon used to investigate brain, liver and other soft tissues [1]. The investigation depends on the energy absorbing and emitting in the radio frequency range of the electromagnetic spectrum. MR images may be corrupted by some degrading phenomena during the acquisition process. Some degrading phenomena may contaminate MR images. It is based on the characteristics of MR phenomenon, image capturing equipment and some environmental influences. In this regard, impulse noise has an important corrupting influence impact on MR images, while the image is capturing.

Removing noise from degraded images is a challenging research field in image processing. It involves estimation procedure of the image corrupted by noise [1]-[3]. Over the years, several filtering techniques have been reported for restoring image, each of which has its own assumptions, advantages and disadvantages [1]. In this regard, nonlinear filters such as median filter are preferred as they can cope with the nonlinear property of the image model [2], [4]. Generally, some properties of the image under corruption process, such as the complexity of the image scene, the applied filter based on the nature of the corruption process, and the parameters and properties of the filter, affect the success of drawing an image close to it [5].

The main approach of this paper is to remove impulse noise from MR images through a median-based filter. Before enhancing MR images, it is substantially important to remove noise from the images. Intensive work has been conducted on the restoration of images degraded by impulse noise. Median filter is the most widely used filter for removing impulse noise because of its good noise suppressing power and computational efficiency [1], [4]-[8]. Median filters are nonlinear filters of rank filters and have highlighted some new promising research avenues in recent years [4], [5]. A median filter is also the most popular filter for removing impulse noise.

Median filter is an effective method for eliminating certain kinds of noise, specifically, impulsive noise. This nonlinear filter is simple, robust, repeatedly applicable and particularly adapted to suppress impulse noise. Based on these advantages, the median filter becomes a popular filter for image processing applications. Although the median filter is well suited for suppressing noise, under the median operation, fine details may be erased and the result may be similar to capillarity when the objects in the image are close enough [4]. Moreover, rounding the corners and mapping texture region to a uniform shade are the other deficiencies of the median filter. To mitigate these disadvantages, various approaches of median filter have been developed such as stack filters, multistage median, weighted median [6], [9], rank conditioned rank selection, and relaxed median [4].

However, this paper has proposed, a novel method for removing impulse noise from gray-level images. The new method is capable of attenuating impulse noise, while it can preserve the high portion of noise-free pixels. In this work, an effective noise detecting method for enhancing the median filter is introduced. It is called decision method (DM) filter. The DM is very simple technique, and does not need an extensive calculation. Conducting intensive simulation reveals that the proposed filter may outperform significantly the standard techniques widely used in image processing. It will be demonstrated that the filter is capable of reducing the impulse noise even in situations with noise density.

The remaining sections of this paper are as follows. Impulse noise is described in section 2. Section 3 represents some types of median filter and their advantages and disadvantages. Section 4

focuses on, the introduced proposed median-based filter. Section 5 is devoted to the analysis of the proposed method depending on the density of impulsive noise. This section also contains a number of simulations, tests and filtering results. Finally, the conclusion and the suggestions for the future research domain are summarized in the last section.

2. Impulse noise

Noise is a phenomenon that contaminates an image (generally a signal). Some kinds of noise affect images during some process of image capturing. In fact, noise can limit the quality of an image during acquisition, formation, storage, and transmission processes [3], [10]. In acquisition process noise can affect the image so that the captured image would not clearly reflect the real scene. Moreover, noise can be produced due to the discrepancies in the hardware such as thermal excitation of CCD sensors, and dirt and scratches on the lenses [3]. Furthermore, noise is added to images when the acquired signal is converting to a digital signal in order to be stored and processed.

Images are often degraded by impulse noise [10] because of malfunction in the CCD sensors, faulty memory locations in hardware, and transmission in a noisy channel [6]. Impulse noise is mathematically given in (1).

$$I_{noisy}(i,j) = \begin{cases} R(i,j), & with \quad probability \quad r \\ I(i,j) & with \quad probability \quad 1-r \end{cases} \quad (1)$$

Where, I, I_{noisy}, and R are the noise-free image, noisy image, and random numbers, respectively. The parameter r is noise ratio [7], [8], [10], [11]. To characterize Equation 1 completely, R component can be any number between n and m as long as [n, and m] are the dynamic range of I. Salt-and-pepper noise and random valued noise are the two common types of impulse noise. Providing that noisy pixels take just n or m, the impulse noise will be called salt-and-pepper noise. Otherwise, the noise is called random valued noise [7], [8], [11].

3. Median filter

Various filtering schemes have been introduced over the last two decades to address impulse noise removal. In this regard median filter is the most popular filter [4]-[8], [10] and significant developments of this filter have been reported such as adaptive median filter [5], weighted median filter (WMF) [6], [9], and recursive weighted median (RWM) filter [6]. Standard median operator ranks the intensities of the pixels within a filtering window and replaces the center pixel with the median value. Despite changing some characteristics of an image, the impulse noise will be significantly suppressed by median filter. However, if the noise level is high (over 50%), the filter will smear the details and edges and may lose in noise removing [6]. To limit this deficiency, first, noisy pixels should be identified and then replaced by the filter operator, while other pixels remain unchanged [5]. Based on this fact, different remedies of the median filter, called decision-based [5], [11], [12] and switching filter [2], good at detecting noise even at a high noise density, have been introduced. In this paper, a novel median-based filter is proposed, which is capable of differentiating among noisy pixels and noise-free pixels which is simple and needs few computations.

4. Proposed method (DBM Filter)

The ideality of the proposed filter is designing a filter in such a way that the identity operator acts on the noise-free samples and noisy pixels are affected by the filter operation. In order to provide a trade-off between the identity filter and the median filter, the proposed method DBM is equipped with a novel significantly simple noise detecting method, namely DM.

In this paper, an image is considered as a vector, made of the rows of the image. In the vector scheme, the followed pixels in the same row are still the followed pixels and the pixel before the last pixel of the row is the followed pixel of the second pixel of the next row. Note that the first row, the last row, the first column, and the last column are skipped in the vector scheme. Therefore, the image $I_{n \times m}$ will be $V_{N \times 1}$ in the vector scheme, where $N = (n-2) \times (m-2)$. A window $W_i(p)$ is a two-dimensional array of pixels with the size $i \times i$, where i is an odd integer and p is the center pixel of the window.

For detecting the noise in DM, the difference between two followed pixels in V is compared with a threshold (d) and the following algorithm is used. The threshold d is not constant and can be changed based on the algorithm provided below. The parameter 'Step' is a predefined value, added to (d) depending on the condition ($|v_{i-1}-v_i|$) $>d$ is satisfied. In some cases, especially when the noise density is less than 50 percent, the probability, which shows how many noisy pixels are immediate neighbors, is very low. Then, providing that a pixel is detected as a noisy pixel, the condition for detecting the next pixel as a noisy one is getting harder by increasing d.

Otherwise, parameter (d) is changed to the pre-defined threshold. The role of 'Step' is very important in detecting noises more accurately and preserving edges.

- Threshold=d
- If ($|v_{i-1}-v_i|>d$) {v_i= median (W_3 (v_i)), d= d + Step}
- Else {d= Threshold}

Where, $|\cdot|$ denotes absolute operator, v_i denotes i^{th} component of V, and W_3 is the filtering window with the size 3×3. Based on the algorithm, if the difference between two followed pixels is greater than the threshold (d), the pixel is noisy and the median operation must be applied to it. Otherwise, the pixel is noise-free and the identity operation can be applied.

5. Simulations and Experimental Results

To evaluate the DBM method in removing noise from MR images, several simulations on an original MR image, shown in Figure 1, are carried out. In this paper, the original image is degraded by impulse noise with the presence of 10 and 20 per cent of noise density shown in Figure 2(a) and Figure 2(b). To set the initial values, the window size is kept 3×3 and the threshold (d) varies from 1 to 180 in order to obtain the best result. Additionally, the parameter 'Step' is 5 in all the experiments. The results, shown in Figure 3 and Figure 4, imply that the method is successful in removing noise and obtaining acceptable result. Moreover, as these results and studies taken up on the other MR images, optimum threshold (d) is in the range of 55-65.

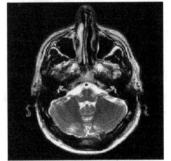

Figure 1. Original image.

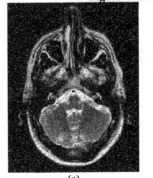 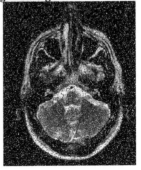
(a)   (b)

Figure 2. Degraded images, (a) 10 per cent noise density; (b) 20 per cent noise density.

Figure 3 (a) and Figure 3 (b) indicate, when the threshold d is less than 35, the edges are not preserved and the image is blurred. In this case, although the noise is removed from noisy pixels visually-acceptable, some other characteristics of the image are faded. Figure 3 (c), shows the noisy pixels become noise free and the characteristics of the image are remained unchanged. Figure 3 (c) also shows the best result among other results where the threshold is in the range of 55 to -65. Regarding Figure 3 (d), where the thresholdis larger than 65, some small spots expanding the size are clear, when the threshold become larger. Consequently, preserving the characteristics of the image and preventing some undesired changes the threshold should be chosen in the range [55, 65]. According to the results shown in Figure 4, all the

above-mentioned results can be gained. In addition, based on our previous study finding and the result in this study shows, the optimum threshold is in the range [55, 65], where the noise reduction rate is maximum.

Figure 5 (a) and Figure (b) show that how many noisy pixels remain after applying the method for 10 and 20 per cent noise, respectively. It is clear that the best thresholds can be obtained in the range [55, 65]. The experiment has been repeated for 50 times and the plots shown in Figure 5(a) and Figure5(b) are the average of the experiments. In addition, all experiments are shown in a small plot on the top of the average plot. According to Figure 5(a) and Figure 5(b), the dynamic of all experiment results are almost the same for each noise density.

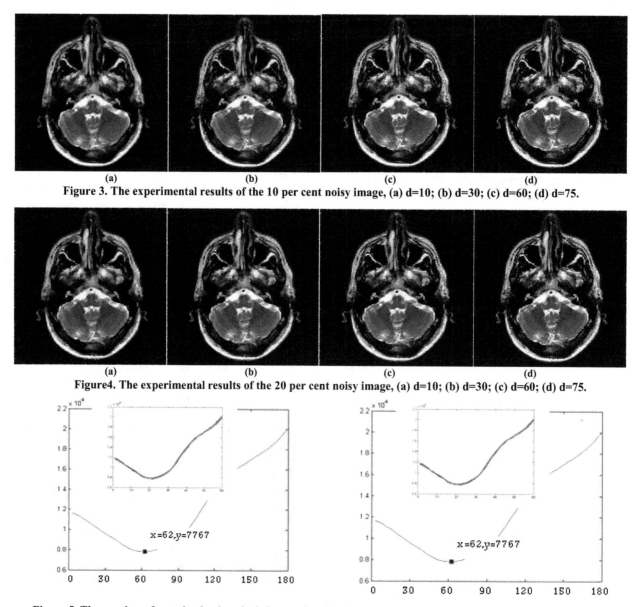

(a)   (b)   (c)   (d)

Figure 3. The experimental results of the 10 per cent noisy image, (a) d=10; (b) d=30; (c) d=60; (d) d=75.

(a)   (b)   (c)   (d)

Figure4. The experimental results of the 20 per cent noisy image, (a) d=10; (b) d=30; (c) d=60; (d) d=75.

Figure 5. The number of remained noisy pixels by varying the threshold d (a) noise density 10%, (b) noise density 2.

6. Conclusion

In this paper, we have proposed a novel method for impulse noise removing in MR images. A new approach is introduced with a novel method, called decision method, for detecting noisy pixels. The proposed decision based on the median filter, applies the median operation to noisy pixels and leaves healthy pixels unchanged. Consequently, redundant operations will be eliminated. In turn, it leads to a fast and accurate approach.

The proposed method attempts to differentiate between noisy and healthy pixels, but this is not guaranteed in all cases. In other words, the method may detect a healthy pixel as a noisy pixel and vice versa. Further studies should be conducted to adjust parameters d and *Step* both locally and adaptively, in order to improve the results in the future domain of the research.

References

[1] Thangavel, K., Manavalan, R., & Laurence Aroquiaraj, I. (2009). Removal of Speckle Noise from Ultrasound Medical Image based on Special Filters:

Comparative Study. ICGST-GVIP Journal, (vol. 9, Issue 3, pp. 25-32).

[2] Pandey, R. (2008). An Improved Switching Median filter for Uniformly Distributed Impulse Noise Removal. WASET (vol.28, pp. 349-351).

[3] Lakshmiprabha, S. (2008). A New Method of Image Denoising Based on Fuzzy Logic. Medwell, International Journal of Software Computing (vol. 3, no. 1, pp. 74-77).

[4] Hamza, A. B., & Krim, H. (2001). Image Denoising: A Nonlinear Robust Statistical Approach. IEEE Transactions on Signal Processing (vol. 49, no. 12, pp. 3045-3054).

[5] Lukac, R., & Smolka, B. (2003). Application of the Adaptive Center-Weighted Vector Median Framework for the Enhancement of cDNA Microarray Images. International Journal of Applied Mathematics and Computer Science (vol. 13, no. 3, pp. 369-383).

[6] Vijay Kumar, V. R., Manikandan, S., Ebenezer, D., Vanathi, P. T., & Kanagasabapathy, P. (2007). High Density Impulse Noise Removal in Color Images Using Median Controlled Adaptive Recursive Weighted Median Filter. IAENG, International Journal of Computer Science.

[7] Chan, R. H., Hu, C., & Nikolova, M. (2004). An Iterative Procedure for Removing Random-Valued Impulse Noise. DRAFT.

[8] Chan, R. H., Ho, C. W., & Nikolova, M. (2004). Salt-and-Pepper Noise Removal by Median-Type Noise Detectors and Detail-Preserving Regularization. DRAFT.

[7] Chan, R. H., Hu, C., & Nikolova, M. (2004). An Iterative Procedure for Removing Random-Valued Impulse Noise. DRAFT.

[8] Chan, R. H., Ho, C. W., & Nikolova, M. (2004). Salt-and-Pepper Noise Removal by Median-Type Noise Detectors and Detail-Preserving Regularization. DRAFT.

[9] Weng, B., Aysal, T. C., & Barner, K. E. (2007). Polynomial Weighted Median Image Sequence Prediction. IEEE Transactions on Circuits Systems and Video Technology (vol. 17, no. 12).

[10] Deepti, G. P., Borker, M. V., & Sivaswamy, J. (2008). Impulse Noise Removal from Color Images with Hopfield Neural Network and Improved Vector Median Filter. IEEE Computer Society 6th Indian Conference of Computer Vision Graphic Image Processing (pp. 17-24).

[11] Cai, J. F., Chan, R. H., & Nikolova, M. (2008). Fast Two-Phase Image Deblurring under Impulse Noise. DRAFT.

[12] Dinet, E., & Robert-Inacio, F. (2007). Color Median Filtering: a Spatially Adaptive Filter. In Proceedings of Image and Vision Computing (pp. 71-76), Hamilton, New Zealand.

21

Dynamic anomaly detection by using incremental approximate PCA in AODV-based MANETs

M. Alikhani[*], M. Ahmadi Livani

Faculty of Electrical and Computer Engineering Tarbiat Modares University

*Corresponding author: m.alikhany@gmail.com (M. Alikhani)

Abstract

Mobile Ad-hoc Networks (MANETs) in contrast to other networks have more vulnerability because of having nature properties, such as dynamic topology and no infrastructure. Therefore, a considerable challenge for these networks, is a method expansion that can specify anomalies with high accuracy at network dynamic topology alternation. In this paper, two methods were proposed for dynamic anomaly detection in MANETs, namely IPAD and IAPAD. The anomaly detection procedure consists of three main phases: Training, detection and updating the two methods. In the IPAD method, to create the normal profile, we used the normal feature vectors and principal components analysis in the training phase. In detection phase, during each time window, anomaly feature vectors based on their projection distance from the first global principal component specified. In updating phase, at end of each time window, normal profile updated by using normal feature vectors in some previous time windows and increasing principal components analysis. IAPAD is similar to IPAD method with a difference that each node use approximate first global principal component to specify anomaly feature vectors. In addition, normal profile will be updated by using approximate singular descriptions in some previous time windows. The simulation results using NS2 simulator for some routing attacks show that an average detection rate and an average false alarm rate in IPAD method had 95.14% and 3.02% respectively. The IAPAD method had 94.20% and 2.84% respectively.

Keywords: MANETs, Dynamic Anomaly Detection, Routing attacks, Incremental Principal Component Analyses.

1. Introduction

Mobile Ad hoc Networks (MANETs) are collections of wireless and mobile nodes that there is not any fixed infrastructure, such as base stations. In recent years, the advent of wireless devices was the cause of these networks potential growth. Today, MANETs are used in military battlefield, emergency rescue and vehicular communications because of its easy and rapid development [1]. In MANETs for sake of nodes mobility, network topology changes rapidly. Due to lack of centralized management in these networks, each node accomplishes routing process.

Intrusion detection methods are divided into two main categories: Signature-based detection and anomaly detection [2]. In signature-based detection methods, known intrusion patterns compared with incoming traffic and if patterns matched, intrusion is recognized. Advantage of this method is low false alarm rate and its disadvantage is lack of new intrusion detection. In anomaly detection methods, first, a profile of network normal behavior created then any traffic deviated from created profile detected as an intrusion. Advantage of this method is new intrusions detection and its disadvantage is the high false alarm rate.

In this paper, we proposed two methods named IPCA and IAPAD, which let normal profile get updated dynamically. Proposed methods contain three phases: Training, Detection and Updating. IPAD method, in training phase, creates network normal profile by using normal feature vectors. In detection and updating phase, a normal profile gets updated by using normal feature vectors in each time window. IAPAD method, in training phase, calculates an approximate singular description for normal feature vectors in each time window, then in detection phase, IAPAD calculates approximate covariance matrix by using approximate singular description.

In the updating phase by approximate covariance matrix, singular value parsing calculates the first approximate global principal component. Evaluations show that proposed methods have significant performance.

In section II, we imply related works in MANETs anomalies detection field. In section III, AODV protocol and in section IV, the attacks against this protocol described shortly. In section V, we have a description about how to select features. In section VI, principal components analysis is explained. In section VII, anomaly detection based on increasing principal components is explained. In section VIII, dynamic anomaly detection based on increasing approximate principal components analysis is represented. In section IV, accomplished simulation results are reported for evaluation. Finally, in section VI, we state the conclusion of this paper.

2. Related works

Huang et al. [3] proposed a method that uses a cross-feature analysis to capture inter-feature correlation patterns in the normal traffic. They create normal profile by using a C classifier and the network normal traffic. C classifier applied on every f_i feature and a C_i classifier will be created as sub model. Finally, these sub models will be used as normal profile. In this method, normal profile just created from training data and always is stable. Regarding to nodes dynamic behavior in MANET, fixed normal profile cannot qualify current network state well.

Huang et al. [4] used both specification-based and statistical-based approaches to detect attacks on AODV. First, they model AODV normal behavior by an extended finite state automaton (EFSA), according to its specifications. EFSA model is utilized for anomaly behaviors detection and they are deviated from descriptions. Statistics training algorithms with statistical properties are used for anomaly behaviors detection that is essentially statistical. In this method, normal profile is always fixed and does not alter with nodes behavior changes.

Sun et al. [5] proposed a method focusing on the mobility in MANETs. In this method, first, in training phase, various models of routing actions mobility has been collected and the link change rate (LCR_{recent}) average will be calculated for each mobility level. Collected routing actions utilized for normal profile creation. Then, in detection phase, each local intrusion detection system calculates link change rate for its own nodes, which are recent routing actions alternatively. Among normal profiles, a profile selected its LCR has less Euclidean distance with LCR_{recent}. In each time slot, each node calculates LCR as for its new and old neighbors. Therefore, LCR calculating does not spot the whole of inter-network nodes. However, attention must be paid for that network estate change and this is because of other network nodes with a sudden appearance and disappearance. When node's behavior in detection phase is different from training phase, using a predefined normal profile cannot describe network behavior well.

Kurosawa et al. [6] proposed a method with dynamic learning to detect anomalies in MANETs. This method updates training data in symmetric time slots. They used three features to model AODV protocol normal behavior that of course the protocol behavior complexity cannot be a model well with these three features. In this method, network normal profile considered as normal data average. Their method is only able to detect Blackhole attack and is not able to detect more attacks.

Nakayama et al. [7] proposed a method to detect dynamic anomaly that use principal components analysis for network normal profile creation. This method used normal data global covariance in sequential time slots for a created profile update. For each time slot, a weight is considered and is used as a factor in covariance calculating. This method uses weigh covariance in principal components calculating (WPCA). In this method, global covariance will be calculated inexactly.

Raj et al. [8] proposed a dynamic learning system to detect Blackhole attack. In this system, the node that received RREP packet compares packet's sequential number with a threshold value that updated dynamically. If the sequential number was greater than threshold value, RREP packet transmitter should be added to black list as an attacker node. This method is just able to detect Blackhole attack and is unable to detect other attacks.

3. AODV routing protocol

AODV protocol is a reactive routing protocol [9]. Protocol uses destination sequence number concept in DSDV routing protocol for maintaining last routing information. Suppose, start node S attempts to communicate with destination node D. In lack of routing information aspect, S starts path discovery via a RREQ packet broadcasting to its neighboring nodes. By receiving RREQ packet having fresh routing information, each neighbor node replies S node via a RREP packet. Otherwise, a hop count field increases RREQ packet unit age and broadcasts this packet again to its neighbors. Also keeps routing information to create inverse path. N_i node to make sure about routing information freshness compares destination sequence number in RREQ packet with a D node's sequence number in its own routing table. If a D node's sequence number in routing table is lesser, this sequence number will be updated with destination sequence number at RREQ packet. If node N receives several RREP packets, select the packet that has greater destination sequence number. If destination sequence number of received RREP packets is equal, the packet will be selected which has lesser hop count. The start node starts a data packet sending as soon as first RREP packet receives. Each node for make sure about active paths validity, broadcasts a HELLO packet alternatively to its neighbors. When a node detects a link fraction, announce that to other nodes by creating a REEP packet. Figure 1 shows routing process in AODV protocol.

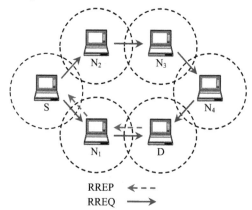

Figure 1. Routing process in AODV protocol

4.Attacks against AODV protocol

A) Classification of attacks

Attacks against AODV protocol are divided into four categories:

1) Route Disruption: A malicious node either destroys an existing route or prevents a new route from getting established.

2) Route Invasion: A malicious node adds itself into route between source and destination nodes.

3) Node Isolation: A given node is prevented from communicating with any other nodes. It differs from route disruption in the route disruption is targeting at a route with two given nodes, while node isolation is targeting at all possible routes to or from a given node.

4) Resource Consumption: The communication bandwidth in the network or storage space at individual nodes is consumed.

In the following, we give a short description of some typical routing attacks on AODV [10].

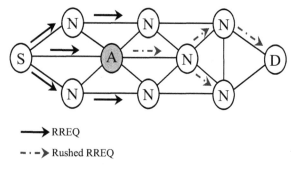

—→ RREQ

—·—► Rushed RREQ

Figure 2. Rushing Attack

B)Typical Attacks

1) Rushing Attack: Each source node establishes routing process by a RREQ packet transmission. In each routing process, each intermediate node just accepts the first received RREQ packet and ignores repetitive packets. Also, each intermediate node leads received RREQ packets after a delay. Malicious node by abusing these properties, immediate after each RREQ packet receiving, sends it to the next node. By this method, probability of malicious node standing between source and destination path will increases [11]. Fig. 2 shows a rushing attack example. In this figure, N_6 and N_7 nodes receive directed RREQ packet faster than other directed packets by malicious node.

2) Neighbor Attack: In AODV protocol, each intermediate node adds its ID in the RREQ/RREP packets before forwarding it to the next node. In neighbor attack, malicious node forward RREQ or RREP packet to the next node without its ID adding. Malicious node's wrong behavior makes other nodes to save false information about its neighbors in routing tables.

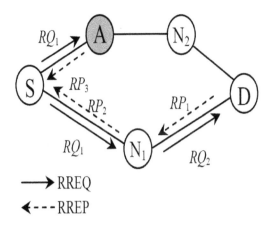

Figure 3. Blackhole Attack

3) Blackhole Attack: Malicious node with false routing information transmission claims that it has an optimized path to destination node. With this false claim, other nodes send their packets to the malicious node [12]. In AODV routing protocol, malicious node can perform this attack by sending a fake RREP packet to the source node. Figure 3 shows a Blackhole attack example. Source node S attempts to communicate with destination node D. Also, suppose, node D sequence number value in node S routing table is 20. Node N_1 by receiving RQ_1 packet forwards that to node D. malicious node A by receiving RQ_1 packet responses to node S with RP_3 packet. Node S according to destination sequence number field selects introduced path by malicious node and transmits its data to invalid node Z. Above packets details are presented in Table 1.

Table 1. The rreq/rrep packet in blackhole attack

	RQ_1	RQ_2	RP_1	RP_2	RP_3
Source IP Address	S	N_1	D	N_1	Z
Destination Sequence Number	20	20	21	21	30
Origin IP Address	S	S	S	S	S
Destination IP Address	D	D	D	D	D
Hop Count	1	2	1	2	1

4)Flooding RREQ Attack: Generally, RREQ packets will be broadcasted for new paths finding. Malicious node broadcasts because of network resources construction and alternatively many of fake RREQ packets.

5.Features definition

The appropriate feature selection for anomalies detection in routing process is the first and the most important action that must be performed. In this paper, nineteen features are used for anomaly detection in MANETs. These features are classified in four categories:

*1) Traffic data related features:*Each node in the network can send, receive and forwards data packet. These actions against data packets can define three features.

*2) Path discovery related features:*RREQ and RREP used for between source and destination nodes path finding and routing tables updating. By using these packets and various actions performed on them can define various features.

*3) Path interruption related features:*Some of paths disrupted cause of node mobility. Paths disrupting will be a cause of RREQ and RREP packets missing. For snatched paths reparation in AODV protocol, RERR packet is used. Proportionate these attributes can define several properties.

*4) AODV protocol specific featur*e: Difference average between destination sequence number in received RREP packet and destination sequence number in transmitted RREQ packet can be defined as a feature in each node.

The first class features are beneficial for data traffic anomaly behavior detection that can be due to a Denial of Service (DoS). The second class features are beneficial for attacks detection creating anomaly in network with routing protocol behavior change. The third class features indicant is seen routing faults rate in the network. Some of attacks alter routing faults rate through creating anomaly in the network. In Blackhole attack, malicious creates anomaly in network normal behavior by fake RREP packets that contains a great destination sequence number transmission. The fourth class features are beneficial for detect of this type of anomaly. In Table 2, name and description of each feature represented.

6.Principal components analysis

Principal component analysis (PCA) is a well-known method for patterns analysis in data [9]. By PCA, the first principal component φ that shows data approximate distribution is calculated. Let X be an $n \times p$ data matrix, whose rows are the feature vectors and columns are the features:

$$X = \begin{bmatrix} x_1^1 & x_1^2 & \cdots & x_1^p \\ x_2^1 & x_2^2 & \cdots & x_2^p \\ \vdots & \vdots & \ddots & \vdots \\ x_n^1 & x_n^2 & \cdots & x_n^p \end{bmatrix}, \qquad (1)$$

Let, $\hat{X}$ is a column-center matrix of X:

$$\hat{X} = (I - \frac{1}{n} e_n e_n^T) X \qquad (2)$$

Principal components of X are obtained by singular vector decomposition (SVD) [9] of $\hat{X}$ matrix [7]:

$$\hat{X} = U\Sigma V^T \tag{3}$$

where U and V are left and right singular vectors of $\hat{X}$ matrix respectively, and $\Sigma = \mathrm{diag}(\sigma_1, ..., \sigma_p)$ is a diagonal matrix with singular values. In this paper, the quadruple (n, V, Σ, μ) is called as s singular description of X and represents with D_X.

Table 2. The features

Type	Feature	Description
CBR Traffic	NumSentCbrPkt	Number of sent CBR data packets
	NumRecvCbrPkt	Number of received CBR data packets
	NumFwdCbrPkt	Number of forwarded CBR data packets
Route Discovery	NumSentRReqPkt	Number of sent RREQ packets
	NumRecvSameSrcRReqPkt	Number of received RREQ packets with the same source address as the node
	NumRecvSameDstRReqPkt	Number of received RREQ packets with the same destination address as the node
	NumRecvDiffSrcDstRReqPkt	Number of received RREQ packets with the different source and destination address of the node
	NumFwdRReqPkt	Number of forwarded RREQ packets
	NumSentSameDstRRepPkt	Number of sent RREP packets with the same destination address as the node
	NumSentDiffDstRRepPkt	Number of sent RREP packets with the different destination address of the node
	NumRecvSameSrcRRepPkt	Number of received RREP packets with the same source address as the node
	NumRecvDiffSrcRRepPkt	Number of received RREP packets with the differentsource address of the node
	NumFwdRRepPkt	Number of forwarded RREP packets
Path Disrupting	NumSentRErrPkt	Number of sent RERR packets
	NumRecvRErrPkt	Number of received RERR packets
	NumFwdRErrPkt	Number of forwarded RERR packets
	NumDropRReqPkt	Number of dropped RREQ packets
	NumDropRRepPkt	Number of dropped RREP packets
Protocol Specific	AvgDiffDstSeqNum	Average difference at each time slot between destination sequence number of received RREP packet and stored sequence number in the node

In this description, V is principal components and μ is a column-center vector of X. We can use the first principal component φ for describes X. Let, C_X is covariance matrix of X:

$$C_X = \frac{1}{n-1} X^T (I - \frac{1}{n} e_n e_n^T) X \tag{4}$$

Right singular vectors of X are equal to principal components of C_X, also the kth special value of C_X is equal to the kth square of $\hat{X}$ matrix singular value:

$$C_X = \frac{1}{n-1} V\Sigma^2 V^T \tag{5}$$

where, V and $\Sigma^2 = \mathrm{diag}(\lambda_1, ..., \lambda_p) = \mathrm{diag}(\sigma_1^2, ..., \sigma_p^2)$ are principal components matrix and eigenvalues matrix of X respectively. According to (5) specified that the equation can gain X singular description by analyze singular values of $(n-1)C_X$ matrix.

7. Dynamic anomaly detection based on ipca

In this section, we proposed an increasing principal components analysis method named IPAD for dynamic anomaly detection in MANETs. In this method, each time window t contains several time slots. In each time slot $t_i \in t$, each node collects a x_{it} feature vector on its traffic.

$$x_{it} = [x_{it}^1, x_{it}^2, ..., x_{it}^p]^T, \tag{6}$$

where each x_{it}^j is a measurable feature. So, each t time window, collects each node of $X(t)$ matrix from feature vectors. In this paper, to establishing normal profile and anomaly detection, 19 mentioned features are used.

A $x_{it} \in X(t)$ feature vector is called normal if agrees with network normal traffic in t time window. Set of normal feature vectors in t time window is represented with $X_N(t)$ and set of whole normal feature vectors in m maximum time window before t is represented with $N_X(t)$.

$$N_X(t) = \bigcup_{\tau=t-m+1}^{t} X_N(\tau) \tag{7}$$

IAPAD method contains three phases: *Training*, *Detection* and *Updating* from which any of these three phases are describe on resumption.

Training Phase:

In this phase, each node collects $N_X(0)$ matrix from feature vectors by its traffic supervision at beginning, then scales each values of $N_X(0)$ features to [0,1] slot. Finally, $\varphi(0)$ first principal component calculating creates a network normal profile. Figure 4 shows the pseudocode of training phase.

Normalization of feature vectors:

The value of each feature vector can have a considerable difference with each other. So, when distance of between two feature vectors is calculated, the features with larges values conquest on features with lower values. For making sure about the whole of features, they have same affection on distance calculation, each $x_{i0}^j \in N_X(0), j=1,...,p$ feature vector values must scale with in [0,1] slot.

$$\hat{x}_{i0}^j = \frac{x_{i0}^j - \min(x^j(0))}{\max(x^j(0)) - \min(x^j(0))} \quad (8)$$

That $\min(x^j(0))$ and $\max(x^j(0))$ are the smallest and greatest j feature values in $N_X(0)$ respectively.

---

procedure Training

---

input:
   A set of normal feature vectors $N_X(0)$
output:
   A normal profile $P(0) = (\varphi(0), \mu(0), d_{max}(0))$
begin
Scale each feature of $N_X(0)$ to the range of [0,1]
Obtain the column-centered matrix $\hat{N}_X(0)$
Obtain the column-means vector $\mu(0)$
Compute the first principal component $\varphi(0)$
for each feature vector $x_{i0} \in N_X(0)$ **do**
      Compute the projection distance $d_p(x_{i0}, \varphi(0))$
   end for
$d_{max}(0) = \max_i \left\{ d_p(x_{i0}, \varphi(0)) \right\}$
end procedure

Figure 4. The training phase

Establishing a Normal Profile:

For the normal profile creation, at first, each node generates $\hat{N}_X(0)$ column-centered matrix for $\hat{N}_X(0)$. Then by $\hat{N}_X(t)$ matrix singular value decomposition calculates the first $\varphi(0)$ principal component and each $x_{i0} \in N_X(0)$ feature vector's projection distance from $\varphi(0)$ is attained.

$$d_p(x_{i0}, \varphi(0)) = (\| x_{i0} - \mu(0) \|^2 - (\varphi(0)^T \cdot (x_{i0} - \mu(0)))^2)^{\frac{1}{2}} \quad (9)$$

where $\mu(0)$ is $N_X(0)$ column-means vector.

On resume, the maximum of projection distance of all x_{i0} feature vectors from $\varphi(0)$ is calculated and uses that for anomaly detection:

$$d_{max}(0) = \max_i \left\{ d_p(x_{i0}, \varphi(0)) \right\} \quad (10)$$

Finally, uses $(\varphi(0), \mu(0), d_{max}(0))$ triplet for $P(0)$ normal profile creation.

Detection Phase:

In this phase, each node during each t time window collects $X(t)$ matrix from feature vectors by its traffic supervision. Then scale features values of each $x_{it} \in X(t)$ feature vector by using minimum and maximum features values in $N_X(t-1)$ and then compares scaled feature vectors with $P(t-1) = (\varphi(t-1), \mu(t-1), d_{max}(t-1))$ normal profile to detect anomaly traffic.

---

procedure Detection

---

input:
   A normal profile $P(t-1) = (\varphi(t-1), \mu(t-1), d_{max}(t-1))$
   A set of feature vectors $X(t)$
output:
   A set of normal feature vectors $X_N(t)$
begin
$X_N(t) = \varnothing$
Scale each feature of $X(t)$ using min and max of $N_X(t-1)$
for each feature vector $x_{it} \in X(t)$ **do**
      Compute the projection distance $d_p(x_{it}, \varphi(t-1))$
   if $d_p(x_{it}, \varphi(t-1)) \leq d_{max}(t-1)$ **then**
      $X_N(t) = X_N(t) \cup \{x_{it}\}$
   end if
end for
end procedure

Figure 5. The detection phase

Anomaly Detection:

For anomaly detection, each node calculates projection distance of each $x_{it} \in X(t)$ feature vector from $\varphi(t-1)$ that $\varphi(t-1)$ is the first global principal component until $t-1$ time window. If calculated projection distance were greater than $d_{max}(t-1)$, x_{it} would be detected as an anomaly feature vector:

$$\begin{cases} d_p(x_{it}, \varphi(t-1)) > d_{max}(t-1) & : \text{Anomaly} \\ d_p(x_{it}, \varphi(t-1)) \leq d_{max}(t-1) & : \text{Normal} \end{cases} \quad (11)$$

Figure 5, shows the pseudo code of detection phase.

Normal Profile Updating Phase:

In this phase, each node at each t time window ending, if normal network state is detected, updates normal profile in this time window by using normal feature vectors. Thus, first, add collected normal feature vectors in t time window to $N_X(t-1)$:

$$N_X(t) = N_X(t-1) \bigcup X_N(t) \qquad (12)$$

That $X_N(t)$ is set of collected normal feature vectors in t time window. Nodes mobility in MANETs is cause of topology similar to network behavior alternation. Each set of feature vectors shows the network state and its connection time. By considering to the rapid behavior changing of network, this feature vectors set cannot show the network state in further times well. So, weight to each set of feature vectors can be useful for dynamic anomaly detection. Assume, $x_{i\tau} \in N_X(t)$ normal feature vector in τ time window be collected, an oblivion relation calculate this feature vector weight in current t time window:

$$w_{i\tau}(t) = \begin{cases} w_0 e^{-\alpha r_m(\tau,t)\Delta T(t-\tau)} & (t-m) \leq \tau \leq t \\ 0 & \text{otherwise} \end{cases} \qquad (13)$$

That $\alpha \in [0,1]$ and w_0 parameters is determined by a user. ΔT is time window length and $r_m(\tau,t)$ is network topology changing rate between τ and t time windows. Network topology changing rate is determined by using neighbor nodes number:

$$r_m(\tau,t) = \frac{|N(\tau) - N(t)| + |N(t) - N(\tau)|}{n}, \qquad (14)$$

That n is the number of whole nodes in the network. $N(\tau)$ and $N(t)$ are neighbor nodes index in τ and t time windows, respectively. Each node just uses a set of collected normal feature vectors in maximum m previous time window. $w_{i\tau}(t)$ weights be bounded by (15) relation:

$$\sum_{\tau=t-m+1}^{t} w_{i\tau}(t) = 1 \qquad (15)$$

If weight of one normal feature vector is lesser from a ε threshold value, the feature vector will be deleted form $N_X(t)$ set.

For normal profile updating, at first, each node by using relation (2), generates $\hat{N}_X(t)$ column-centered matrix for $N_X(t)$, then by $\hat{N}_X(t)$ matrix singular value analysis, calculates the first $\varphi(t)$ global principal component and finally the maximum projection distance of whole $x_{i\tau} \in N_X(t)$ feature vectors from $\varphi(t)$ is attained:

$$d_{\max}(t) = \max_{i,\tau} \left\{ d_p(x_{i\tau}, \varphi(t)) \right\} \qquad (16)$$

The $(\varphi(t), \mu(t), d_{\max}(t))$ triplet shows $P(t)$ updated normal profile. In Figure 6, represent normal profile updating in each node.

---

procedure Updating

input:
     A set of normal feature vectors $N_X(t)$
output:
A normal profile $P(t) = (\varphi(t), \mu(t), d_{\max}(t))$
begin
     for each feature vector $x_{i\tau} \in N_X(t)$ **do**
         Update the weight $w_{i\tau}(t)$
   if $w_{i\tau}(t) < \varepsilon$ **then**
   $N_X(t) = N_X(t) \backslash \{x_{i\tau}\}$
   endif
     end for
Obtain the column-centered matrix $\hat{N}_X(t)$
Obtain the column-means vector $\mu(t)$
     Find the global first principal component $\varphi(t)$
for each feature vector $x_{i\tau} \in N_X(t)$ **do**
     Compute the projection distance $d_p(x_{i\tau}, \varphi(t))$
     end for
$d_{\max}(t) = \max_i \left\{ d_p(x_{i\tau}, \varphi(t)) \right\}$
end procedure

Figure 6. The updating phase

8. Increasing proximate components analysis based dynamic anomaly detection:

In IPAD method, first global principal component calculating is accomplished strictly. In this method, at each time window ending for normal profile updating, a set of normal feature vectors in previous time windows is used. This problem is cause of calculating complexity and memory usage in crescent in each node. For this problem solution, an increasing proximate principal components analysis based method is proposed which named IAPAD that decreases calculating complexity and memory usage in each node. In this method, each node in current time window t, calculates $\tilde{D}_N(t) = (n(t), \tilde{V}(t), \tilde{\Sigma}(t), \mu(t))$ proximate singular description for $X_N(t)$ normal feature vectors. The time window in this description, $n(t)$ is number of normal feature vectors, $\tilde{V}(t)$ is the matrix which contains k is the most important principal component, $\widetilde{\Sigma}(t)$ is the matrix contains k the greatest special value and μ is $X_N(t)$ column-means vector. The k is the minimum value that relation (17) confirmed that:

$$\frac{\sum_{j=1}^{k}\lambda_j^2}{\sum_{j=1}^{p}\lambda_j^2} \geq T_\alpha \tag{17}$$

where p and λ_j^2 are the number of features and $X_N(t)$ matrix special value, respectively. T_α Named as proximate quality threshold bound and thus by using k the most important principal component can describe T_α percent of data dispersion. The set of proximate singular descriptions in maximum m time window before t is presented with $\widetilde{N}_D(t)$:

$$\widetilde{N}_D(t) = \bigcup_{\tau=t-m+1}^{t}\widetilde{D}_N(\tau) \tag{18}$$

Each node instead of $N_X(t)$ normal feature vectors set maintaining, and keeps $\widetilde{N}_D(t)$ singular description set.

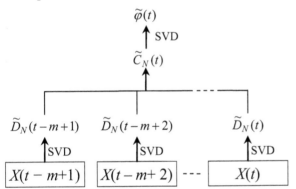

Figure 7. IAPAD Description

IAPAD method contains three phases: *Training, Detection* and *Updating* noted above are similar to IPAD method with a difference that instead of $\varphi(t)$ first global principal component, used from $\widetilde{\varphi}(t)$ first proximate global principal component. For calculation of $\widetilde{\varphi}(t)$, first, $\widetilde{C}_N(t)$ proximate covariance matrix for normal feature vectors in maximum m previous time window calculated [13]:

$$\widetilde{C}_N(t) = \frac{1}{n-1}\sum_{\tau=t-m+1}^{t}\begin{pmatrix}(\widetilde{V}(\tau)\widetilde{\Sigma}^2(\tau)\widetilde{V}^T(\tau)+\\ n(\tau)(\mu(\tau)-\mu)(\mu(\tau)-\mu)^T)\end{pmatrix} \tag{19}$$

where μ is global column-means vector.

$$\mu = \frac{1}{n}\sum_{\tau=t-m+1}^{t}n(\tau)\mu(\tau) \tag{20}$$

Value of n is equal to normal feature vectors total in maximum m time window:

$$n = \sum_{\tau=t-m+1}^{t}n(\tau) \tag{21}$$

Then, by $\widetilde{C}_N(t)$ matrix singular value analysis, the first $\widetilde{\varphi}(t)$ proximate global principal component is calculated. Figure 7 shows a description for this method.

9. Time complexity analysis:

In this section, the first $\varphi(t)$ global principal component time complexity calculating in IPAD method and the first $\widetilde{\varphi}(t)$ proximate global principal component in IAPAD will be compared with each other.

In IPAD method, in each t time window, each node, first, generates $\hat{N}_X(t)$ column-centered matrix for $N_X(t)$. This matrix generation is done in time of $O(mnp)$, that n is normal feature vectors number average in each time window, then by $\hat{N}_X(t)$ matrix singular value analysis, calculates the first $\varphi(t)$ global principal component in time of $O(mnp^2)$. Therefore, $\varphi(t)$ calculating has $O(mnp^2)$ time complexity.

In IAPAD method, in each t time window, each node, at first, calculates $\widetilde{D}_N(t)$ proximate singular description for normal feature vectors in this time window. This singular description calculating is accomplished in time of $O(np^2)$. Then calculates $\widetilde{C}_N(t)$ proximate covariance matrix by using singular description in maximum m previous time window. This covariance matrix calculating is accomplished in time of $O(np^2)$. Finally, by $\widetilde{C}_N(t)$ matrix singular value analysis, calculates the first $\widetilde{\varphi}(t)$ proximate global principal component in time of $O(p^3)$. Therefore, $\widetilde{\varphi}(t)$ calculating has $O(np^2)$ time complexity. Mention is require that $p < n$ and $m < n$.

10. Experiment results:

In this section, at first, impact of routing attacks on MANETs performance will be studied, and then accomplished experiment results are described for proposed IPAD and IAPAD performance evaluation.

Simulation Environment:

We conducted MANET simulations using the NS2 simulator [14]. In this simulation, CBR traffic model with 512-byte data packet length generated through *cbrgen.tcl* program and RWP [15] mobility model in a region dimensioned 1000m×1000m and 5sec pause time, generated by the *setdest* program. The number of whole network nodes, includes 30 nodes. Table 3 shows a detail of simulation parameters represented.

Table 3. Simulation Parameters

Parameter	Value
Simulation Time	10000(s)
Mobility Model	RWP
Pause Time	5(s)
Maximum Mobility	35(m/s)
Maximum Connections	30
Maximum bandwidth	2(Mbps)
Number of Malicious Nodes	1
Simulation Area	1000(m) × 1000(m)
Transmission Rate	250(m)
Traffic Model	CBR
Routing Protocol	AODV

In RWP mobility model, each node for a specific time length (pause time) locates in a simulation region and after this time ending, a random destination selection with a steady speed moves from [0, *maxspeed*] slot to the destination. The node after reaching to a new location, positions there within pause time and then begins mobility process again.

Figure 8 shows malicious node and a node of the network mobility model. In this figure, pause time 5 seconds and speed bound [0, 35m/s] has been selected. Regarding to Figure 8(a) specified that malicious node attends steady in different location of simulation environment. Therefore, any anomaly behavior from malicious affects entire network. This local distribution is also seen for other network nodes (Figure 8(b)).

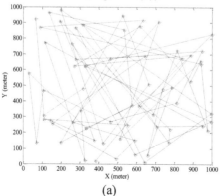

(a)

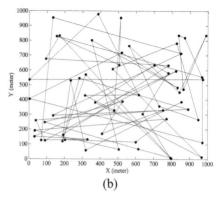

(b)

Figure 8. Mobility model in RWP: a) Malicious Node b) A Node of The Network

Impact of routing attacks on Network Performance

In this section, we will study about impact of routing attacks on MANET performance by using NS2 simulator. There are many parameters such as End-To-End Delay and Packet Delivery Ratio for MANET performance measurement [16]. End-To-End Delay refers to the time taken for a packet to be transmitted across a network from source to destination. The packet delivery ratio of a receiver is defined as the ratio of the number of data packets, which actually received over the number of data packets transmitted by the senders. Routing attacks are cause of network performance decrement by anomaly creation in the network.

Figure 9 shows, impact of blackhole attack on End-To-End Delay parameters and Packet Delivery Ratio represented respectively. As seen on this figure, in the above attack occurrence time, network performance decreased noticeably.

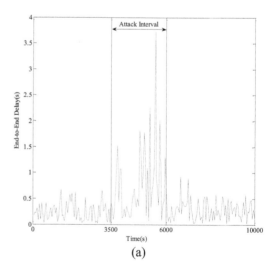

(a)

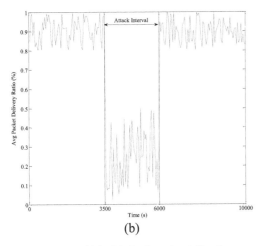

(b)

Figure 9. Impact of Blackhole Attack: a) On the average End-To-End Delay Parameter b) On the average Packet Delivery Ratio

Performance Evaluation

To establish the normal profile, a set of feature vectors are collected by each node of network normal traffic. This set of feature vectors collecting time length are considered 1000sec and time slot length for any feature vector collecting considered 5sec. One of the nodes selected is a malicious node. This node, accomplished rushing, neighbor, blackhole and flooding RREQ attacks is distinctly in 3500-6000sec-time interval. An experiment, used for normal feature vectors sets and proximates singular descriptions in maximum $m=5$ previous time window, and the length of time window is also selected $\Delta T=200$s.

For performance evaluation of anomaly detection methods, two measures used detection rate (DR) and false alarm rate (FAR). Detection rate is a percent of anomaly feature vectors that have been detected successfully. False alarm rate is a percent of normal feature vectors that have been detected as anomaly feature vectors inaccuracy.

Figure 10 shows detection rate and false alarm rate averages in IPAD and IAPAD have been compared within different values of time window length $\Delta T=500$, 400, 300, 350, 200, 150, 100s represented detection rate and false alarm rate in this figure. This calculated as blackhole, rushing, neighbor and flooding RREQ attacks detection rate and false alarm rate averages.

Regarding to the above figure specified that by time window length decrement or by the other hand, by normal profile rapid updating, detection rate increases. In addition, IAPAD method has similar performance with IPAD method and it has lesser time complexity and lesser usage memory. Table 4 shows detection rate and false alarm rate

averages in IAPAD method has been compared by the m parameter different values. Regarding to this table specified that by m value decrement, for normal profile updating used from lesser singular description. Therefore, the updated normal profile cannot model current time network normal traffic well with regarding to the low number of singular description, false alarm rate increased. By m value increasing, using from old singular descriptions to normal profile is updated. Therefore, the updated normal profile cannot model current time network normal traffic well with regarding to the high number of old singular descriptions, and detection rate are decreased.

In Figure 11, for one of network nodes, feature vectors projection distance from the first proximate global principal component during blackhole attack represented. In 3500-6000sec-time distance, projection distance of many collected feature vectors during each time window from the first proximate global principal component calculated to its prior time window is greater than a threshold bound. So, this feature vectors detected as anomaly and above time distance is considered as attacks time distance.

Figure 12 shows detection rate and false alarm rate averages in IAPAD method compared with each other through different time window length values. Regarding to this figure, specified that by time window length decrement to 200 seconds, detection rate increases noticeably. For time windows with under 200sec, detection rate against false alarm rate is so fiddling. So, in accomplished experiment, time window length selected as $\Delta T=200$.

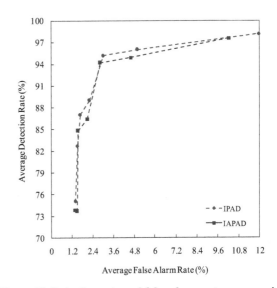

Figure 10. Detection rate and false alarm rate averages in IPAD and IAPAD

Table 4. Detection rate and false alarm rate averages in IAPAD

m	Rushing		Neighbor		Blackhole		Flooding	
	DR	FAR	DR	FAR	DR	FAR	DR	FAR
1	100	36.07	100	29.02	100	30	100	31.21
3	95.83	8.76	97.5	6.06	95.42	5.99	95.17	7.81
5	95.83	3.27	96.53	2.63	92.22	2.29	92.23	3.16
10	87.5	1.38	93.75	2.02	85	1.13	89.95	1.80

determines importance level of each principal component to complex variance percent calculating for each i principal component used the relation (22):

$$CPV_i = \frac{\lambda_i}{\sum_{j=1}^{p} \lambda_j} \qquad (22)$$

where λ_i is special value corresponding with ith principal component.

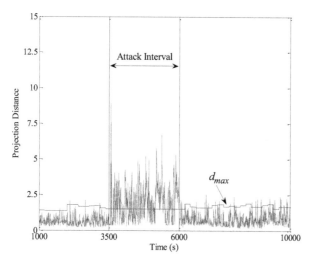

Figure 11. Projection distance from the first proximate global principal component during blackhole attack

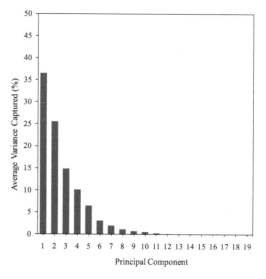

Figure 13. CPV average in detection phase represented for each principal component in IAPAD method

Figure 13 shows, cumulative percent variance average in detection phase represented for each principal component in IAPAD method. Regarding to this figure specified that the first principal component describes only 36.46 percent of total variance. Therefore, for better data dispersal modeling, it is necessary the second principal component considered with 25.45 percent of total variance in proximate singular description calculation time. In this face, with $k=2$ principal component can describe 69.91 percent of data dispersal. In accomplished experiment, threshold bound of approximation quality considered equal to $T_\alpha = 50\%$.

Table 5 shows impact of updating in performance on the IAPAD method represented for various type of attacks. Regarding to this table, the detection rate and false alarm rate averages in IAPAD method in the face of normal profile updating are 94.20 and 2.84 percent, respectively and in the face of nonupdating are 59.72 and 1.70 percent in respectively.

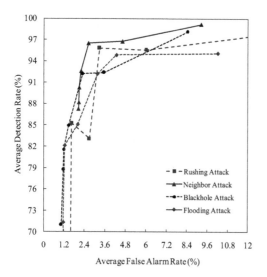

Figure 12. Detection rate and false alarm rate averages in IAPAD method compared with each other by different time window length values

Cumulative Percent Variance (CPV) [17] is a standard that represents the described variance percent by the most important principal components. In fact, complex variance percent

Table 5. Impact of updating in performance on the IAPAD method

	With Updating		Without Updating	
	DR	*FAR*	*DR*	*FAR*
Rushing	95.83	3.27	38.60	0.64
Neighbor	96.53	2.63	74.60	2.88
Blackhole	92.22	2.29	58.4	1.32
Flooding	92.23	3.16	67.28	1.98
Average	94.20	2.84	59.72	1.70

Figure 14 shows detection rate and false alarm rate in IPAD, IAPD and WPCA [7] methods compared with each other. Regarding to this figure specified that detection rate average in IPAD and IAPAD methods is 4/40 and 3/46 percent better than WPCA method, when false alarm rate average in WPCA method is 0/53 and 0/35 percent better than IPAD and IAPAD methods.

Table 6 shows detection rate and false alarm rate averages in IPAD and IAPAD and WPCA methods compared with each other by the breakdown of each rushing, neighbor, blackhole and flooding RREQ attacks.

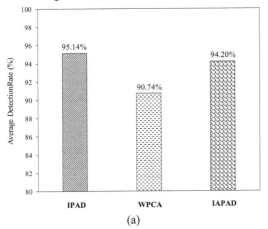

(a)

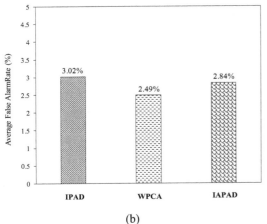

(b)

Figure 14. Comparison of the performance of IPAD, IAPD and WPCA: a) average detection rate b) average false alarm rate.

Table 6. Comparison of the performance of IPAD and IAPAD and WPCA methods

	Rushing		Neighbor		Blackhole		Flooding	
	DR	*FAR*	*DR*	*FAR*	*DR*	*FAR*	*DR*	*FAR*
IPAD	**98.33**	4.6	**96.53**	2.84	91.88	2.35	**93.83**	**2.27**
IAPAD	95.83	3.27	96.53	2.63	**92.22**	**2.29**	92.23	3.16
WPCA [7]	90.83	**2.18**	95.34	**2.22**	86.52	2.39	90.25	3.18

11. Conclusion

Regarding to dynamic topology in MANETs, the cause of alternation in network behavior, using from a predefined normal profile cannot describe network behavior well. Therefore, it is necessary to update normal profile coincident with network nodes and topology behavior alternations. In this paper, two increasing principal components analysis based on methods named IPAD and IAPD proposed for dynamic anomaly detection in MANETs. Proposed methods contain 3 phases: Education, detection and normal profile updating. In IPAD method, in education phase, by using normal feature vectors and principal component analysis, network traffic usual profile will be created. In detection phase, during each time window, a set of feature vectors to be collected and anomaly feature vectors based on their projection distance detected from the first global principal component. In the updating phase, in each time window ending, usual profile will be updated by using normal feature vectors in this time window and previous time windows. Updating is accomplished by using increasingly principal components analysis and an oblivion relation. IAPAD method is similar to IPAD method with this difference that any node in any time window calculates a proximate singular description of normal feature vectors in the time window. In addition, instead of the first global principal component used from the first proximate global principal component for anomaly feature vectors detection. Usual profile updated by using proximate singular description in current and previous time windows. For MANETs implementation and also rushing, neighbor, blackhole and flooding RREQ attacks used from NS2 simulator. Routing attacks are the cause of network performance decrement through creating anomaly in the network. By using the End-To-End Delay and Packet Delivery Rate parameters, impact of above attacks network performance is studied. The performance evaluation of proposed IPAD and IPAD methods used two standards, which are detection and false alarm rate. Regarding to the accomplished experiment results, IAPAD method has a similar performance with IPAD method when it has less time complexity and usage memory.

Time windows length in the usual profile updating time can be affective on the detection rate and false alarm rate increment of decrement. The IAPAD method performance is evaluated by various values of time window length. Regarding to experiment results in this method, $\Delta T=200s$ time window length establishes a better balance between detection rate and false alarm rate. In IAPAD method for proximate singular description, calculation is used for k the most important principal component. Using standard of Cumulative Percent Variance (CPV) importance level of each principal component in detection phase is calculated. Regarding to experiment results in normal face, $k=2$ principal components can describe 61.91 percent of data dispersal. Various experiment accomplishments, performance of IPAD and IAPAD methods are compared with WPCA method for rushing, neighbor, blackhole and flooding RREQ attacks detection. Experiment results show that detection rate average in IPAD and IAPAD methods respectively 4.40 and 3.46 percent better than WPCA method. False alarm rate average in WPCA method is only 0.53 and 0.35 percent better than IPAD and IAPD methods.

Acknowledgment

This work was supported by Iran Telecommunication Research Center (ITRC) under contract number 88-12-128.

References

[1] Chlamtac, I., Conti, M. and. Liu, J. J.-N. (2003). Mobile ad hoc networking: imperatives and challenges. Ad Hoc Networks, 1(1), 13–64.

[2] Debar, H., Dacier, M. and Wespi, A. (2000). A revised taxonomy for intrusion detection systems," Annals of Telecommunications. 55(7–8), 361–78.

[3] Huang, Y. A., Fan, W., Lee, W. and Yu, P. S. (2003) Cross-feature analysis for detecting ad-hoc routing anomalies, in Proceedings of the 23rd International Conference on Distributed Computing Systems. 478–487, Washington DC, USA.

[4] Huang, Y. A. and Lee, W. (2004) Attack analysis and detection for ad hoc routing protocols, in Proceedings of the 7th International Symposium on Recent Advances in Intrusion Detection (RAID'04), 125–145, Riviera, French.

[5] Sun, B., Wu, K. and Pooch, U. (2004). Towards adaptive intrusion detection in mobile ad hoc networks," in Proceedings of the IEEE Global Telecommunications Conference (GLOBECOM'04), 6, 3551–3555, Dallas, TX, USA.

[6] Kurosawa, S., Nakayama, H., Kato, N., Jamalipour, A. and Nemoto, Y. (2007). Detecting blackhole attack on AODV-based mobile ad hoc networks by dynamic learning method," International Journal of Network Security, 5(3), 338–346.

[7] Nakayama, H., Kurosawa, S., Jamalipour, A., Nemoto, Y. and Kato, N. (2009). A dynamic anomaly detection scheme for AODV-based mobile ad hoc networks," IEEE Transactions on Vehicular Technology, 58(5), 2471–2481.

[8] Raj, P. N. and Swadas, P. B. (2009). DPRAODV: A dynamic learning system against blackhole attack in AODV-based MANET," International Journal of Computer Science Issues, 2(1), 54–59.

[9] Perkins, C. E., Royer, E. M. B. and Das, S. R. (2003). Ad hoc on-demand distance vector (AODV) routing. RFC 3561, July 2003.

[10] Ning, P. and Sun, K. (2003). How to misuse AODV: A case study of insider attacks against mobile ad-hoc routing protocols," in Proceedings of the 4th Annual IEEE Information Assurance Workshop, pp. 60–67, West Point, NY, USA, June 2003.

[11] Chun Hu, Perrig, A. and johnson, D. B. (2003). Rushing attacks and defense in wireless ad hoc network routing protocols," in Proceeding of the 2nd ACM workshop on Wireless security, pp. 30–40, San Diego, CA, USA, September 2003.

[12] Hongsong, Y. C., Zhenzhou, J. and Mingzeng, H. (2006). A novel security agent scheme for AODV routing protocol based on thread state transition. Asia Journal of Information Technology. 5(1), 54–60.

[13] Qu, Y., Ostrouchov, G., Samatova, N. and Geist, A. (2002). Principal component analysis for dimension reduction in massive distributed data sets, in Proceedings of the SIAM International Conference on Data Mining, Washington, DC, USA, April 2002.

[14] Fall, K. and Varadhan, K. (2002). The NS manual, The VINT Project, UC Berkeley, LBL, USC/ISI, and Xerox PARC, April 2002.

[15] Camp, T., Boleng, J. and Davies, V. (2002). A survey of mobility models for ad hoc network research," Wireless Communications and Mobile Computing. 2(5), 483–502.

[16] Nguyen, H. L. and Nguyen, U. T. (2008). A study of different types of attacks on multicast in mobile ad hoc networks," Ad Hoc Networks, 6(1), 32–46.

[17] Jolliffe, I. T. (2002). Principal Component Analysis, Second Edition, New York: Springer-Verlag.

22

On improving APIT algorithm for better localization in WSN

S. M. Hosseinirad [1*], M. Niazi [2], J. Pourdeilami [2], S. K. Basu [1], and A. A. Pouyan [2]

1. Department of Computer Science, Banaras Hindu University, India.
2. Department of Computer Engineering, Shahrood University of Technology, Shahrood, Iran.

*Corresponding author: hosseinirad@gmail.com (S. M. Hosseinirad).

Abstract

In Wireless Sensor Networks (WSNs), localization algorithms could be range-based or range-free. The Approximate Point in Triangle (APIT) is a range-free approach. We propose modification of the APIT algorithm and refer as modified-APIT. We select suitable triangles with appropriate distance between anchors to reduce PIT test errors (edge effect and non-uniform placement of neighbours) in APIT algorithm. To reduce the computational load and avoid useless anchors selection, we propose to segment the application area to four non-overlapping and four overlapping sub-regions. Our results show that the modified-APIT has better estimation's performance of localization for different sizes of network for both grid and random deployments in terms of average error and time requirement. For increasing the accuracy of localization and reduction of computation time, every sub-region should contain minimum 5 anchors. Variations of the size of a network and radio communication radius of anchors affect the value of average error and time requirement. To have more accurate location estimation, 5 to 10 anchors per sub-region are effective in modified-APIT.

Keywords: *WSN, Localization, APIT, Anchor, Coverage.*

1. Introduction

WSNs contain tiny and smart sensors nodes which are battery-operated (limited life-time) [1]. They have limited storage, processing, communication capacity to sense various physical phenomena in the environment. WSNs greatly extend our ability to track, monitor and control a physical phenomenon [2]. Applications include industrial process monitoring and control, military and civilian applications, healthcare, environment and habitat monitoring, home automation, traffic control, etc. [3]. The typical tasks of networked sensor nodes are to collaborate and aggregate huge amount of sensed data from the physical environment. Sensors are deployed either inside a phenomenon being monitored or very close to it. WSNs are highly distributed self-organized systems [4].

WSNs have attracted a lot of research attention in the recent years. It offers a rich area of research, in which a variety of multi-disciplinary tools and concepts are employed [5]. WSN protocols and algorithms must possess self-organizing capabilities. This allows random deployment in inaccessible terrains or hostile terrains.

Localization issue in WSN has attracted a lot of research effort in the recent years [6]. Estimation of the physical positions of the nodes is one of the fundamental and critical issues in Geographical Positional System (GPS) [7]. Accurate estimation of location is useful in sensor network services such as information processing, sensing coverage [8], location directory service [9], management and operation of the network [10], location-based routing protocols [11], etc.

The positional information is essential to many location-aware sensor network communication protocols, such as packet routing and sensing coverage [12]. When an abnormal event occurs, the sensor node detecting the event needs the positional information to locate the abnormal event and report to the special node called the Base Station (BS) or sink(s). BS has higher capability compared to an ordinary sensor node.

Many different protocols and algorithms were proposed for localization in WSN. It is a challenging task to design practical algorithms for node localization, given the constraints that are usually imposed on the sensors [13].

Sensors may be deployed in an application area manually or randomly. Manual sensor deployment is applicable when the size of network is not large. Generally, in the case of harsh or hostile environment large number of sensors is randomly deployed. Positions of sensors are unknown because of random distribution, while applications in this type of networks need to know the source of the received information.

The Approximate Point in Triangle (APIT) is a range-free approach [14]. The main idea of APIT is to consider overlapping triangles. Localization with APIT algorithm leads to PIT test problem and the issue of time. In this paper, to reduce the computational load and avoid useless anchors selection, and increase the location estimation accuracy in APIT algorithm, we propose modification of the APIT algorithm and refer as modified-APIT. The paper is organized as: section 2 deals with localization algorithms, section 3 deals with APIT algorithm, section 4 deals with results and discussion, and section 5 concludes the paper.

2. Localization algorithms

The proposed localization protocols may be divided into two categories: range-based and range-free [15]. The range information can be acquired by using different protocols. These protocols use absolute point-to-point distance estimates (range) or angle estimates for calculating location [16]. The simplest possible localization solution is to attach a GPS. Time of Arrival (TOA) technique is used to estimate distance based on measurement of signal propagation time between two communicating nodes. It uses GPS as the basic localization system [17]. The Time Difference of Arrival (TDOA) measurement uses ultrasound signals to make the distance information estimation possible for nodes [18]. Measurements that are based on signal propagation time can be affected by multipath fading and noise interference; therefore, TOA and TDOA are impractical solutions for WSN localization. To augment and complement TDOA and TOA technologies, an Arrival of Angle (AOA) technique has been proposed that allows nodes to estimate and map relative angles between neighbours. It needs additional expensive hardware like a directional antenna or a digital compass [19]. So, AOA is not a good choice for

resource limited networks. Received Signal Strength Indicator (RSSI) technology has been proposed for hardware-constrained systems. It is another method based on signal strength and distance relation [20]. All range-based localization algorithms are relatively precise, but present a costly solution (expensive and energy consuming) for localization in large scale WSN [21].

Considering the hardware limitations of WSN devices, solutions using range-free localization are being pursued as a cost-effective alternative to the more expensive range-based approaches [22]. Generally, the positions of sensor nodes are not to be engineered or predetermined. The range-free protocols make no assumption about the availability or validity of such information as are required in the range-based estimates.

The centroid algorithm is simple and economic. It requires a lot of anchor nodes broadcasting their positions (via GPS) to compute position as the center of the connected anchor nodes. All the sensor nodes should be connected to the anchor node for good localization results [23]. However, it results in large errors in the case of low anchor ratio or distribution of them is not even, since the nodes are not uniformly distributed and the relationship between hop counts and geographic distances is very weak [24]; therefore, estimated locations tend to be inaccurate.

Distance Vector-Hop (DV-Hop) algorithm has been proposed based on distance vector routing concept [25]. It assumes a heterogeneous network consisting of sensing nodes and anchors. Instead of single-hop broadcasts, anchors flood and broadcast their location information throughout the network maintaining a running hop-count at each node along the way [26]. Consequently, other anchors can obtain minimum hop count to other anchors.

3. APIT algorithm and its modification

The APIT algorithm requires a small percentage of anchors and employs a novel area-based approach to perform location estimation by segmentation of the field. Moreover, these nodes can be equipped with high-powered radio transmitter.

The main idea of APIT for localization of nodes is to consider overlapping triangles. The vertices of these triangles are anchors. Bounding triangles are obtained using any group of three reference nodes, rather than the coverage area of a single node. In the APIT algorithm, the sensor nodes receive location information from the nearby anchors initially.

Second, the Point in Triangulation (PIT) test checks whether a sensor node is in a virtual triangle that is formed by connecting the three anchors from which signals are received. After the PIT test is done, the APIT algorithm aggregates the results through a grid SCAN algorithm [27]. The APIT algorithm calculates the Centre of Gravity (COG) of the intersections of all the overlapped triangles in which the node resides to determine its location.

Localization with APIT algorithm leads to two major issues: (i) PIT test problem, and (ii) anchor selection problem leading to increased time requirement. To solve these issues, we modify the APIT algorithm and call it the modified-APIT algorithm. By selecting suitable triangles with appropriate distance (discussed later) between anchors, we reduce PIT test errors (edge effect and non-uniform placement of neighbours) in APIT algorithm. To reduce the computational load and avoid selection of useless anchors, we propose to segment the application area to four non-overlapping and four overlapping sub-regions.

3.1. PIT test
The purpose of PIT test is to check whether a node is inside a triangle that is formed by three anchors. Every time, the node selects three possible anchors and apply the PIT test. When a node M is inside $\triangle ABC$, if M is shifted in any direction, the new position must be nearer to (or further from) at least one of the anchors A, B or C. Also, when a node M is outside of $\triangle ABC$ and M is shifted, there must exist a direction in which the position of M is closer to (or further from) all the three anchors A, B and C. When there is a direction such that a point adjacent to node M is closer to (or further from) anchors A, B and C simultaneously, then M is outside of $\triangle ABC$. Otherwise, M is inside $\triangle ABC$. This is named Perfect PIT test (PPIT). It can correctly determine whether node M is inside $\triangle ABC$ or not.

To perform PIT algorithm in WSN without the need of node movement, approximate PIT test method has been proposed that takes advantage of high node density in WSNs. To emulate the movement of a node in the PPIT, node uses neighbor information, exchanged via beaconing. If no neighbor of node M is closer to (or further from) all the three anchors A, B and C simultaneously, it is assumed that M is inside $\triangle ABC$. Otherwise, M is outside this triangle. APIT can only check a few directions (neighbors).

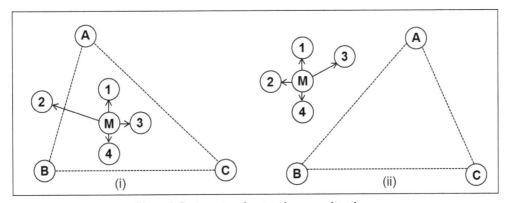

Figure1. In-to-out and out-to-in error situations.

It may be incorrect in the selection of its decisions (Figure 1) to determine the node's position. Although, node M is inside the triangle but APIT decides that it is outside.

The node is near to the edges and some of its neighbors are outside the triangle and further from all anchors in relation to node M. Consequently, node M mistakenly considers it is outside the triangle due to edge effect (In-to-out error, Figure 1 (node A). Although, node M is outside the triangle but since none of its neighbors are closer to (or further from) all anchors simultaneously, node M assumes it is inside the triangle (Out-to-in error, Figure 1 (node B).

3.2. Removing anomalies in PIT test
Selecting suitable triangles of anchors in PIT test is an important issue. In-to-out and out-to-in errors in PIT test is caused by edge effect and non-uniform placement of neighbors. When the triangles formed do not have appropriate sides and areas, these errors mostly occur (Figure 2).

The triangles of anchors should satisfy two conditions. These are: (i) sides of triangles should be comparable within a range. Narrow triangles should be eliminated from the considered set of triangles, because few number of nodes reside inside a very narrow triangle (one of its sides is short and the other two are very long)

Most of the neighbors of a node are located outside the triangle. Sides (x, y, z) of a triangle are to satisfy (1), where α and β are scalars.

$$(\alpha \times z \leq x + y \leq \beta \times z \text{ and } \alpha \times y \leq x + z \leq \beta \times y)$$

where $\alpha = 0.7$ and $\beta = 1.4$.   (1)

(ii) Because of random deployment of anchors in the environment, short distances among anchors are possible. In such a situation, they may form triangles with very small areas where a few nodes only can reside inside these triangles. They do not have utility in node localization process. Consequently, triangles with area less than a threshold are eliminated from the considered set of triangles. The area size should satisfy (2), where λ and γ are scalars.

$$\lambda \times A_{\text{Application}} \leq A_{\text{Triangle}} \leq \gamma \times A_{\text{Application}}$$

where $\lambda = \frac{1}{16}$ and $\gamma = \frac{1}{4}$ (2)

$A_{\text{Application}}$ is the area of the field of interest and A_{Triangle} is the area of the selected triangle.

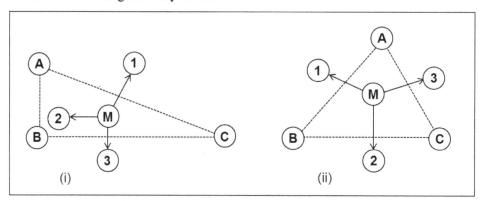

(i)   (ii)

Figure 2. Two instances of inappropriate triangles.

3.3. Appropriate anchor selection problem

Extension of covering area can lead to discontinuity of coverage, computational overload, and increase in localization errors. In APIT algorithm, anchors advertise their locations by using maximum power of radio communication. In addition to consumption of energy, it wastes the sensor nodes resources as well. Possibility of useless anchors selection is one of the major problems that may occur while using APIT algorithm in large area increasing the system cost. Receiving of signal by a sensor node from an anchor is not adequate for selection in localization. To reduce computational load and useless anchors selection, we propose that a new device named Super Anchors (SA) should be used in the environment. SAs are high-powered equipment with wide radio communication range and it broadcasts signal in the whole environment. They help other sensors to conserve energy and prevent wastage of resources. Segmenting the application area to four sub-regions, four SAs are located in the four corners.

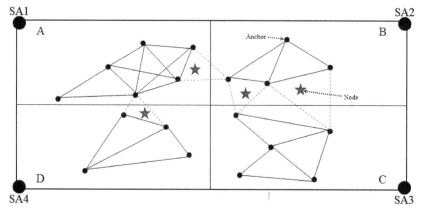

Figure 3. Non-formation of triangles because of residence of anchors in different sub-regions.

By comparing received signal strength of SAs, every node can determine its location in the sub-regions. Sensor nodes select only close by anchors co-located in the sub-region to estimate their location. With wide radio communications range, an anchor broadcasts its location information over a long distance.

Sometimes, more than one triangle may be formed in APIT algorithm for the specified nodes which are located near the external borders, but the nodes maybe outside of all of these triangles. Whole of the covering area except the formed triangle could be determined as a possible node location and COG (Centre of Gravity) is calculated for a large but wrong region. After the environment is equipped with SAs, the effect of location miscalculation error is decreased. The maximum error may be equal to the distance of the sub-region corners from its center (Figure 3). After addition of the SAs, same miscalculation error may happen for the nodes located near to the internal sub-region borders and it has negative effect on localization algorithm. The maximum error may be equal to the distance of the sub-region corner and its center. Triangles with dashed lines (Figure 3) can be used to localize the specified node.

To solve miscalculation of the nodes located near the internal sub-region borders, we propose to segment the environment to four non-overlapping and four overlapping regions. Each overlapping region covers about 30% of regions. Based on the received signals from the SAs, every node is able to determine its location in a sub-region through comparison of the received signal strengths. A node is co-located with a SA from which it has received signal of highest strength. After determination of the nearest SA, every node can estimate its sub-region (including overlapping and non-overlapping sub-region) location in the application area through comparison of the strengths of received signals. If the received signal strength from SA 'A' is greater than 70%

of the signal strength received from SA 'B' and if the signal strength of SA 'B' be greater than 70% of the signal strength of SA 'A' then the node is located in the overlapping region. Otherwise, it is located in the sub-region corresponding to the greater signal strength of the SAs. Through the same rule, a node determines the left or the right half of the environment. Based on the proposed method, every node may be located in a sub-region or an overlapping region. The anchors which are least common in one region are selected for triangle formation. Figure 4 shows non-localized nodes (□ and □) in the domain with four sub- regions, because they are located near the internal borders of the sub-regions (no triangles are formed). The nodes □ and □ have been successfully localized after segmenting the environment to four overlapping sub-regions in addition to considering four sub-regions (Figure 4).

The anchors #1, #2 and #3 have been used to localize the node □. Figure 4 shows that the anchor #1 is located in regions 4 and 8, and anchor #2 is located in regions 4, 7 and 8, and anchor #3 is located in regions 1, 5 and 8. These anchors are common in region 8, so they can be used to form triangles. Anchors #4, #5 and #6 have participated in node ★ localization. Anchor #4 is placed in regions 3, 6 and 7, and anchors #5 is placed in regions 3 and 7, and anchor #6 is placed in regions 2, 5 and 6. The common region of these anchors in region 6, they can be used to localize the node ★.

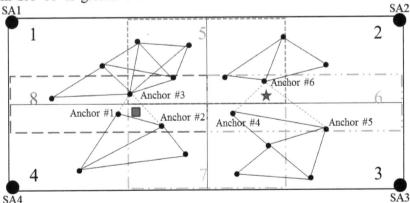

Figure 4. Localization of nodes ★ and ■ after segmentation of field to four non-overlapping and four overlapping sub-regions.

4. Results and discussion

In our study we applied APIT and modified-APIT algorithms on three different network sizes (100, 225, and 400) in a square shaped application area. Figures 5(a) and (b) show the localized sensors with APIT and modified-APIT respectively for a WSN with 100 sensors (the blue sensors determine locations of localized anchors sensors

and black sensors determine locations of localized ordinary sensors).

The algorithms are coded in MATLAB version 7 on Intel(R) core *i*5 CPU 650 3.2 GHz running Windows 7 professional. In APIT algorithm every sensor node is able to receive all anchors' signals to estimate its location. We assume limited percentage of sensor nodes (almost 10%) is equipped with GPS (anchors) to find and advertise its location. When the size of network is low, modified-APIT algorithm is not useful. For example, in a network with 100 sensor nodes, 10 sensors are used as anchors (10%). Therefore, in

every sub-region 2.5 anchors probably are deployed but to form a triangle three anchors are required. Also, for estimation accuracy we need more than one triangle for every sensor node.

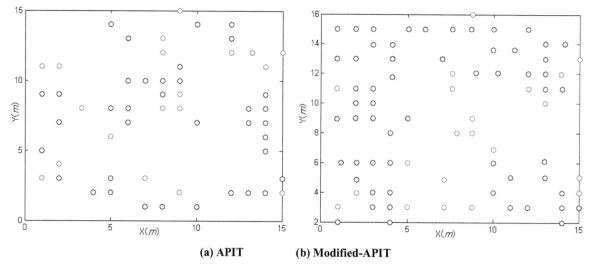

(a) APIT   (b) Modified-APIT

Figure 5. Localized sensors with APIT and modified-APIT.

We define a threshold for the number of anchors in every sub-region and we use minimum 5 anchors in every sub-region. Based on this, we assume that in a network of size 100, 20% of the sensor nodes are anchors. In addition to estimation accuracy, to conserve the energy, we find the threshold value for anchors' radio communication radius based on the number of localized sensors. We compare the APIT and modified-APIT algorithms based on average error and computational time. Average error is calculated by (3).

$$\text{Average error} = \frac{\sum_{i=1}^{n} | \text{Exact Location}_i - \text{Estimated Location}_i |}{n} \quad (3)$$

In the first part of this study, we apply APIT algorithm for three different sizes of network (100, 225, and 400) with grid and random deployments. Table 1 shows that the APIT algorithm has better performance for all sizes of network with random deployment in terms of average error and time requirement.

Table 1. Result of APIT algorithm.

WSN Size	Grid Deployment			Random Deployment		
	Time (s)	Avg. Error	No. of Sen.	Time (s)	Avg. Error	No. of Sen.
100	62.96	3.12	80	52.07	2.97	80
225	1245.48	3.83	202	1246.36	4.67	202
400	110039.1	6.82	360	109949.36	6.11	360

By increasing the size of the network, average error increases linearly and the time requirement increases non-linearly. In a large size network, sensors localization needs lots of time to calculate their location through the APIT algorithm. In the second part of this study we apply the modified-APIT algorithm on three different sizes of network (100, 225, and 400) with grid and random deployments (Table 2).
APIT consumes more time for sensors localization with more average error compared

with modified-APIT algorithm. Also, anchors have to consume more energy for location advertisement. In modified-APIT algorithm, by varying radio communication radius of anchors between 6m and 9m, all sensor nodes are localized. In the modified-APIT algorithm, the average value of this radius is 8m for grid and random deployments. Variation of the size of a network and the value of radio communication radius of anchors affect value of average error and localization time. Increasing the size of the network, the average error increased linearly but the amount of time required increased non-linearly. When the size of a network is increased, the number of anchor nodes in every sub-region is also increased. For example in a network with 225 sensors, every sub-region has 5 anchors and every sensor node can use 10 triangles for location estimation. When the size of the network is 400, every sub-region contains 10 anchors and sensors can use at least 120 triangles for localization. The results illustrate that with increment of anchors in every sub-region, the average error and time requirement are also increased. Therefore, for having more location estimation accuracy, we propose that 5 to 10 anchors per sub-region be used.

Table 2. Result of modified-APIT algorithm.

WSN Size	Grid Deployment				Random Deployment			
	R(m)	Time (s)	Avg. Error	No. of Sen.	R(m)	Time (s)	Avg. Error	No. of Sen.
	5	1.18	1.81	78	6	2.43	1.75	66
100	**6**	**2.05**	**1.83**	**80**	**7**	**3.57**	**1.83**	**80**
	7	2.51	1.87	80	8	3.67	1.85	80
	7.5	19.63	2.8	201.4	7.5	25.33	2.84	195
225	**8.5**	**24.05**	**2.83**	**202**	**8.5**	**27.73**	**2.93**	**202**
	9.5	34.42	2.96	202	9.5	30.64	2.72	202
	8	66.83	3.53	358	7	70.19	2.74	348
400	**9**	**92.46**	**3.63**	**360**	**8**	**105.41**	**3.12**	**360**
	10	103.27	3.73	360	9	18622	3.83	360

5. Conclusion

We proposed modification of the APIT algorithm and studied efficacy of the modified algorithm in terms of average error and computational time and compare with those of APIT with segmentation of the application area to four non-overlapping and four overlapping sub-regions. Our results show that the modified-APIT algorithm has better performance in terms of average error and time requirement for all sizes of network with random and grid deployments. To increasing accuracy of localization and prevention of localization complexity, every sub-region should contain minimum 5 anchors. Variations in the size of a network and radio communication radius of anchors affect average error and time requirement. Localization in a large size network using APIT algorithm needs lots of time compared to modified-APIT algorithm. APIT algorithm localizes sensor nodes with more average error compared with the modified-APIT algorithm. Also, in APIT algorithm, anchors consume more energy to advertise their locations. It reduces anchors' lifetime. For more accurate location estimation, 5 to 10 anchors per sub-region are effective in modified-APIT. Sensors localization based on the modified-APIT algorithm through clustering approach is our future plan of study.

References

[1] Akyildiz, I. F., Su, W., Sankarasubramaniam, Y. & Cayirci, E. (2002). Wireless sensor networks: a survey. Journal of Computer Networks, vol. 38, pp. 393-422, DOI: 10.1016/S1389-1286(01)00302-4.

[2] Anastasi, G., Conti, M., Di Francesco, M. & Passarella, A. (2009). Energy conservation in wireless sensor networks: A survey. Journal of Ad Hoc Networks, vol. 7, no. 3, pp. 537–568, DOI: 10.1016/j.adhoc.2008.06.003.

[3] Arampatzis, T., Lygeros, J. & Manesis, S. (2005). A Survey of Applications of Wireless Sensors and Wireless Sensor Networks. In: the Proceeding of 13th Mediterranean Conference on Control and Automation Limassol, pp. 27-29, DOI:10.1109/.2005.1467103.

[4] Akyildiz, I. F. & Kasimoglu, I. H. (2004). Wireless Sensor and actor Networks: Research Challenges. Journal of Ad Hoc Networks, vol. 2, no. 4, pp. 351-367, DOI: 10.1016/j.adhoc.2004.04.003.

[5] Zheng J. & Jamalipour, A. (2009). Wireless Sensor Networks, a networking perspective. Wiley, New York.

[6] Pal, A. (2010). Localization Algorithms in Wireless Sensor Networks: Current Approaches and Future Challenges. Journal of Network Protocols and Algorithms (Macrothink Institute), vol. 2, no. 1, DOI: 10.5296/npa.v2i1.279.

[7] Hofmann-Wellenhof, B., Lichtenegger, H. & Collins, J. (1993). Global Positioning System: Theory and Practice. Springer, New York.

[8] Yan, T., He, T. & Stankovic, J. A. (2003). Differentiated Surveillance Service for Sensor Networks. Proceedings of the 1st international

conference on Embedded networked sensor systems, USA, pp. 51-62.

[9] Li, J., Jannotti, J., De Couto, D. S. J., Karger, D. R. & Morris, R. A. (2000). Scalable location service for geographic ad-hoc routing. In: the Proceeding of International Conference on Mobile Computing and Networking (MOBICOM), pp. 120-130, DOI: 10.1145/345910.345931.

[10] Gengzhong, Z. & Qiumei, L. (2010). A Survey on Topology Control in Wireless Sensor Networks. In: the Proceeding of Second International Conference on Future Networks (ICFN 2010), pp. 376-380, DOI: 10.1109/ICFN.2010.31.

[11] Ko, Y. B. & Vaidya, N. H. (1998). Location-Aided Routing (LAR) in Mobile Ad Hoc Networks. In: the Proceeding of International Conference on Mobile Computing and Networking (MOBICOM) (1998), DOI: 10.1145/288235.288252.

[12] Xu, Y., Heidemann, J. & Estrin, D. (2001). Geography-informed Energy Conservation for Ad Hoc Routing. In: the Proceeding of International Conference on Mobile Computing and Networking (MOBICOM), vol. 1, DOI: 10.1145/381677.381685.

[13] Yu, K., Hedley, M., Sharp, I. & Guo, Y. J. (2006). Node Positioning in Ad Hoc Wireless Sensor Networks. Journal of IEEE International Conference on Industrial Informatics (2006), pp. 641-646, DOI: 10.1109/INDIN.2006.275636.

[14] He, T., Huang, C., Blum, B. M., Stankovic, J. A. & Abdelzaher, T. (2005). Range-Free Localization and Its Impact on Large Scale Sensor Networks. ACM Transactions on Embedded Computing Systems, vol. 4, no. 4, pp. 877-906, DOI: 10.1145/1113830.1113837.

[15] Datta, S., Klinowski, C., Rudafshani, M. & Khaleque S. (2006). Distributed localization in static and mobile sensor networks. In: the Proceeding of IEEE International Conference on Wireless and Mobile Computing, Networking and Communications, (WiMob'2006), pp. 69-76, DOI: 10.1109/WIMOB.2006.1696397.

[16] Garcia-Morchon, O. & Baldus, H. (2009). The ANGEL WSN Security Architecture. In: the Proceeding of third International Conference on Sensor Technologies and Applications (SENSORCOMM), pp. 430-435, DOI: 10.1109/SENSORCOMM.2009.71.

[17] Patwari, N., Hero, A., Perkins, M., Correal, N. & Dea, R. (2003). Relative location estimation in Wireless Sensor Networks. Journal of IEEE Transactions on Signal Processing (2003), pp. 2137-2148, DOI: 10.1109/TSP.2003.814469.

[18] Doherty, L., Pister, K. S. J. & El Ghaoui, L. (2001). Convex Position Estimation in Wireless Sensor Networks. In: the Proceeding of twentieth Annual Joint Conference of the IEEE Computer and Communications Societies (INFOCOM), vol. 3, pp. 1655-1663, DOI: 10.1109/INFCOM.2001.916662.

[19] Niculescu, D. & Nath, B. (2003). Ad Hoc Positioning System (APS) using AoA. In: Twenty-Second Annual Joint Conference of the IEEE Computer and Communications. IEEE Societies (INFOCOM), vol. 3, pp. 1734-1743, DOI: 10.1109/INFCOM.2003.1209196.

[20] Kumar, P., Reddy, L. & Varma, S. (2009). Distance measurement and error estimation scheme for RSSI based localization in Wireless Sensor Networks. In: the Proceeding of Fifth International Conference on Wireless Communication and Sensor Networks (WCSN), pp. 1-4, DOI: 10.1109/WCSN.2009.5434802.

[21] Liu, C., Wu, K. & He, T. (2004). Sensor Localization with Ring Overlapping Based on Comparison of Received Signal Strength Indicator. In: the Proceeding of IEEE International Conference on Mobile Ad-hoc and Sensor Systems (IEEE Cat. No.04EX975 2004), pp. 516-518, DOI: 10.1109/MAHSS.2004.1392193.

[22] Le, V. D., Dang, V. H., Lee, S. & Lee, S. H. (2008). Distributed localization in wireless sensor networks based on force-vectors. In: the Proceeding of International Conference on Intelligent Sensors, Sensor Networks and Information Processing (2008), pp. 31-36, DOI: 10.1109/ISSNIP.2008.4761958.

[23] Meguerdichian, S., Koushanfar, F., Potkonjak, M. & Srivastava, M. B. (2001). Coverage problems in wireless ad-hoc sensor networks. In: the Proceeding of twentieth Annual Joint Conference of the IEEE Computer and Communications Societies (INFOCOM), vol. 3, pp. 1380-1387, DOI: 10.1109/INFCOM.2001.916633.

[24] Sheu, J. P., Li, J. M. & Hsu, C. S. (2006). A distributed location estimating algorithm for wireless sensor networks. In: the Proceeding of IEEE International Conference on Sensor Networks, Ubiquitous, and Trustworthy Computing (SUTC). vol. 1, DOI: 10.1109/SUTC.2006.1636179.

[25] Rudafshani, M. & Datta, S. (2007). Localization in Wireless Sensor Networks. In: the Proceedings of the 6th international conference on Information processing in sensor networks (IPSN'07), pp. 51-60, DOI: 10.1145/1236360.1236368.

[26] Tian, S., Zhang, X., Liu, P., Sun, P. & Wang, X. (2007). A RSSI-based DV-hop Algorithm for Wireless Sensor Networks. In: the Proceeding of International Conference on Digital Object Identifier (WICOM 2007), pp. 2555-2558, DOI: 10.1109/WICOM.2007.636.

23

Designing stable neural identifier based on Lyapunov method

F. Alibakhshi[1*], M. Teshnehlab[2], M. Alibakhshi[3] and M. Mansouri[4]

1. Control Department, Islamic Azad University South Tehran Branch, Tehran, Iran.
2. Center of Excellence in Industrial Control, K.N. Toosi University, Tehran, Iran.
3. Young Researchers & Elite Club, Borujerd Branch, Islamic Azad University, Borujerd, Iran.
4. Intelligent System Laboratory (ISLAB), Electrical & Computer engineering department, K.N. Toosi University, Tehran, Iran.

*Corresponding author: Alibakhshi.fatemeh@gmail.com (F. Alibakhshi)

Abstract

The stability of learning rate in neural network identifiers and controllers is one of the challenging issues, which attract many researchers' interest in neural networks. This paper suggests adaptive gradient descent algorithm with stable learning laws for modified dynamic neural network (MDNN) and studies the stability of this algorithm. Also, stable learning algorithm for parameters of MDNN is proposed. By the proposed method, some constraints are obtained for learning rate. Lyapunov stability theory is applied to study the stability of the proposed algorithm. The Lyapunov stability theory guaranteed the stability of the learning algorithm. In the proposed method, the learning rate can be calculated online and will provide an adaptive learning rate for the MDNN structure. Simulation results are given to validate the results.

Keywords: *Gradient Descent Algorithm, Identifier, Learning Rate, Lyapunov Stability Theory.*

1. Introduction

In recent decades, soft computing is frequently used in business and industry. Artificial neural networks are essential parts of any computing software [4]. The most widely used neural network architecture is the multilayer feed forward neural network. The most popular approach for training the multilayer feed-forward neural network (FNN) is the backpropagation (BP) algorithm based on gradient descent (GD) method. Determining an appropriate learning rate for this algorithm is important. The training algorithms (learning rules) could be defined as "a procedure for modifying the weights and biases of a network in order to train the network to perform some tasks" [6,11]. The network model having a good function approximation capability through the training samples can well reflect the complex nonlinear relationship between objects [17].

However, one problem inherent within them is their convergence to local minima and the user set acceleration rates and inertia factor parameters that are sensitive to the learning process [1–3]. The FNNs with the BP learning algorithm have been used successfully in pattern recognition, optimization, classification, modeling,

identification and controlling [13,31]. However, the problems of the slow convergence rate, local minimum and instability are the most challenging issues in this algorithm.

In recent decades, many efforts have been made to improve the convergence of the BP algorithm. There are some works to improve BP algorithm in order to have online training [9,19-21]. For this algorithm determining, an appropriate learning rate is necessary, so that the learning process become stable. If the learning rate is large, learning may happen rapidly, but it may also become unstable. To ensure stable learning, the learning rate is small enough. Small learning rate may also lead to a long training time. These problems are inherent to the basic learning rule of FNN that are based on GD optimization methods [15,30]. The convergence properties of such algorithms are discussed in [5,7,12,15,16,18], and [22]. Learning algorithms based on GD includes real-time recurrent learning (RTRL), ordered derivative learning and so on [1].

Derivative-based methods have the advantage of fast convergence, but they tend to converge to local minima [2]. In addition, due to their dependence on the analytical derivatives, they are limited to specific objective functions, inferences, and MFs [2].

Some papers [1-3,25,26] have investigated the stability of fuzzy neural networks. The popular method for stability analysis is Lyapunov stability. Also, in [8,10,27,28] Lyapunov stability theorem is considered.

The learning algorithm in neural and fuzzy neural networks not only has the role of updating parameters but also has influence on stability and convergence. The stability and convergence of learning algorithms are rarely investigated in the papers. In this study, the stability of learning algorithm is addressed in dynamic neural networks.

In this paper, the main concern is using Lyapunov stability approach for determining stable learning rate in system identification via modified dynamic neural network. The GD training the parameters of update rule for MDNN is considered.

The rest of article is organized as follows: in section 2, the structure of the dynamic neural network is discussed. In section 3, MDNN learning algorithm applied to process. Simulations and results for three nonlinear systems are presented in section 4. Section 5 presents conclusions.

2. Dynamic neural network

In the feed forward artificial neural, a neuron receives its inputs from other neurons. The weight sum of these signals is the input to the activation function. The resulting value of the activation function is the output of a neuron. This output is branched out to other processing units. This simple model of the artificial neuron ignores many of the characteristics of its biological counterpart. For example, it does not take into account time delays that affect the dynamics of the system [23]. The dynamic neural network (DNN) for the first time proposed by Gupta [24]. The basic structure of dynamic neuron (DN) is shown in figure 1.

Each neuron composed of two units: the inhibitory (negative) unit and excitatory (positive) unit. The inhibitory units received the summation of positive inputs, a delay of own outputs and abstraction a delay of excitatory outputs by multiple to determined weights. The excitatory units received the summation of negative inputs, a delay of own outputs and abstraction a delay of initiatory outputs by multiple to the determined weights [29].

The final output of the neuron can be written as follow:

$$O_T(t) = O_E(t) + O_I(t) \qquad (1)$$

where, O_E, O_I are represent the output of excitatory (net_E) and inhibitory units (net_I), respectively and can be written as:

$$net_E(t) = a_0 X_E(t) + a_{11} net_E(t-1) - b_{12} net_I(t-1) \quad (2)$$

$$net_I(t) = b_0 X_I(t) + b_{11} net_I(t-1) - a_{12} net_E(t-1) \quad (3)$$

And:

$$net_T(t) = net_E(t) + net_I(t) \qquad (4)$$

where, X_E, X_I are the positive and negative inputs, respectively and the parameters of a_0, a_{11}, a_{12}, b_0, b_{11}, b_{12} are the weights of DN.

3. Stability analysis of learning algorithm

Suppose an MDNN as an identifier shown in figure 2.

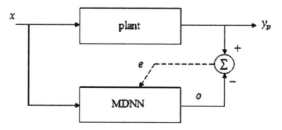

Figure 2. Modified dynamic neural network as the identifier.

Details of the MDNN network are illustrated in the figure 3.

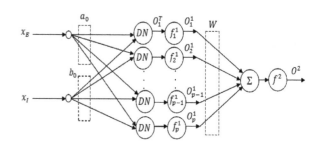

Figure 3. Modified dynamic neural network architecture.

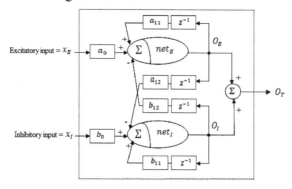

Figure 1. Structure of dynamic neuron [29].

Assume that the parameters of the MDNN are changed with time. In figure 3, $W(k)=[w_1(k),w_2(k),\ldots,w_p(k)]^T$ the is the weight vector of the MDNN output layer, $O^2(k)$ is the final output of MDNN and $O^1(k)$ is the output of hidden layer of MDNN, $O^T(k)$ is the output of DN neuron. DN structure of neurons is shown in figure 1. This network has n inputs in the input layer, p DN in the hidden layer and one conventional neuron in the output layer. $f^1(.)$ and $f^2(.)$ are nonlinear activation functions. According to figure 3 it is obvious that:

$$O^1(k)=f^1\left(net_T(k)\right),\ O^2(k)=f^2\left(WO^1(k)\right) \quad (5)$$

$$O(k)=O^2(k)=f^2\left(Wf^1\left(net_T(k)\right)\right) \quad (6)$$

The cost function for the training algorithm is defined as:

$$e(k)=y_p(k)-O(k),\ E(k)=\frac{1}{2}e^2(k) \quad (7)$$

where, $e(k)$ is real output error, $y_p(k)$ is the output of plant, $O(k)$ is the final output of MDNN. Weights of output layer are updated by GD method as follows:

$$W(k+1)=W(k)+\eta^o(k)\left(-\frac{\partial E(k)}{\partial W(k)}\right) \quad (8)$$

where, $\eta^o(k)$ is the learning rate parameters of the output layer, and we have:

$$\frac{\partial E(k)}{\partial W(k)}=\left(\frac{\partial E(k)}{\partial e(k)}\right)\times\left(\frac{\partial e(k)}{\partial O(k)}\right)\times\left(\frac{\partial O(k)}{\partial W(k)}\right) \quad (9)$$

$$=-e(k)\left(\frac{\partial O(k)}{\partial W(k)}\right)$$

From (8) and (9), it will be inferred that:

$$W(k+1)=W(k)+\eta^o(k)e(k)\left(\frac{\partial O(k)}{\partial W(k)}\right) \quad (10)$$

$$\Delta W(k)=\eta^o(k)e(k)\left(\frac{\partial O(k)}{\partial W(k)}\right)$$

$$D_W(k)=\frac{\partial O(k)}{\partial W(k)} \quad (11)$$

And the updating rule for hidden layer parameters by GD method is as follows:

$$\Gamma(k+1)=\Gamma(k)+\eta^h(k)\left(-\frac{\partial E(k)}{\partial \Gamma(k)}\right) \quad (12)$$

where, $\Gamma=[a_0\ a_{11}\ a_{12}\ b_0\ b_{11}\ b_{12}]$ is the weight

vector and, $\eta^h(k)$ is the learning rate of DN. Assuming $\Delta\Gamma(k)=\Gamma(k+1)-\Gamma(k)$ the weights are updated as follows:

$$a_0(k+1)=a_0(k)+\eta^h(k)\left(-\frac{\partial E(k)}{\partial a_0(k)}\right) \quad (13)$$

$$\frac{\partial E(k)}{\partial a_0(k)}=\left(\frac{\partial E(k)}{\partial e(k)}\right)\times\left(\frac{\partial e(k)}{\partial O(k)}\right)\times\left(\frac{\partial O(k)}{\partial a_0(k)}\right) \quad (14)$$

$$=-e(k)\left(\frac{\partial O(k)}{\partial a_0(k)}\right)$$

From (13) and (14), it will be inferred that:

$$\Delta a_0(k)=\eta^h(k)e(k)\left(\frac{\partial O(k)}{\partial a_0(k)}\right) \quad (15)$$

It can also be written as:

$$\Delta a_{11}(k)=\eta^h(k)e(k)\left(\frac{\partial O(k)}{\partial a_{11}(k)}\right) \quad (16)$$

$$\Delta a_{12}(k)=\eta^h(k)e(k)\left(\frac{\partial O(k)}{\partial a_{12}(k)}\right) \quad (17)$$

$$\Delta b_0(k)=\eta^h(k)e(k)\left(\frac{\partial O(k)}{\partial b_0(k)}\right) \quad (18)$$

$$\Delta b_{11}(k)=\eta^h(k)e(k)\left(\frac{\partial O(k)}{\partial b_{11}(k)}\right) \quad (19)$$

$$\Delta b_{12}(k)=\eta^h(k)e(k)\left(\frac{\partial O(k)}{\partial b_{12}(k)}\right) \quad (20)$$

$$D_\Gamma(k)=\frac{\partial O(k)}{\partial \Gamma(k)} \quad \Gamma=[a_0\ a_{11}\ a_{12}\ b_0\ b_{11}\ b_{12}] \quad (21)$$

In this paper, candidate Lyapunov function is a function of error which is associated with GD based learning algorithms. This means when Lyapunov function converges to zero GD based learning algorithm is converged to zero too. Now a discrete Lyapunov function is considered as follows:

$$V(k)=\frac{1}{2}e^2(k) \quad (22)$$

Then, the variation of Lyapunov function on each iteration will be:

$$\Delta V(k)=V(k+1)-V(k) \quad (23)$$

$$=\frac{1}{2}\left(e^2(k+1)-e^2(k)\right)$$

$$=\frac{1}{2}\left(e(k+1)-e(k)\right)\left(e(k+1)+e(k)\right)$$

$$=\frac{1}{2}\Delta e(k)\left(2e(k)+\Delta e(k)\right)$$

The variation of error can be approximated by:

$$\Delta e(k) = \left\{ \left(\frac{\partial e(k)}{\partial W(k)} \right)^T \Delta W(k) + \overbrace{tr\left[\left(\frac{\partial e(k)}{\partial a_0(k)} \right)^T \Delta a_0(k) \right]}^{\alpha_1} + \overbrace{tr\left[\left(\frac{\partial e(k)}{\partial a_{11}(k)} \right)^T \Delta a_{11}(k) \right]}^{\alpha_2} + \overbrace{tr\left[\left(\frac{\partial e(k)}{\partial a_{12}(k)} \right)^T \Delta a_{12}(k) \right]}^{\alpha_3} \right. \tag{24}$$

$$\left. + \overbrace{tr\left[\left(\frac{\partial e(k)}{\partial b_0(k)} \right)^T \Delta b_0(k) \right]}^{\alpha_4} + \overbrace{tr\left[\left(\frac{\partial e(k)}{\partial b_{11}(k)} \right)^T \Delta b_{11}(k) \right]}^{\alpha_5} + \overbrace{tr\left[\left(\frac{\partial e(k)}{\partial b_{12}(k)} \right)^T \Delta b_{12}(k) \right]}^{\alpha_6} \right\}$$

where, the $tr(.)$ is the trace of matrices. From (10) it will be concluded that:

$$\left(\frac{\partial e(k)}{\partial W(k)} \right)^T \Delta W(k) = \left(\frac{\partial e(k)}{\partial O(k)} \right)^T \tag{25}$$

$$\times \left(\frac{\partial O(k)}{\partial W(k)} \right)^T \times \eta^o(k) e(k) \left(\frac{\partial O(k)}{\partial W(k)} \right)$$

$$= -\eta^o(k) e(k) \left(\frac{\partial O(k)}{\partial W(k)} \right)^T \times \left(\frac{\partial O(k)}{\partial W(k)} \right)$$

$$= -\eta^o(k) e(k) \| D_W(k) \|^2$$

From (15) and (21), α_1 obtained as follows:

$$\alpha_1 = tr\left[\left(\frac{\partial e(k)}{\partial a_0(k)} \right)^T \Delta a_0(k) \right] \tag{26}$$

$$= tr\left[\left(\frac{\partial e(k)}{\partial O(k)} \right)^T \times \left(\frac{\partial O(k)}{\partial a_0(k)} \right)^T \right.$$

$$\left. \times \eta^h(k) e(k) \left(\frac{\partial O(k)}{\partial a_0(k)} \right) \right]$$

$$= tr\left[-\eta^h(k) e(k) \left(\frac{\partial O(k)}{\partial a_0(k)} \right)^T \times \left(\frac{\partial O(k)}{\partial a_0(k)} \right) \right]$$

$$= -\eta^h(k) e(k) tr\left[\left(\frac{\partial O(k)}{\partial a_0(k)} \right)^T \times \left(\frac{\partial O(k)}{\partial a_0(k)} \right) \right]$$

$$= -\eta^h(k) e(k) \| D_{a_0}(k) \|_F^2$$

Let $\| . \|_F$ be Frobenius norm. Thus, using (16) to (20) and (21), the following equations are obtained:

$$\alpha_2 = -\eta^h(k) e(k) \| D_{a_{11}}(k) \|_F^2 \tag{27}$$

$$\alpha_3 = -\eta^h(k) e(k) \| D_{a_{12}}(k) \|_F^2 \tag{28}$$

$$\alpha_4 = -\eta^h(k) e(k) \| D_{b_0}(k) \|_F^2 \tag{29}$$

$$\alpha_5 = -\eta^h(k) e(k) \| D_{b_{11}}(k) \|_F^2 \tag{30}$$

$$\alpha_6 = -\eta^h(k) e(k) \| D_{b_{12}}(k) \|_F^2 \tag{31}$$

So, it can be written as:

$$\Delta e(k) = -\eta^o(k) e(k) \| D_W(k) \|^2 \tag{32}$$

$$-\eta^h(k) e(k) \left\{ \| D_{a_0}(k) \|_F^2 + \| D_{a_{11}}(k) \|_F^2 \right.$$

$$+ \| D_{a_{12}}(k) \|_F^2 + \| D_{b_0}(k) \|_F^2$$

$$\left. + \| D_{b_{11}}(k) \|_F^2 + \| D_{b_{12}}(k) \|_F^2 \right\}$$

From (23) and (32), it will be inferred that:

$$\Delta V(k) = \frac{1}{2} \Delta e(k) \left(2e(k) + \Delta e(k) \right) \tag{33}$$

$$= \frac{1}{2} \left(-\eta^o(k) e(k) \| D_W(k) \|^2 - \eta^h(k) e(k) \left\{ \| D_{a_0}(k) \|_F^2 + \| D_{a_{11}}(k) \|_F^2 + \| D_{a_{12}}(k) \|_F^2 + \| D_{b_0}(k) \|_F^2 + \| D_{b_{11}}(k) \|_F^2 + \| D_{b_{12}}(k) \|_F^2 \right\} \right)$$

$$\times \left(2e(k) - \eta^o(k) e(k) \| D_W(k) \|^2 - \eta^h(k) e(k) \left\{ \| D_{a_0}(k) \|_F^2 + \| D_{a_{11}}(k) \|_F^2 + \| D_{a_{12}}(k) \|_F^2 + \| D_{b_0}(k) \|_F^2 + \| D_{b_{11}}(k) \|_F^2 + \| D_{b_{12}}(k) \|_F^2 \right\} \right)$$

$$= -\frac{1}{2} e^2(k) \left(\eta^o(k) \| D_W(k) \|^2 + \eta^h(k) \left\{ \| D_{a_0}(k) \|_F^2 + \| D_{a_{11}}(k) \|_F^2 + \| D_{a_{12}}(k) \|_F^2 + \| D_{b_0}(k) \|_F^2 + \| D_{b_{11}}(k) \|_F^2 + \| D_{b_{12}}(k) \|_F^2 \right\} \right)$$

$$\times \left(2 - \eta^o(k) \| D_W(k) \|^2 - \eta^h(k) \left\{ \| D_{a_0}(k) \|_F^2 + \| D_{a_{11}}(k) \|_F^2 + \| D_{a_{12}}(k) \|_F^2 + \| D_{b_0}(k) \|_F^2 + \| D_{b_{11}}(k) \|_F^2 + \| D_{b_{12}}(k) \|_F^2 \right\} \right) < 0$$

Then:

$$\Delta V(k) < 0 \Rightarrow 0 < \eta^o(k) \| D_W(k) \|^2 + \eta^h(k) \tag{34}$$

$$\left\{ \| D_{a_0}(k) \|_F^2 + \| D_{a_{11}}(k) \|_F^2 + \| D_{a_{12}}(k) \|_F^2 + \| D_{b_0}(k) \|_F^2 + \| D_{b_{11}}(k) \|_F^2 + \| D_{b_{12}}(k) \|_F^2 \right\} < 2$$

If we choose $\eta^o(k) = \eta^h(k)$ then:

$$0 < \eta^o(k) = \eta^h(k) < \frac{2}{\left\|D_W(k)\right\|^2 + \left\|D_{a_0}(k)\right\|_F^2 + \left\|D_{a_{11}}(k)\right\|_F^2 + \left\|D_{a_{12}}(k)\right\|_F^2 + \left\|D_{b_0}(k)\right\|_F^2 + \left\|D_{b_{11}}(k)\right\|_F^2 + \left\|D_{b_{12}}(k)\right\|_F^2} \tag{35}$$

From (35) we choose the learning rates as follows:

$$0 < \eta^o(k) < \frac{2}{\left\|D_W(k)\right\|^2} \tag{36}$$

$$0 < \eta^h(k) < \frac{2}{6\left(\left\|D_W(k)\right\|^2 + \left\|D_{a_0}(k)\right\|_F^2 + \left\|D_{a_{11}}(k)\right\|_F^2 + \left\|D_{a_{12}}(k)\right\|_F^2 + \left\|D_{b_0}(k)\right\|_F^2 + \left\|D_{b_{11}}(k)\right\|_F^2 + \left\|D_{b_{12}}(k)\right\|_F^2\right)} \tag{37}$$

4. Simulation and results

In this section, the proposed algorithm in sections 3 is simulated on three nonlinear systems as examples 1, 2 and 3.

In each example, there are 1000 random numbers which divide to training and test data sets. Dynamic neural network is used as identifier as illustrated in figure 2.

Example 1: Identification of a nonlinear dynamical system. In this example, the nonlinear plant with multiple time-delays is described as [3]:

$$y(k+1) = f\left(y(k), y(k-1), y(k-2), \right. \tag{38}$$
$$\left. u(k), u(k-1)\right)$$

where, $u(k)$ and $y(k)$ are the system input and output, respectively.

Where:

$$f(x_1, x_2, x_3, x_4, x_5) = \frac{x_1 x_2 x_3 x_5 (x_3 - 1) + x_4}{1 + x_2^2 + x_3^3} \tag{39}$$

For simulation of this nonlinear system, a neural network with the structure depicted in figure 2 is employed, where n is assumed to be 5, and p is taken as 15. In this neural network, it has been assumed that f^2 is a linear function, and f^1 is a symmetric sigmoid function defined as below:

$$f^1(net) = \frac{1 - e^{-net}}{1 + e^{-net}} \tag{40}$$

where, net is the weighted sum of the inputs. For comparison, the mean square error (MSE) criterion has been used.

In the simulation results, figure 4 indicates convergence with fulfillment of the stability conditions.

Example 2: This system of equation is as follows [14]:

$$y(k+1) = \frac{y(k)}{1 + y^2(k)} + u^2(k) \tag{41}$$

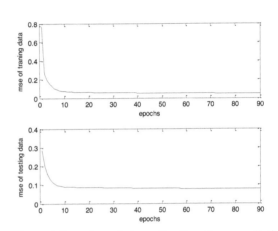

Figure 4. Learning rate is smaller than the upper limit bound.

where, $u(k)$ and $y(k)$ are the system input and output, respectively.

For simulation of this nonlinear system, a neural network with the structure depicted in figure 2 is employed, where n is assumed to be 2, and p is taken as 10.

In the simulation results, figure 5 indicates convergence with fulfillment of the stability conditions.

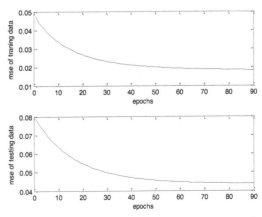

Figure 5. Learning rate is smaller than the upper limit bound.

Example 3: This system of equation is as follows [1-3]:

$$y(k+1) = 0.3y(k) + 0.6y(k-1) + f(u(k)) \quad (42)$$

where, $u(k)$ and $y(k)$ are the system input and output, respectively. The unknown function $f(.)$ is described as follows:

$$f(u) = 0.6\sin(\pi u) + 0.3\sin(3\pi u) + 0.1\sin(3\pi u) \quad (43)$$

For simulation of this nonlinear system, a neural network with the structure depicted in figure 2 is employed, where n is assumed to be 3, and p is taken as 15. In the simulation results, figure 6 indicates convergence with fulfillment of the stability conditions.

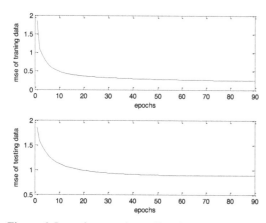

Figure 6. Learning rate is smaller than the upper limit bound.

5. Conclusions

In this paper, for permanent learning of modified dynamic neural network parameters online, Lyapunov stability theory is employed. In this learning algorithm, the associated parameters are trained according to descending gradient. Taking advantage of Lyapunov stability theory, some regions are defined, and through selection of the permanent training rate out of these regions, it can be guaranteed that the learning algorithm is stable throughout the identification process. The results of the obtained theory have been simulated for three examples. The simulation results suggest that in the training process, the system is stable and the convergence rate is desirable. This procedure can be employed in neural controllers.

References

[1] AliyariShoorehdeli, M., Teshnehlab, M., KhakiSedigh, A. & AhmadiehKhanesar M. (2009). Identification using ANFIS with intelligent hybrid stable learning algorithm approaches and stability analysis of training methods. Elsevier, Applied Soft Computing 9, pp. 833–850.

[2] AliyariShoorehdeli, M., Teshnehlab, M. & KhakiSedigh, A. (2009). Training ANFIS as an identifier with intelligent hybrid stable learning algorithm based on particle swarm optimization and extended Kalman filter. Elsevier, Fuzzy SetsandSystems160, pp. 922–948.

[3] AliyariShoorehdeli, M., Teshnehlab, M. & KhakiSedigh, A. (2009). Identification using ANFIS with intelligent hybrid stable learning algorithm approaches. Springer, Neural Comput & Applic 18, pp. 157–174.

[4] Bonissone, P. P., Goebl, K. Y. T. & khedkar, P. S. (1999). Parameter convergence and learning curves for neural networks. Proc, of IEEE, vol. 87, no. 9, pp. 1641-1667.

[5] Fine, T. L., Goebl, S. & khedkar, P. S. (1997). Hybrid Soft Computing System: Industrial and Commercial Application. Neural Computation, pp. 747-769.

[6] Hagan, M. T., Demuth, H. B. & Beale, M. (1996). Neural network design, McGraw – Hill publishing company. First edition.

[7] Hagan, M. T. & Menhaj, M. (1994). Training feedforward networks with Marquardt algorithm. IEEE Transactions on Neural Networks, vol. 5, no. 6, pp. 989-993.

[8] Zhang, T., Ge, S. S. & Hang, C. C. (May 2000). Adaptive neural network control for strict-feedback nonlinear systems using back stepping design. Elsevier Science Ltd., pp. 1835-1846.

[9] Hedjar, R. (2007). Online Adaptive Control of Nonlinear Plants Using Neural Networks with Application to Temperature Control System. J. King Saud Univ., vol. 19, Comp. & Info. Sci, pp. 75-94.

[10] Ge, S. S., Hang, C. C. & Zhang, T. (June 2000). Stable Adaptive Control for Nonlinear Multivariable Systems with a Triangular Control Structure. IEEE Transactions on Automatic Control, vol. 45, no. 6.

[11] Kazem, B. I. & Zangana, N. F. H. (2007). A Neural Network Based Real Time Controller for Turning Process. Jordan Journal of Mechanical and Industrial Engineering, ISSN 1995-6665, pp 43 – 55.

[12] Kuan, C. M. & Hornik, K. (1991). Dynamical systems using neural networks. IEEE Transactions on Neural Networks, vol. 1, no. 1, pp. 4-27.

[13] Meireles, M. R. G., Almeida, P. E. M. & Simões, M .G. (2003). A Comrehensive Review For Industrial Applicability Of Artifical Neural Networks. IEEE Trans. Ind. Electron, vol. 50, no. 3, pp. 585 – 601.

[14] Mandic, D. P., Hanna, A. I. & Razaz, Moe. (2001). A Normalized GraDient Descent Algorithm For Nonlinear Adaptive Filters Using A Gradient Adaptive Step Size. IEEE Signal Processing, Letters . vol. 1, no. 1.

[15] Sha, D. & Bajic, V. B. (2011). An Optimized Recursive Learning Algorithm for Three-Layer Feed forward Neural Networks For MIMO Nonlinear System Identifications. Intelligent Automation and Soft Computing, vol. 17, no. x, pp. 1-15.

[16] Song, Q. & Xiao, J. (1997). On the Convergence Performance of Multilayered NN Tracking Controller. Neural & Parallel Computation, vol. 5, no. 3, pp. 461-470.

[17] Sun, X., Liu, Q. & Zhang, L. (2011). A BP Neural Network Model Based on Genetic Algorithm for Comprehensive Evaluation. IEEE, 978-1-4577-0856.

[18] Torii, M. & Hagan, M. T. (2002). Stability of steepest descent with momentum for quadratic functions. IEEE Trans. On Neural Networks, vol. 13, no. 3, pp. 752-756.

[19] Velagic, J., Osmic N. & Lacevic, B. (2008). Neural Network Controller for Mobile Robot Motion Control, World Academy of Science. Engineering and Technology 47.

[20] Velagic, J. & Hebibovic, M. (2004). Neuro-Fuzzy Architecture for Identification and Tracking Control of a Robot. In Proc, The World Automation Congress - 5th International Symposium on Soft Computing for Industry ISSCI2004, June 28 - July 1, Sevilla Spain, paper no. ISSCI-032, pp. 1-9.

[21] Velagic, J., Lacevic, B. & Hebibovic, M. (2005). On-Line Identification of a Robot Manipulator Using Neural Network with an Adaptive Learning Rate. in Proc. 16th IFAC World Congress, 03-08 June, Prague, Czech Republic, no. 2684, pp. 1-6.

[22] Wu, W., Feng, G. R., Li, Z. X. & Xu, Y. S. (2005). Deterministic Convergence of an Online Gradient Method for BP Neural Networks. IEEE Transaction on Neural Networks, vol. 16, no. 3, pp. 533-540.

[23] Wasserman, P. D. (1989). Neural Computing: Theory and Practice, Van Nostrand, New York.

[24] Gupta, M. M. & Rae, D. H. (1993). Dynamic Neural Units with Applications to the Control of Unknown Nonlinear Systems. 7th Journal of intelligent and Fuzzy Systems, vol. 1, no. 1, pp. 73-92, Jan.

[25] Kim, W. C., Ahn, S. C. & Kwon, W. H. (1995). Stability Analysis and Stabilization of Fuzzy State Space Models. Fuzzy Sets Syst. 71 (April (1)), pp.131–142.

[26] Yu, W. & Li, X. (June 2003), Fuzzy neural modeling using stable learning algorithm. In: Proceedings of the American Control Conference, pp. 4542–4547.

[27] Jafarov, E. M. (August 2013). On Stability Delay Bounds of Simple Input-delayed Linear and Non-Linear systems: Computational Results. International Journal of Automation and Computing (IJAC), vol. 10, no. 4, pp. 327–334.

[28] Sun, H. Y., Li, N., Zhao, De. P. & Zhang, Q. L. (August 2013). Synchronization of Complex Networks with Coupling Delays via Adaptive Pinning Intermittent Control. International Journal of Automation and Computing (IJAC), vol. 10, no. 4, pp. 312–318.

[29] Sabahi, K., Nekoui, M. A., Teshnehlab, M., Aliyari M. & Mansouri, M. (July 2007). Load Frequency Control in Interconnected Power System Using Modified Dynamic Neural Networks. Proceedings of the 15th Mediterranean Conference on Control & Automation, Athens - Greece.

[30] Widrow, B. & Lehr, M. A. (1990). Adaptive Neural Networks: Perceptron, Madaline, and Back propagation. Proceedings of the IEEE, Special Issue on Neural Networks, I: Theory & Modeling; 78(9), pp.1415-1442.

[31] Heydari, A. & Balakrishnan, S. N. (2014). Optimal Switching and Control of Nonlinear Switching Systems Using Approximate Dynamic Programming. IEEE Transactions on Neural Networks and Learning Systems, vol. 25, no. 6, pp. 1106-1117.

24

Modified CLPSO-based fuzzy classification system: Color image segmentation

M. Shafiee[1*] and A. Latif[2]

1. Department of Computer Engineering, Kerman Branch, Islamic Azad University, Kerman, Iran
2. Department of Electrical and Computer Engineering, Yazd University, Yazd, Iran.

*Corresponding author: a.shafiee@iauk.ac.ir (M. Shafiee).

Abstract

Fuzzy segmentation is an effective way of segmenting out objects in images containing varying illumination. In this paper, a modified method based on the Comprehensive Learning Particle Swarm Optimization (CLPSO) is proposed for pixel classification in HSI color space by selecting a fuzzy classification system with minimum number of fuzzy rules and minimum number of incorrectly classified patterns. In the CLPSO-based method, each individual of population is considered to automatically generate a fuzzy classification system. Afterwards, an individual member tries to maximize a fitness criterion which is high classification rate and small number of fuzzy rules. To reduce the multidimensional search space for an M-class classification problem, the centroid of each class is calculated and then fixed in membership function of fuzzy system. The performance of the proposed method is evaluated in terms of future classification within the RoboCup soccer environment with spatially varying illumination intensities on the scene. The results present 85.8% accuracy in terms of classification.

Keywords: *Comprehensive Learning Particle Swarm Optimization, Fuzzy Classification, Image Segmentation, Robotics, RoboCup, LUT Generation, Pattern Recognition.*

1. Introduction

The process of partitioning an image into regions is called image segmentation. The result of the image segmentation is a set of regions that cover the image. All of the pixels in a region are similar with respect to some characteristics, such as color, intensity, or texture. Image segmentation methods divided into five categories: pixel based segmentation [1,2], region based segmentation [3], edge based segmentation [4], edge and region hybrid segmentation [5], and clustering based segmentation [4,6,7]. Color image segmentation using fuzzy classification system is a pixel based segmentation method. A pixel is assigned to a specific color by the fuzzy system, which partitions the color space into segments. Any given pixel is then classified according to the segments it lies in.

Fuzzy rule-based systems applied to solve many classification problems. In many of them, fuzzy classification rules are derived from human experts. Because it is not easy to derive fuzzy rules from human experts, many approaches have been proposed to generate fuzzy rules automatically from the training patterns of the main classification problem [1,2,8,9,10,11].

Solving classification problems with high-dimensional pattern spaces has a significant shortcoming, the more the number of fuzzy rules are, the more the number of dimensions are and the learning time is too high. The Particle Swarm Optimizer (PSO) [12,13] is a computational method that optimizes a problem by iteratively trying to improve a candidate solution with regard to a given measure of quality. Although PSO shares many similarities with evolutionary computation techniques, the standard PSO does not use evolution operators such as crossover and mutation.

PSO emulates the swarm behavior of insects, birds flocking, and fish schooling where these swarms search for food in a collaborative manner. Each member in the swarm adapts its search patterns by learning from its own experience and other members' experiences.

In PSO, a member in the swarm represents a potential solution which is a point in the search space. The global optimum is regarded as the location of food. Each particle has a fitness value and a velocity to adjust its flying direction according to the best experiences of the swarm. The PSO algorithm is easy to implement and has been empirically shown to perform well on many optimization problems [14]. However, it may easily get trapped in a local optimum. In order to improve PSO's performance, we adopt the modified comprehensive learning particle swarm optimizer utilizing a new learning strategy.

In recent years, different methods have been proposed for tuning membership parameters and generating fuzzy rules such as genetic algorithm and PSO. Shamir [15] introduced a human perception based approach to pixel color segmentation using fuzzy systems. Fuzzy sets are defined on the H, S and V components of the HSV color space. The fuzzy rules in this model are defined based on human observations. Tuning fuzzy rules parameters by human expert, significantly affects the classification results and it is a time consuming problem. Marquesan et al. design a color classification system using CLPSO [16]. Image segmentation with the least number of rules and minimum error rate was the main purpose of his work. Enormous search space caused the learning process slow and also his proposed algorithm needed human supervision for defining output color classes. The similar approach using PSO variant algorithm was applied for color image segmentation in [1,2,8,13]. Casillas et al. presented a genetic feature selection process that can be integrated in multistage genetic learning method to obtain fuzzy rule based classification system. It composed a set of comprehensible fuzzy rules with high-classification ability [9]. Yuan et al. designed a fuzzy genetic algorithm to generate classification rules with several techniques such as multi-value logic coding, viability check and composite [10].

Although many color classification methods have been proposed using optimization technique

[1,2,8,13,16] and many unsupervised methods for clustering introduced [6,7,17,18,19], no solution have an optimal solution for color image classification to have both high accuracy and time efficiency simultaneously.

In this paper, a modified method based on the Comprehensive Learning Particle Swarm Optimization (CLPSO) is implemented to select an appropriate fuzzy classification system with minimum number of incorrect classified patterns and minimum number of fuzzy rules. In this approach, Centroid of each class is calculated and then fixed in membership function of fuzzy system. As the consequence the search space reduces. Each individual in the population is considered to represent a fuzzy classification system. Then, a fitness function is used to guide the search procedure to select an appropriate fuzzy classification system.

The rest of this paper is organized as follows. Section 2 describes the structure of the fuzzy classification system. Section 3 proposes a modified CLPSO-based method to adjust the fuzzy classification system parameters for pixel classification problem. Section 4 considers classification problems of a humanoid robot vision data to illustrate the learning and the generalization ability of the proposed approach, respectively. Finally, section 5 demonstrates conclusions about the proposed method for solving the classification problem.

2. Fuzzy color classification system

Fuzzy color pixel classification is a supervised learning method for segmentation of color images. In this method, each pixel of an input image assigns to a color class by applying a set of fuzzy rules on it. A set of training pixels, for which the colors class are known, are used to train the fuzzy system.

Figure 1 shows a fuzzy classification system with color pixel on HSI color space as an input. Unlike RGB, HSI separates luminance, from Chroma. This is useful for robustness to lighting changes, or removing shadows.

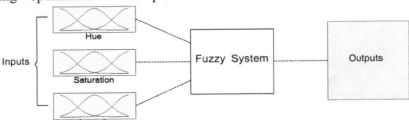

Figure 1. Fuzzy color pixel classification system.

For an M-class classification problem, a rule base of fuzzy classification system considered as follows [12]:

jth Rule:
if x_1 is A_{j1} and x_2 is A_{j2} and ...
and x_m is A_{jm}
then $\underline{x} = (x_1, x_2, ..., x_m)$ belongs to   (1)
class H_j with $CF = CF_j$ $j = 1, 2, ..., R$

Where R is the number of fuzzy rules and A_{ji} $i = 1, 2, ..., m$, are the premise fuzzy sets of the jth fuzzy rule, $H_j \epsilon \{1, 2, ..., M\}$, is the consequent class output of the th fuzzy rule, and $CF_j \epsilon [0,1]$ is the grade of certainty of the th fuzzy rule.
Fuzzy sets are defined on the H, S and I channels with Gaussian membership functions, which are described by (2):

$$\mu_{A_{ji}}\left(m_{(ji,1)}, m_{(ji,2)}, m_{(ji,3)}; x_i\right)$$
$$= \begin{cases} \exp\left(-\left(\frac{x_i - m_{(ji,1)}}{m_{(ji,2)}}\right)^2\right), & \text{if } x_i \leq m_{(ji,1)} \\ \exp\left(-\left(\frac{x_i - m_{(ji,1)}}{m_{(ji,3)}}\right)^2\right), & \text{if } x_i > m_{(ji,1)} \end{cases}$$
(2)

Where $m_{(ji,1)}$ determines the center position, $m_{(ji,2)}$ and $m_{(ji,3)}$ are the left and right width values of the membership function, respectively. Hence, the shape of membership function is defined by a parameter vector $\underline{m_{ji}} = [m_{(ji,1)}, m_{(ji,2)}, m_{(ji,3)}]$.
The th rule is determined by a parameter vector $\underline{r}_j = [m_{j1}, m_{j2}, ..., m_{jM}]$. Also, the set of parameters in the premise part of the rule base is defined as $r = [\underline{r}_1, \underline{r}_2, ..., \underline{r}_R]$.
According to (1), the set of parameters in the consequent part of the rule is defined as $\underline{a} = [H_1, CF_1, H_2, CF_2, ..., H_R, CF_R]$. When the input $x = (x_1, x_2, ..., x_m)$ is given the premise of the jth rule is calculated by the (3).
The class output of the fuzzy classification system with respect to the input x can be determined by (4).

$$q_j(x) = \prod_{i=1}^{M} \mu_{A_{ji}}(x_i) \qquad (3)$$

$$y = \arg \max_{j=1} q_j(x) . CF_j \qquad (4)$$

According to the above description, a fuzzy classification system determines by a set of premise and consequent parameters.

Different parameter sets determine different fuzzy classification systems and so the generated fuzzy classification systems have different performances.
The goal is to find an appropriate fuzzy classification system to have both minimum number of fuzzy rules and maximum number of correct classified pattern.
In the next section, to select an appropriate fuzzy classification system a modified CLPSO is applied.

3. Modified CLPSO-based fuzzy classification system

3.1. Particle swarm optimization
As mentioned before, PSO emulates a swarm behavior and each individual represents some points in the multi-dimensional search space. A particle is a potential solution.
The velocity V_i^d and position X_i^d of the dth dimension of the ith particle are updated as follows:

$$V_i^d \leftarrow V_i^d + c_1 * rand1_i^d * \left(pbest_i^d - X_i^d\right) + c_2 * rand2_i^d * \left(gbest_i^d - X_i^d\right) \qquad (5)$$

$$X_i^d \leftarrow X_i^d + V_i^d \qquad (6)$$

Where $X_i = (X_i^1, X_i^2, ..., X_i^D)$ is the position of the ith particle, $V_i = (V_i^1, V_i^2, ..., V_i^D)$ represents velocity of ith particle. $pbest_i = (pbest_i^1, pbest_i^2, ..., pbest_i^D)$ is the best previous position yielding the best fitness value for the ith particle; and $gbest = (gbest^1, gbest^2, ..., gbest^D)$ is the best position discovered by the whole population.
c_1 and c_2 are the acceleration constants reflecting the weighting of stochastic acceleration in terms that pull each particle toward pbest and gbest positions, respectively. $rand1_i^d$ and $rand2_i^d$ are two random numbers in the interval of [0, 1].
Although there are numerous variants for the PSO, premature convergence for multimodal problems is the main deficiency of the PSO.
In the original PSO, each particle learns from pbest and gbest simultaneously; restricting the social learning aspect to only to gbest, makes the original PSO converge fast.
Since all particles learn from the gbest even if the current gbest is far from the global optimum, particles may easily be attracted to the gbest region and get trapped in a local optimum.
This matter is critical if the search environment is complex with numerous local solutions.

3.2. Comprehensive learning particle swarm optimization

In the CLPSO, velocity is updated according to (7):

$$V_i^d \leftarrow w * V_i^d + c * rand_i^d \\ * \left(pbest_{fi(d)}^d - X_i^d\right) \qquad (7)$$

Where $f_i = [f_i(1), f_i(2), \dots, f_i(D)]$ defines which particles' pbest, the particle i should follow. $pbest_{fi(d)}^d$ can be the corresponding dimension of any particle's pbest including its own pbest, and the decision depends on probability P_{c_i}, referred to as the learning probability, which can take different values for different particles.

For each dimension of particle i, a random number is generated. If this random number is larger than P_{c_i}, the corresponding dimension will learn from its own pbest; otherwise, it will learn from another particles' pbest as follows:

1) First two particles randomly choose out of population.
2) The fitness of these two particles pbest are compared and the better one is selected. In CLPSO, the larger the fitness value is, the better the pbest is defined.

3) The winner's pbest is used as the exemplar to learn from that dimension. The details of choosing f_i are given in Figure 2.

4. Proposed modified CLPSO with fuzzy classification system

Training data contains a mapping from HIS color space **S** to a set of colors **M** which assigns a class label $\mathbf{m_i} \in \mathbf{M}$ to every point $\mathbf{s_j} \in \mathbf{S}$ in color space. If each channel is represented by an n-bit value and k = |M| represents the number of defined class labels, then $\mathbf{S} \rightarrow \mathbf{M}$, where $\mathbf{S} = \{\mathbf{0, 1, \dots, 2^n - 1}\}^3$ and $\mathbf{M} = \{\mathbf{m_0, m_1, \dots, m_{k-1}}\}$. Assuming we have **M** cluster in data set, the centroid of each cluster **C** can be determined by the following equation:

$$C_x = \frac{1}{np} \sum_{j=1}^{n_p} s_{xj} , x \in \{H, S, I\} \qquad (8)$$

Where n_p is the number of points in training set and s_{xj} represents the value of x-channel of the jth point in the training set. Using the cluster

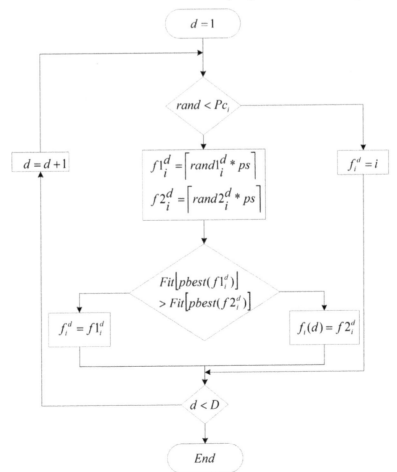

Figure 2. Selection of exemplar dimensions for particle i.

centroids, the center position of the Gaussian membership function of the fuzzy rule system, $m_{(ji,1)}$, can be fixed and therefore, we have a search space reduction. In addition, by having the number of clusters, minimum number of fuzzy rules is calculable and fitness function can be improved.

In the proposed method, each individual is represented to determine a fuzzy classification system. The individual is used to partition the input space so that the rule number and the premise part of the generated fuzzy classification system are determined. Subsequently, the consequent parameters of the corresponding fuzzy system are obtained by the premise fuzzy sets of the generated fuzzy classification system.

A set of L individuals, P which is called population is expressed in the following:

$$
\begin{bmatrix} \underline{P_1} \\ \underline{P_2} \\ \underline{P_3} \\ \vdots \\ \underline{P_h} \\ \vdots \\ \underline{P_L} \end{bmatrix} = \begin{bmatrix} \underline{r_1} & \underline{g_1} \\ \underline{r_2} & \underline{g_2} \\ \underline{r_3} & \underline{g_3} \\ \vdots & \\ \underline{r_h} & \underline{g_h} \\ \vdots & \\ \underline{r_L} & \underline{g_L} \end{bmatrix} \qquad (9)
$$

In order to evolutionarily determine the parameters of the fuzzy classification system, the individual $\underline{P_h}$ contains two parameter vectors: $\underline{r_h}$ and $\underline{g_h}$. The parameter vector $\underline{r_h} = [r_1^h \ r_2^h \ \cdots r_j^h \ \cdots r_B^h]$ consists of the premise parameters of the candidate fuzzy rules, where B is a positive integer to decide the maximum number of fuzzy rules in the rule base generated by the individual $\underline{P_h}$. B is all possible combination of clusters centroid for each channel which is $B = C_H \times C_S \times C_I$ where C_H, C_S, C_I is calculated by Eq.8. Likewise, the minimum number of fuzzy rules is equal to the number of main clusters, which is called Q.

Here, $\underline{r_j^h} = [m_{j1}^h \ m_{j2}^h \dots m_{ji}^h \dots m_{jM}^h]$ is the parameter vector to determine the membership functions of the jth fuzzy rule, where $\underline{m_{ij}^h} = [m_{(ji,1)} \ \_{(ji,2)} \ \_{(ji,P)}^h]$ is the parameter vector to determine the membership function for the ith input variable.

The parameter vector $\underline{g_h} = [g_1^h \ g_2^h \dots g_j^h \dots g_B^h]$ is used to select the fuzzy rules from the candidate rules $\underline{r_h} = [r_1^h \ r_2^h \ \cdots r_j^h \cdots r_B^h]$ so that the fuzzy rule base is generated. $g_j^h \in [0,1]$ decides whether the jth candidate rule $\underline{r_j^h}$ is added to the rule base of the generated fuzzy system or not. If $g_j^h \geq 0.5$,

then the jth candidate rule $\underline{r_j^h}$ is added to the rule base. Consequently, the total number of g_j^h ($j = 1,2, \dots, B$) whose value is greater than or equal to 0.5 is the number of fuzzy rules in the generated rule base.

In order to generate the rule base, the index j of g_j^h ($j = 1,2, \dots, B$) whose value is greater than or equal to 0.5 is defined as $I_r^h \in \{1, 2, \dots, B\}$, $r = 1, 2, \dots, r_h$ where r_h represents the number of the fuzzy rules in the generated rule base. $\{r_{I_1^h}^h, r_{I_2^h}^h \qquad {}_h^h\}$ generates the premise part of the fuzzy rule base which is generated by the individual $\underline{P_h} = [\underline{r_h} \ \underline{g_h}]$.

For example, assume that $\underline{r_h}$ and $\underline{g_h}$ are denoted as $[r_1 \ r_2 \ r_3 \ r_4 \ r_5 \ r_6]$ and $[0.12 \ 0.72 \ 0.82 \ 0.35 \ 0.29 \ 0.8]$, respectively. According to $\underline{g_h}$, the generated rule base has three fuzzy rules $\{I_1^h, I_2^h, I_3^h\} = \{2,3,6\}$; therefore, $\{r_2 \ r_3 \ r_6\}$ determines the premise part of the generated rule base.

The rule base of the generated fuzzy classification system is described as follows:

rth Rule:
if x_1 is $A_{I_r^h 1}^h$ and x_2 is $A_{I_r^h 2}^h$ and ...
and x_m is $A_{I_r^h m}^h$ (10)
then $\underline{x} = (x_1, x_2, \dots, x_m)$ belongs to
class H_r with $CF = CF_r$ $j = 1,2, \dots, r_h$,

Where $A_{I_r^h i}^h$, $i = 1,2, \dots, m$, are the fuzzy sets of the generated rth fuzzy rule. The membership function associated with the fuzzy set is described as follows:

$$
\mu_{A_{I_r^h i}^h} \left(m_{(I_r^h i,1)}^h, m_{(I_r^h i,2)}^h, m_{(I_r^h i,3)}^h; x_i \right)
$$
$$
= \begin{cases} exp\left(-\left(\dfrac{x_i - m_{(I_r^h i,1)}^h}{m_{(I_r^h i,2)}^h} \right)^2 \right), & if \ x_i \leq m_{(I_r^h i,1)}^h \\ \\ exp\left(-\left(\dfrac{x_i - m_{(I_r^h i,1)}^h}{m_{(I_r^h i,3)}^h} \right)^2 \right), & if \ x_i > m_{(I_r^h i,1)}^h \end{cases} \qquad (11)
$$

Assume that N training patterns $(\underline{x_n}, y_n)$, $n = 1,2, \dots, N$, are gathered from the observation of the considered M-class classification problem, where $\underline{x_n} = (x_{n1}, x_{n2}, \dots, x_{nm})$ is the input vector of the nth training pattern and $y_n \in \{1,2, \dots, M\}$, where M is the total number of classes, is the corresponding class output.

In order to determine the consequent parameters H_r and CF_r of the rth fuzzy rule, a procedure is proposed as follows [1]:

Step1. Calculate θ_t, $t = 1, 2, \dots, M$ for the rth fuzzy rule as follows:

$$\theta_t = \sum_{\underline{x}_p \in Class\ t} q_r(\underline{x}_p), \qquad t = 1, 2, \dots, M. \tag{12}$$

Step2. Determine H_r for the rth fuzzy rule by:

$$H_r = \underset{t = 1}{arg\ max}^{M}\ \theta_t. \tag{13}$$

Step3. Determine the grade of certainty CF_r of the rth fuzzy rule by:

$$CF_r = \frac{\theta_{H_r} - \bar{\theta}}{\sum_{t=1}^{M} \theta_t} \tag{14}$$

$$\bar{\theta} = \sum_{\substack{t=1 \\ t \neq H_r}}^{M} \frac{\theta_t}{M-1} \tag{15}$$

In order to construct a fuzzy classification system which has an appropriate number of fuzzy rules and minimize incorrectly classified patterns simultaneously, the fitness function is defined as follows:

$$f_h = fit(\underline{p}_h) = g_1(\underline{p}_h) * g_2(\underline{p}_h) \tag{16}$$

$$g_1(\underline{p}_h) = \text{NCCP} \tag{17}$$

$$g_2(\underline{p}_h) = \begin{cases} \left(\dfrac{B - r_h}{B - Q}\right) & B \neq Q \\ \left(\dfrac{r_h}{B}\right) & B = Q \end{cases} \tag{18}$$

Where NCCP $(\underline{p}_h)$ is the number of correctly classified patterns, r_h is the number of fuzzy rules in the rule base of the generated fuzzy classification system.

The fitness function is designed to maximize the number of correctly classified patterns and minimize the number of fuzzy rules.

In this way, as the fitness function value increases as much as possible, the fuzzy classification system corresponding to the individual will satisfy the desired objective as well as possible.

CLPSO-based method is proposed to find an appropriate individual so that the corresponding fuzzy classification system has the desired performance. The modified proposed procedure is described as follows:

Step1. Initialize the CLPSO-based method.
(a) Set the number of individuals (L), the maximum number of rules (B), the number of generations (K), and the constants for the PSO algorithm (ω_0, ω_1, c).

(b) Generate randomly initial population P. Each individual of the population is expressed as follows:

$$\underline{p}_h = [\underline{r}_h\ \underline{g}_h]$$

where

$$\underline{r}_h = [m^h_{(11,1)}\ m^h_{(11,2)}\ m^h_{(11,3)} \cdots$$
$$m^h_{(1m,1)}\ m^h_{(1m,2)}\ m^h_{(1m,3)} \cdots$$
$$m^h_{(B1,1)}\ m^h_{(B1,2)}\ m^h_{(B1,3)} \cdots$$
$$m^h_{(Bm,1)}\ m^h_{(Bm,2)}\ m^h_{(Bm,3)}] \tag{19}$$
$$m^h_{(ji,k)}, j \in \{1,2,\dots,B\}, i \in \{1,2,\dots,M\},$$
$$k \in \{1,2,3\}$$

and

$$\underline{g}_h = [g^h_1\ g^h_2 \cdots g^h_j \cdots g^h_B]. m^h_{(ji,k)},$$
$$j \in \{1,2,\dots,B\}$$
$m^h_{(ji,k)}$ is randomly generated as follow:

$$m^h_{(ji,k)} = m^{min}_{(ji,k)} + \left(m^{max}_{(ji,k)} - m^{min}_{(ji,k)}\right) \times rand \tag{20}$$

Where the range of the parameter $m^h_{(ji,k)}$ is defined as $[m^{min}_{(ji,k)}, m^{max}_{(ji,k)}]$ and $rand$ is a uniformly distributed random numbers in $[0,1]$, also g^h_j is randomly generated.

(c) Generate randomly initial velocity vectors $\underline{v}_h$, $h = 1, 2, \dots, L$. Each velocity vector is expressed as follows:

$$\underline{v}_h = [\underline{\alpha}_h\ \underline{\beta}_h]$$

where

$$\underline{\alpha}_h = [\alpha^h_{(11,1)}\ \alpha^h_{(11,2)}\ \alpha^h_{(11,3)} \cdots$$
$$\alpha^h_{(1m,1)}\ \alpha^h_{(1m,2)}\ \alpha^h_{(1m,3)} \cdots$$
$$\alpha^h_{(B1,1)}\ \alpha^h_{(B1,2)}\ \alpha^h_{(B1,3)} \cdots \tag{21}$$
$$\alpha^h_{(Bm,1)}\ \alpha^h_{(Bm,2)}\ \alpha^h_{(Bm,3)}]$$
$$\alpha^h_{(ji,k)},\ j \in \{1,2,\dots,B\},\ i \in \{1,2,\dots,M\},$$
$$k \in \{1,2,3\}\ and$$
$$\underline{\beta}_h = [\beta^h_1\ \beta^h_2 \cdots \beta^h_B]$$

$\alpha^h_{(ji,k)}$ is randomly generated as follows:

$$\alpha^h_{(ji,k)} = \frac{\left(\alpha^{max}_{(ji,k)} - \alpha^{min}_{(ji,k)}\right)}{20} \times rand \tag{22}$$

β^h_j is randomly generated as follows:

$$\beta^h_j = \frac{rand}{20} \tag{23}$$

(d) The fitness value for each particle of the population is calculated and saved. It is being noted that to calculate the fitness value, the fuzzy systems of each particle is tested with training data, individually.

Step2. Generate f_i for each particle as in.

Step3. Update the vector $\underline{g_h} = [g_1^h\ g_2^h\ ...\ g_j^h\ ...\ g_B^h]$, as follows:

$$g_{j^*}^h = 1 - g_{j^*}^h, \qquad j^* = rand([1, B]) \qquad (24)$$

Where $rand$ generates an integer random number in interval of $[1, B]$.

Step4. Update velocity and position of each particle according to (6 and 7).

Step5. Mutate the population randomly. At any stage an integer random number, called mutation indicator in range of $[1, L]$, is generated. Particle associated with the selected indicator is selected and its $\underline{g_h}$ vector is replaced by Max-Score vector.

To obtain Max-Score, the total value of all existing rules regardless of $\underline{g_h}$ is achieved using fitness function. Since the fuzzy rules of each cluster is distinctive, the rule with maximum fitness value receives score 1 in Max-Score and the rest of the rules related to the cluster receive score 0. If the particle does not acquire a better fitness value after the mutation, $\underline{g_h}$ will be restored to the previous values before mutation.

Step6. If Max-gen > K then K = K+1 and go to step 2 or it; otherwise stops.

Step7. Based on the individual with the best fitness, the desired fuzzy classification system can be determined.

The flowchart of the modified-CLPSO is given in figure 3.

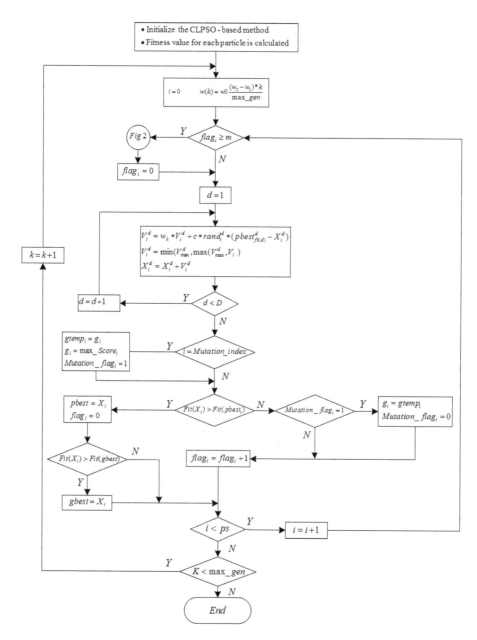

Figure 3. Flowchart of the modified CLPSO.

5. Experimental results

For evaluating the algorithm, one set of images (50 images) was obtained from reference [20] and also we obtain another set (117 images) in varying light condition to measure the robustness of the classifier against the light changes. In providing these images; fluorescent lights and also natural light of ambient without applying any filter were used. A lux-meter with 12 to 12000 lux sensitivity was used and ambient light level for each image was recorded. Light of obtained images was in the range of 100 to 1200 lux.

We implement our scheme on MATLAB R2013 installed on a computer with a Corei7 processor and 8GB RAM. The general parameters of the proposed CLPSO algorithm are listed in Table 1.

Table 1. Proposed method parameters.

Parameters	Symbol	Initialization value
Population size	L	0
Max number of rules	B	$C_{Hn} \times C_{Sn} \times C_{In}$
Min number of rules	Q	Variable
Max number of iterations	K	500
Constants of CLPSO	$(\omega_0, \omega_1, c, m)$	(0.9,0.4,1.49445,4)

For comparison and evaluation of fuzzy classification system, the first set of images was used. After training a fuzzy system with proposed method, its precision was evaluated; table 2 presents the results of this step and Table shows the result of fuzzy pixel classification on 7 samples of data set.

Table 2. Performance of the proposed classification system.

No.	No. of samples	Sensitivity	Specificity	Precision	Accuracy
1	50	0.7312	0.9644	0.6762	0.8582

5.1. Performance of the proposed fuzzy classification system against light changes

To evaluate the robustness of the proposed system against lights changes, set of 117 images in the range of 0 to 1000 lux were used (see Figure 4).

To train the system, a set of pixels in the range of 400 to 700 lux selected and the fuzzy system trained.

Numbers of obtained rules after training were 9 and general precision of classification system was 90%.

Figure 4. Five samples of increasing illumination recorded by lux meter.

To test the system, a set of pixels in the range of 0 to 1000 lux selected and system performance presented in table 4 according to the color and light.

The first column is standard colors defined by RoboCup; the second column is the range of light levels in which the images are taken, the next three columns are the minimum and maximum value of each channel of HSI color space, the result of classification with the proposed fuzzy system is shown in column six, last column shows increase or decrease in classification performance.

As shown in the table 4, in the range of 400 to 700 lux, the lowest classification precision related to green, orange and yellow, respectively.

In the range of 0-400 lux, the most decrease in classification precision related to cyan with 37.92

percent, yellow with 20.62 percent and orange with 7.68 percent, respectively.

In this range, it is noticeable that the classification precision for green color increased to 37.09 percent, because of light levels severely reduced in the range of 0-400 lux which places all the data in the correct class.

In the range of 700-1000 lux, classification precision of yellow, green, blue and cyan reduced to 18.33%, 7.5%, 19.58% and 1.2 %, respectively. Therefore, the most robust color to the light changes is pink and the most sensitive color to the light changes is green.

The surveying colors according to robustness against the light changes are pink with 100%, blue with 92.63%, cyan with 86.96%, yellow with 84.92%, orange with 81.37% and green with 77.35%.

Table 3. Result of fuzzy pixel classification tuned by proposed modified CLPSO algorithm.

No.	Input Image	Fuzzy pixel classification output image	Sensitivity	Specificity	Precision	Accuracy
1			0.6099	0.9942	0.9562	0.9799
2			0.6044	0.9791	0.8821	0.8866
3			0.7224	0.9904	0.8997	0.9667
4			0.5949	0.9685	0.7217	0.7827
5			0.7229	0.9824	0.8375	0.8870
6			0.6440	0.9761	0.6629	0.8058
7			0.7747	0.9814	0.6821	0.9276

Table 4. The effect of light changes on system performance.

Color	Lux	Hue Min	Hue Max	Saturation Min	Saturation Max	Intensity Min	Intensity Max	Classification True	Classification False	Performance
Orange	400-0	3.78	19.27	191.56	232.02	120.00	230.00	75.62	24.37	-7.68
Orange	700-400	7.57	30.47	189.01	234.18	140.00	238.00	83.3	16.6	0
Orange	1000-700	15.14	39.77	76.26	230.44	140.00	243.00	85.20	14.79	+1.9
Yellow	400-0	29.30	42.50	154.06	218.51	116.00	226.00	77.29	22.70	-20.62
Yellow	700-400	34.99	43.50	190.85	219.71	153.00	234.00	97.91	2.08	0
Yellow	1000-700	36.21	43.86	119.22	219.71	180.00	236.00	79.58	20.41	-18.33
Green	400-0	70.26	108.15	130.00	217.00	84.00	171.00	100	0	+37.09
Green	700-400	79.90	109.51	107.05	221.45	152.00	212.00	62.91	37.09	0
Green	1000-700	75.65	111.25	95.21	225.32	163.00	235.00	69.16	30.83	-7.5
Blue	400-0	152.86	170.00	138.70	227.06	80.00	166.00	97.5	2.5	-2.5
Blue	700-400	151.41	158.88	140.03	225.45	120.00	173.00	100	0	0
Blue	1000-700	149.10	157.68	99.41	199.27	144.00	223.00	80.41	19.58	-19.58
Cyan	400-0	115.36	136.45	93.95	221.45	106.00	211.00	62.08	37.92	-37.92
Cyan	700-400	118.77	132.19	91.15	218.57	158.00	221.00	100	0	0
Cyan	1000-700	115.78	133.84	91.15	219.39	171.00	234.00	98.8	1.2	-1.2
Pink	400-0	229.35	251.7	151.17	221.00	73.00	172.00	100	0	0
Pink	700-400	233.75	246.11	138.68	201.45	94.00	195.00	100	0	0
Pink	1000-700	229.96	79.69	79.69	163.36	127.00	231.00	100	0	0

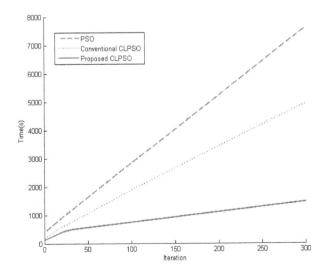

Figure 5. Consumed time graph of PSO, conventional CLPSO and proposed CLPSO methods.

6. Comparison of the proposed segmentation of the algorithm performance with the existing methods

One of the problems related to optimization techniques is that they are time-consuming. The proposed method has a higher speed compared with the conventional methods.

Figure 5 shows the iteration time table. Firstly, it is observed that all three slopes are approximately equal.

Due to iteration 20, mutations in the particles and the reduction of rules cause the decrease in the calculation complexity and the slope graph.

In figure 6, the overall precision of the existing methods is compared. For this comparison, the results of references [20,21,22] have been used.

In all methods, except for the reference method [20], an optimization algorithm is used to adjust the fuzzy classification system.

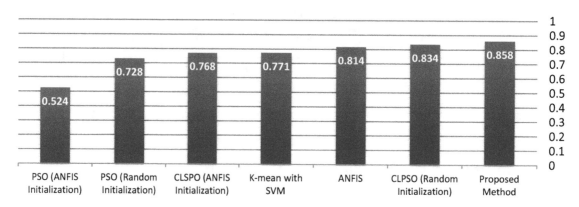

Figure 6. Accuracy of the existing methods.

In all methods, the Gaussian membership function is used, and the goal is to set up a classification system for Robocop competitions.

The main difference of the proposed method with the reference [21] is mainly the modified fitness function and the fixed centroids of the fuzzy membership function.

In [20], the overall precision of classification was not presented and the precision of positive and negative classes were used for expressing the results. For calculating the overall precision of this method, the following equation was used.

$$Balanced\ Accuracy = \frac{Sensitivity + Specificity}{2} \quad (25)$$

The proposed method with 0.858 precision for classifying 8 classes allocated the most precision method among the existing ones.

It is observed that the primary initialization has considerable effects on increasing the accuracy. In addition to the reported accuracy of different methods, the result of classification of each method is shown in figure 7.

Figure 7. (a) original image, the rest are segmentation result of the test image produced by the following algorithms: (b) PSO random initialization, (c) k-mean with SVM, (d) ANFIS, (e) CLPSO random initialization, (f) proposed method.

One of the important parameters of fuzzy classification system is the number of rules.
As mentioned erliear, the reduction of rules in the fitness function has been taken into consideration and has been one of the main differences between the particle swarm optimization method and ANFIS. In figure 8, the number of obtained rules for various methods has been studied. Due to the

lack of fuzzy methods in reference [20], this method has not been studied in figure 8. Calculations of the number and the cluster centers and using mutation in particles are the main reasons for the dramatic drop off in the number of proposed method rules.

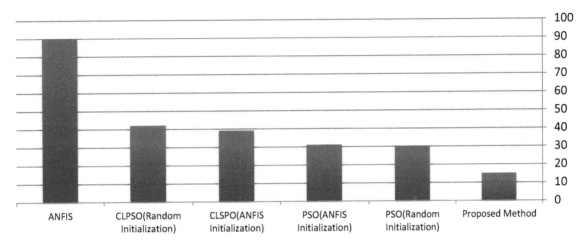

Figure 8. The number of fuzzy rules of the existing methods.

7. Conclusion

In this paper, a comprehensive learning particle swarm optimization (CLPSO) technique with some modifications was proposed to find optimal fuzzy rules and membership functions. Each particle of the swarm codes a set of fuzzy rules. During evolution, a population member tries to maximize a fitness criterion which is here high classification rate and small number of rules. The simulation results show that the selected fuzzy classification system not only has an appropriate number of rules for the considered classification problem but also has a low number of incorrectly classified patterns.

References

[1] Sowmya, B. & Sheela Rani, B. (2011). Colour image segmentation using fuzzy clustering techniques and competitive neural network. Applied Soft Computing, vol. 11, no. 3, pp. 3170-3178.

[2] Reyes, N. H. & Dadios, E. P. (2004). Dynamic Color Object Recognition Using Fuzzy Logic. JACIII, vol. 8, no. 1, pp. 29-38.

[3] Gould, S., Gao, T. & Koller, D. (2009). Region-based segmentation and object detection. Advances in neural information processing systems 22, 2009.

[4] Gupta, A., Ganguly, A. & Bhateja, V. (2013). A Novel Color Edge Detection Technique Using Hilbert Transform. Proceedings of the International Conference on Frontiers of Intelligent Computing: Theory and Applications (FICTA). Springer Berlin Heidelberg, pp. 725-732.

[5] Othmani, A., et al. (2013). Hybrid segmentation of depth images using a watershed and region merging based method for tree species recognition. IVMSP Workshop, 2013 IEEE 11th, pp. 1-4.

[6] Wang, X. Y., Zhang, X. J., Yang, H. Y. & Bu, J. (2012). A pixel-based color image segmentation using support vector machine and fuzzy C-means. Neural Networks, vol. 33, pp. 148-159.

[7] Ji, Z., Xia, Y., Chen, Q., Sun, Q., Xia, D. & Feng, D. D. (2012). Fuzzy c-means clustering with weighted image patch for image segmentation. Applied Soft Computing, vol. 12, no. 6, pp. 1659-1667.

[8] Reyes, N. H. & Messom, C. (2005). Identifying colour objects with fuzzy colour contrast fusion. In 3rd International conference on computational intelligence, robotics and autonomous systems, and FIRA roboworld congress.

[9] Casillas, J., Cordón, O., Del Jesus, M. J. & Herrera, F. (2001). Genetic feature selection in a fuzzy rule-based classification system learning process for high-dimensional problems. Information Sciences, vol. 136, no. 1, pp. 135-157.

[10] Yuan, Y. & Zhuang, H. (1996). A genetic algorithm for generating fuzzy classification rules. Fuzzy sets and systems, vol. 84, no. 1, pp. 1-19.

[11] Borji, A., Hamidi, M. & Moghadam, A. M. E. (2007). CLPSO-based fuzzy color image segmentation. In Proceedings of North American Fuzzy Information Processing Society, pp. 508-513.

[12] Puranik, P., Bajaj, P., Abraham, A., Palsodkar, P. & Deshmukh, A. (2009, December). Human perception-based color image segmentation using comprehensive learning particle swarm optimization. 2nd International Conference on Emerging Trends in Engineering and Technology, pp. 630-635.

[13] Murugesan, K. M. & Palaniswami, S. (2010). Efficient colour image segmentation using exponential particle swarm optimization. In Proceedings of the 12th international conference on Networking, VLSI and signal processing. World Scientific and Engineering Academy and Society (WSEAS), pp. 240-244.

[14] Hu, M., Wu, T. & Weir, J. D. (2012). An intelligent augmentation of particle swarm optimization with multiple adaptive methods. Information Sciences., vol. 213, pp. 68-83.

[15] Shamir, L. (2006, June). Human Perception-based Color Segmentation Using Fuzzy Logic. In IPCV, pp. 496-502.

[16] Maitra, M. & Chatterjee, A. (2008). A hybrid cooperative–comprehensive learning based PSO algorithm for image segmentation using multilevel thresholding. Expert Systems with Applications, vol. 34, no. 2, pp. 1341-1350.

[17] Mishra, S., Satapathy, S. K. & Mishra, D. (2012). CLPSO-Fuzzy Frequent Pattern Mining from Gene Expression Data. Procedia Technology, vol. 4, pp. 807-811.

[18] Yu, Z., Au, O. C., Zou, R., Yu, W. & Tian, J. (2010). An adaptive unsupervised approach toward pixel clustering and color image segmentation. Pattern Recognition, vol. 43, no. 5, pp. 1889-1906.

[19] Wang, X. Y., Wang, Q. Y., Yang, H. Y. & Bu, J. (2011). Color image segmentation using automatic pixel classification with support vector machine. Neurocomputing, vol. 74, no. 18, pp. 3898-3911.

[20] Ishibuchi, H., Nozaki, K., Yamamoto, N. & Tanaka, H. (1995). Selecting fuzzy if-then rules for classification problems using genetic algorithms. IEEE Transactions on Fuzzy Systems, vol. 3, no. 3, pp. 260-270.

[21] Hamidi, M. & Borji, A. (2007). Color image segmentation with CLPSO-based fuzzy. International Journal of Computer Science and Network Security (IJCSNS), vol. 7, no. 6, pp. 215-221.

[22] Budden, D. & Mendes, A. (2014). Unsupervised recognition of salient colour for real-time image processing. RoboCup 2013: Robot Soccer World Cup XVII, vol. 8371, pp. 373-384.

[23] Tan, K. S., Mat Isa, N. A. & Lim, W. H. (2013). Color image segmentation using adaptive unsupervised clustering approach. Applied Soft Computing, vol. 13, no. 4, pp. 2017-2036.

[24] Kashanipour, A., Milani, N. S., Kashanipour, A. R. & Eghrary, H. H. (2008, May). Robust color classification using fuzzy rule-based particle swarm optimization. In Image and Signal Processing, CISP'08, vol. 2, pp. 110-114.

25

Adaptive RBF network control for robot manipulators

M. M. Fateh[1*], S. M. Ahmadi[2] and S. Khorashadizadeh[1]

1. *Department of Electrical Engineering, University of Shahrood, Shahrood, Iran.*
2. *Department of Mechanical Engineering, University of Shahrood, Shahrood, Iran.*

Corresponding author: mmfateh@shahroodut.ac.ir (M. M. Fateh).

Abstract

The uncertainty estimation and compensation are challenging problems for the robust control of robot manipulators which are complex systems. This paper presents a novel decentralized model-free robust controller for electrically driven robot manipulators. As a novelty, the proposed controller employs a simple Gaussian Radial-Basis-Function network (RBF network) as an uncertainty estimator. The proposed network includes a hidden layer with one node, two inputs and a single output. In comparison with other model-free estimators such as multilayer neural networks and fuzzy systems, the proposed estimator is simpler, less computational and more effective. The weights of the RBF network are tuned online using an adaptation law derived by stability analysis. Despite the majority of previous control approaches which are the torque-based control, the proposed control design is the voltage-based control. Simulations and comparisons with a robust neural network control approach show the efficiency of the proposed control approach applied on the articulated robot manipulator driven by permanent magnet DC motors.

Keywords: *Adaptive Uncertainty Estimator, RBF Network Control, Robust Control, Electrically Driven Robot Manipulators.*

1. Introduction

Torque Control Strategy (TCS) has attracted many research efforts in the field of robot control [1-3]. The robust torque-based control tries to overcome problems such as nonlinearity, coupling between inputs and outputs and uncertainty raised from manipulator dynamics. It is also assumed that the actuators can perfectly generate the proposed torque control laws for the joints. This assumption may not be satisfied due to the dynamics, saturation and some practical limitations associated with actuators. The problems associated with manipulator dynamics will be removed if a robust control approach can be free from manipulator model. Considering this fact, Voltage Control Strategy (VCS) [4-5] was presented for electrically driven robot manipulators. This control strategy is free from manipulator model but is dependent on actuator model. Nevertheless, the uncertainty estimation and compensation can be effective in VCS to improve the control performance [6]. Using the

estimation of uncertainty, this paper presents a voltage-based robust neural-network control for electrically driven robot manipulators which is model-free from both manipulator and actuators. The proposed design has a simpler design compared with alternative valuable voltage-based robust control approaches such as fuzzy estimation-based control [7], observer-based control [8], adaptive fuzzy control [9], neural-network control [10], fuzzy-neural-network control [11] and intelligent control [12] were presented for electrically driven robot manipulators. The simplicity and efficiency of the proposed control approach is shown through a comparison with the robust neural network control approach given by [10].

In most conventional robust approaches such as sliding mode control, the uncertainty bound parameter should be known in advance or estimated. The tracking error and smoothness of the control input are significantly affected by this parameter. The switching control laws resulted from these robust control methods may cause the chattering problem which will excite the un-modeled dynamics and degrade the system performance. As a result, too high estimation of the bounds may cause saturation of input, higher frequency of chattering in the switching control laws, and thus a bad behavior of the whole system, while too low estimation of the bounds may cause a higher tracking error [13].

Generally, uncertainty estimation and compensation are essential in robust tracking control of robots and the control performance is entirely enhanced by these crucial tasks. Function approximation methods play an important role in this stage and various tools such as fuzzy logic, neural networks, optimization algorithms, trigonometric function and orthogonal functions series have been used. In the two past decades, fuzzy logic [14-17] and neural networks [18-20] and neuro-fuzzy control [21] have been frequently employed in control systems and different control objectives have been successfully fulfilled due to their powerful capability in function approximation [22]. As important criteria, the simplicity and efficiency of the estimator should be paid attention since complex estimators require excessive memory, computational burden and many parameters. Tuning or online adaptation of these parameters significantly influences the estimator performance and increases the computations, as well.

One of the effective tools to approximate a function is the Radial-Basis-Function (RBF) networks. Applications of RBF networks in the robust control of nonlinear systems can be classified into direct and indirect adaptive control [23-26]. In direct adaptive control, RBF networks are employed as controllers. The network parameters are tuned online using adaptation laws derived from stability analysis.

Indirect application of RBF networks consists of two stages. In the first stage, the system dynamics are estimated using RBF networks and in the second stage, the estimated functions are used to design the control laws.

The novelty of this paper is to propose a robust model-free control for electrically driven robot manipulators using a simple RBF network as an uncertainty estimator in the decentralized controller. The simplicity of estimator is for using RBF network which consists of a hidden layer with one node, two inputs and a single output. Compared with the conventional robust control, the proposed robust control requires neither the uncertainty bound parameter nor the bounding

functions. In addition, it is free from the chattering problem.

The robust RBF network control is compared with a robust Neural Network control (robust NN control) given by [10]. The robust NN control has two interior loops. The inner loop is a voltage controller for motor using two-layer neural networks whereas the outer loop is a current controller using two-layer neural networks for providing the desired current. The robust RBF network control has a simpler design by using only one control loop and a RBF network.

The structure and design of the proposed Gaussian RBF network used as an adaptive uncertainty estimator in this paper is simpler than the fuzzy system used in [27] as an adaptive fuzzy controller [27]. These two designs have different structures. An interesting result is that fuzzy systems and neural networks can be designed somehow to perform the same behavior.

This paper is organized as follows. Section 2 explains modeling of the robotic system including the robot manipulator and motors. Section 3 develops the robust RBF network control approach. Section 4 describes the RBF network for estimation of the uncertainty. Section 5 presents the stability analysis. Section 6 illustrates the simulation results. Finally, section 7 concludes the paper.

2. Modeling

The robot manipulator consists of n links interconnected at n joints into an open kinematic chain. The mechanical system is assumed to be perfectly rigid. Each link is driven by a permanent magnet DC motor through the gears. The dynamics is described [28] as

$$\mathbf{D(q)\ddot{q}+C(q,\dot{q})\dot{q}+g(q)=\tau_r-\tau_f(\dot{q})} \qquad (1)$$

Where $\mathbf{q} \in R^n$ is the vector of joint positions, $\mathbf{D(q)}$ the $n \times n$ matrix of manipulator inertia, $\mathbf{C(q,\dot{q})\dot{q}} \in R^n$ the vector of centrifugal and Coriolis torques, $\mathbf{g(q)} \in R^n$ the vector of gravitational torques, $\boldsymbol{\tau}_f(\dot{\mathbf{q}}) \in R^n$ the vector of friction torques and $\boldsymbol{\tau}_r \in R^n$ the joint torque vector of robot.

Note that vectors and matrices are represented in bold form for clarity. The electric motors provide the joint torque vector as follows [28]

$$\mathbf{Jr^{-1}\ddot{q}+Br^{-1}\dot{q}+r\tau_r=\tau_m} \qquad (2)$$

Where $\boldsymbol{\tau}_m \in R^n$ is the torque vector of motors, $\mathbf{J}$, $\mathbf{B}$ and $\mathbf{r}$ are the $n \times n$ diagonal matrices for motor coefficients namely the inertia, damping, and reduction gear, respectively. The joint velocity vector $\dot{\mathbf{q}}$ and the motor velocity vector $\dot{\mathbf{q}}_m \in R^n$ are related through the gears to yield

$$\mathbf{r}\dot{\mathbf{q}}_m = \dot{\mathbf{q}} \tag{3}$$

In order to obtain the motor voltages as the inputs of system, we consider the electrical equation of geared permanent magnet DC motors in the matrix form,

$$\mathbf{R}\mathbf{I}_a + \mathbf{L}\dot{\mathbf{I}}_a + \mathbf{K}_b\mathbf{r}^{-1}\dot{\mathbf{q}} + \boldsymbol{\varphi} = \mathbf{v} \tag{4}$$

Where $\mathbf{v} \in R^n$ is the vector of motor voltages, $\mathbf{I}_a \in R^n$ is the vector of motor currents and $\boldsymbol{\varphi} \in R^n$ is a vector of external disturbances. $\mathbf{R}$, $\mathbf{L}$ and $\mathbf{K}_b$ represent the $n \times n$ diagonal matrices for the coefficients of armature resistance, inductance, and back-emf constant, respectively.

The motor torque vector $\boldsymbol{\tau}_m$ as the input for dynamic (2) is produced by the motor current vector,

$$\mathbf{K}_m\mathbf{I}_a = \boldsymbol{\tau}_m \tag{5}$$

Where $\mathbf{K}_m$ is a diagonal matrix of the torque constants. Using (1-5), obtains the state-space model

$$\dot{\mathbf{x}} = \mathbf{f}(\mathbf{x}) + \mathbf{b}\mathbf{v} - \mathbf{b}\boldsymbol{\varphi} \tag{6}$$

Where $\mathbf{v}$ is considered as the inputs, $\mathbf{x}$ is the state vector and $\mathbf{f}(\mathbf{x})$ is of the form of

$$\mathbf{f}(\mathbf{x}) = \begin{bmatrix} \mathbf{x}_2 \\ \left(\mathbf{J}\mathbf{r}^{-1} + \mathbf{r}\mathbf{D}(\mathbf{x}_1)\right)^{-1}. \\ \left(-\left(\mathbf{B}\mathbf{r}^{-1} + \mathbf{r}\mathbf{C}(\mathbf{x}_1,\mathbf{x}_2)\right)\mathbf{x}_2 - \mathbf{r}\mathbf{g}(\mathbf{x}_1) + \mathbf{K}_m\mathbf{x}_3 - \mathbf{r}\boldsymbol{\tau}_f(\mathbf{x}_2)\right) \\ -\mathbf{L}^{-1}\left(\mathbf{K}_b\mathbf{r}^{-1}\mathbf{x}_2 + \mathbf{R}\mathbf{x}_3\right) \end{bmatrix}$$

$$\mathbf{b} = \begin{bmatrix} \mathbf{0} \\ \mathbf{0} \\ \mathbf{L}^{-1} \end{bmatrix}, \quad \mathbf{x} = \begin{bmatrix} \mathbf{q} \\ \dot{\mathbf{q}} \\ \mathbf{I}_a \end{bmatrix} \tag{7}$$

The state-space (6) shows a highly coupled nonlinear system in a non-companion form. The complexity of model is a serious challenge for the control of the robot.

To avoid much more complexity, many works have ignored the motors' dynamics. However, considering the motors' dynamics is required in high-speed and high-accuracy applications.

3. Robust control design

By substituting (2), (3) and (5) into (4), the voltage equation of the i th motor in the scalar form can be expressed by

$$RK_m^{-1}Jr^{-1}\ddot{q} + (RK_m^{-1}Br^{-1} + K_b r^{-1})\dot{q} \tag{8}$$
$$+RK_m^{-1}r\tau_r + L\dot{I}_a + \varphi = v$$

Where $\ddot{q}$, $\dot{q}$, τ_r, $\dot{I}_a$ and φ are the ith element of the vectors $\ddot{\mathbf{q}}$, $\dot{\mathbf{q}}$, $\boldsymbol{\tau}_r$, $\mathbf{I}_a$ and φ, respectively.

Equation (8) can be rewritten as

$$\ddot{q} + F = v \tag{9}$$

Where F is referred to as the lumped uncertainty expressed by

$$F = (RK_m^{-1}Jr^{-1} - 1)\ddot{q} + L\dot{I}_a + \varphi + \tag{10}$$
$$(RK_m^{-1}Br^{-1} + K_b r^{-1})\dot{q} + RK_m^{-1}r\tau_r$$

Let us define

$$u = \ddot{q}_d + k_d(\dot{q}_d - \dot{q}) + k_p(q_d - q) + \hat{F} \tag{11}$$

Where $\hat{F}$ is the estimate of F, q_d is the desired joint position, k_p and k_d are the control design parameters. In order to estimate F, this paper designs a simple RBF network as an uncertainty estimator. In order to protect the motor from over voltage, the motor voltage must be under a permitted value v_{max}.

Therefore, a voltage limiter is used for each motor to hold the voltage under the value v_{max}. Then, a robust control law is proposed as

$$v(t) = v_{max} sat(u / v_{max}) \tag{12}$$

Where

$$sat(u / v_{max}) = \begin{cases} 1 & if \quad u > v_{max} \\ u / v_{max} & if \quad |u| \le v_{max} \\ -1 & if \quad u < -v_{max} \end{cases} \tag{13}$$

The control scheme is presented in figure1.

4. Adaptive uncertainty estimator

Applying control law (12) to the system (9) obtains the closed loop system

$$\ddot{q} + F = v_{max} sat(u / v_{max}) \tag{14}$$

In the case of $u > v_{max}$, according to (13) we have

$$\ddot{q} + F = v_{max} \tag{15}$$

Therefore, the estimator $\hat{F}$ is not effective in the closed loop system.

In the case of $u < -v_{max}$, according to (13) we have

$$\ddot{q} + F = -v_{max} \tag{16}$$

Therefore, the estimator $\hat{F}$ is not effective in the closed loop system.

In the case of $|u| \le v_{max}$, according to (9), (11) and (13) we have

$$\ddot{q} + F = (\ddot{q}_d + k_d(\dot{q}_d - \dot{q}) + k_p(q_d - q)) \tag{17}$$
$$+ \hat{F}$$

Therefore, the closed loop system can be written as

$$\ddot{e} + k_d\dot{e} + k_p e = F - \hat{F} \tag{18}$$

Where e is the tracking error expressed by

$$e = q_d - q \tag{19}$$

This paper suggests a simple RBF estimator for every joint as

$$\hat{F} = \hat{p}\exp(-(e^2 + \dot{e}^2)) \tag{20}$$

Where $\hat{p}$ is an adaptive gain. One can easily represent (20) as

$$\hat{F} = \hat{p}\zeta \tag{21}$$

Where ζ is expressed as

$$\zeta = \exp(-(e^2 + \dot{e}^2)) \tag{22}$$

The estimator $\hat{F}$ defined by (21) can approximate F adaptively based on the universal approximation of RBF networks [22]. Thus,

$$|F - \hat{F}| \leq \rho \tag{23}$$

Where ρ is a positive scalar. Suppose that F can be modeled as

$$F = p\zeta + \varepsilon$$

Where ε is the approximation error and vector p is constant. Assume that

$$|F - p\zeta| \leq \beta \tag{25}$$

Considering (24) and (25) shows that $|\varepsilon| \leq \beta$ in which β is the upper bound of approximation error. The dynamics of tracking error can be expressed by substituting (24) and (21) into (18) to have

$$\ddot{e} + k_d\dot{e} + k_p e = (p - \hat{p})\zeta + \varepsilon \tag{26}$$

The state space equation in the tracking space is obtained using (26) as

$$\dot{E} = AE + B\omega \tag{27}$$

Where

$$A = \begin{bmatrix} 0 & 1 \\ -k_p & -k_d \end{bmatrix}, \; B = \begin{bmatrix} 0 \\ 1 \end{bmatrix}, \; E = \begin{bmatrix} e \\ \dot{e} \end{bmatrix}$$

$$\omega = (p - \hat{p})\zeta + \varepsilon \tag{28}$$

Consider the following positive definite function [27]

$$V = 0.5E^T SE + \frac{1}{2\gamma}(p - \hat{p})^2 \tag{29}$$

Where γ is a positive scalar, S and Q are the unique symmetric positive definite matrices satisfying the matrix Lyapunov equation as

$$A^T S + SA = -Q \tag{30}$$

Taking the time derivative of V gives that

$$\dot{V} = 0.5\dot{E}^T SE + 0.5E^T S\dot{E} - (p - \hat{p})\dot{\hat{p}}/\gamma \tag{31}$$

Substituting (27), (28) and (30) into (31) yields to

$$\dot{V} = (p - \hat{p})\left(E^T S_2 \zeta - \frac{1}{\gamma}\dot{\hat{p}} \right) \tag{32}$$

$$+ E^T S_2 \varepsilon - 0.5 E^T Q E$$

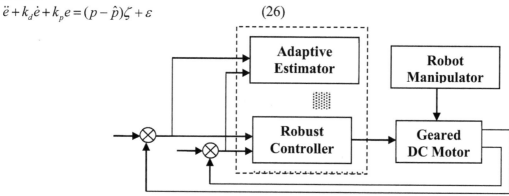

Figure 1. Proposed robust RBF network control.

Where S_2 is the second column of S. Since $-0.5E^T Q E < 0$ for $E \neq 0$, if the adaptation law is given by

$$\dot{\hat{p}} = \gamma E^T S_2 \zeta \tag{33}$$

Then

$$\dot{V} = -0.5E^T Q E + E^T S_2 \varepsilon \tag{34}$$

The tracking error is reduced if $\dot{V} < 0$. Therefore, the convergence of E is guaranteed if

$$E^T S_2 \varepsilon < 0.5 E^T Q E$$

Using the Cauchy–Schwartz inequality and $|\varepsilon| \leq \beta$, we can obtain,

$$E^T S_2 \varepsilon \leq \|E\| . \|S_2\| . |\varepsilon| < \beta \|E\| . \|S_2\| \tag{36}$$

Since $\lambda_{min}(Q)\|E\|^2 \leq E^T Q E \leq \lambda_{max}(Q)\|E\|^2$, in order to satisfy (35), it is sufficient that

$$\beta\|S_2\| < 0.5\lambda_{min}(Q)\|E\| \quad \text{or} \tag{37}$$

$$2\beta\|S_2\|/\lambda_{min}(Q) \; \square \; \delta_0 < \|E\|$$

Where δ_0 is a positive constant, $\lambda_{min}(Q)$ and $\lambda_{max}(Q)$ are the minimum and maximum eigenvalues of Q, respectively. Thus, we have $\dot{V} < 0$ as long as $\delta_0 < \|E\|$. This means that the tracking error becomes smaller out of the ball with the radius of δ_0. As a result, the tracking error ultimately enters into the ball. On the other hand $\dot{V} > 0$ if $\delta_0 > \| E \|$. This means that the tracking error does not converge to zero.

According to (33), the parameter of the RBF network estimator is calculated by

$$\hat{p}(t) = \hat{p}(0) + \int_0^t \gamma \mathbf{E}^T \mathbf{S}_2 \zeta d\tau \quad (38)$$

Where $\hat{p}(0)$ is the initial value.

Result 1: The tracking error e and its time derivatives $\dot{e}$ are bounded and ultimately enters into a ball with a radius of δ_0.

To evaluate the final size of error, it is worthy to note that it depends on the upper bound of approximation error, β, and the control design parameters k_p and k_d. Selecting large values for k_p and k_d, will provide a small size of tracking error. To evaluate the size of estimation error ρ in (23), one can substitute (24) into (23) to have

$$|p\zeta + \varepsilon - \hat{p}\zeta| \le |(p-\hat{p})\zeta| + |\varepsilon| \quad (39)$$

Thus, to satisfy (23), ρ can be given by

$$\rho = |(p-\hat{p})\zeta| + \beta \quad (40)$$

5. Stability analysis

A proof for the boundedness of the state variables $\mathbf{\theta}$, $\dot{\mathbf{\theta}}$ and $\mathbf{I_a}$ is given by stability analysis. In order to analyze the stability, the following assumptions are made:

Assumption 1 The desired trajectory q_d must be smooth in the sense that q_d and its derivatives up to a necessary order are available and all uniformly bounded [28].

As a necessary condition to design a robust control, the external disturbance must be bounded. Thus, the following assumption is made:

Assumption 2 The external disturbance φ is bounded as $|\varphi(t)| \le \varphi_{max}$.

Control law (12) makes the following assumption.

Assumption 3 The motor voltage is bounded as $|v| \le v_{max}$.

The motor should be sufficiently strong to drive the robot for tracking the desired joint velocity under the maximum permitted voltages. According to result1, $\mathbf{E} = [q_d - q \quad \dot{q}_d - \dot{q}]^T$ is bounded. Since q_d and $\dot{q}_d$ are bounded in assumption 1,

Result 2: The joint position q and joint velocity $\dot{q}$ are bounded.

From (4), we can write for every motor

$$RI_a + L\dot{I}_a + K_b r^{-1}\dot{q} + \varphi = v \quad (41)$$

Substituting control law (12) into (41) yields

$$RI_a + L\dot{I}_a + K_b r^{-1}\dot{q} + \varphi = v_{max} sat(\frac{u}{v_{max}}) \quad (42)$$

That is

$$RI_a + L\dot{I}_a = w \quad (43)$$

$$w = v_{max} sat(u / v_{max}) - k_b r^{-1}\dot{q} - \phi \quad (44)$$

The variables $\dot{q}$ and ϕ are bounded according to result 2 and assumption 2, respectively. Additionally, $|v_{max} sat(u / v_{max})| \le v_{max}$.

Consequently, the input w in (43) is bounded. The linear differential (43) is a stable linear system based on the Routh-Hurwitz criterion. Since the input w is bounded, the output I_a is bounded.

Result 3: The current I_a is bounded.

As a result of this reasoning, for every joint, the joint position q, the joint velocity $\dot{q}$ and the motor current I_a are bounded. Therefore, the system states $\mathbf{q}$, $\dot{\mathbf{q}}$ and $\mathbf{I_a}$ are bounded and the stability of system is guaranteed.

6. Simulation results

The robust RBF network control is simulated using an articulated robot driven by permanent magnet DC motors.

The details of robot is given by [6]. The maximum voltage of each motor is set to $u_{max} = 40$ V. The parameters of motors are given in table 1. The desired joint trajectory for all joints is shown in figure 1. The desired position for every joint is given by

$$\theta_d = 1 - \cos(\pi t / 5) \quad \text{for} \quad 0 \le t < 10 \quad (45)$$

Table 1. Specifications of DC motors.

u_{max} (V)	R (Ω)	K_b ($\frac{V.s}{rad}$)	L (H)	J_m ($\frac{Nm.s^2}{rad}$)	B_m ($\frac{Nm.s}{rad}$)	r
40	1.26	0.26	0.001	0.0002	0.001	0.01

The external disturbance φ in (8) for every joint is given by

$$\varphi = \begin{cases} 0 & 0 \le t \le 2 \text{ and } 4 \le t \le 6 \text{ and } 8 \le t \le 10 \\ 1 & 2 \le t \le 4 \text{ and } 6 \le t \le 8 \end{cases} \quad (46)$$

Tracking performance: The robust RBF network control in (12) is simulated with adaptive law (38) and the following parameters

$$A = \begin{bmatrix} 0 & 1 \\ -100 & -20 \end{bmatrix}, S_2 = \begin{bmatrix} 50 \\ 6 \end{bmatrix},$$

$$\gamma = 5000, \hat{p}(0) = 0 \quad (47)$$

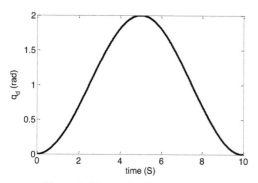

Figure 2. The desired joint trajectory.

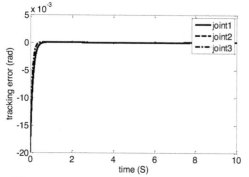

Figure 3. Performance of the proposed control.

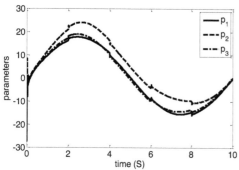

Figure 4. Adaptation of parameters.

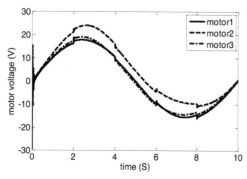

Figure 5. Control efforts of the proposed control.

The initial errors for all joints are given $0.02\,rad$. The tacking performance is very good as shown in figure 3. All joint errors finally go under $4.2 \times 10^{-5}\,rad$ without overshoot.

The adaptation of parameters for all joints is shown in figure 4. All parameters are varied to cover all effects of higher order terms in RBF

network estimators. Motors behave well under the permitted voltages as shown in figure 5.

The control efforts are increased when starting because of the initial tracking error. Simulation results confirm the effectiveness of the robust RBF network control.

A comparison: The robust RBF network control is compared with a robust Neural Network control (robust NN control) given by [10]. The control structure has two interior loops. The inner loop is a voltage controller for motor using two-layer neural networks whereas the outer loop is a current controller using two-layer neural networks for providing the desired current.

The control design is based on the stability analysis using Lyapunov theory. As a comparison it is noted that the robust RBF network control is much simpler since it has only one control loop using a RBF network.

The parameters of the robust NN control are set to $\Lambda = 100$, $k_\tau = 30$, $k_v = 1$, $k_1 = 0.1$, $k_\omega = 1$, $\Gamma = 1000$, $\hat{W}_1(0) = 0$ and $\hat{W}_2(0) = 0$. The initial errors and external disturbances for all joints are the same as ones used in Simulation 1.

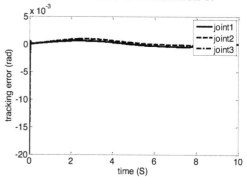

Figure 6. Performance of the robust NN control.

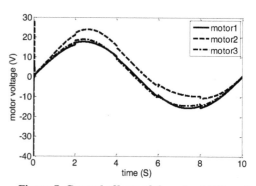

Figure 7. Control efforts of the robust NN control.

The control performance of [10] is shown in figure 6. Both control approaches are robust with a good tracking performance. Figure 8 shows voltages applied to the motors.

The control efforts in figure 7 are smooth and permitted. The robust RBF network control is much simpler, less computational, less number of design parameters and has better control performance. On the other hand, the tracking error of the robust NN control will be decreased by increasing the gains however the chattering phenomenon will be increased.

7. Conclusion

This paper has presented a novel robust model-free control approach for electrically driven robot manipulators. It has been found that the complex dynamics of the robotic system can be estimated by using a RBF network in a decentralized structure as an estimator of uncertainty. The robust controller has become model-free by using this estimator to compensate the uncertainty. The proposed adaptive mechanism has guaranteed the stability and provided a good tracking performance. The performance of the proposed estimator in the robust control system has been very good as shown by simulations. In order to have a simple design with easy implementation yet good performance it has been confirmed that using only the tracking error and its time derivatives is sufficient to form the estimator. A comparison with a robust NN control has shown that the proposed control approach is simpler in design, less computational and better control performance.

References

[1] Abdallah, C., Dawson, D., Dorato, P. & Jamshidi, M. (1991). Survey of robust control for rigid robots. IEEE Control System Magazine, vol. 11, no. 2, pp. 24-30.

[2] Qu, Z. & Dawson, D. (1996). Robust tracking control of robot manipulators. IEEE Press, Inc., New York.

[3] Sage, H. G., De Mathelin, M. F. & Ostertag, E. (1999). Robust control of robot manipulators: A survey. International Journal of Control, vol. 72, no. 16, pp. 1498-1522.

[4] Fateh, M. M. (2008). On the voltage-based control of robot manipulators. International Journal of Control and Automation System, vol. 6, no. 5, pp. 702-712.

[5] Fateh, M. M. (2010). Robust voltage control of electrical manipulators in task-space. International Journal of Innovative Computing Information and Control, vol. 6, no. 6, pp. 2691-2700.

[6] Fateh, M. M. & Khorashadizadeh, S. (2012). Robust control of electrically driven robots by adaptive fuzzy estimation of uncertainty. Nonlinear Dynamics, vol. 69, pp. 1465-1477.

[7] Chang, Y. C. & Yen, H. M. (2009). Robust tracking control for a class of uncertain electrically driven robots. Control Theory & Applications, IET, vol. 3, pp. 519-532.

[8] Oya, M., Chun-Yi, S. & Kobayashi, T. (2004). State observer-based robust control scheme for electrically driven robot manipulators. IEEE Transactions on Robotics, vol. 20, pp. 796-804.

[9] Jae Pil, H. and Euntai, K. (2006). Robust tracking control of an electrically driven robot: adaptive fuzzy logic approach. IEEE Transactions on Fuzzy systems, vol. 14, pp. 232-247.

[10] Kwan, C., Lewis, F. L. & Dawson, D. (1998). Robust neural-network control of rigid-link electrically driven robots. IEEE Transactions on Neural Networks, vol. 9, no. 4, pp. 581-588.

[11] Rong-Jong, W. & Muthusamy, R. (2013). Fuzzy-Neural-Network Inherited Sliding-Mode Control for Robot Manipulator Including Actuator Dynamics. IEEE Transactions on Neural Networks and Learning Systems, vol. 24, pp. 274-287.

[12] Chang, Y. C., Yen, H. M. & Wu, M. F. (2008). An intelligent robust tracking control for electrically-driven robot systems. International Journal of Systems Science, vol. 39, pp. 497-511.

[13] Fateh, M. M. (2010). Proper uncertainty bound parameter to robust control of electrical manipulators using nominal model. Nonlinear Dynamics, vol. 61, no. 4, pp. 655-666.

[14] Kim, E. (2004). Output feedback tracking control of robot manipulator with model uncertainty via adaptive fuzzy logic. IEEE Transactions on Fuzzy Systems, vol. 12, no. 3, pp. 368-376.

[15] Hwang, J. P. & Kim, E. (2006). Robust tracking control of an electrically driven robot: adaptive fuzzy logic approach. IEEE Transactions on Fuzzy Systems, vol. 14, no. 2, pp. 232-247.

[16] Ho, H. F., Wong Y. K. & Rad, A. B. (2008). Adaptive fuzzy approach for a class of uncertain nonlinear systems in strict-feedback form. ISA Transactions, vol. 47, pp. 286-299.

[17] Senthilkumar, D. & Mahanta, C. (2010). Identification of uncertain nonlinear systems for robust fuzzy control. ISA Transactions, vol. 49, pp. 27-38.

[18] Peng, J. & Dubay, R. (2011). Identification and adaptive neural network control of a DC motor system with dead-zone characteristics. ISA Transactions, vol. 50, no. 4, pp. 588-598.

[19] Huang, S. N., Tan, K. K. & Lee, T. H. (2008). Adaptive neural network algorithm for control design of rigid-link electrically driven robots. Neurocomputing, vol. 71, pp. 885-894.

[20] Sun, T., Pei, H., Yan, Y., Zhou, H. & Zhang, C. (2011). Neural network-based sliding mode adaptive control for robot manipulators. Neurocomputing, vol. 74, pp. 2377-2384.

[21] Alavandar, S. & Nigam, M. J. (2009). New hybrid adaptive neuro-fuzzy algorithms for manipulator

control with uncertainties–comparative study. ISA Transactions, vol. 48, no. 4, pp. 497-502.

[22] Park, J. & Sandberg, J. W. (1991). Universal approximation using radial-basis-function Network. Neural Computation, vol. 3, pp. 246-257.

[23] Sanner, R. M. & Slotine, J. E. (1992). Gaussian networks for direct adaptive control. IEEE Transactions on Neural Networks, vol. 3, pp. 837-863.

[24] Ge, S. S. & Wang, C. (2002). Direct Adaptive NN Control of a Class of Nonlinear Systems. IEEE Transactions on Neural Networks, vol. 13, no. 1, pp. 214-221.

[25] Sridhar, S. & Hassan, K. K. (2000). Output feedback control of nonlinear systems using RBF neural networks. IEEE Transactions on Neural Networks, vol. 11, no. 1, pp. 69-79.

[26] Yang, Y. & Wang, X. (2007). Adaptive H∞ tracking control for a class of uncertain nonlinear systems using radial-basis-function neural networks. Neurocomputing, vol. 70, pp. 932-941.

[27] Fateh, M. M. & Fateh, S. (2012). Decentralized direct adaptive fuzzy control of robots using voltage control strategy. Nonlinear Dynamics, vol. 70, pp. 919-1930.

[28] Spong, M. W., Hutchinson, S. & Vidyasagar, M. (2006). Robot Modelling and Control: Wiley. Hoboken.

Permissions

All chapters in this book were first published in JAIDM, by Shahrood University of Technology; hereby published with permission under the Creative Commons Attribution License or equivalent. Every chapter published in this book has been scrutinized by our experts. Their significance has been extensively debated. The topics covered herein carry significant findings which will fuel the growth of the discipline. They may even be implemented as practical applications or may be referred to as a beginning point for another development.

The contributors of this book come from diverse backgrounds, making this book a truly international effort. This book will bring forth new frontiers with its revolutionizing research information and detailed analysis of the nascent developments around the world.

We would like to thank all the contributing authors for lending their expertise to make the book truly unique. They have played a crucial role in the development of this book. Without their invaluable contributions this book wouldn't have been possible. They have made vital efforts to compile up to date information on the varied aspects of this subject to make this book a valuable addition to the collection of many professionals and students.

This book was conceptualized with the vision of imparting up-to-date information and advanced data in this field. To ensure the same, a matchless editorial board was set up. Every individual on the board went through rigorous rounds of assessment to prove their worth. After which they invested a large part of their time researching and compiling the most relevant data for our readers.

The editorial board has been involved in producing this book since its inception. They have spent rigorous hours researching and exploring the diverse topics which have resulted in the successful publishing of this book. They have passed on their knowledge of decades through this book. To expedite this challenging task, the publisher supported the team at every step. A small team of assistant editors was also appointed to further simplify the editing procedure and attain best results for the readers.

Apart from the editorial board, the designing team has also invested a significant amount of their time in understanding the subject and creating the most relevant covers. They scrutinized every image to scout for the most suitable representation of the subject and create an appropriate cover for the book.

The publishing team has been an ardent support to the editorial, designing and production team. Their endless efforts to recruit the best for this project, has resulted in the accomplishment of this book. They are a veteran in the field of academics and their pool of knowledge is as vast as their experience in printing. Their expertise and guidance has proved useful at every step. Their uncompromising quality standards have made this book an exceptional effort. Their encouragement from time to time has been an inspiration for everyone.

The publisher and the editorial board hope that this book will prove to be a valuable piece of knowledge for researchers, students, practitioners and scholars across the globe.

List of Contributors

M. M. Hosseini and J. Hassanian
Islamic Azad University, Shahrood branch, Shahroodt, Iran

V. Khoshdel and A. Akbarzadeh
Center of Excellence on Soft Computing & Intelligent Information Processing, Mechanical Engineering Department, Ferdowsi University of Mashhad, Mashhad

Z. Imani and A. R. Ahmadyfard
Electrical Engineering Department, University of Shahrood, Shahrood, Iran

A. Zohrevand
Computer Engineering & Information Technology Department, University of Shahrood, Shahrood, Iran

M. Banejad and H. Ijadi
Electrical Engineering Department, Shahrood University of Technology, Shahrood, Iran

S. Shafeipour Yourdeshahi and H. Seyedarabi
Faculty of Electrical and Computer Engineering, University of Tabriz, Tabriz, Iran

A. Aghagolzadeh
Faculty of Electrical and Computer Engineering, Babol University of Technology, Babol, Iran

L. Yu and D. Qian
School of Control & Computer Engineering, North China Electric Power University, Changping District, Beijing, China

M. Heidarian, H. Jalalifar and A. Rafati
Department of Petroleum Engineering, Shahid Bahonar University, Kerman, Iran

J. Hamidzadeh
Faculty of Computer Engineering & Information Technology, Sadjad University of Technology, Mashhad, Iran

M. Amin-Naji
Faculty of Electrical & Computer Engineering, Babol Noshirvani University of Technology, Babol, Iran

M. Azarbad and A. Ebrahimzadeh
Department of Electrical and Computer Engineering, Babol University of Technology, Babol, Iran

H. Azami
Department of Electrical Engineering, Iran University of Science and Technology, Tehran, Iran

M. Imani and H. Ghassemian
Faculty of Electrical & Computer Engineering, Tarbiat Modares University, Tehran, Iran

R. Davarzani
Department of Electrical & Computer Engineering, College of Engineering, Shahrood Branch, Islamic Azad University, Shahrood, Iran

S. Mozaffari and Kh.Yaghmaie
Faculty of Electrical and Computer Engineering, Semnan University, Semnan, Iran

M. Baluchzadeh
Department of Electrical and Robotic Engineering, University of Shahrood, Shahrood, Iran

V. Abolghasemi and S. Ferdowsi
Department of Electrical Engineering & Robotics, University of Shahrood, Shahrood, Iran

S. Sanei
Faculty of Engineering and Physical Sciences, University of Surrey, Guildford, United Kingdom

A. Goshvarpour, A. Abbasi and A. Goshvarpour
Department of Biomedical Engineering, Faculty of Electrical Engineering, Sahand University of Technology, Tabriz, Iran

V. Ghasemi and A. A. Pouyan
Department of Computer and IT Engineering, Shahrood University of Technology, Shahrood, Iran

M. Sharifi
Department of Computer Engineering, Iran University of Science and Technology, Tehran, Iran

V. Majidnezhad
United Institute of Informatics Problems, National Academy of Science of Belarus, Minsk, Belarus

M. Alikhani and M. Ahmadi Livani
Faculty of Electrical and Computer Engineering Tarbiat Modares University

S. M. Hosseinirad and S. K. Basu
Department of Computer Science, Banaras Hindu University, India

M. Niazi, J. Pourdeilami and A. A. Pouyan
Department of Computer Engineering, Shahrood University of Technology, Shahrood, Iran

M. Shafiee
Department of Computer Engineering, Kerman Branch, Islamic Azad University, Kerman, Iran

A. Latif
Department of Electrical and Computer Engineering, Yazd University, Yazd, Iran

M. M. Fateh and S. Khorashadizadeh
Department of Electrical Engineering, University of Shahrood, Shahrood, Iran

S. M. Ahmadi
Department of Mechanical Engineering, University of Shahrood, Shahrood, Iran

Index

Printed in the USA
CPSIA information can be obtained
at www.ICGtesting.com
JSHW051431221024
72173JS00006B/1441